Scars on the Land

Scars on the Land

An Environmental History of Slavery in the American South

DAVID SILKENAT

OXFORD
UNIVERSITY PRESS

OXFORD
UNIVERSITY PRESS

Oxford University Press is a department of the University of Oxford. It furthers
the University's objective of excellence in research, scholarship, and education
by publishing worldwide. Oxford is a registered trade mark of Oxford University
Press in the UK and certain other countries.

Published in the United States of America by Oxford University Press
198 Madison Avenue, New York, NY 10016, United States of America.

CIP data is on file at the Library of Congress

ISBN 978–0–19–756422–6

DOI: 10.1093/oso/9780197564226.001.0001

1 3 5 7 9 8 6 4 2

Printed by Sheridan Books, Inc., United States of America

Contents

Scars on the Land

Introduction

A FUGITIVE FROM bondage in Mississippi, William Anderson observed in 1857 that "it is almost impossible for slaves to escape from that part of the South, to the Northern States. There are a great many things to encounter in escaping, vis: large and small rivers, lakes, panthers, bears, snakes, alligators, white and black men, blood hounds, guns, and, above all, the dangers of starvation."[1] In enumerating the many barriers to freedom, Anderson lumped together natural and human obstacles. He understood that slavery's shackles were not just man-made; enslaved people toiled in an environment that conspired with slave owners to keep African Americans in bondage. At the same time, Anderson and other enslaved people knew the Southern environment in a way their enslavers never could. By day, they plucked worms from tobacco leaves, trod barefoot in the mud as they hoed rice fields, and felt the late summer sun on their backs as they picked cotton. By night, they clandestinely took to the woods and swamps to trap opossums and turtles, to visit relatives living on adjacent plantations, and to escape to freedom.

While the Southern environment provided the context for the peculiar institution, enslaved labor remade the landscape. One simple calculation had profound consequences: rather than measuring productivity based on outputs per acre, Southern planters sought to maximize how much labor they could extract from their enslaved workforce. They saw the landscape as disposable, relocating to more fertile prospects once they had leached the soils and cut down the forests. The expanding enslaved frontier irrevocably transformed the environment. On its leading edge, slavery laid waste to fragile ecosystems, draining swamps and clearing forests to plant crops and fuel steamships. On its trailing edge, slavery left eroded hillsides, rivers clogged with sterile soil, and the extinction of native species. Although the precise mechanisms and effects varied in Virginia's tobacco fields, Louisiana's swamps, and North

Scars on the Land. David Silkenat, Oxford University Press. © Oxford University Press 2022.
DOI: 10.1093/oso/9780197564226.003.0001

Carolina's pine forests, slavery exacted the same swift price. While environmental destruction fueled slavery's expansion, no environment could long survive intensive slave labor. The scars manifested themselves in different ways, but the land too fell victim to the slave owner's lash.

Slavery more than nature defined the South as a region. Geographers have identified dozens of distinct ecosystems within the American South, encompassing a vast variety of soil types, weather patterns, and biota. Two centuries of human bondage cemented these diverse biomes into a distinct cultural region. When they sought to establish a slaveholders' republic in 1861, Southern partisans saw enslaved labor as the thread that linked the Eastern Coastal Plain, the Appalachian Piedmont, and the Mississippi Delta. "The South is now in the formation of a *Slave* Republic," wrote L. W. Spratt, the editor of the *Charleston Mercury*, in February 1861. Its commitment to human bondage defined "the South as a geographical section" and provided what Confederate vice president Alexander Stephens described as the "cornerstone" of the new republic. Its advocates championed the South's ecological diversity as an asset, one that enslaved labor could exploit. "What a soil, and climate, and variety of productions," boasted Daniel M. Barringer in April 1861, shortly after the firing on Fort Sumter. Urging his fellow North Carolinians to join the newly established Southern Confederacy, Barringer saw its future in the expanding slave frontier, where "almost everywhere an inviting soil, capable of every variety of production and, in many portions of the Confederacy, still of virgin fertility—with every good climate of the world, and very little of the bad." For Spratt, Stephens, Barringer, and other Confederate nationalists, slavery undergirded the world they hoped to defend. As historian Ira Berlin has observed, the ethos of a slave society infused and infected all aspects of its social order: law, family, custom, religion, politics, and art. Slavery also shaped how white and Black Southerners came to view the land itself and their relationship to it.[2]

This book begins from a simple premise: between 1665 and 1865 the environment fundamentally shaped American slavery, and slavery remade the Southern landscape. The complex interplay between slavery and the environment in the American South over two centuries does not lend itself to easy or straightforward narratives. Each of this book's first six chapters adopts a feature of the Southern landscape as a vehicle for understanding how the environment shaped the lives of enslaved people and how they shaped their environment: soil, animals, trees, rivers, weather, and swamps. Although treated separately, these facets naturally intersect in intricate and powerful ways, as the environmental effects of enslaved labor cascaded throughout the ecosystem. The final chapter examines how the environmental factors during the Civil War shaped emancipation, demonstrating how African Americans drew upon accumulated environmental knowledge to liberate themselves. This thematic approach does not purport to provide an exhaustive or encyclopedic account, but rather to create a framework for understanding the relationship between slavery and the environment for others to expand upon, improve, and challenge.

To some degree, historians of American slavery have always recognized that environmental conditions mattered. In 1929, Ulrich B. Phillips opened his *Life and Labor in the Old South* by noting, "Let us begin by discussing the weather, for that has been the chief agency in making the South distinctive." If not for the climate, Philips argued, plantation agriculture and thus slavery would never have developed. Historians also recognized that enslaved labor reshaped the landscape. Beginning with Avery Craven's 1926 *Soil Exhaustion as a Factor in the Agricultural History of Virginia and Maryland, 1606–1860*, agricultural historians have recognized that the profitability of slave labor prompted plantation owners to abuse the land, favoring short-term financial gains over long-term sustainability.[3] In the near century since Phillips and Craven, historians' understanding of slavery, agriculture, and the environment of the South has changed profoundly, each evolving into its own distinct field within Southern history. In recent decades, they have flourished, although not always in full dialogue with each other. *Scars on the Land* attempts to weave together these scholarly threads together.[4]

This study draws upon some familiar sources such as fugitive slave narratives that recounted not only the horrors of human bondage but also how the Southern landscape shaped the contours of their enslavement. The particular demands of Virginia's tobacco fields, South Carolina's rice marshes, and the Black Belt's cotton plantations defined how slaves labored, each environment exacting a particular type of torture on the enslaved body and soul. The Southern landscape also determined their routes of escape. In evading slave patrols, fugitives hid in loblolly forests, pocosin swamps, alligator-infested rivers, and Smoky Mountain caves. Formerly enslaved people recalled their memories of these experiences and recounted them in WPA interviews conducted in the late 1930s. More than six decades after emancipation, elderly men and women vividly described how the soil, the weather, and the wilderness defined and confined their early lives.[5]

Of the many accounts by formerly enslaved people, a few voices stand out for their environmental insights. Foremost among them, Charles Ball's *Slavery in the United States* highlighted the diversity of the enslaved experience and showed how environmental factors shaped the lives of those held in bondage. Born in 1781 in Calvert County, Maryland, Ball labored under many enslavers, as sales, inheritances, and hirings repeatedly tore him from friends and family and took him from the tobacco fields of the Chesapeake to the rice and cotton fields of South Carolina and Georgia. Ball's peripatetic life enabled him into explore Southern swamps, forests, and rivers, observing the flora and fauna with a naturalist's eye. He managed to escape from slavery twice, using his knowledge of the land to aid him in his quest for freedom. First published in 1837, Ball's memoir became a template for many of the narratives that followed. Only a few fugitive slave narratives rival the breadth of Ball's ecological vision, though Henry Bibb, John Parker, Solomon Northup, and Frederick Douglass come close. Like Ball, they recognized how the natural environment shaped their lives in bondage and how enslaved labor effected profound changes in the Southern landscape.

In addition to listening to the voices of the enslaved, this study also draws upon the writings of planters and agricultural reformers, such as Thomas Jefferson and Edmund Ruffin, who wrestled with how to reconcile the demands of mastery, the market, and Mother Nature. In seeking to extract labor from their slaves and fertility from the soil, they created a brutal capitalism that laid waste to the Southern landscape and to Black bodies.[6] Visitors to the American South also chronicled their observations of slavery and environment. Although divided in their interests, prejudices, and backgrounds, scientists and naturalists like William Bartram, Charles Lyell, John James Audubon, and Frederick Law Olmsted each traveled through the slave South and recognized the complex relationships linking slavery and the environment. In addition to these textual sources, this book draws upon the work of archaeologists, environmental scientists, and historical geographers and climatologists to illuminate how the South's built and natural environments shaped enslaved people's lives and how in turn they remade the landscape.[7]

Two caveats: First, centuries of human occupation had transformed and molded the Southern landscape prior to the introduction of chattel slavery. Although white commentators often described the land beyond the slave frontier as natural, wild, and unsettled, the plantation revolution built upon ecosystems already profoundly altered by Native farming and hunting practices.[8] Second, this book should not be read as a work of environmental determinism. Nothing in the Southern environment made slavery necessary. Rather, both enslavers and the enslaved made choices about how to approach their natural environs. Slavery in the American South existed within

an environmental context that provided the contours of the enslaved experience and was remade by the work of enslaved hands. The environmental
devastation chronicled in this book pales in comparison to the brutality of
American slavery on human bodies and souls. Yet looking at slavery through
an environmental lens reveals how the chattel principle poisoned everything
it touched.

I

An Exhausted Soil

IN 1805, CHARLES BALL marched in a coffle from his native Maryland to Georgia. An iron chain, one hundred feet long, bound Ball to fifty-one other enslaved people, as they shuffled, handcuffed and collared, along a dirt road. Crossing the Potomac into Virginia, Ball noted that they "traversed a region, which had been deserted by the occupants—being no longer worth culture—and immense thickets of young red cedars, now occupied the fields, in digging of which thousands of wretched slaves had worn out their lives in the service of merciless masters." A century earlier, these abandoned fields stood at the epicenter of Virginia's tobacco boom, creating America's first planter class, some of whose names still marked the land: Carter, Lee, Byrd, and Washington. Ball could see the history of the region written on the landscape. The soil "had originally been highly fertile and productive . . . but the gentlemen who become the early proprietors of this fine region, supplied themselves with slaves from Africa, cleared large plantations of many thousands of acres—cultivated tobacco—and became suddenly wealthy." The region's prosperity proved fleeting, as slave owners "valued their lands less than their slaves, [and] exhausted the kindly soil by unremitting crops of tobacco." Once they had leached the soil, planters abandoned them, moving themselves and their enslaved people to the latest slavery frontier, where the process could be repeated.[1]

Southern planters' insatiable appetite for fertile land pushed slavery west and prompted an aggressive foreign policy bent on territorial acquisition. Slave-owning presidents expanded the frontier by purchase (Louisiana), annexation (Texas), and force (the Mexican Cession). Opening new lands to slavery required emptying them of native peoples, a quest that Southern slave owners pursued with vigor. The legal and military expulsion of Native peoples took on new urgency with the post-1812 cotton boom, as planters in Atlantic

Scars on the Land. David Silkenat, Oxford University Press. © Oxford University Press 2022.
DOI: 10.1093/oso/9780197564226.003.0002

states developed "Alabama Fever." Soil exhaustion not only pushed slavery's territorial expansion but also drove the internal slave trade. By the time the Atlantic trade closed in 1808, soil exhaustion and erosion in the Chesapeake had reached a critical state. The demand for slaves on the cotton frontier led to the forced relocation of more than one million slaves by 1860, a commerce that divided enslaved families and communities.[2]

The idea that Southern monoculture depleted the soil has deep roots. Decades ago, pioneering scholarship demonstrated how agricultural practices embraced by Southern planters leached the soil of nutrients and promoted erosion.[3] More recent scholarship has modified this thesis in two important respects. First, Southern soils may not have been so fertile initially. While the South benefited from a long growing season and abundant rainfall, the soil itself proved low in phosphorus and too acidic for sustained cultivation. Therefore, rather than depleting fertile soil through environmentally insensitive farming techniques, Southern plantation agriculture began on a fragile ecosystem. Second, regional and local variation in soil fertility and resilience meant that the same farming techniques could have radically different effects on the landscape. Even if plantation monoculture generally prompted erosion and soil infertility across the Slave South, some locales proved more resilient than others. Ecologically aware planters could maintain soil fertility through careful application of traditional and innovative agricultural techniques, including crop rotation and the use of fertilizers.[4]

This chapter situates soil depletion and erosion within a broader ecosystem. Planters' choices and enslaved laborers' actions had consequences not only for the soil but also for the rivers that eroded topsoil washed into and for the native species of plants and animals that depended upon the soil. Declining soil fertility not only affected agricultural output but had dramatic repercussions throughout the ecosystem. Enslaved mining in southern Appalachia also poisoned the soil. Thousands of enslaved people labored in gold mines in North Carolina and Georgia and in coal mines in Virginia that extracted wealth from the earth but devasted the environment. Both enslaved monoculture and mining had transformative effects on the local ecosystems and entire regions, as soil runoff and mining byproducts changed the composition of streams, forests, and biomes. This chapter attempts to put the voices and experiences of the enslaved at the center of the story. For Charles Ball and six million other enslaved men and women, their lives never took them far from the earth. They labored in the Southern soil from sunup to sundown: plowing, planting, hoeing, and harvesting left them caked in dirt. Many enslaved slept on straw pallets laid on packed dirt floors, burying treasured items in subterranean pits for safekeeping. When they died, they were buried in the same soil that dominated their lives, often committed to unmarked graves.

The ruined landscape that Charles Ball witnessed in 1805 had its roots more than a century earlier, as Chesapeake planters embraced a land and labor regime designed to maximize tobacco production. Of all the crops cultivated using enslaved labor, tobacco had a particular reputation for exhausting the soil. Sustained tobacco cultivation in the Chesapeake leached the soil of nitrogen, phosphorus, calcium, and potassium, reducing the topsoil to a dusty powder. Root rot and crippling fungi flourished in the depleted soil, choking the growing plants of nutrients. During the tobacco boom of the 1620s and 1630s, planters observed that tobacco grew best on fresh soils, prompting an aggressive policy of land accumulation and prospecting. Conventional wisdom among Chesapeake tobacco barons held that a field could productively support the noxious weed for three years, after which it would require two decades fallow before another planting. The rise of tobacco agriculture prompted Chesapeake planters to abandon European agricultural practices that sought to retain soil fertility. The expansive geography and the chronic labor shortage enabled them to view land as disposable. Crop rotation, manuring, and deep plowing seemed like poor investments in time and manpower when productive fresh lands could be cleared. Those planters who commanded the largest enslaved labor force could best exploit the abundant land, tasking some with planting tobacco on established fields and others with clearing the wilderness for the next year's planting.[5]

As enslaved Africans replaced English indentured servants as the dominant unfree agricultural labor force at the end of the seventeenth century, the planter class consolidated its power. In the half century after Bacon's Rebellion, Chesapeake's gentry engaged in a recursive process of purchasing more land and enslaved people to produce more tobacco. In 1701, a new arrival in Virginia noted how tobacco cultivation dominated the economic, social, and environmental landscape. "Tobacco is the principle [sic] article," he wrote. "It passes for money." The constant subject of discussion, tobacco drove enslavers to embrace a frantic, peripatetic life in search of "new soil." He quickly grasped the iterative power of enslaved labor, land, and tobacco. "Most of the wealth consists in slaves or negroes," he observed, "for if one has many workmen, much food-stuff and tobacco can be produced." By 1730, this quest for new tobacco lands pushed planters into more marginal soils, prompting a significant decline in productivity per acre and per enslaved worker. At the same time, tobacco overproduction had caused the price of tobacco to plummet. Many of largest planters responded by expanding their lands under cultivation, believing they could make up for low prices. Working as a tutor on Robert Carter III's Nomini Hall plantation, Philip Fithian remarked in 1774, "Their method of farming is slovenly, without any regard to continue their Land in heart, for future Crops—They plant large Quantities of Land, without any Manure & work it very hard to make the best of the Crop, and when the Crop comes off they take away the Fences to enclose another Piece of Land."[6]

By the mid-eighteenth century, some planters had begun to diversify their production, with many embracing wheat as an alternative to tobacco. A series of poor harvests in Europe elevated the price of grain, offering further entice-ment to shift production. The transition happened gradually and in a piece-meal fashion across the Chesapeake. An early adopter, George Washington had largely abandoned tobacco by 1760, though his enslaved workers con-tinued to grow small quantities throughout his lifetime. Despite embracing diversified agriculture early, he wished that he had not cultivated tobacco so long. "I never ride to my plantations," Washington wrote to a friend in 1785, "without seeing something which makes me regret having [continued] so long in the ruinous mode of farming." Thomas Jefferson stuck with tobacco far longer, only abandoning it in 1794. Shifting to diversified agriculture pushed Jefferson to reconfigure the landscape of enslavement at Monticello. From large multifamily cabins clustered near the overseer's house, enslaved families moved into smaller cabins distributed around the plantation, where they could be closer to Jefferson's various agricultural experiments.[7]

The shift to wheat brought its own set of environmental problems. When clearing a field for tobacco cultivation, enslaved laborers cut down trees but usually left the stumps and roots intact. Touring Virginia plantations in the late 1790s, architect and artist Benjamin Henry Latrobe observed that overseers used tree stumps to elevate themselves above enslaved laborers, surveilling them while they worked the soil with hoes. Planting tobacco in this manner expedited the opening of new fields for cultivation but also kept the arboreal root system in place, which helped to anchor the topsoil. Wheat cultivation, however, required plowing, which meant removing impediments such as stumps from the soil. Untethered by subterranean root systems, the soil on Virginia wheat fields eroded that much more quickly. When planted on old tobacco fields, wheat usually only sustained a few harvests before planters deemed the land worthless for agriculture.[8]

FIGURE 1.1. *An Overseer Doing His Duty*, 1798, Benjamin Henry Latrobe Sketch book, III, 33, Maryland Center for History and Culture, Baltimore. Note that the overseer stands on a tree stump, allowing him to surveil the enslaved women. Chesapeake tobacco plantations often left tree stumps in situ, and their roots helped to prevent erosion. The shift to wheat and intensive plowing required removing the stumps.

Erosion proved even more environmentally destructive than soil deg-radation. Without the protection of grasses or other native vegetation, exposed topsoil fell victim to the endemic heavy rainfall common in most of the Slave South. While the effect of intense afternoon thunderstorms on the Piedmont's red clay and Mississippi's sandy loam differed because of the slope and permeability of the soil, the resulting runoff often took with it the most nutrient-rich organic material, leaving behind a gullied and sterile land-scape. In Virginia, the runoff after intense thunderstorms was evident to even the casual observer, especially as cultivation spread to the hillier Piedmont. A British officer held captive in Virginia at the confluence of the James and Fluvanna Rivers noted in 1779 that heavy rain in the Piedmont "washes away the earth, which being of a red cast, appears like a torrent of blood."[9] Thomas Jefferson noted how Virginia's torrential storms quickly washed away top-soil from exposed fields. "Every rain," Jefferson wrote in an 1817 letter, "did permanent evil by carrying off our soil: and fields were no sooner cleared than wasted." Jefferson had taken steps to mitigate the erosion at Monticello, embracing contour (or horizontal) plowing, in which furrows follow the curves of the land, creating terraces to slow the runoff. Compared to traditional straight plowing, contour plowing required more labor and precision. Using a ten-foot rafter level, Thruston Hern, a fifteen-year-old enslaved boy, marked the contours at Monticello. While Jefferson adopted contour plowing, he used it inconsistently, and most of his contemporaries felt that the technique was too slow and labor intensive. Although the merits of various plows and plowing strategies filled the pages of agricultural journals, most planters continued to use traditional techniques, even if they knew the consequences. They responded to soil erosion and exhaustion by seeking out new lands further west. In 1831, one North Carolina planter complained that many of his neighbors refused to adopt erosion prevention techniques and "his land [was] soon washing way. As that goes down the rivers, he goes over the mountains."[10]

Despite the piecemeal transition to wheat, Virginia planters never entirely gave up on tobacco, a crop that maintained its economic and cultural importance. By the time of the American Revolution, tobacco planters' hunger for fresh soil had become one of their defining traits. "There is no plant in the world that requires richer land," a 1775 agricultural handbook advised, "than tobacco." The handbook linked tobacco cultivation, virgin land use, and enslaved labor, noting that tobacco "will grow on poorer soils, but not yield crops that are sufficiently profitable to pay the expences of negroes." Instead, it recommended that planters acquire "fresh woodlands, where many ages have formed a stratum of rich black mould. Such land will, after clearing, bear tobacco." The constant demand for fresh lands, the handbook concluded, "makes the tobacco planters more solicitous for new land than any other people in America." This made them an unusual aristocratic class. Rather than consolidate wealth and power in a particular locale, many planters saw land as a disposable commodity to consume and abandon: "When they have exhausted their grounds, [they] will sell them to new settlers for corn-fields, and move backwards with their negroes, cattle, and tools, to take up fresh land for tobacco." The handbook predicted that this pattern would "continue so as long as good land is to be had upon navigable rivers." The upheaval of the American Revolution threw Virginia's tobacco industry into chaos, as Dunmore's Proclamation and Cornwallis's army prompted thousands of enslaved people to seek freedom under the British flag and planters temporarily lost access to European markets. After Yorktown, however, most tobacco planters resumed their land-exhaustive practices. "The Virginians in the lower country are very easy and negligent husbandmen," noted one traveler in 1783. "New land is taken up, the best to be had, tobacco is grown on it 3–4 years, and then Indian corn as long as any will come. And in the end, if the soil is thoroughly impoverished, they begin again with a new piece and go through the rotation."[11]

By the early decades of the nineteenth century, many Virginians lamented the damage they had done to the landscape. Tobacco had created an ecological crisis that agricultural reformers sought to meet head-on. In 1818, planter and politician James M. Garnett decried "land-killers" who had transformed "a new country, almost boundless, . . . fresh lands of great fertility" and caused "the exhaustion of our soil." Rather than embrace agricultural reform, the "land-killer . . . according to his arithmetic" chose to settle "new lands" on the slave frontier. The following year, North Carolina planter George W. Jeffreys employed similar language, claiming that the common practice of "cutting down their woods and exhausting their lands" amounted to a "land-killing system." Garnett and Jeffreys joined reformers like Edmund Ruffin and John Taylor in calling for a scientific approach to tobacco agriculture. In farming journals and conventions, these reformers sought to demonstrate what "Virginia farmers and planters can accomplish on the good old soil of their forefathers" and "check that mad spirit of expatriation which is desolating our homes and fire-sides like a raging pestilence."[12]

Virginia planters knew their farming practices wore out the land. Despite persistent pleas by agricultural reformers to adopt crop rotation or use fertilizer to replenish the soils, they saw short-term profits as preferable to sustainable practices. Thomas Jefferson noted in 1793 that he did not use manure to fertilize his tobacco fields "because we can buy an acre of new land cheaper than we can manure an old acre." Twenty years later, Jefferson could see the consequences of his choice: "constant culture without any aid of manure" had rendered his soils inert. His neighbors, Jefferson noted, had "run away to Alibama [sic], as so many of our countrymen are doing, who find it easier to resolve on quitting their country, than to change the practices in husbandry to which they have been brought up."[13] When Frederick Law Olmsted challenged one Virginia tobacco planter about his destructive agricultural practices, he replied that he was "well-paid for it and did not know why he should not wear out his land." As tobacco planters moved west into the Piedmont, their problems only increased, as the clay-rich soils and steeper gradients prompted even faster erosion and soil degradation. Many planters discovered that these new soils could manage only two harvests before exhaustion. In an 1859 article in the *Southern Planter*, John Hartwell Cocke decried tobacco as "the Bane of Virginia Husbandry." All agreed, Cocke claimed, that tobacco was "the most exhausting of all crops." Its persistent cultivation had left "impoverished fields of the whole State . . . a standing monument against the ruthless destroyer."[14]

Desperate tobacco planters experimented with additives to rejuvenate their exhausted fields. In the 1840s, Edmund Ruffin experimented with marl (a calcium-rich clay), greensand (sandstone), and gypsum plaster, hoping to revitalize his Coggins Point plantation. From January through March, Ruffin allocated more than half of his enslaved labor force to the task, excavating calcium-rich clays from one part of his holdings and spreading them on his fields. "Two carts have been kept pretty constantly hauling marl," Ruffin wrote in February 1841. Ruffin had his strongest enslaved men quarry the marl and greensand from nearby riverbanks and assigned enslaved women and children with spreading it on his fields. Ruffin's experiments with soil additives made what had usually been a slow part of the agricultural calendar into one of the most grueling. Two days after "the worst snow storm we have had," Ruffin noted, he had the "marl carts at work all day." When spring rains filled marl trenches, Ruffin ordered enslaved laborers with buckets to bail the muddy water, sometimes for days. Ruffin's meticulous records suggested that this extra labor had done little to improve the soil's productivity. In May 1842, he noted laconically that his experiments had been "without any effect." Despite his own modest results, Ruffin became a leading proponent of using marl to improve depleted soils, claiming that "the most exhausted lands . . . have been greatly and rapidly improved" with its application. Ruffin's advocacy, however, did little to transform how most Chesapeake planters approached the issue of soil exhaustion. As long as new fertile soils remained available, they saw little benefit to Ruffin's expensive and time-consuming program.[15]

In the two decades prior to the Civil War, Chesapeake planters hoped to salvage their depleted fields with a new miracle cure, imported guano, deposited by centuries of seabirds on the Chincha Islands off the coast of Peru. Throughout the 1850s, Southern agricultural journals heralded the importance of guano in revitalizing worn out soils. The *American Farmer* noted that "amongst all the new-fangled manures introduced by experimenting agriculturalists, during the last twenty years, not one has been so rapidly and universally adopted as guano." The guano craze proved inescapable, especially in the Chesapeake. A passenger onboard the steamboat *Virginia* traveling from Baltimore to Fredericksburg in 1854 felt overcome by the odor, claiming that there was "now a guano epidemic among the planters of the Old Dominion. No vessel, I hear, leaves Baltimore for 'long shore' at this season, which is not freighted with it." The *Virginia*'s decks bore "hundreds of bags" such that "I shall never forget the bouquet: it was inhaled by me with every

thing I ate." Southerner planters' demand for guano reached such a pitch that
some advocated military and political pressure on the government of Peru,
the main source of American guano, to secure the fertilizer at a lower price.
In 1843, the first notable shipment of Peruvian guano arrived in Baltimore,
which would become the major Southern port for the fertilizer trade. During
its first decade, the quantity of guano imported in Baltimore rose from 445
tons to more than 25,000 tons.[16]

Despite its miraculous properties, imported guano proved too expensive for extensive use. Agricultural guides recommended up to eight hundred pounds of guano per acre, and at forty to fifty dollars per ton, even
the wealthiest planters only used it selectively. Moreover, guano proved an
incomplete fertilizer: nitrogen-rich but potassium-poor, guano temporary
revived exhausted soils but did not provide a long-term solution. The introduction of guano added to the demands placed upon enslaved workers. One
eastern North Carolina planter claimed that judicious use of imported guano
and domestic manure doubled his cotton and corn production. He warned,
however, that the process of improving the worn-out soil on his Edgecombe
County plantation exacted a heavy toll on his enslaved labor force. During
the two-week window between "fodder pulling and cotton picking," his
thirty-four enslaved men, women, and children shoveled compost, "filling up
our cattle and hog lots." Later, after the cotton had been picked, they returned
to manure duty, "composting cotton seed, and ditch bank, stable manure
and low ground soil, and hauling again into the cattle and hog lots." The following March, his slaves "commenced the troublesome and laborious job of
hauling out" and spreading the manure, which they mixed with twelve tons of
Peruvian guano. A single application of fertilizer, he warned, would do little
to improve the quality of the soil, arguing that the "the process of making
poor land fertile is the work of years, long years." Despite guano's popularity
in agricultural journals, many planters felt that increased productivity per acre
did not justify the added expense and labor. In 1858, North Carolina's official
geological survey found that many of the state's largest land and slave owners
dismissed the guano craze, believing they could replenish their fields with less
expensive alternatives, such as clover, or simply by acquiring virgin soil to re-
place that which had been leached from tobacco and cotton planting. Guano,
the report concluded, was "a drain upon the pockets of planters."[17]

The devastation in tobacco country sent ripples throughout the ecosystem.
Runoff clogged and polluted streams and rivers, turning pristine waterways
muddy and sterile. Native flora and fauna vanished. One Virginian lamented
in 1838 that "the lands naturally the best in the world have become worn and

exhausted by the culture of tobacco. The bitter weed has laid the forest low and left us with nothing but gall and gullies and dwarf pine. Our ridges have become so barren, they do not afford cover for the partridges and they have followed the soil down branches and creeks, hovering in the flats." As scrub forest reclaimed the land, many observers noted the absence of deer, bear, and other wildlife in the barren landscape. Visiting Virginia in 1834, three decades after Charles Ball witnessed how enslaved labor had left the soil barren, British abolitionist Edward Abdy observed that the landscape "exhibited the effects of slavery in every part of it:—an exhausted soil, miserable hovels, thinly peopled villages, half ploughed fields, and spontaneous vegetation in rank fertility, usurping the place of healthy and profitable crops." In contrast with the vibrant agriculture of the North, Abdy thought Virginia would become "a wilderness again."[18]

Cotton

If tobacco cultivation destroyed the soils in the Chesapeake and Piedmont, it paled in comparison to damage wrought by the cotton boom after 1800. Like wheat, cotton cultivation required plowing, untethering the topsoil from the clay below. Although agricultural journals chastised the practice, planters tended to arrange rows of cotton east to west to maximize sun exposure, ignoring the natural contours of the land. Heavy rains could turn cotton furrows into canals, swiftly eroding the topsoil. Cotton also required less labor per acre. Agricultural handbooks indicated that an enslaved man could tend only an acre or two of tobacco but eight to ten acres of cotton.[19]

"Cotton and negroes are the constant theme," wrote Joseph Holt Ingraham, a Northern-born teacher in Washington, Mississippi. "Not till every acre is purchased and cultivated—not till Mississippi becomes one vast cotton field, will this mania, which has entered into the very marrow, bone and sinew of a Mississippian's system, pass away." He foresaw the end result of the region's obsession with cotton and slavery: "The lands become exhausted and wholly unfit for farther cultivation." He could read in the landscape the foreshadowing of its own destruction: "The rich loam which forms the upland soil of this state is of a very slight depth—and after a few years is worn away by constant culture and the actions of the winds and rain. The fields are 'thrown out' as useless. Every plough furrow becomes the bed of a rivulet after heavy rains—these uniting are increased into torrents before which the impalpable soil dissolves like ice under a summer's sun. By degrees, acre after acre, of what was a few years previous beautifully undulating ground . . . presents

a wild scene of frightful precipices, and yawning chasms." By 1835, still early
in the state's cotton boom, Ingraham saw evidence of the environmental destruction wrought by enslaved agriculture. Soil erosion had transformed the
area around Natchez, "the earliest cultivated portions of the country," into
"wild desolation."[20]

As the cotton-slave frontier spread westward, it left devastated soils in its
wake and drove the domestic slave trade. In 1827, a traveler departed Augusta,
Georgia, and "overtook hordes of cotton planters from North Carolina,
South Carolina, and Georgia with large gangs of negroes, bound for Alabama,
Mississippi, and Louisiana; 'where the cotton land is not worn out.'" A decade
later, a Georgia newspaper complained that thousands of acres of broken land
"that were once fertile, and richly re-paid labour" now stood "worthless to
the last degree—nothing but sterile red clay." Between 1850 and 1860, nearly
60 percent of planters in the Cotton Belt had relocated. In 1853, newspaper
editor James D. B. DeBow lamented that the South's failure to embrace agricultural reform had produced a peripatetic planter class, as "the lands which
were the most fertile, became at last, almost irretrievably barren; and the
sons, whose fathers grew wealthy, scarcely with an effort, are forced to submit
themselves to exile from the paternal estates, sacrificing them or abandoning
them, to seek in new and virgin soils the support they cannot find at home."
When they cast their ballots in 1860, many Mississippi planters foresaw soil
degradation and the collapse of cotton production in the Delta and pondered
where the next slave frontier would lead them.[21]

While some tobacco planters embraced the rejuvenating effects of manure
and marl, cotton planters saw little value in trying to preserve the fertility of
their soil. "No one who has been attentive to the cotton culture, as pursued
in the south-western States," lamented Alabama politician Philip Phillips in
1849, "but recognizes its exhaustive culture." An advocate for railroads and
other internal improvements, Phillips saw planters enriching themselves at
the cost of the soil and broader economic development. "The opinion is generally prevalent among our cotton planters, that it is cheaper to purchase new
lands than to manure old ones," he noted; "like the locust, they settle only to
destroy." With fresh land selling for four dollars per acre, it made little sense
to invest in expensive reclamation projects; fertilizing an old field cost more
than twice as much as buying virgin soil. Yet Phillips argued that slave owners'
practice of abandoning worn-out cotton fields inhibited the development of
robust transportation networks. Without a stable population and markets,
railroads could not plan or invest. It created a feedback loop: planters refused
to use manure, citing high transportation costs, but their quest for fertile

virgin soils made it difficult to build infrastructure that would lower transportation costs. Only by breaking this cycle, Phillips argued, could Alabama take advantage of its great mineral wealth in iron, coal, limestone, and marble.[22]

Enslaved people drew connections between the abuse of the soil and their own experiences in bondage. Laboring on several Maryland plantations, John Thompson saw parallels between enslavers' brutality and their treatment of the land. After experiencing torture at the hands of several owners, he was hired to a plantation where the owner did not practice wanton violence, which Thompson deemed "humane." He believed that "the land being less cursed by cruelty, was rich and fertile; producing in abundance corn, wheat, and tobacco." Charles Ball made a similar observation, noting that the regions where he saw the most cruelty also had the most degraded soil. In upcountry South Carolina, he witnessed the "half-naked condition of the negroes. . . . Their wan complexions, proved to me that they had too much work, or not enough food," toiling where the "fields were destitute." In Virginia, he observed the "long since worn out and exhausted soil . . . tortured into barrenness by the double curse of slavery and tobacco." Enslaved in Kentucky, Lewis Clarke put it simply: slavery "curses the soil."[23]

While the expanding slave frontier leached the soil of nutrients, it also introduced new pathogens into the soil. Imported from Africa aboard slave ships, hookworms flourished in the ecosystem of the American South. The parasite's larvae hatch in warm, moist dirt and burrow into their host through the skin. The microscopic organisms then travel though the bloodstream to the lungs, induce coughing fits, and thus enter the digestive system, where they mature to full size and mate. Attaching themselves to the walls of the small intestine, hookworms can live from one to five years, during which they can produce up to 25,000 eggs per day. Distributed via the host's feces, the eggs return to the soil to begin the lifecycle. Enslaved people proved the ideal host for spreading hookworm throughout Southern soils. The tiny hookworm causes persistent anemia, so although not fatal, an infection causes a panoply of maladies, including diarrhea, vomiting, constipation, chronic fatigue, edema, and hypoalbuminemia (protein deficiency). Infection sites, where the hookworm burrowed into the skin, can develop chronic inflammation, a phenomenon slaves called "ground itch." In children, hookworm infestation prompts delayed physical and mental development; in pregnant women, it produces low-birthweight babies.[24]

Some scholars have hypothesized a relationship between hookworm infestation and geophagia, the cultural practice of clay-eating, among enslaved people. Plantation owners frequently commented in horror on the practice, punishing enslaved people for engaging in what they conceived of as a barbaric behavior. Slaves, they believed, had a preternatural attraction to dirt eating, a compulsion they compared to tobacco or alcohol addiction. Dr. William M. Carpenter, one of the foremost white authorities on slave medicine, labeled the practice "cachexia Africana," claiming that slaves felt "a depraved appetite causing an invisible craving for earthy substances." Yet clay-eating may have had a therapeutic effect, replacing nutrients lost due to anemia and easing intestinal pain caused by the hookworm infestation. While clay-eating may have caused hookworm reinfection, the practice may also have provided needed calcium, magnesium, and iron, all deficient in the enslaved diet. The transatlantic and internal slave trade allowed the worm to travel from Africa to Virginia and South Carolina and Texas, infecting millions of enslaved people and acres of soil.[25]

The soil provided a venue for other parasitic worms to infect enslaved people. Antebellum physicians identified at least five varieties of intestinal parasites, including two varieties of threadworm, two varieties of tapeworm, and roundworm, though they frequently misdiagnosed or misidentified the resulting illnesses. Each of these parasites exploited the unhygienic conditions in the slave quarters and fields. Spread by human and animal feces, these parasites contributed to a range of physical maladies, including anemia, abdominal pain, diarrhea, and vomiting. In rare cases, they prompted fatal intestinal blockages.[26] In 1758, Windsor, an enslaved man on Landon Carter's Sabine Hall plantation, experienced violent abdominal pains from a tapeworm infection. Delirious, Windsor had to be restrained "from killing himself." Carter administered powerful purgatives, which "brought off large quantitys of Slimy . . . parts of the Joint worm." Working with the enslaved near Fredericksburg, Virginia, in the 1820s, Dr. James Carmichael found parasitic worms endemic among enslaved children, who customarily did not receive shoes until adulthood. Prior to approaching Carmichael, Virginia planters usually administered calomel, a mercury-based purgative, to treat enslaved children. Only when this treatment failed did they seek professional medical advice. One wrote that an eighteen-month-old enslaved child was "no better [after calomel] but several worms have crept from it—all live and from the mouth." Another wrote that a six-year-old enslaved boy suffered every evening from high fever and had "a good many worms come from him." Laboring in the soil, slaves found themselves constantly re-exposed to worm larvae. Cramped living conditions and inadequate sanitation in slave quarters reinforced the parasitic relationship between enslaved African Americans and worms.[27]

Enslaved people left the fields with their bodies and clothes drenched in sweat, dirt, and grime. Physically exhausted from toiling since sunrise and without the time, energy, or facilities to properly clean themselves, many enslaved people went to sleep with dirt encrusted on their skin and under their nails. Growing up enslaved on a cotton and cattle plantation in Texas, Adeline Cunningham recalled that "de slaves comes in from de fields and dey hands is all dirty." She vividly remembered that the laborers returned so depleted and hungry that "dey dips de dirty hands right in de trough" that held their communal meal. For Charlie Davenport, enslaved on a Mississippi cotton plantation, working in the soil amounted to his only education. Sent into the fields to pick cotton as a young child, he said, "When I growed up, I was a ploughman." He prided himself on his ability to pick cotton as well any anyone. "Us fiel' han's never knowed nothin'," he recalled, "'cept weather an' dirt."[28]

Mining

In 1833, Henry Barnard, a recent Yale graduate touring the South, noted that the prosperous gold mines near Morganton, North Carolina, generated massive but short-term profits for their owners. "These mines will be exhausted in a few years and then the land will be good for nothing, and this mining land is the only land that can be cultivated," he observed. "There are 5000 slaves engaged in mining in this county." While enslaved labor prompted soil depletion and erosion across the plantation South, extractive mining in southern Appalachia swiftly laid waste to a local ecosystem. Barnard witnessed firsthand how the work of enslaved gold miners transformed the landscape. They dug through four to eight feet of topsoil to reach a layer of gravel where "gold is diffused in very minute particles." To extract the gold, enslaved men shoveled tons of crushed gravel into a rocker box, a large inclined cradle where "a constant stream of water is kept running on it." The addition of quicksilver (mercury) to the rocker caused the tiny gold flecks to congeal into an amalgam, which could then be picked from the rocker. When heated, the mercury evaporated, leaving behind relatively pure gold. The entire process poisoned the workers, the waterways, and the soil.[29]

Prior to the California Gold Rush, the epicenter of American gold mining sat in the mountains of northern Georgia and western North and South Carolina, with tendrils stretching into western Virginia, eastern Tennessee, and northern Alabama. Although gold was first discovered in the region in 1799, systematic extraction only began in the 1820s. In the three decades prior

FIGURE 1.2. Rocking Cradles. Porte Crayon [David Hunter Strother], "North Carolina Illustrated: The Gold Region." *Harper's New Monthly Magazine* 15 (1857): 297.

to the Civil War, mining in Southern Appalachia produced approximately forty million dollars in gold, much of it extracted by enslaved laborers, nearly ten thousand of whom toiled with shovel, pick, and rocker at its apex in the 1830s. Enslaved miners handled the dirtiest and most dangerous jobs because, as one mine manger explained, "Negroes are found to be among the most efficient laborers."[30]

Enslaved gold mining passed through three distinct phases, with escalating environmental effects. Placer mining dominated during the first two decades of the nineteenth century, when most of the southern Piedmont and Appalachia remained in Cherokee hands, despite significant white encroachment in the region. Placer miners took advantage of the natural erosion caused by mountain streams, which exposed alluvial deposits. In geologic time, the force of water separated the dense and malleable gold from the surrounding rock, leaving creek beds strewn with the precious metal. From the very beginning, gold-hungry prospectors envisioned drawing upon the enslaved labor force. "Blacks who have been accustomed to the hoe will consider the search [for gold] more as amusement than work," posited Dr. William Thornton, who surveyed the North Carolina backcountry in 1805. A physician and architect (famous for designing the original 1793 plan for the US Capitol), Thornton proposed a joint stock company that would use enslaved labor to gather gold from mountain streambeds. He envisioned that gold harvesting would run alongside agricultural production, with slaves tending corn and wheat fields and "orchards of apples, peaches, &c." Gold extraction, therefore, would work in tandem with a form of "safety-first" farming already taking root in the Appalachian frontier. While Thornton's efforts never came to fruition, other prospectors did successfully profit using enslaved workers. Foremost among them was North Carolinian John Reed, whose twelve-year-old son, according to local legend, discovered a seventeen-pound gold nugget in 1799, setting off the first gold rush. In 1803, the elder Reed, a former Hessian soldier who deserted his regiment at Savannah, formed a partnership with three other local farmers, each contributing the labor of two enslaved men to scour streambanks during slow periods of the agricultural calendar, especially in the winter, when the creeks ran dry. Although Reed's corporation made some profitable discoveries, including a twenty-eight-pound nugget found by an enslaved man named Peter, the capricious nature of the work and the region's remoteness retarded the growth of gold extraction. Even Reed and his partners saw gold harvesting as a sideline to their agricultural pursuits, a hedge in case of drought or blight. One letter from 1807 noted that slave owners in Burke County, North Carolina, deployed their enslaved workers to hunt for gold "whenever the corn is hoed, the cotton is weeded, and the agriculture duties which engage them will permit."[31]

In 1825, the discovery of underground veins transformed gold extraction in southern Appalachia. First identified in western North Carolina's Montgomery County and subsequently in nearby counties in South Carolina and Georgia, subterranean deposits created a gold rush and helped to establish a robust enslaved mining industry. Unlike placer mining, subterranean hard-rock mining required a substantial labor supply to extract and process the gold grains from tons of gravel. While Southern gold mining companies employed some free white workers, often immigrants from mining regions of Britain and Germany, many local whites disdained mining, which they associated with drudgery. Mine owners, therefore, relied heavily upon enslaved men, both owned and rented, for the most difficult and dangerous work. Enslaved men provided at least a third of the mining labor in the region and the majority on the largest industrial mines.[32]

The Georgia Gold Rush of 1829 exacerbated tensions between Cherokees and white gold hunters. During "the winter of 1829 and 30," noted one Georgia newspaper, "when the precious metals having been discovered in great abundance upon our Cherokee soil, great numbers of people from Georgia and other States rushed to the Territory in search of its treasures." Boom towns sprung up overnight: Auraria and Dahlonega in Georgia and Morganton, Rutherfordton, and Gold Hill in North Carolina. By 1830, the year Congress passed the Indian Removal Act, thousands of miners had descended upon the southern Appalachian gold fields. The earliest '29ers were placer miners, who scoured the riverbanks for gold, but within a year, capital- and labor-intensive industrial mining operations had set up operation. The Cherokee called this influx the Great Intrusion. "Our neighbors who regard no law and pay no respects to the laws of humanity are now reaping a plentiful harvest," complained one writer in the *Cherokee Phoenix*. "We are an abused people. If we can receive no redress, we can feel deeply the injustice done to our rights." In 1832 and 1833, the state of Georgia ran a series of land lotteries to distribute Cherokee land to white settlers, including many speculators who hoped to draw a golden allotment. In 1835, the Federal Mint opened branches in Dahlonega and Charlotte to capitalize on the southern Appalachian Gold Rush, signaling the Federal government's approval of the land seizure. After the fraudulent Treaty of New Echota in 1838, the Federal army forcibly relocated most Cherokee in southern Appalachia from their homeland to Indian Territory.[33]

In a mountainous region unsuitable for plantation agriculture, mine owners ranked among the largest enslavers in southern Appalachia. Throughout the 1830s and 1840s, advertisements for renting slaves for work in the mines became a staple in North Carolina and Georgia newspapers. Although the mines operated year-round, extraction intensified during the winter, between planting and harvest seasons, or when cotton prices were low, when planters reallocated enslaved labor from the cotton fields to the gold mines. "Farming and gold-digging went, in many cases, hand in hand," observed geologists H. B. C. Nitze and H. A. J. Wilkens. "When the crops were laid by, the slaves and the farmhands were turned into the creek-bottoms, thus utilizing their prime during the dull season. When mining proved more profitable than planting, the former superseded the latter entirely."[34]

The Appalachian Gold Rush attracted interest and investment from across the country and around the world, but many of its largest proprietors came from the South and had deep ties to the institution of slavery. "Numbers of our most intelligent, wealthy, and enterprising citizens from the eastern and middle counties," one North Carolinian observed in April 1830, "are withdrawing their slaves entirely from the cultivation of cotton and tobacco, and removing them to the deposit mines." Foremost among the planter class to embrace gold mining was South Carolina senator John C. Calhoun. In 1833, at the height of the gold rush and shortly after his resignation as Andrew Jackson's vice president, Calhoun purchased the O'Barr mine in Lumpkin County, Georgia. Compared to his other sites of enslaved labor, the 239-acre mine proved highly profitable, despite its relatively small size. Between 1833 and 1835, Calhoun's twenty enslaved miners extracted enough gold that Calhoun pocketed approximately five hundred dollars per person each year, a rate of return that greatly outpaced his cotton plantations. Pleased with his investment, Calhoun claimed that "the gold business is universally doing well" and saw "no reason why it should not continue to yield at the same rate" for the foreseeable future. With politics keeping him in Washington, Calhoun tasked his son-in-law, Thomas Clemson, a mining engineer by training, with its management. "The amount of labor that has been expended in this region is prodigious," Clemson noted in 1844. "The streams have been turned from their courses, and the banks and alluvion have been dug down to the slate."[35]

These enormous profits came at a tremendous environmental cost and risk to enslaved miners. Accessing the subterranean veins required tunneling deep into the Appalachian hillsides, with the mining shafts reaching a depth of 150 feet and horizontal tunnels extending "a great distance." During his visit to North Carolina, Henry Barnard ventured into a gold mine near Charlotte. Candle in hand, he "descended the perpendicular shaft nearly 100 ft . . . [that] then penetrates the mines 100 yards in various directions." Like many in the region, the mine used black powder to blast through granite, slate, and quartz, which dazed Barnard with "a stunning noise." Navigating underground proved challenging, as "we were obliged in some places to slide, in others to creep and stoop, which is very trying to the back." As Barnard's account indicates, working in Appalachian gold mines exposed enslaved workers to profoundly dangerous conditions, where they could be injured, maimed, or killed. At one North Carolina mine, two enslaved men were "engaged in blowing up rock, when one of the blasts went off unexpectedly, putting out the eyes of the negroes and inflicting other injuries." Both of the men had been rented to the mine and became a cautionary tale for planters seeking to profit from the rental market. The worst documented mining disaster took place at the Franklin Mine in Cherokee County, Georgia, when a timber beam supporting the roof collapsed, killing an entire enslaved mining crew. Knowing the danger, some slave owners explicitly prohibited mine work in rental contracts. "There is a general prejudice against letting [enslaved] hands work in the mines," wrote one mine operator in Brackettown, North Carolina, as many planters worried about the health and safety of their enslaved property. Not infrequently rented enslaved men complained to their owners about conditions in the mines and begged to be allowed to return home.[36]

Extracted from the depths of the mines by bucketloads, dirt and gravel laced with minute particles of gold required extensive processing. At most industrial mines, enslaved miners fed the excavated material into a Chilean mill, a water-, horse-, or steam-powered machine for crushing the gold-laden rocks beneath heavy stone wheels. Next, enslaved miners, working either alone or in pairs, manned a rocker box, a long, riffled sluice that used water to separate the gold from the detritus and mercury to cause the gold to amalgamate. Effectively operating the rocker box required both skill and patience. Then, in a process known as retorting, the gold could be separated from the mercury amalgam by adding heat in a still or an open flame. While much of the mercury could be recovered, significant amounts were lost in both the washing and distilling processes, leaving concentrated amounts of the toxin in the spoil piles and mountain streams. Mercury mixed with the sulfuric acid created when deep earth soils came into contact with oxygen poisoned the watershed, its effects reaching far beyond mining territory. Enslaved miners suffered from mercury poisoning, both from working with the liquid form with their bare hands and from inhaling fumes during distillation. Such exposure had both short- and long-term consequences, including skin irritation, numbness in the hands and feet, kidney problems, memory loss, and impaired speech, hearing, and sight.[37]

Contemporaries were not blind to the environmental destruction that mining wrought. "On approaching Dahlonega," wrote one visitor in 1848, "I notice that the water-coarses had all been mutilated with the spade and pickaxe, and that their waters were of a deep yellow; and having explored the country since then, I find that such is the condition of all streams within a circuit of many miles." The two decades since the start of the gold rush had left the surrounding hillsides pockmarked, "riddled with shafts and tunnels." In an article extolling Georgia's natural beauty, painter George Cooke offered Dahlonega as a cautionary tale. The site may once have been a "Paradise," but now "the whole population is engaged in digging for gold; and the face of the country for many miles presents the appearance of new made graves." Contemporaries also recognized that the conditions under which enslaved miners lived and worked were extraordinarily harsh. "I staid at the mines untill I was convinced that Money was the Root of all Evil, and that slavery would prove a curse to our Nation if nott its Ruin," wrote a Kentucky man passing through North Carolina's gold fields. "Thousands of Slaves was engaged in these Mines under Cruel Masters who had a Great thirst for filthy Lucre."[38]

Despite the conditions, some enslaved people preferred working in the mines to life in the cotton or tobacco fields. One visitor to the region noted that the mines in Haywood County, North Carolina, were "conducted almost entirely by the negroes, without supervision." Many of the enslaved workers had been hired seasonally and were "greatly pleased with the mining life & would not willingly revert to the labour of tillage." He believed that they preferred mining because work ended at sundown and "they have no tax on their time or exertions for the night."[39]

Part of the work's appeal, at least for some enslaved miners, was the opportunity to smuggle gold out of the mine. Mine managers knew that preventing such clandestine trafficking required constant vigilance, as enslaved miners could conceal gold dust in the seams of their clothes. Physical inspections at the end of the day became common practice at many mines, with those found with gold on their person punished severely. "The black men employed in washing [the gold-laden gravel] were slaves" who "were closely watched to prevent their secreting any pieces of gold they might find," noted one traveler. In 1830, a frustrated Georgia mine overseer ordered his enslaved workers shaved before they left the mine, uncovering several ounces of gold that they had secreted in their hair. Some mine proprietors tried to discourage such subterfuge by allowing enslaved miners to keep gold they procured outside of normal working hours. "Many of the negroes search for gold on Sunday and holidays," noted one newspaper, "and several have found so much as to pay for the freedom of themselves and families." At his mine near Frogtown, Georgia, Jacob Scudder permitted enslaved miners to keep gold secured after nightfall, provided they only sold the gold to him. Panning "after sundown by light from rich pine torches," Dan Riley managed to accumulate enough gold to purchase freedom for himself and his wife, Lucinda. In Goochland County, Virginia, Bill Easton purchased his freedom with $2,000 he had accumulated from his work in the Waller mine. Such examples of self-purchase, however, proved rare.[40]

Gold fueled the underground economy that linked the enslaved with poor white farmers and merchants willing to overlook legal prohibitions. Appalachian mining towns hosted "gambling houses, dancing houses, drinking saloons, houses of ill fame, billiard saloons, and tenpin alleys [that] were open day and night," a few of which opened their doors to enslaved miners. Those businesses catering to enslaved miners charged exorbitant prices to fleece their clientele. One journalist noted that "at the surrounding groceries and liquors shops, the negroes employed in the mines" exchanged "for a pint of brandy or whiskey a pint of gold, which they abstracted from their masters, or collected at night." Local courts occasionally cracked down on this illicit traffic, though never to the extent that it curtailed the robust underground economy.[41]

Enslaved miners used commandeered gold not only to purchase freedom and participate in the underground economy but also to facilitate escape. A few ounces of purloined gold helped them make it to freedom and establish themselves afterward. Runaway advertisements suggest that enslaved miners often tried to run away. While some headed north, relying on the Appalachian wilderness for concealment, leased slaves often ran away to return home, reuniting with family and complaining of the dangerous working conditions in the mines. Runaway advertisements also reveal that plantation owners suspected that runaways fled to the gold fields as a refuge. In North Carolina, they believed that fugitives might be "about the gold mines," "lurking about the gold mines," "in the neighborhood of the Harris Mine," or "lurking about Reed's Gold Mine." The transient nature of the mining population allowed runaways to blend in and escape detection. Born enslaved in Richmond, Wash Ingram recalled that his father "was a fightin' man and he run off and got a job in a gold mine in Virgini.'"[42]

While mine operators concentrated their efforts on preventing enslaved miners from running away and from smuggling gold, the broader white community of southern Appalachia grew increasingly concerned about the presence of so many enslaved people in the region. The concentration in mining camps of enslaved adult men, most of them young and without families, seemed like a powder keg. In 1830, panicked rumors spread in western North Carolina about a fugitive slave called Big George who reportedly had murdered a white South Carolinian and had been sighted in the gold region.[43]

Nat Turner's Rebellion in 1831 only served to amplify white residents' paranoia. Across the South, rumors of possible enslaved conspiracies metastasized, as did violence against enslaved and free African Americans. In late September, a month after the rebellion but prior to Turner's capture, white residents of Rutherford and Burke Counties, North Carolina, began to hear that Black miners, led by an enslaved preacher named Fed, were plotting to attack and overrun Morganton and Rutherfordton, sowing death and destruction. "The excitement amongst the people is considerable," warned one local newspaper. "The development of an intended Insurrection, among the Slaves working at some of the Gold Mines in this County . . . appears to call for prompt, efficient, and uniform exertions to be adopted . . . to put down this insurrectionary spirit," noting that "the plot is much more extensive than has yet been brought to light." Because so many of the enslaved miners were recent arrivals, the newspaper pinned the purported insurrections on the "introduction to this County of negroes of bad, doubtful, or suspicious character."[44]

Not everyone, however, was caught up in the panic. Isaac T. Avery, the owner of one of the region's largest gold mines and ninety enslaved people, wrote to his sister that "a Negro Preacher" had been "charged with mediating an insurrection, in the neighborhood of the mines," and inflamed "a state of uncommon excitement." He had doubts, however, about the extent of the plot and indeed if a conspiracy existed at all. "The great number of Slaves employed about the mines, would render vigilance among Managers and Patrollers proper at all times," Avery opined, "but from the information I can get, there is just no ground for the Panic that has existed. The Negroes of the Country, are as orderly and submissive, as I ever knew them & I really believe that the alarm is alltogether imaginary." He told his sister that she had no reason to be concerned. Yet over the next six months, mountain whites uncovered at least two other alleged conspiracies among enslaved miners, a testament to their paranoia after Nat Turner.[45]

The Nat Turner panic coincided with the apex of gold production in southern Appalachia. By 1840, prospectors had secured most of the surface gold from creek banks, and hard rock miners had extracted much of the easily accessible subterranean veins. While the output of the southern Appalachian gold region gradually declined, enslaved miners became an increasingly important part of the labor force, as white prospectors in search of a quick fortune abandoned mining for other pursuits or left for California in the 1849 Gold Rush. By 1850, what remained of the southern Appalachian gold industry centered on the large industrial mines in North Carolina and Georgia, highly capitalized and technologically complex enterprises that relied on enslaved labor. This third and final phase of antebellum gold mining in southern Appalachia witnessed increasing concentration of wealth in the hands of the remaining mining magnates. Yet many suspected that southern Appalachia's gold mining days were coming to a close. Diminishing returns prompted one geologist to claim in 1854 that "the future operations in the mines, must, if they be permanently productive, be carried to a far greater depth."[46]

By the late 1850s, technologies first introduced in northern California's gold fields had made their way to the Appalachian mines. New Yorker

William Phipps Blake promoted hydraulic mining to Southern mine owners, promising "that by introducing water by canals, as in California, and washing down the hills by the hydraulic process, a new era of mining will be inaugurated." If subterranean mining sought to remove the gold from the hills through burrowing into its depths, hydraulic mining aimed to remove the hills from the gold, blasting away tons of earth in the process. Blake presented this environmentally devasting technique as a form of technological modernity: "The water issuing in a continuous stream, with great force, from a large hose-pipe, like that of a fire engine, is directed against the base of a bank of earth and gravel, and tears it away. The bank is rapidly undermining, the gravel is loosened and violently rolled together, and cleansed from any adhering particles of gold, while the fine sand and clay are carried off in the water." Using this technique, Blake argued, "square acres of earth on the hillsides may thus be swept away into the hollows, without the aid of a pick or shovel in excavating." Without referencing slavery explicitly, Blake touted hydraulic mining as a "labor-saving process," an appealing option considering the escalating value attached to enslaved men. By 1858, several mines in Georgia, especially along the Yahoola and Chestatee Rivers, had embraced hydraulic mining, revitalizing a dying industry, By 1861, however, its environmental effects had become apparent, as the "tailings from their mills" had been "emptied into this stream [the Yahoola], with a considerable quantity of auriferous sulphides."[47]

In 1857, a *Harper's Weekly* reporter and illustrator visited the North Carolina gold hills to see what remained of the once vibrant industry. Writing under the pen-name "Porte Crayon," David H. Strother observed that "at the present day the surface gold is very scare, and the precious ore is found principally in veins of quartz, bedded in the hardest black slate." En route to Gold Hill from Salisbury, he observed the ruins of a dying industry: "heaps of red earth, broken rocks, decaying windlasses, and roofless sheds, designating the spots where men had wasted time and money in searching for the 'earth's most operant poison.'" When he arrived in Gold Hill, he found "nothing in the appearance of the place or its inhabitants to remind one of its auriferous origin, but, on the contrary, a deal of dirt and shabbiness."

Unimpressed with the surface, Strother persuaded a mine operator to allow him to tour one of the mines. Donning mining apparel, he descended a series of "narrow slippery ladders, and nothing between us and the bottom but four hundred feet of unsubstantial darkness." Halfway through their descent, Strother "found a couple of negroes boring in the rock with iron sledge and auger," excavating a new branch of the mine. "Heated and reeling with fatigue," Strother eventually made it to the mine's gallery, where the enslaved miners were preparing to use black powder. Huddled in a safe location, he heard of series of blasts and was "soon enveloped in an atmosphere of sulphurous smoke." Having seen enough, Strother asked to be returned to the surface, exhausted and overwhelmed by his brief venture into the mine.[48]

Surveying the region in the aftermath of Cherokee Removal, government geologist George William Featherstonhaugh remarked upon the environmental destruction. "I could not but be sorry to see the destruction which awaited all these beautiful valleys," he wrote. "The fine trees with which they were covered were all in a way of being rooted up; the soil, after being washed left in rude heaps, and the streams diverted from their courses." Sympathetic to the plight of the Cherokee, whom he believed had been illegally stripped of their land, Featherstonhaugh observed how the land was "once the favourite resort of the red man when pursuing his game; but which the white man has converted into a picture of perfect desolation. To obtain a small quantity of

FIGURE 1.3. Boring. Porte Crayon [David Hunter Strother], "North Carolina Illustrated: The Gold Region," *Harper's New Monthly Magazine* 15 (1857): 294.

gold for the wants of the present generation, the most fertile bottoms are rendered barren for countless generations."[49]

Other extractive industries wrought environmental destruction across the Slave South. By the 1840s, southern Appalachia boasted robust coal, iron, copper, salt, and potassium nitrate mining operations, enterprises that relied on enslaved labor to carry out the dirtiest and most dangerous work and left an indelible imprint on the landscape. Intensive mining, even if only done for a few years, polluted topsoil with toxic detritus, contaminated mountain streams, and consumed millions of acres of forest for fuel.[50]

Mine operators insisted that only enslaved labor could do this dangerous work. An Alabama coal mine owner claimed in 1859 that it was "impossible to prosecute my mining interest successfully with free labor. . . . I must have a negro force or give up my business." When these mines collapsed, flooded, or exploded, enslaved miners paid the price. Enslaved workers in the coal mines near Richmond, Virginia, knew that their lives were at risk every time they went underground, as a series of disasters had killed hundreds. In 1839, a gas explosion seven hundred feet below ground killed forty-five enslaved miners at the Black Heath Mine. "The laborers were all colored men," noted the *Richmond Enquirer*, which attributed the explosion to poor safety precautions. In 1855, an explosion in the Midlothian mines killed between thirty-four and fifty-five miners, nearly all enslaved, and left "a number of others so badly burned that little or no hopes are entertained of their recovery. . . . Some of the dead men, the flesh charred on their bones, held their shovels in their hands. . . . Those who were not dead . . . begged earnestly not to be left, and then prayed loudly for a few drops of cold water to quench their burning thirsts." The following year, the Midlothian mines flooded, killing seven enslaved men and one white overseer. Beyond these disasters, Virginia's coal fields had a reputation for killing and crippling their enslaved workers, prompting many enslavers to fear renting to mining operations. "From the impending danger they supposed to exist," one Richmond mine manger wrote in 1858, "slave-owners could not be induced to engage their hands without first effecting an insurance upon them." However, due to recent subterranean disasters in which "life had been sacrificed," he found no insurance company willing to issue a policy. While enslavers and insurance companies balked at the dangerous conditions in coal mines, those with the most to lose, the enslaved miners themselves, voiced the loudest objections. One enslaver had pledged six men to work in a Virginia mine in 1815 but reconsidered after learning of the perilous conditions and their adamant refusal: "The negroes themselves also positively object to going to the pits," he wrote. Like their brethren in the gold fields, enslaved people sent into the coal mines had a reputation for running away.[51]

Generations of enslaved people were buried in the same soil they worked in life. Across the plantation South, secluded grounds on the periphery became a kind of eternal slave quarters, an anonymous chronicle of their lives. Demarcated only by hollow depressions in the soil and local oral tradition, many of these graveyards for the enslaved have recently revealed their secrets to archaeologists, who have used ground penetrating radar to document their subterranean contents. When Allen Parker's mother died in eastern North Carolina in August 1861, a month after the Battle of Bull Run, she was buried unceremoniously in an unmarked shallow grave, "the sandy earth heaped above it." Parker could not mourn her publicly. "Not a prayer was said nor a hymn sung," Parker recalled, "for the white folks seemed to feel that the sooner the matter was over the more time the slaves would have for work, and the slaves—well they were not supposed to feel at all, they were only cattle." He hoped that one day he would "meet her in that land where all shall be free, and where there shall be no night nor any sorrow, and where there shall be none to oppress."[52]

2
———

An Animal without Hope

"THE REAL INJURY" of slavery, wrote runaway John Parker, was that it made "a human being an animal without hope." Throughout his autobiography, Parker compared his experience in bondage with the lives of wild and domestic animals. Born in Virginia in 1827, Parker was "sold south like their mules" to Alabama. Running away, he took to the swamp, "full of wolves and catamounts" and the "ugly and dreaded water moccasins." His owners, who saw him as "a beast of labor in revolt" and "an animal worth $2,000," pursued him. During his flight, Parker lived in dread of hearing the "yelping of the hounds, the despair of fugitive slaves."[1] For John Parker, the parallels between his own status as an enslaved person and the animal kingdom came naturally. Enslaved people, after all, lived in an ecosystem in which they interacted with animals every day. They plowed fields with mules, beasts of burden that they both loved and resented. They hunted, fished, and trapped wild animals to supplement the meager rations provided by their owners. They lived in fear of wild animals—alligators, rattlesnakes, bears—which served as a powerful disincentive to leave the plantation. Slave owners used animals, especially horses and dogs, as instruments of control and punishment. In short, a menagerie of wild and domesticated animals created a complex zoological framework for slavery in the American South, one that shaped and was shaped by the peculiar institution.

Not all enslaved Black Southerners had the same exposure and access to the South's vast faunal diversity. The connections between them and animals varied significantly based on geography, occupation, and gender. Urban and house slaves, for instance, encountered far fewer wild animals than field slaves. Enslaved people on South Carolina rice plantations confronted a very different faunal landscape than those in Alabama's Black Belt. Enslaved men tended to have a larger geographical footprint, charged with caring for

Scars on the Land. David Silkenat, Oxford University Press. © Oxford University Press 2022.
DOI: 10.1093/oso/9780197564226.003.0003

livestock and permitted to hunt, trap, and fish, while enslaved women had a much more constrained geographic boundary, limited to the fields and slave quarters. Enslaved men, therefore, tended to have far more frequent and meaningful interactions with both wild and domesticated animals.[2]

Pigs and Cattle

Although white Southerners sometimes referred to slavery as their "peculiar institution," many visitors to the antebellum South found their animal husbandry practices equally curious. While farmers throughout colonial British America allowed their livestock to roam, practicing free-range husbandry, by the time of the American Revolution, farmers outside the South had largely adopted animal enclosure, penning their livestock or allowing them to graze in fenced pastures. Careful breeding allowed farmers in New England and the Midwest to produce larger, more docile animals. Southern farmers maintained the older practice of allowing their livestock to roam unfettered by fences.[3] Slavery helped to perpetuate open-range husbandry when the broader Western world had turned against it. Permitting livestock to roam in the vast tracts of undeveloped land that bordered agricultural fields allowed slave owners to direct their labor force toward the production of cash crops. While the quality of Southern livestock suffered significantly—visiting Northerners and Europeans mocked their pigs and cattle—planters saw it as in their economic best interest to prioritize and maximize their production of cotton, tobacco, sugar, and rice. Every enslaved person assigned to tend livestock, they knew, would be one fewer hand in the fields; every acre devoted to growing animal fodder would be one fewer acre of the crops that mattered.[4]

Except for a few months in the winter, cattle in the plantation South were "left to shift for themselves in the woods." By allowing cattle to roam, plantation masters expanded their environmental impact. Touring central Tennessee in 1802, French botanist Francois Michaux marveled at the enormous canebrakes, where native bamboo grew along riverbanks, providing a unique shelter for a variety of species, including Bachman's warbler (now extinct) and the Florida panther. Michaux noted in dismay that "as new plantations are formed, these canes in a few years disappear, as the cattle prefer the leaves of them to any other kind of vegetables, and destroy them still more by breaking the body of the plant while browsing on the top of the stalks." In 1828, geologist Elisha Mitchell came to a similar conclusion about the destructive effects of free-roaming cattle in western North Carolina, noting that the plants preferred by the cattle, such as "pea-vine and natural grasses are fast devoured." In their place, Mitchell noted, flourished "bitter unpalatable weeds."[5]

Responsibility for tending cattle often fell to boys not yet old enough to work in the fields. One of the first jobs assigned to Frederick Douglass was to "drive up the cows at evening." Shortly after arriving on a South Carolina rice plantation, Charles Ball found himself ordered to join the plantation's cattle tender, a boy named Toney, to retrieve some of the animals for slaughter. To Ball's surprise, he discovered that most of the plantation's cattle were not penned with the milch cows but allowed to roam in a "long savannah" three miles away. Traipsing through mosquito-infested woods to reach the "long savannah," Ball found a "low, swampy ground, several miles in extent, . . . a natural meadow." Ball searched this vast expanse for his master's cattle, but in vain. Toney concluded that the mosquitoes had driven the cattle from the meadow, and the pair "proceeded into the woods and thickets, and after wandering about for an hour or more, we found the cattle," a few of whom they dragged back to the plantation for slaughter.[6]

Visitors to the plantation South often disparaged local cattle as inferior. A New Englander wrote to a friend at home that "the cows are the meanest looking animals you ever saw," claiming that "four of them are not as good as one of ours." She attributed the animals' poor condition to their inadequate diet. One Swiss traveler noted that "the Cattle of *Carolina* are very fat in Summer, but as lean in Winter, because they can find very little to eat, and have no cover to shelter them from the cold Rains, Frosts, and Snows. . . . The last Winter being very severe, about 10,000 horned Cattle died of Hunger and Cold." While the quality of Southern cattle varied somewhat, reflecting local availability of wild foods, they usually weighed less and produced less milk than Northern varieties.[7]

Although visitors found Southern cattle distinctive, the domesticated species that garnered the most attention was the hog. Since early in the colonial era, pork had served as a mainstay in the Southern diet across class and color lines. "The flesh of the hog," noted British journalist and social reformer James Silk Buckingham, "is the universal food of all classes in the interior, and we have never yet sat down to any meal, where pork or bacon did not form the principal, and often the only dish of animal food on the table." Buckingham found Southern pork inedible, paling in comparison to its British counterpart. He found the animal's appearance just as loathsome as its taste. "Hogs were everywhere abundant," he wrote. "These are among the ugliest of their species, with long thin heads, long legs, arched back, large lapping ears, lank bodies, and long thin tails." By 1860, most Southern states had more pigs than people.[8]

Pork played a particularly prominent role in the enslaved diet. Although plantation owners often provided less, slave management experts advocated three and a half pounds of bacon per week for an enslaved adult man, with smaller rations for women and children. During "hog killing time," usually November or December, they received fresh pork rations. For the remainder of the year, the pork came preserved, soaked in salt brine and smoked. During butchering season, enslaved peopled tracked down the pigs from the forests, swamps, and wastelands adjacent to the plantation and herded them into pens for slaughter. On the largest plantations, this meant rounding up hundreds of animals, many of which had wandered miles into the wilderness. Shade Richards, a slave in Pike County, Georgia, recalled that "when the 'hog kill' time come' it took 150 nigger men a week to do it."[9]

While Southern farmers attempted to maintain nominal ownership over these roaming hogs, using distinguishing earmarks for identification, feral hog populations flourished in the wilderness, untagged and unfettered. Living and breeding in the woods and swamps, Southern hogs adapted to environmental pressures, becoming leaner and more aggressive. In the wild, piglets became prey for many local species, including gray and red foxes, bobcats, cougars, and alligators. Predation culled the slowest and most vulnerable, transforming the Southern hog into an animal quite different from its carefully bred domestic counterpart. Visiting Alabama in 1838, British naturalist Philip Gosse observed that "the southern hogs are a queer breed; very singular creatures indeed; . . . [with] their sharp thin backs, long heads, and tall legs, looking so little like hogs and so much like greyhounds." These hogs, Gosse noted, lacked the docility of their domesticated counterpart but adopted a "shrewd look, half alarm, half defiance." Gosse concluded that "from the amount of liberty which is granted them, and their consequent habits of self-protection and self-dependence, they are very wild; indeed, many are found in the woods which are as really wild, in every sense of the word, as any panther; perfectly ownerless, swift of foot, and fierce and strong withal." Frederick Law Olmsted found the feral hogs terrifying. Traveling through rural Virginia, he came across "long, lank, bony, snake-headed, hairy, wild beasts [that] would come dashing across our path, in packs of from three to a dozen, with short, hasty grunts, almost always at a gallop, . . . as if they were quite ready to fight if we advanced any further." Later that day, Olmsted decided to stop his travels at sunset rather than pushing on to his intended destination, for fear of "knocking about among those fierce hogs in the pine-forest, if I should be lost."[10]

Olmsted's fears proved justified. Enslaved people knew that feral hogs could and would injure them. In Missouri, Henry Bruce observed, "The most vicious wild animal I met or encountered was the hog," which thrived in the woods near the plantation, where they feasted on the abundant hickory nuts. Bruce and other enslaved people also frequented these woods to collect nuts, competing with the feral hogs. He vividly recalled one occasion when "a drove of wild hogs" bore down on their party. They scampered up the trees, narrowly escaping. "From my safe position in the tree," Bruce wrote, "I looked down on those vicious wild animals," relieved that "we had escaped immediate death," as "one minute later and . . . those hogs would have torn and eaten me in short order." Bruce and his companions remained tree-bound until the hogs lost interest and moved on.[11]

Roaming domesticated and feral hogs had a much more significant effect on the Southern ecosystem than frightening Northern journalists and terrifying nut-gathering enslaved foragers. Opportunistic omnivores, hogs can rapidly increase in population when unchecked; sows can give birth twice per year, with average litters of six piglets. Traveling in packs, feral pigs can decimate indigenous vegetation with their rooting and trampling. Feasting on acorns, hickory nuts, and beechnuts, they can inhibit the growth of new trees. Using sapling and mature trees for scratching and scent marking, hogs can strip the bark, exposing the trees to disease. Hogs also feast on the eggs of turtles and ground-nesting birds, and on salamanders, frogs, snakes, and crabs, all of which can be indicator species for the health of the ecosystem. They compete with native fauna such as white-tailed deer, quail, and turkey for food. Their rooting and wallowing along river- and streambanks encourage erosion. In brief, the rapid spread of unfettered domesticated pigs and feral hogs could transform an ecosystem.[12]

Hogs could also wreak havoc on agriculture. Although they generally ignored cotton and tobacco fields, a sounder of hogs could destroy a grain field overnight. In 1859, Virginia planter Richard Eppes complained in his diary that he had become "much annoyed by a wild hog that infests ou[r] oat & corn fields." Despite him setting traps for the miscreant hog and arming an enslaved boy with an old gun to kill it, hogs continued to ravage Eppes's crops over the following months, prompting his overseer to note "depredations had been committed by wild hogs, the same as injured us last spring." Increasingly agitated and "perfectly horrified to see the destruction done to the growing crop of corn by the wild hogs," Eppes ordered "some Strycnine with shelled corn" to kill the hogs. Some agricultural reformers, including Virginians John Taylor and Edmund Ruffin, promoted closing the open range and

unsuccessfully urged the passage of new fence laws to restrict the pig population. While planters debated the merits of building fences to contain pigs or
fences to protect crops from pigs, enslaved people feared that their gardens
would fall victim to the nighttime foraging of unrestrained hogs.[13]

Although the practice varied regionally, some planters found it easier
to allow enslaved people to own and raise their own pigs rather than issue
weekly pork rations. This practice seems to have been particularly common
among South Carolina rice planters, who also purchased surplus pork from
them. "We don't look at our hogs every day," noted one enslaved pig owner.
"Sometimes [we] don't see them for two (2) months at a time." Like other
Southern pig owners, enslaved people allowed their animals to forage in the
wild areas adjoining the plantation and used earmarks to identify their animals. "The negroes' swine are allowed to run in woods," Olmsted observed
when visiting the Lowcountry, "each owner having his own distinguished by
a peculiar mark." Although pig ownership gave bondspeople a degree of independence and autonomy—causing some masters to fret about vulnerable
paternalism—in practice, it served the interests of slave owners more than the
slaves themselves. Although delegating pig ownership facilitated the growth
of internal and underground slave economies, it also relieved planters of the
burden of maintaining pork rations.[14]

For runaway and maroon slaves, open-range husbandry provided access
to a much needed source of food. In the Great Dismal Swamp, straddling the
border of eastern Virginia and North Carolina, maroons relied on pigs and
cattle that, like them, had taken refuge in the swamp. In 1775, Dr. John F. Smyth,
a Scottish immigrant and Loyalist, noted that in the Dismal Swamp, "Runaway Negroes" fed "themselves in the swamp upon corn, hogs, and fowls."
Shortly after the Revolution, German naturalist Johann David Schoepf, who
had traveled to America as a physician attending Hessian soldiers, observed
"runaway slaves, who have lived many years in the swamp, . . . raising hogs and
fowls which they stole from their neighbors." Although the Dismal Swamp
sheltered the largest and best-documented maroon community in the United
States, smaller settlements in Louisiana and South Carolina also relied heavily
on captured hogs. Given the tenuous nature of maroon communities, sustainability depended on regular access to open range and feral animals.[15]

Hunting and Fishing

Paternalistic enslavers claimed that they generously provided for their
enslaved community, supplying them with ample rations. "Slaves should be

well fed," an 1856 pro-slavery tome argued. "Every right-minded master," it claimed, had a duty to provide "a sufficient quantity of good substantial food," including generous servings of meat and the occasional "delicacies of the 'great house.'" Yet, as many historians have documented, the customary rations usually fell well short of the caloric and nutritional needs of agricultural laborers. For many enslaved people, food obtained by hunting, trapping, and fishing formed the core of their diet. These activities allowed plantation owners to transfer much of the responsibility for feeding their enslaved workforce to the slaves themselves. "If we want[ed] meat," noted Jeff Calhoun, "we went to the woods after it." Growing up on plantations in Alabama and Texas, Calhoun saw hunting as essential, adding "deer, turkey, buffalo, and some bear," plus the occasional "skunk, crow, and hawk" to his meager rations.[16]

Archaeological evidence from across the plantation South indicates that wild foods often formed as much as half of an enslaved person's diet. Excavations of one Virginia slave cabin revealed hundreds of bone fragments from a wide variety of wild fauna, including deer, opossum, rabbit, squirrel, raccoon, crow, and mallard. The enslaved inhabitants also harvested catfish, sturgeon, striped bass, gar, snapping turtle, oysters, freshwater mussels, and marine clams from the nearby James River. Intermixed with the detritus from hunting and fishing were hundreds of pig bone fragments. At the Saragossa Plantation near Natchez, Mississippi, archaeologists found a similarly diverse diet. Alongside bone fragments from domesticated pigs, chickens, and cattle were those of white-tailed deer, box turtle, oyster, raccoon, swamp rabbit, squirrel, gar, Canada goose, and blue and channel catfish.[17]

Most slave owners generally tolerated the people they enslaved hunting, trapping, and fishing. Not only did it transfer the responsibility for procuring food to the enslaved people themselves, but it also thinned the ranks of pest species attracted to the plantation. "No objections are made to hunting," Solomon Northup noted, as "it dispenses with drafts upon the smoke-house, and because every marauding coon that is killed is so much saved from the standing corn." Northup noted that enslaved people across Louisiana hunted in swamps for raccoon and opossum to make up for inadequate rations, "at night, after the day's work is accomplished." Northup had no illusions about why slave owners, who usually tightly controlled slave mobility, carved out an exception for hunting: enslaved people who could hunt and trap their meat could be fed much more cheaply. "There are planters whose slaves, for months at time," Northup noted, "have no other meat" except that which they procured for themselves.[18]

Although most planters permitted hunting and fishing, they recognized that allowing enslaved people access to wilderness opened the door for a panoply of problems. Hunting formed the core of the independent enslaved economy, one that threatened paternalistic dependence and opened up new areas of negotiation. Skilled hunters, trappers, and fishermen could barter or sell their surpluses to the enslaved community, to their owners, or beyond the plantation. They could also use hunting and fishing as a pretext for meeting and exchanging information with friends and relatives from neighboring plantations, creating a vital link in the grapevine telegraph that enslaved Southerners used to communicate and plot. Even more problematic for planters, hunting, trapping, and fishing taught enslaved people how to navigate the woods and swamps, geographic information that they used to escape and find wild resources to feed and shelter themselves off the plantation. Thomas Cole successfully escaped from bondage in Alabama in large part due to his experience hunting. When meat on his plantation ran short, his overseer gave permission for slaves to "kill a deer or wild hawgs or jes' any kind of game." As soon as he got to the "huntin' ground," Cole began to make his way north to freedom. En route, he sustained himself with the skills he learned over a lifetime of harvesting wild resources. He recalled that he staved off hunger during his flight by gathering "all de nuts and kill[ing] a few swamp rabbits and cotch[ing] a few fish."[19]

Weighing the costs and benefits of enslaved people's hunting, trapping, and fishing, most slave owners permitted these activities. When they attempted to restrict enslaved people's access to wild game, they usually failed. Jenny Proctor, born enslaved in Alabama in 1850, noted, "Our marster, he wouldn' 'low us to go fishing, he say dat too easy on a nigger and wouldn' 'low us to hunt none neither." Despite the prohibition, Proctor recalled, "Some time we slips off at night and ketch 'possums." Similarly, James Bolton recalled that on his Georgia plantation, "slaves warn't spozen to go huntin' at night and everybody know you can't ketch no 'possums 'ceppin' at night!," but "jus' the same, we had plenty 'possums and nobody ax how we cotch 'em."[20]

Some enslaved men managed to procure firearms for hunting, usually with the knowledge and consent of their owners. Planters sometimes issued guns to slaves to kill or scare away pests. On South Carolina and Georgia plantations, select enslaved men used the crack of old flintlocks to disperse flocks of birds—bobolinks, red-winged blackbirds, and grackles—that feasted on rice fields. Other planters found it profitable to arm slaves to procure game, either for the big table or to feed the enslaved population. Alex Woods, an enslaved man in the North Carolina Piedmont, recalled, "Dey 'lowed my father hunt

wid a gun. He wus a good hunter an' he brought a lot o' game to the de plantation." Other slave owners dispensed firearms as a reward for good behavior.
Around 1810, Charles Ball's owner gave him "an old gun that had seen much
hard service," probably a relic from the Revolution. The musket was unus-
able when he received it—the "stock was quite shattered to pieces, and the
lock would not strike fire"—but Ball repaired it with the aid of a blacksmith,
allowing him "for the first time in my life" to become a "hunter, in the proper
sense of the word." Hunting at night or during time off on Saturdays, Ball
managed to radically improve the quality of his diet. From a tree-top perch,
Ball shot deer, lured to a salt lick, as well as raccoons. Hunting provided Ball
with more than a needed supplement to his meager slave rations and the
ability to share with other enslaved people; it also enabled him, he said, to
"feel myself, in some measure, an independent man."[21]

Most enslaved hunters, however, relied on traps, snares, and especially
dogs to help them catch prey. Effective hunting without the use of firearms
required detailed knowledge of the local ecosystem. Enslaved hunters possessed an encyclopedic mental map of the proximate wilderness. From his
time hunting and trapping, Charles Ball became "well acquainted with the
woods and swamps, for several miles round our plantation," knowledge that
allowed him to procure more food for himself.[22]

Effective hunting or trapping required enslaved people to possess an intimate understanding of animal behavior. "Us had good food mos' time," noted
Amos Lincoln, recalling his childhood in Louisiana. Studying the habits and
preferences of local fauna allowed enslaved trappers to catch a wide variety
of game that lived on the periphery of the plantation. Lincoln remembered
setting "steel an' log traps fo' big game; dig pit traps in de woods 'bout so
long an' se deep, an' kiver dem wid bresh an' leaves. Dat kotch 'possum, 'coon,
an' uder t'ings w'at come 'long in d' night." Lincoln also learned how to trap
birds, which he would roast in lard, salt, and pepper. Enslaved parents often
taught their young children how to make and use traps and nets, showing
them how to decode the landscape for subtle clues to track their quarry. In
North Carolina, Julius Nelson recalled that the defining feature of effective
enslaved hunters was their intelligence: "De smart nigger et a heap o' possums
an' coons dar bein' plenty o' dem an' rabbits an' squirrels in abundance." As
Lincoln's and Nelson's accounts suggest, slaves primarily hunted and trapped
small game. Indeed, small game became so associated with enslaved hunters
that planters often categorically distinguished their pursuit of deer and other
prestige animals from those hunted by slaves. Although this artificial divide
existed primarily in the minds of planter class—poor whites often trapped

raccoon and opossum, and enslaved men occasionally hunted deer—it helped to bolster ideas of mastery and racial superiority.[23]

Depending on the local geography, fishing proved just as important as trapping and hunting for providing protein. In South Carolina and Georgia rice plantations and on the cotton plantations of the Sea Islands, slaves relied heavily on fishing and gathering shellfish to supplement their diets. "No meat whatsoever was issued," recalled former Georgia slave Julia Rush. "It was up to the slaves to catch fish, oysters and other sea food for their meat supply." Rice plantation canals doubled as fishponds for bowfin, gar, freshwater catfish, and turtles, which slaves could harvest during spare hours. "Dar wuz a ribber nearby de plantation," recalled Midge Burnett of her childhood in Georgia. "We fished dar a heap too. We ketched a big mess of fish ever' week an' dese come in good an' helped ter save rations ter boot." According to Burnett, her owner encouraged fishing to save money on meat rations.[24]

Like hunting, fishing proved instrumental to the enslaved economy. Using homemade hooks fashioned from pins, George Rogers fished in Brier Creek in Wake County, North Carolina. "We caught a lot o' fish," he recalled. "We would trade our fish to missus for molasses to make candy out uv." While Rogers engaged in sanctioned trading, many other enslaved people used fishing to participate in illicit commerce. "Expert fisherman," noted Charles Ball, "caught and sold as many fish and oysters, as enabled them to buy coffee, sugar, and other luxuries for their wives besides keeping themselves and their families in Sunday clothes." Ball himself "had all [his] life been accustomed to fishing" and believed fishing a better investment than hunting. Sold from his native Maryland to South Carolina, he persuaded his new owner to allow him to construct a fishery on the Congaree River. Weaving a seine and clearing the riverbed of debris, Ball hoped, he said, "I should be able to gain some advantage to myself, by disposing of a part of the small fish that might be taken at the fishery." He traded shad for bacon with white men aboard a passing keel-boat, who charged a premium because of the "hazard of being prosecuted for dealing with slaves." Ball and the other enslaved men at the fishery feasted on shad, catfish, perch, and mullets, as well as the purchased bacon, until recalled to the cotton fields. "To the end of the fishing season," Ball recalled, "we all lived well."[25]

Wild Animals

While hunting and the possibility of escape attracted enslaved people to the wilderness, fear of wild animals kept many of them from venturing beyond the plantation. Visiting her new husband's plantation on St. Simon's Island, Georgia, for the first time, Fanny Kemble found the enslaved people there terrified of snakes. Jack, "my peculiar slave" whom her husband "appointed to attend me in my roamings about the island," had developed a particular phobia. "Jack is in such deadly terror about snakes," she wrote, "which are now beginning to glide about with a freedom and frequency certainly not pleasing." Although Kemble expressed a desire to see the wild parts of the island, Jack steadfastly refused to "follow me off the open road." Touring the slave quarters, Kemble found Jack's fears justified. She met an enslaved woman whose son had been killed by a rattlesnake's bite. Attempted to defend her child, the mother too had been bitten. A driver stopped the snake's venom from spreading by cutting off her bitten finger, leaving her hand "badly maimed." Kemble found this fear of snakes almost universal among her husband's slaves, a paralyzing terror that kept them on the plantation. When Kemble asked an elderly enslaved woman named Molly about running away, she replied that it was futile: "Snake eat 'em up, or dey starve to def in a swamp. Massa's niggers dey don't' neber run away."[26]

Because of his extensive experience hunting and trapping, Charles Ball often encountered venomous snakes. "Serpents of various kinds swarmed in this country," Ball claimed. He boasted, "I have killed more than twenty rattle-snakes in a day, and copper-heads were innumerable." Enslaved in swampy coastal South Carolina, Ball had learned to fear and respect venomous snakes, particularly the water moccasin, "the snake that I most dreaded," because it was "quite as venomous as the copper-head or rattle-snake, and much more active and malicious." While venomous snakes posed the most ubiquitous threat to hunters, Ball knew that other perils loomed in the wilderness. In addition to snakes, he noted that "panthers, wolves, and other beasts of prey, were common in the woods." During one hunting expedition, Ball found "a huge panther creeping along the path after me, in the manner that a cat creeps when stealing upon her prey." Ball slowly retreated from the animal, but was pursued all the way until he returned to the plantation and safety. Even on the plantation, many enslaved people felt threatened by venomous snakes. When he went out to the cotton fields in the morning, Charles Ball observed that most enslaved women "laid their children at the side of the fence, or under the shade of the cotton plants, whilst they were at work," but one woman did not, preferring to carry her infant in a "rude knapsack" on her back while she worked. When Ball asked why, she replied, "I cannot leave my child in the weeds amongst the snakes. What would be my feelings if I should leave it there, and a scorpion were to bite it?"[27]

While many enslaved people feared snakes creeping among the cotton rows, rats exacted a much higher death toll. Overcrowding and poor sanitation in slave quarters attracted rats, whose bites were common, especially among slave children. Harriet Jacobs described a captured runaway in North Carolina punished by a severe whipping and confinement "between the screws of the cotton gin." When a stench arose from the tiny prison, "the dead body was found partly eaten by rats and vermin." Some hypothesized that the rats had "gnawed him before life was extinct." South Carolinian John Andrew Jackson claimed that rats feasted on slaves' feet, which barefoot labor had encrusted with a layer of dead skin. On rising in the morning, he often found that "rats had actually eaten a part of our feet." Jackson noted that "slaves cannot *feel* the rats eating it until their teeth touch the more tender part of the feet. During the day, that part of the foot which has been skinned by the rats is very tender and causes great pain." Slaves knew that rats served as a harbinger of snakes. "The presence of rats in our houses brought venomous snakes," noted Jackson, "who frequented them for the purpose of swallowing the rats, and who sometimes bit the negroes." Irving Lowery remembered that his enslaved grandmother worked as a plantation cook, and her cramped kitchen had become "a den for rats, and, in consequence of this, a place for snakes. The rats came in search of food and the snakes came in search of rats." The ubiquitous rats served as vectors for a variety of diseases, including murine typhus, tuberculous, leptospirosis, and plague.[28]

When Solomon Northup attempted to escape from slavery in Louisiana by fleeing to the swamp, he became keenly aware of the peril around him. While he had temporarily escaped the terrors of slavery, he had entered a realm in which "for thirty or forty miles it is without inhabitants, save wild beasts—the bear, the wild-cat, the tiger, and great slimy reptiles, that are crawling through it everywhere. . . . I saw hundreds of moccasin snakes. Every log and bog—every trunk of a fallen tree, over which I was compelled to step or climb, was alive with them. They crawled away at my approach, but sometimes in my haste, I almost placed my hand or foot upon them. They are poisonous serpents—their bite more fatal than the rattlesnake's." Like many runaway slaves, Northup feared approaching water, where alligators lurked undetected in the murky darkness. During his flight into the swamp, Northup encountered "many alligators, great and small, lying in the water. . . . I staggered on, fearing every instant I should feel the dreadful sting of the moccasin, or be crushed within the jaws of some disturbed alligator." Charles Ball had a similar experience during one escape attempt. Swimming across the Appalachie River, he found "a large alligator was moving in full pursuit of me, with his nose just above the surface." Ball knew that an "alligator can swim more than twice as fast as a man," and he only narrowly made it across. "Had I been ten seconds longer in the river," he noted, "I should have been dragged to the bottom, and never again been heard of."[29]

Horses and Mules

One of Wes Brady's earliest memories of growing up on a Texas cotton plantation was of a white man towering over him on horseback. "The overseer was 'straddle his big horse at three o'clock in the mornin'," Brady recalled, "roustin' the hands off to the field." He also had vivid image of "long lines of slaves chained together driv by a white man on a hoss." Horses made American slavery's "carceral landscape" possible, giving slave owners, overseers, and patrollers two key advantages. They provided height, enabling their riders to survey fields and forests, observing enslaved people at work and in flight, and they provided speed, allowing white authorities to overcome the tyranny of distance. Horses enabled a handful of white men to patrol vast areas in an evening, monitoring and disciplining slaves' nocturnal movements. They also allowed an owner or overseer to effectively supervise dozens of enslaved laborers. Solomon Northrup noted the terror and implied threat they faced while hoeing cotton fields as "the overseer . . . follows the slaves on horseback with a whip." When an enslaved person ran away, white pursuers on horseback could run down the fugitive, who had few options once spotted. During one escape attempt with his family, Henry Bibb recalled, they were caught when "the soul drivers came charging up on their horses, commanding us to stand still or they would shoot us down." In addition to the power that horses gave to the white men astride them, the animals themselves could terrify bondspeople, who feared being trampled under their hooves. Frederick Douglass recalled as a young man being "literally dragged . . . behind horses, a distance of fifteen miles."[30]

When it served their slave owners' interests, many enslaved people worked closely with horses. As carriage drivers, messengers, draymen, groomers, and jockeys, some enslaved men managed to escape laboring in the fields because of their skill as equestrians. From the seventeenth century onward, enslaved cowboys on horseback herded cattle on the frontier. In colonial South Carolina, "the cattle ranged for miles," and enslaved cattlemen on horseback periodically herded them into cow pens, becoming "better acquainted with the land than any other set of men." In 1731, a visitor to South Carolina noted that "Horses, the best Kind in the World, are so plentiful that you seldom

see any body travel on foot, except *Negroes*, and they often on horseback."
As slavery spread westward and into the interior, so too did ranching, with
enslaved cowboys on horseback forming the vanguard of the slave frontier.[31]

Enslaved ranching flourished in antebellum Texas. On the largest plantations along the Sabine, Neches, Brazos, Colorado, and Trinity Rivers,
ranching stood on equal footing with corn and cotton as a source of revenue
and a site of enslaved labor. Born in 1849 on a plantation on the Colorado,
Sam Jones Washington learned to ride, he said, "soon's I's could sit de hoss"
and become a cattle hand prior to emancipation. For Washington and
other enslaved cowboys, he found his life in the saddle preferrable to the
alternatives. "I stays out with de cattle mos' de time and I's tickled," he told
a WPA interviewer. "I sho' likes to ride and rope dem cattle." He recognized
the danger that came with working with large animals. The cattle frequently
stampeded, requiring Washington, only an adolescent, to ride aggres-
sively to corral them. "Dat sho' dangerous ridin'," Washington recalled. "If
de hoss throw you off dem cattle stamp you to death." Despite the danger,
Washington boasted that he was "never skeert w'en I's roundin' de cattle,
'cause I's sho ob my ridin'."[32]

While horses served as an instrument of control and domination, enslaved
people recognized their own ability to subvert that power. Many enslaved
people used horses to visit friends and relatives. In 1829, sixteen-year-old
enslaved groomsman Jacob Green appropriated his owner's horse to attend a
clandestine dance twelve miles away. When he arrived, Green found "about
one hundred horses tied round the fence—for some of them were far from
home, and, like myself, they were all runaways, and their horses, like mine, had
to be home and cleaned before their masters were up in the morning." Green
knew that, if caught, he would face whipping, but he decided that the opportunity worth the risk. The practice of horseback social visits had become so
common that an 1857 article in *DeBow's Review* recommended that enslavers
adopt a rule that "no negro will be allowed to ride the horses . . . without
permission; and the habit of riding about on Sundays and at night must be
discontinued."[33]

Enslavers recognized that the real threat from enslaved people on horseback far exceeded their capacity to attend a dance or visit neighboring plantations. One observer of the German Coast slave rebellion in 1811 noted
that half of the two hundred insurgents rode on horseback. Runaways who
stole horses could cover much more ground than fugitives who escaped on
foot, putting distance between themselves and the plantation before their
owners discovered their departure. One Tennessee fugitive traversed more

than sixty-five miles on horseback in two and a half days before his owner discovered him missing. Horses allowed those enslaved people unable to walk due to age or disability to escape. They also made it harder for slave-hunting dogs to track fugitives, as horses disguised their scent and outpaced their pursuers. Because of the threat posed by enslaved people on horseback, white Southerners took steps to keep the reins of power firmly under their control. As Black abolitionist William Wells Brown noted, state law often prohibited slaves from riding horses. Louisiana, for instance, decreed that "every slave found on horseback, without a written permission from his master, shall receive twenty-five lashes."[34]

While enslaved people tended to see horses as a symbol of the master's tyranny and power, mules evoked both sympathy and hostility. By 1830, planters were increasingly buying mules to pull their plows and wagons, displacing oxen and horses. Although it was hotly debated in Southern agricultural journals, many planters saw the adoption of the mule as a progressive reform. Although slightly smaller on average, mules provided essentially the same draft power as horses but consumed less forage. Moreover, planters believed that mules could pull a plow at a younger age, lived longer, and could sustain the Southern heat better than horses or oxen. Probably most importantly, however, mules were thought to better sustain slaves' rough handling. An 1858 article in the *Southern Planter* claimed that mules "are better for our servants to handle, as they can stand neglect and violent treatment better than the horse." Visiting Richmond in 1852, New Yorker Frederick Law Olmsted asked "why mules are so universally substituted for horses on the farm, the first reason given, and confessedly the most conclusive one, is, that horses cannot bear the treatment that they always must get from negroes; horses are always soon foundered or crippled by them, while mules will bear cudgeling, and lose a meal or two now and then, and not be materially injured, and they do not take cold or get sick if neglected or overworked." Several years later in Fauquier County, Virginia, James Redpath, a New York journalist, saw an enslaved wagon driver abuse his draft horses, noting, "Whenever we came to a hill, especially if it was very steep, he dismounted, lashed the horses with all his strength, varying his performances by picking up stones, none of them smaller than half a brick, and throwing them with all his force at the horses' legs." Declaring that "this is a fair specimen of the style in which slaves treat stock," Redpath attributed the wagon driver's abuse of his horses to the chronic physical cruelty of bondage. If masters relied on torture to compel their slaves to labor, Redpath reasoned, one should not be surprised that the enslaved, lash in hand, would replicate that brutality on beasts under their control.[35]

The obvious downside of using mules rather than horses was their ste-
rility. The hybrid offspring of a male donkey (a jack) and a female horse (a
mare), mules needed to be bred, usually by specialized mule breeders. Among
the earliest mule breeders in the South was George Washington, who after
Yorktown became convinced that mules would be particularly well suited
to plantation agriculture. In 1785, learning of Washington's interest, King
Charles III sent a Spanish jack named Royal Gift to Mount Vernon. The following year, Lafayette gave Washington a Maltese mule, reputed second only
to Spanish mules in their quality. Washington subsequently purchased additional jacks from Europe, and by 1787 he began advertising them as studs
in Southern newspapers. At the time of his death in 1799, Washington had
fifty-eight mules and had become the leading mule breeder in the country.
However, mule breeding did not take off until the 1830s, when Kentucky and
Tennessee became the epicenter of the Southern mule trade, which exported
thousands of animals across the South. Between 1850 and 1860, the number
of mules of the Deep South increased from 266,000 to 529,000, a population
growth that exceeded the rapidly expanding enslaved demographic. However,
because mules cost more than either work horses or oxen, non-slave-owning
white Southerners continued to prefer the traditional beasts of burden.[36]

Working with mules sometimes proved dangerous. Although generally
docile, mules developed a reputation for stubbornness. Prone to kicking
and biting, they left many enslaved mule drivers with serious injuries. One
former slave recalled that her husband's uncle Cal had "his face all mashed
in . . . broken by the kick of a mule." Another recalled that a bolting mule
killed her husband, dragging him behind the plow and leaving his face and
chest "crushed, and mashed." One Alabama slave owner saw that he could use
the mule as an instrument of torture, punishing an enslaved woman named
Delphia by compelling "her day after day to plow with her mule at a trot. She
dare not stop, for his eye was ever on her." After weeks of overwork, she died
from exhaustion.[37]

If mules injured enslaved people, enslaved people also injured mules.
Although some historians have claimed that enslaved people intentionally
maimed mules and other draft animals as a form of resistance, little evidence
supports this claim. However, mules did bear the brunt of some rough handling, as much from overwork and neglect as abuse. South Carolina planter
Charles Manigault urged his overseers to regularly inspect mules for signs
of mistreatment. Manigault knew that slaves often allowed the chains connecting the animal to the plow to "wound the Side or the Legs of the mule."
He also instructed that slaves should not be allowed to "strike the mule in the

same spot to make it raw." Despite the harsh treatment that some enslaved people inflicted on mules, many expressed sincere affection for the animals. Interviewed in 1938 by the WPA, Marshal Butler's most positive memories of slavery revolved around his mule. "I had a mule named George—I know my mule—he was a good mule," Butler recalled. When questioned by his interviewer about his recall of an individual animal, Butler, eighty-eight years of age, reiterated firmly, "Ye[s], Bossman, I remembers my mule."[38]

More than any other animal, enslaved people saw profound similarities between their own lives and those of the mules they worked with. Like mules, they knew their primary, if not exclusive, value to their owner was as a laborer, sentenced to toil and sweat in the dirt. Charles Ball observed, "Mules that I saw at work in the cotton-fields, were poor and badly harnessed, and the half-naked condition of the negroes, who drove them, or followed with the hoe, together with their wan complexions, proved to me that they had too much work, or not enough food."[39]

Dogs

Of all the animals that enslaved people encountered regularly, dogs engendered both the most heartfelt expressions of devotion and visceral hatred. Visitors to the plantation South often commented on the ubiquity and diversity of Southern canines: hunting and herding dogs, coon dogs, bloodhounds, bulldogs, and lap dogs, each with a particular function and valiance. "A traveler in passing through our country," noted one planter, "cannot but be struck with surprise at our taste for dogs." Every farm, no matter how poor, seemed to have its own kennel of dogs. One Georgia planter noted in 1848 that "every man in Carolina, and I suppose in Georgia also, keeps one or more dogs." Estimates of the number of dogs in the antebellum South vary widely, but conservative calculations place the figure at over a million.[40]

While most dogs belonged to white masters, many enslaved people also owned dogs and considered them their closest ally and most valuable piece of property. "The slave loves his dog," argued one white abolitionist in 1857. "They are constant companions. He talks with him by day and hunts with him at night, and shares with him his scanty meals. His dog is the only thing under the sun that he can call his own; for the master claims the woman that is called his wife, his offspring, his hut, his pig, his own body—and his very soul." Sold from South Carolina to Georgia, Charles Ball found himself separated from everything and everyone, except his dog Trueman. "I had a dog of my own which I had brought with me from Carolina, and which was an excellent hunting dog," Ball wrote. "He would tree rackoons and bears, and chase deer, and was so faithful, that I thought he would lose his life, if necessary, in my defence." Although Ball never explained the origin of Trueman's name, it may have reflected the dog's companionship and loyalty. Trueman accompanied Ball everywhere for four years, an element of stability in a life dominated by uncertainty and capricious cruelty.[41]

Ball attributed most of his success as a hunter to Trueman. Enslaved Black hunters may have depended on their dogs more than their free white counterparts. Denied access to firearms, most enslaved hunters depended on their dogs not only to track their quarry but also to kill it. Slaves in Louisiana relied on hunting raccoon and opossum for their meat, Solomon Northup observed. "They are hunted with dogs and clubs, slaves not being allowed the use of fire-arms." Enslaved hunters had to limit their choice of prey to those animals that their dogs could catch. Allen Parker, a slave in eastern North Carolina, noted that although "bear meat was considered good eating, the slaves gave the bears a very wide berth, for in order to hunt him a gun was needed, and the slaves were not allowed to have any such weapons." While they could not pursue large game, enslaved people with trained dogs could hunt small mammals, including rabbits, opossum, and raccoons. As raccoons were known for their vicious temperament, hunting them required tenacious hunting dogs. "It takes a good dog to kill a coon," noted Virginia slave Isaac Williams. "It will fall on its back and scratch and bite to the last."[42]

Masters had decidedly mixed feelings about their slaves' dogs. Enslaved people who owned dogs, they believed, would be better able to feed themselves. Moreover, concern for a dog's welfare could make recalcitrant slaves more docile and less likely to run away. Dog ownership, they believed, would tether slaves to the plantation.[43] Indeed, Charles Ball's greatest hesitation when running away was abandoning his faithful dog. "This poor animal had been my constant companion for more than four years," Ball noted, "without ever showing cowardice or infidelity." Ball found himself "anxious to bring my dog with me; but as I knew the success of my undertaking depended on secrecy and silence, I thought it safest to abandon my last friend, and engage in my perilous enterprise alone." On the day he ran away, he shared his last meal with Trueman, "dividing the contents of my basket with my dog." Before heading off, Ball "turned to take a last farewell of my poor dog, that stood by the tree to which he was bound, looking wistfully at me. When I approached him, he licked my hands, and then rising on his hind feet, and placing his fore paws on my breast, he uttered a long howl, which thrilled through my heart, as if he had said, 'My master, do not leave me behind you.' All the affection that the poor animal had testified for me in the course of his life, now rose fresh in my memory." If Charles Ball ever questioned his decision to escape, the moment he parted from Trueman made him reconsider what he had to leave behind. In his narrative, Ball addressed his dog in a lengthy soliloquy, undoubtedly a narrative creation, but one that reflected his deep love and affection for the animal: "Poor Trueman, faithful Trueman, fare thee well. Thou hast been an honest dog, and sure friend to thy master in all his shades of fortune. . . . In the day of my adversity, when all the world had forsaken me, . . . and I had no friend to protect me, still, poor Trueman, thou wert the same. Thou laidest thyself down at my feet when the world had united to oppress me. How often, when I was sick, and the fever raged in my veins, didst thou come at the going down of the sun, and lick my feet in token of thy faith; and how patiently didst thou watch with thy poor master through the long and lonely night."[44]

From the Revolution onward, slave owners increasingly expressed frustration and hostility toward slave ownership of dogs. Planters often complained that slaves' dogs preyed on sheep and hogs or aided slaves in stealing food. In 1792 George Washington wrote to his farm manager, "It is not for any good purpose Negros raise, or keep dogs; but to aid them in their night robberies." Therefore, Washington ordered the immediate execution of their dogs: "I not only approve of your killing those Dogs which have been the occasion of the late loss [of sheep], & of thinning the Plantations of others, but give it as a positive order, that after saying what dog, or dogs shall remain, if any negro presumes under any pretence whatsoever, to preserve, or bring one into the family, that he shall be severely punished, and the dog hanged." In 1808, Thomas Jefferson wrote to his overseer at Monticello that to protect his sheep from predation, "the negroes dogs must all be killed. Do no spare a single one." While Washington and Jefferson sought to rid their plantations of slaves' dogs, both planters kept substantial personal kennels.[45]

White Southerners' hostility to Black dog ownership increased in the 1840s and 1850s. Slaveholders and non-slaveholders alike saw the animals as a threat to livestock. In October 1845, Louisiana planter Bennet Barrow complained in his diary that his driver "caught a dog killing one of my Hogs on the creek." The guilty animal, Barrow recorded in his diary, "belongs to Mrs Sterlings negro." In 1858, a meeting of South Carolina farmers concluded, "We allow our negroes to have dogs which prevents us from raising sheep." The state's senator, James Henry Hammond, agreed, arguing that "a man should not let his negroes have dogs." To dissuade slave owners from permitting their bondsmen to have dogs, several Southern states passed legislation in the 1850s making slave owners responsible for livestock predation carried out by their slaves' dogs. As an added burden to enslaved dog ownership, South Carolina placed an annual one-dollar tax "upon every dog kept by a slave . . . to be paid by the owner of such slave." Some Lowcountry planters ordered their slaves to kill their dogs rather than pay the tax.[46]

While slaves expressed deep and sincere affection for their own dogs, they loathed and feared their owners' canine associates. Across the plantation South, slave owners used dogs as their primary weapon to track and pursue runaway slaves. Although they regularly encountered larger and more vicious animals, slaves feared dogs above all others. When he attempted to run away, Solomon Northup noted that within the swamp lived many "wild beasts—the bear, the wild-cat, the tiger, and great slimy reptiles, that are crawling through it everywhere. I staggered on, fearing every instant I should feel the dreadful sting of the moccasin, or be crushed within the jaws of some disturbed alligator. The dread of them now almost equaled the fear of the pursuing hounds." Northup's belief that he had more to fear from slave-catching dogs than from the perils of the swamp reveals the abject terror that dogs could provoke.[47]

Some slave owners kept dogs specifically for tracking fugitive slaves. "They keep a great many hounds on purpose to hunt runaways. They call them 'nigger dogs,'" observed one South Carolina runaway. "They teach them to run colored people when they are pups." Slave-hunting dogs "were always taught to hate a negro, never permitted to see one unless to be put in chase of him." According to Frederick Law Olmsted, who questioned a slave-tracker about how the animals were trained: "A negro is made to run from them, and they are encouraged to follow him until he gets into a tree, when meat is given them. Afterwards they learn to follow any particular negro by scent, and then a shoe or a piece of clothing is taken off a negro, and they learn to find by scent who it belongs to, and to tree him." Some slave owners bred dogs especially for the purpose of hunting runaway slaves. Imported from Cuba, bloodhounds—dogs bred to track fugitive slaves—became widespread in the South after 1840. Larger and more vicious than hunting dogs, bloodhounds struck terror into many slaves. For fugitives, no sound made the stomach drop like "shrill yelling of the savage blood hounds as they drew nigh." According to William Anderson, slave owners kept "savage dogs, trained to hunt and follow the track of the poor colored fugitive, day and night, till they catch him." Those who did not own their own bloodhounds could "hire them for the purpose" of catching fugitives. Freelance "negro-hunters" could charge a hefty commission to lead their trained dogs in search of runaways. One such

slave hunter, a man named Elliott, offered his services to planters in central
Kentucky, "bringing with him his trained dogs—seven hounds and a bull-
dog." Like many slave hunters, Elliott boasted that his dogs would take no
more than a day or two to recover runaway slaves. Another slave-hunting
professional reminded readers of the *Lexington Democratic* in 1855, "I still
have my Nigger Dogs, and they are in prime training, and ready to attend all
calls of Hunting and Catching runaway Niggers." While professional slave
hunters relied on bloodhounds, local slave patrols usually relied on hunting
dogs. Function and training distinguished these two classes of canine more
than biology. Professional slave hunters emphasized the difference between
bloodhounds and hunting dogs, lauding their dogs' slave-tracking abilities.
However, slaves themselves usually did not see a meaningful difference between trained bloodhounds employed by professional slave catchers and
hunting dogs used by slave patrols.[48]

Slaves hated bloodhounds not only because of their ability to track fugitives
but also because of their capacity to inflict pain. A pack of bloodhounds was
able to maim and kill a fugitive slave. William Anderson recalled that one
enraged slave owner "hunted and caught" a fugitive "with bloodhounds, and
allowed the dogs to kill him. Then he cut his body up and fed the fragments to
the hounds." Most slave owners sought to capture their runaway slaves alive,
but unleashed bloodhounds could inflict serious wounds in minutes. One
Alabama planter wrote to his overseer to use dogs to track a runaway "but

FIGURE 2.1. Richard Ansdell, *The Hunted Slaves*, 1861, oil on canvas, WAG 3070.
National Museums of Liverpool.

dont want *dogs* to go and Ketch him. It is to[o] dangerous. They may kill a man in a very short time. Last time they had nearly torn him up." Some masters saw the violence done by dogs as part of the punishment due to rebellious slaves. Over the course of ten weeks in 1845, Louisiana planter Bennet Barrow noted in his diary three occasions when bloodhounds attacked runaway slaves. First, they caught a runaway named Ginny Jerry, who sought refuge in the branches before the "negro hunters . . . made the dogs pull him out of the tree, Bit him very badly, think he will stay home a while." Second, a few weeks later, while pursuing another truant, Barrow "came across Williams runaway," who found himself found himself cornered by bloodhounds, and the "Dogs nearly et his legs off—near killing him." Finally, an unnamed third runaway managed to elude the hounds for half a mile before the "dogs soon tore him naked." When he returned to the plantation, Barrow "made the dogs give him another overhauling" in front of the assembled enslaved community as a deterrent. Although Barrow may have taken unusual pleasure in watching dogs attack runaway slaves, his diary reveals that slave owners used dogs to track fugitives and torture them. In bloodhounds, slaves saw the lash transformed into animal form, a snarling implement of torture. Runaway Isaac Williams noted that "many a poor fugitive slave has been torn limb from limb by those ferocious brutes." More than seventy years after emancipation, former Georgia slave Ferebe Rogers recalled, "When slaves run away, dey always put de bloodhounds on de tracks." She had vivid memories of her owner's bloodhound, Rock, whose services he would employ whenever a slave strayed from the plantation. Rock stuck in Rogers's memory not only because he served as a constant reminder of the territorial bounds of her enslavement but also because of the vicious wounds he inflicted on runaway slaves. "Dey had de dogs trained to keep dey teeth out you till dey told 'em to bring you down," she remembered. "Den de dogs would go at your throat, and dey'd tear you to pieces, too."[49]

Unlike the lash, however, dogs had a will of their own, and many slaves recognized that they could manipulate their canine adversaries. In their plotting to escape, some runaway slaves planned and equipped themselves with the tools to evade pursuing bloodhounds. When Isaac Williams heard the "dread baying of the bloodhounds," he and his companions knew that their trackers approached. They "had taken the precaution to bring with us some red onions and spruce pine for the purpose of rubbing our boots so as to divert the scent of the dogs." They also "commenced rubbing our backs vigorously against the bark" of a nearby tree to make "the dogs think we had climbed it." A slave on a Louisiana plantation, Sam Wilson frequently sought refuge from his abusive owner in the swamp, going truant for months at a time. When his owner sought to reclaim him, Wilson "greased his feet with rabbit-grease, and that kept the dogs from him." Another slave opined that "Sam could go off and stay as long as he wanted," so long as he kept the dogs off his scent. During the Civil War, when the trickle of slave runaways became a flood, fugitives drew upon generations of knowledge about how to throw off pursuing dogs. When a band of runaway Mississippi slaves heard the howl of bloodhounds, its leader applied an "ointment made of turpentine and onions, a preparation used to throw the hounds off the trail." Slaves who did not practice olfactory deception by masking their odor knew that bloodhounds had difficulty tracking their scent through water. One former Texas slave recalled that her father fled from a particularly sadistic owner, who would try to "track papa with he [sic] dogs, but papa wade in water and dey can't track him." When he heard the "frightful baying" of hounds, Kentucky slave Andrew Jackson began "running back and forth across the stream, as often as I dared, and then along in the edge of the stream, to embarrass the dogs."[50]

When surrounded by bloodhounds, some fugitive slaves fought back. Relentlessly pursued by slave catchers and bloodhounds, Isaac Williams fashioned "a weapon out of an old carving knife blade and tied it on the end of a stout pole." When the dogs finally tracked him down and "two bloodhounds sprang upon me, I slashed at the foremost one and swung the heavy pole around as he sprang at my throat, cutting off his fore legs and laying him writhing and moaning on the ground." In the tumult, Williams dropped the weapon, but managed to dispatch the second dog by "seizing a large stone" with which he pummeled it "by a perfect shower of blows until he was dead." The ordeal left him covered with the animals' blood.[51]

White and Black Southerners frequently invoked comparisons between slavery and animals, particularly domesticated animals. Indeed, as the dominant metaphor for slavery, the slave-as-animal had profoundly deep roots and wide branches, stretching all the way back to antiquity and finding purchase throughout the Atlantic world. It reached its apex, however, in the antebellum South, as white Southerners evoked this metaphor to justify treating slaves as less than fully human. A slave should be treated, an article in the *Southern Cultivator* opined, to "understand that he is merely a mule, and possessing only the instincts of brute creation." When Frederick Law Olmsted asked one overseer if he found whipping slaves unethical or unpleasant, he replied, "I think nothing of it. . . . I wouldn't mind killing a nigger more than I would a dog."[52]

Slaves drew upon the same metaphor to explain the dehumanizing effects of slavery, drawing parallels between their experience and those of the animals around them. Like livestock, they could be bought and sold "just like a pack of mules," or "like an ox," or "like cattle," or "like a cow or horse." They had to work "lak a mule" and could be beaten "like a dog." If they ran away, they would be hunted "like a beast" or "like a wolf by a hundred blood hounds." Interviewed in 1949, 101-year-old Fountain Hughes tried to explain what slavery felt like, eight decades after emancipation. Time and again, he compared his experience with those of domesticated animals. "They'd sell us like they sell horses and cows and hogs and all like that," he said. "Bid on you just same as you bidding on cattle." Asked at the end of the interview whether he preferred slavery or freedom, Hughes replied that if he had "any idea that I'd ever be a slave again, I'd take a gun and just end it all right away! Because you're nothing but a dog. You're not a thing but a dog!"[53]

Although both slaves and slave owners used the comparison with domesticated animals to describe the dehumanizing features of the peculiar institution, when enslaved parents taught their children about how to maintain their humanity and survive in a system designed to crush their spirits, they told stories about wild animals. Codified by Joel Chandler Harris in his Uncle Remus books, animal trickster tales had their roots in African folklore, but the animals that populated them came from the American South: rabbit, deer, cooter (turtle), opossum, fox, alligator, racoon, squirrel, buzzard, and bear—animals that enslaved people knew intimately. Slaves valued these stories in part because they demonstrated the ability of the weak (Brer Rabbit) to overcome the powerful (Brer Bear). Although historians and literary critics have debated how enslaved people understood these stories and their complex moral landscape, at a very elementary level, the stories demonstrate admiration and respect for wild animals. Brer Rabbit, Brer Fox, and the other animals act autonomously, express and act on their desires, and trick and are tricked. The wild animals are free and demonstrate the full range of human emotions. By contrast, when domesticated animals appear in the trickster tales, they do so as mute animals and as property: when Brer Rabbit and Brer Wolf fight over a horse, the horse remains silent and passive. At their core, these stories reflected the profound reverence and fear that enslaved people had for the beasts of the briar patch.[54]

3

Dragged Out by the Roots

IN 1853, JOURNALIST and landscape architect Frederick Law Olmsted witnessed how enslaved labor nearly brought a once widespread tree species to extinction. Less than a decade before he designed an artificial wilderness in New York's Central Park, Olmsted had traveled to North Carolina's turpentine forests, where he saw enslaved men extract the valuable sap from longleaf pines. Olmsted saw brutality in both labor that enslaved people performed and its effect upon the trees. Extensive extraction over the previous decades had left the forest a shell of its former self, littered with dead trees that had been leached by repeated tapping. Many of these trees were old; Olmsted counted eighty-five rings on one felled longleaf pine. The process had left the trees with a series of deep incisions, "scarified" like the backs of enslaved people who had been repeatedly whipped. Olmsted noted that turpentine forests rarely recovered. "When the original long-leafed pine has been destroyed," he observed, "a bastard variety springs up, which grows very rapidly, but is of no value for turpentine, and of but little use for timber. The true variety, rich in turpentine, is of very slow growth." He had arrived at precisely the moment when market forces, technological innovation, and slavery conspired to destroy a native forest. By the time of his visit, more than a century of intensive enslaved lumbering had devastated forests across the South. From the early eighteenth century onward, enslaved men formed the backbone of a timber industry.[1]

The Southern timber industry served multiple masters. During the colonial era, demand from Britain and the West Indies helped to jumpstart it, as Southern wood helped to panel Georgian mansions, roof Jamaican plantations, and barrel Barbadian sugar. Forestry products proved second only to tobacco in Virginia exports, with shiploads of shingles, lumber, and staves departing from Norfolk. Timber production in the Carolinas followed suit,

Scars on the Land. David Silkenat, Oxford University Press. © Oxford University Press 2022.
DOI: 10.1093/oso/9780197564226.003.0004

FIGURE 3.1. "Scraping or gathering hard turpentine, Sampson County, N.C.," Commercial Museum (Philadelphia, Pa.) Collection of North Carolina Photographs, North Carolina Collection, University of North Carolina Library at Chapel Hill.

such that by 1764 approximately 750,000 shingles left Charles Town for St. Kitts alone. The export business only grew after the Revolution; by 1850, more than six million board feet of lumber left Charleston for the West Indies and northern Europe. Shipbuilding constituted a second major consumer of Southern timber. Although overshadowed by New England and the mid-Atlantic colonies, shipwrights in the Chesapeake and South Carolina relied on Southern timber for masts and decking. "We have in plenty a sort of wood called the live oak for timbers which seem admirably adapted to that use," wrote South Carolina governor James Glen in 1751. "Builders prefer it even to

the best Oak that can be met with in the yards of England and we have great
quantities of yellow pine for planking, now are we in want of plenty of Masts
and Naval Stores."[2]

Insatiable domestic demand proved the largest consumer of Southern
timber. Plantation houses and slave quarters alike were constructed from
yellow pine, white oak, and cypress. Worm fences required approximately five
thousand cedar and chestnut rails per mile, rails that needed to be regularly
replaced due to rot and breakage. Hogsheads for tobacco and barrels for rice
and indigo required a constant supply of white oak for staves. Moreover, wood
provided the main source for heat in the winter and for cooking year-round.
In 1770, Virginia planter Landon Carter observed, "We now have full ¾ of the
year in which we are obliged to keep constant fires; we must fence our ground
in with rails[,] build and repair our houses with timber and every cooking
room must have its fire the year through." Carter deployed some of his four
hundred slaves every winter to his upriver holdings to fell trees, floating the
logs down the Rappahannock to his plantation. With each passing year, he
found it increasing difficult to procure enough fuel, as the indigenous forests
in eastern Virginia had largely been cleared. "I must think that in a few years,"
he concluded, "the lower parts of this Country will be without firewood."[3]

In April 1776, naturalist William Bartram observed enslaved lumbermen
firsthand. Traveling west from Charleston into the Georgia backcountry, he
came across a slave lumber camp on the Savannah River where he found "slaves
comparatively of a gigantic stature, fat and muscular, mounted on the massive
timber logs, the regular heavy strokes of their gleaming axes re-echo in the
deep forests." Bartram observed that "the log or timber landing is a capacious
open area, the lofty pines having been felled and cleared away for a considerable distance round about." The enslaved lumbermen rolled the logs "down
the banks into the river, where being formed into rafts, they are conducted
by slaves down to Savanna[h], about fifty miles below this place," where they
would be processed into boards.[4]

The lumber camp that Bartram observed resembled countless others on
the edge of the slave frontier on the eve of the Revolution. Upriver from the
plantation belt, enslaved men wielded axes, exacting a heavy toll on the virgin
forest. Separated from their families, they worked in dangerous and difficult
conditions, but at the same time had less direct supervision than plantation
slaves. According to one colonial surveyor in South Carolina, eight enslaved
men could clear-cut an acre of forest per day. Once the usable lumber had been
felled, "The Planters set their weak Hands, (Women and Boys) to cut down
the Bushes and Shrubs with Hoes and Hatchets." Gathering the detritus into

small piles, they would light low-intensity fires that would consume the waste
without burning the soil. The "lopping and burning" took place after sunset,
when calmer night-time winds reduced the danger that fires would spread
uncontrollably. The ashes had an added benefit of fertilizing the soil with potassium and calcium.[5]

With each passing decade, these lumber camps moved further upriver,
causing many coastal planters to worry that they had denuded the region of
usable woodlands. In 1770, Maryland governor William Eddis observed that,
"notwithstanding the extensive forests that abound throughout this vast continent," the cost of river transport and slave labor made firewood "an expensive article in all the considerable towns." By the first decade of the nineteenth
century, Revolutionary physician and politician David Ramsay reported that
Charlestonians used thirty thousand cords of wood annually "and much
more cut down, burnt, and destroyed in the country." Ramsay attributed this
deforestation not only to Charlestonians' insatiable appetite for lumber but
also to the recent boom in short-staple cotton. "So great is the eagerness to
plant cotton," Ramsay observed, "that forests containing immense quantities
of useful wood are yearly cut down." Writing only a decade after the invention
of the cotton gin made short-staple cotton profitable, Ramsay could foresee
the consequences "when Carolina, stript of its trees, will . . . present an unshaded surface to the direct action of the sun." Indeed, the lumber frontier
had already stretched into Appalachia.[6]

The rate of deforestation only increased as slavery spread into the Lower
South. Early white visitors to Alabama's Black Belt described a region rich in
old-growth forests. In 1818, a surveyor documented that along the Alabama
River rested "an extensive body of level, rich land, of fine black, or chocolate
coloured soil. The principal growth is hickory: black oak, post oak, dogwood,
and poplar, are also common," but pine trees were rare. Many other early Black
Belt settlers noted the extensive hardwood forests interspersed with prairies.
However, in less than two decades, cotton plantations had displaced these
forests. Arriving in Alabama at the head of a coffle, one slave trader observed
in 1832 that the landscape was in the process of rapid transformation. Near
Montgomery, he saw slaves "picking cotton and clearing land—the axes were
cutting until midnight, and an hour before day next morning," and on some
settlements near Marion, "negroes were cutting timber all night until sunrise."
That same year, a surveyor in Sumter County documented a land rich in oaks
and hickories but an almost total absence of pines and cedars.[7]

Twenty years later, visitors found a different landscape. When Frederick
Law Olmsted visited Montgomery in 1853, he saw "in every direction upon a

dense forest, boundless as the sea." However, this was a different forest than the one confronted by settlers a generation earlier. The old-growth oak and hickory had largely been replaced by quick-growing pines and cedars. Much of this land had been cleared for cotton cultivation but subsequently abandoned when the soil had been exhausted. Olmsted pointed to a speech by Alabama senator C. C. Clay to explain "the sad memorials of the artless and exhausting culture of cotton." A pro-slavery ideologue who would later become a Confederate nationalist, Clay did not blame slavery per se for the region's ecological collapse but recognized that the economics of cotton slavery exacted a heavy cost. "Our small planters, after taking the cream off their lands, unable to restore them by rest, manures, or otherwise, are going further west and south, in search of other virgin lands, which they may and will despoil and impoverish in like manner," he observed. "Our wealthier planters, with greater means and no more skill, are buying out their poorer neighbors, extending their plantations, and adding to their slave force." Clay knew that such a path would be unsustainable. The explosive growth and rapid decline of Alabama's Black Belt, Clay lamented, was tragic for "a country in its infancy, where, fifty years ago, scarce a forest tree had been felled by the axe of the pioneer" and that was "already exhibiting the painful signs of senility and decay, apparent in Virginia and the Carolinas; the freshness of its agricultural glory is gone; the vigor of its youth is extinct, and the spirit of desolation seems brooding over it."[8]

Located on riverbanks, slave lumber camps transformed the riverine ecosystem. Without tree roots to stabilize the soil, the banks eroded and muddied the current. Water levels dropped, and some tributaries went dry in summer months. Higher water temperatures made many waterways inhospitable to fish and amphibians. Treeless rivers also became more prone to flooding; without trees to absorb spring and summer rains, freshets became increasingly prevalent. After decades of clear-cutting on their Virginia plantations to power mills and a forge, the Jerdone family found their properties threatened by flooding. "The water [is] rising so fast," John Jerdone wrote to his father in 1830, "the quantity of water we have to encounter prevents anything like effectual operation. It has been by far the most difficult and dangerous work of the sort we have ever had to encounter with here." Flooding had already destroyed their wheat crop. To prevent further disaster, he had his slaves hastily reinforce a dam to protect the forge and upper fields. The following year, flooding breached the dam and ruined another crop, prompting Jerdone to have his enslaved labor force work through the night on repairs. In 1833, flooding left "corn and wheat . . . underwater, buried in mud & sand

& washed up by the roots." While the Jerdones worried about the effects of flooding on their finances, their enslaved labor force bore the brunt of the destruction. Intense flooding destroyed some slave cabins and left the others caked in muck. When flood waters washed away their profits, the Jerdones balanced their books by selling off their human property.[9]

The deforestation of the Mississippi Delta between 1840 and 1860 illustrated how the expanding slave frontier prompted an ecological collapse. The Delta's virgin forests contained some of the most diverse amalgamations of tree species anywhere in the United States: bald cypress, southern magnolia, sweetgum, willows, laurel oak, American elm, shagbark hickory, white oak, dogwood, and walnut, among others. Thousands of animal species made their home within this complex and diverse habitat, and its destruction radically constrained their range and numbers. By the eve of the Civil War, once plentiful white-tailed deer, black bear, and cougars had essentially disappeared from the Delta. Riparian species that depended on the complex interplay between the water and trees suffered significantly: frogs, salamanders, turtles, and crayfish all felt the ecological pressure on their habitats, as did the hundreds of bird species who made their homes in the woods. Indeed, the slave frontier's deforestation contributed to the extinction or near extinction of several species, including the ivory-billed woodpecker, the Mississippi sandhill crane, Bachman's warbler, the Carolina parakeet, and the Pine Barrens tree frog.[10]

The Mississippi

Along the lower Mississippi, extensive enslaved lumbering had transformed the landscape for more than a century prior to the Louisiana Purchase. Until the development of sugar as a cash crop in the 1790s, French and Spanish settlers saw lumber (as well as indigo) as the region's primary export commodity, hoping to exploit its vast stocks of cypress, oak, and pine. Throughout the eighteenth century, Louisiana exported boatloads of planks, shingles, and barrel staves to Martinique, Saint-Domingue, and other French Caribbean colonies, many of which had already been deforested and relied on imported timber. Longtime French governor Jean-Baptiste Le Moyne de Bienville promoted the timber trade, observing that "it is well known how scarce dressed timber is in Santo Domingo." After experiments on local timber on Dauphin Island in 1709, French settlers discovered the utility of Louisiana cypress. Even after immersion in seawater for several months, cypress proved immune to the marine worms that riddled its rivals. Moreover, cypress demonstrated unusual resistance to rot and insects, definite virtues in humid Louisiana and the Caribbean. Carpenters and sawyers appreciated that cypress could be as easily worked as pine, leading one observer to claim in 1723 that "there is no negro or convict who is not capable of sawing plank." By the 1730s, French lumber barons established water-powered and horse-drawn sawmills in Biloxi and New Orleans. Tall and straight, cypress logs were in high demand for ship masts and planking. Cypress wood also proved invaluable in the construction of vats for steeping indigo. However, roof shingles, the most important product derived from Louisiana cypress, did not require a sawmill for production, just a floe ax and a mallet. Durable and resistant to splitting and warping, cypress shingles became the preferred roofing material across the Gulf South, the Caribbean, and the British Atlantic colonies. As one visitor from Martinique noted in 1753, enslaved cypress extraction proved immensely profitable. "Some plantations have a sawmill which once started with ten or twelve slaves will result in a net revenue of ten to twelve thousand livres per year," roughly the salary of the French imperial governor. In the years to come, slave owners in Virginia, the Carolinas, and Florida used Louisiana as an example, sending enslaved lumbermen into cypress swamps to turn timber into shingles.[11]

Working in cypress swamps posed particular problems for enslaved lumbermen. More than one hundred feet tall and weighing in excess of thirty tons, cypress trees could only be moved with "three or four pair of horses dragging them." Even during the dry season, draft animals and timber carts became mired in thick umber mud. During the wet season, the swamps became inaccessible except by boat, making cutting down trees nearly impossible. Moreover, green cypress sank, so freshly cut timber could not be floated to market. By 1730, cypress logging in Louisiana had developed seasonal patterns: felling the trees in October and November, the driest months of the year, allowing them to cure in situ, then floating the trees out of the swamp in June and July. The seasonal nature of cypress extraction allowed slave owners to assign their enslaved lumbermen to food production and construction when the swamps proved inaccessible. Other problems proved more intractable. In cypress swamps, lumbermen confronted alligators, snapping turtles, canebrake rattlesnakes, cottonmouths, and copperheads. Drenched in sweat, they were often injured by falling trees and slipping axes.[12]

Conditions within the cypress swamps dissuaded slave owners and overseers from closely supervising enslaved lumbermen. Using clandestine paths that snaked through the swamps, enslaved workers could meet and trade with each other. During logging season, many enslaved lumbermen lived for weeks in the swamp in a kind of quasi-freedom, building cabins and social and economic networks. As historian Gwendolyn Midlo Hall has documented, cypress lumbering in colonial Louisiana created the framework for a kind of marronage that would become common in other industrial swamps across the slave South. Runaway slaves established communities in the swamp, living and working not far from enslaved lumbermen, with whom they regularly met and traded. Farming in high clearings in the swamp, maroons cultivated corn and vegetables and hunted alligators and turtles. Although white officials made periodic efforts to suppress the maroon population, many sawmill owners traded with runaway slaves, who exchanged cypress logs for firearms, axes, and silver Spanish reales. One recaptured fugitive named Zéphir testified in 1781 that maroons worked closely with sawmill owners for "the agreed stipend," which they divided "in accordance with the work which each of us performed." They also traded regularly with slaves, "giving them baskets, sifters, and other items which we wove from willow which they brought to the city to sell, and in return for their value and price, they brought us the provisions we ordered."[13]

When the United States purchased Louisiana in 1803, nearly a century of intensive lumbering had already devastated the colony's cypress stock. More than fifty years earlier, French authorities began to worry that unfettered cultivation would exhaust the precious resource. "The cypresses were formerly very common in Louisiana," noted one French planter in 1751, "but they have wasted them so imprudently, that they are now somewhat rare. . . . They sawed the wood into planks which they exported at different places. The price of the wood now is three times as much as it was formerly." To find cypress, enslaved lumbermen had to venture farther into the swamp. Under Spanish control after 1766, demand for Louisiana cypress became volatile, as shifting international trade barriers opened and closed markets and new sources of cypress closer to Caribbean markets, including North Carolina's Great Dismal Swamp, undercut prices. With the development of sugar as a cash crop in the 1790s, much the enslaved labor in the region became reassigned to cut and process cane. By the time the United States took possession of Louisiana, cypress exports had dwindled to a trickle.[14]

North of the sugar belt, frontier planters saw the Mississippi River primarily for its timber resources. Settling near Baton Rouge in 1771, then under Spanish control, Scottish immigrant William Dunbar imported fourteen slaves from Jamaica and assigned them to clear the forests along the Mississippi, producing thousands of white-oak barrel staves every week, which he then exported to the Caribbean. In 1784, he moved upriver to Natchez, purchasing a plantation he called "the Forest." Although Dunbar eventually diversified his holdings to include rice, indigo, and cotton, his account books make clear that he built his fortune on enslaved lumbering. By the time of his death in 1810, he had become one of the wealthiest men in the Mississippi territory.[15]

Dunbar's timber empire foreshadowed the deforestation that would take place along the Mississippi with the cotton revolution. Gangs of enslaved men formed the vanguard of the plantation system, with full hands cutting an eighth of an acre per day. A fugitive from bondage in Mississippi, Louis Hughes recalled, "When additional land was required for cultivation the first step was to go into the forest in summer and 'deaden' or girdle the trees on a given tract. This was cutting through the bark all around the trunk about thirty inches from the ground. The trees so treated soon died and in a year or two were in condition to be removed." More impatient planters hired enslaved logging crews, who specialized in clearing land for cotton planting. Knickerbocker novelist and former secretary of the Navy James K. Paulding observed that in Mississippi "the more recent plantations are invariably indicated by masses of dead trees, presenting an abrupt and disagreeable transition from the rich vendure [sic] of the living forest, to the dreary aspect of decay and ruin."[16]

The expansion of the cotton frontier to the Mississippi coincided with technological changes that made clearing forests faster and more profitable. Until 1830, most planters processed their own timber, assigning slaves to saw felled trees into boards by hand. Working in pairs, enslaved sawyers used a whipsaw to split logs into boards. Usually, one enslaved sawyer stood alongside the log on a "scaffold, about ten feet high," sharing the saw with "another below, who [would] alternately pull and push the saw." Alternatively, they "dug a deep trench in the ground, and laid the log to be sawed into boards lengthwise over the trench, and one of us would stand in the trench under the log and the other on top of the log." In either arrangement, the man in the bottom position found himself inundated with sawdust and risked significant injury from falling logs. Performing this slow and backbreaking work, experienced sawyers could produce only one hundred board feet per day. Water-powered sawmills provided only a slight improvement: the slow-moving sash blades were said to cut "up today and down tomorrow." Slave owners interested in converting their forestlands to finished lumber therefore found themselves limited by the speed at which logs could be cut into boards.[17]

In the 1830s, innovations in sawmill technology dramatically increased their speed, efficiency, and quality. The introduction of steam power and circular saws removed the proverbial logjam in lumber production, facilitating lumber production and profit at unprecedented levels. Between 1830 and 1860, the number of Southern sawmills doubled every decade. By the eve of the Civil War nearly five thousand dotted the landscape, generating more than $23 million in lumber per year. Exported to northeastern cities, the West Indies, and Britain, processed lumber outpaced cotton as a growth industry, prompting some planters to see untamed forests not as a barrier to be overcome before planting could commence but as a valuable resource for extraction.[18]

Clear-cutting forests served the immediate needs of plantation construction. Slaves split harvested lumber into fence rails and boards for slave cabins and smokehouses. Kidnapped into slavery in 1841, Solomon Northup witnessed firsthand how slavery's expansion prompted the destruction of native forests. Northup's first owner, Rev. William Prince Ford, lived in the Great Pine Woods on Louisiana's Red River, which speculators saw as the next cotton frontier. While he was en route from New Orleans, his first impression of the region was of unbroken forest: "This upland is covered with numerous trees—the white oak, the chincopin, resembling chestnut, but principally the yellow pine. They are of great size, running up sixty feet, and perfectly straight." Northup described Ford's nascent plantation as "entirely surrounded by woods, and covered with a carpet of rich, rank verdure. It was a quiet, lonely, pleasant place—literally a green spot in the wilderness." Like many frontier planters, Ford had accrued significant debts and needed to quickly transform this wilderness into profitable cotton fields. During his first summer in bondage, Northup toiled "in piling lumber, and chopping logs." When Ford's debts caught up with him, he sold Northup to John Tibaut, a carpenter to whom he owed money. Tibaut treated Northup cruelly, but Northup's skills as a lumberman prompted a neighboring planter to hire him. Sent to the "wild lands of Mr. Eldret, where he contemplated clearing up an extensive plantation," Northup found himself "in the midst of trees of enormous growth, whose wide-spreading branches almost shut out the light of the sun, while the space between the trunks was an impervious mass of cane, with here and there an occasional palmetto." Northup found the dense forest both beautiful and intimidating. "The bay and the sycamore, the oak and the cypress, reach a growth unparalleled," he observed, "in those fertile lowlands bordering the Red River." His new master, however, wasted no time in setting his band of enslaved lumbermen to work, as "we cut down oaks, split them into rails, and with these erected temporary cabins." Northup found the work physically grueling, leaving him "weary and fatigued" and plagued by mosquitoes and biting flies. Eager to clear the land as quickly as possible,

Eldret brought in addition slaves over the coming weeks, including four
women, whose skill impressed Northup. "They were excellent choppers, the
largest oak or sycamore standing but a brief season before their heavy and
well-directed blows," Northup observed. "At piling logs, they were equal to
any man. There are lumberwomen as well as lumbermen in the forests of the
South."[19]

More sustained demand for lumber came from the growing steamboat
traffic on the Mississippi. The number of steamboats plying the river doubled
every decade after their introduction in 1811. Intense competition prompted
steamboat owners to adopt high pressure engines. Nominally faster upriver,
these new engines proved enormously fuel inefficient, burning twelve to
seventy-five cords of wood per day, depending on conditions and the direction of travel. Compelled to stop multiple times per day to refuel, steamboats
had an insatiable appetite, consuming thousands of acres of forestland each
year. By 1850, one could travel down the Mississippi from Cairo to New
Orleans without a forest in sight. "On either bank of the Mississippi," noted
one downriver steamboat passenger in 1858, "every four or five miles' distances
[were] piles of wood . . . cut by the negroes for their masters."[20] Working on a
steamboat on the Alabama River between Mobile and Montgomery, Cudjo
Lewis recalled, "Oh Lor,! I workee so hard! Every landing, you understand
me, I tote wood on de boat." Born Oulale Kossula around 1840 in West
Africa, he had been kidnapped and illegally imported into the United States
aboard the slave ship *Clotilda* in 1860. When he recounted his experience to
anthropologist and novelist Zora Neale Hurston in 1931, he could vividly recall each of the twenty stops that the steamship made. "De steamboat didn't
used to burnee de coal," he reminded her. "It burnee de wood an' it usee so
muchee wood!"[21]

For planters hoping to establish themselves on the Mississippi, selling
fuel to steamboats provided an important source of startup capital. In his
response to Harriet Beecher Stowe's *Uncle Tom's Cabin*, Mississippi novelist
Joseph Holt Ingraham described how the use of enslaved lumbermen enabled
a young Natchez planter to enrich himself while he built his cotton plantation: he received "at twenty-one years of age, thirty slaves from his father,
and fourteen hundred acres of wild forest land on the Mississippi. He took
his hands there, and commenced clearing. Thirty axes do vast execution in a
wood. As he cleared, he piled up the cloven timber into a fire-wood length,
and sold it to passing steamers at $2.50 a cord. The first year he took $12,000
in cash for wood alone." The following year, he planted cotton on the cleared
land but continued to derive most of his income from selling steamboat

timber. Only after four years did his income from cotton exceed that from timber, such that "the young man, not yet twenty-nine, is now a rich planter, with a hundred slaves, and is making 500 bales of cotton at a crop." This fictional example mirrored the account books of many Mississippi planters and the guidance given in agricultural journals. "Nothing pays so well," noted one steamboat traveler, "as wooding up and down the river."[22]

Fuel for the Forge

Forests remote from the steamboat routes did not escape the ax, as iron works in Virginia, the Carolinas, Kentucky, and Tennessee proved insatiable consumers of fuel. Although iron production in the South had its roots in the colonial era, demand for both pig and wrought iron increased dramatically in the 1830s, prompting the construction of iron plantations across the mountain South. Small antebellum iron furnaces required 360 bushels of charcoal per day, roughly an acre of forestland, to produce two tons of pig iron. By 1860, more than 240 charcoal-burning iron furnaces dotted the Southern landscape, often located near Appalachian iron mining sites. Usually built into hillsides, iron furnaces stood twenty-five to forty feet tall, near the top of which enslaved workers shoveled iron ore, limestone, and charcoal. At most Southern iron furnaces, the owner procured his own raw materials and stopped production when local supplies ran out. In most cases, the supply of charcoal proved the more tenuous component. Made from seasoned timber burnt in a low-oxygen kiln, charcoal made from Southern pine and oak required a substantial enslaved labor force to cut the wood and attend the kilns. Most furnaces employed over fifty enslaved lumbermen, while the largest corporate iron operations in Appalachia commanded the labor of five hundred men. By one estimate, approximately ten thousand slaves worked in the Southern iron industry, mostly to maintain the steady supply of charcoal.

Ironworks left a large footprint on the landscape. In many mountain counties, iron planters had the largest land and human property holdings. One East Tennessee iron planter observed, "To keep a smelting furnace in operation making about twenty tons of metal per week, require[s] 7,000 to 10,000 acres of common mountain land" simply to provide enough lumber for charcoal. Built in 1827, Virginia's Lucy Selina forge relied on the ample forests in the foothills of the Alleghenies, owning forty thousand acres of woodlands. In 1830, the firm owned six enslaved men, who attended the forge itself, but hired the labor of an additional thirty-two men to cut wood and produce charcoal. In the decades prior to the Civil War, southern Appalachia

lost upwards of three hundred thousand acres of forest to charcoal production. Once the timberland had been exhausted, the furnace was usually
abandoned, leaving a barren landscape. "For miles on either side of the iron
works, the whole country has been laid waste, presenting as far as the eye can
reach the most desolate and gloomy appearance," noted one upland traveler,
"the lands having all been bought up by the Company for the sake of fuel."
Within a decade, these abandoned lands became overwhelmed by dwarf pine,
cedar, and scrub oak, creating a dense unnatural thicket. Local tradition in
Spotsylvania County, Virginia, attributed the impenetrable undergrowth at
the Wilderness, the site of the May 1864 Civil War battle, to its former use as
a charcoal forest for an iron furnace abandoned nearly twenty years earlier.

Some of the largest iron plantations had forges on site to convert the pig
iron to wrought iron, but most furnace owners sold their product to industrial forges, such as Richmond's Tredegar Iron Works. Like smelting, forging
required charcoal to fuel the intense fires needed to remove carbon and other
impurities. Although some Southern forges experimented with using mineral coal in the 1850s in lieu of charcoal, already common practice in the
North and in Europe, most continued to rely on charcoal as their primary
fuel. Beyond iron, many Southern industries relied on slave-produced charcoal for fuel, including salt furnaces, which used charcoal to boil and dry the
salt brine, and tobacco cultivation, which used charcoal to cure the leaf to a
bright yellow color. A calculation of the cumulative effect of charcoal production and consumption on Southern forests may prove elusive, but its extensive use demonstrates the deep connections between industrial slavery in a
modernizing South and its profound environmental consequences.[23]

Turpentine Forests

In North Carolina longleaf pine forests, the growth of industrial capitalism
drove another kind of ecological destruction. Within these old-growth
forests, enslaved lumberjacks extracted turpentine—a valuable but non-
renewable resource that would leave permanent scars upon the landscape.
Reaching one hundred feet tall, longleaf pines flourished in sandy soil along
a crescent-shaped band that stretched from Virginia to east Texas. Covering
130 million acres, this one-hundred-mile-wide strip of trees had its strongest
concentration in the eastern counties of North Carolina, which by 1840
produced 96 percent of all turpentine, tar, and rosin in the United States.

Although the naval stores industry—an umbrella term for turpentine,
tar, pitch, rosin, and related products—had begun in North Carolina's pine

FIGURE 3.2. "Lower Salt-Works." *Harper's New Monthly Magazine* 15 (1857): 450.

forests in the 1720s, demand exploded after 1830 when industrialists found
new uses for turpentine, including in rubber production, as a soap additive, as
an industrial solvent, and especially as a component in camphene, a popular
lamp oil. In response to increased demand, North Carolina slave owners expanded and intensified turpentine production, up to eight hundred thousand
barrels per year. The collapse of the cotton market in 1837 and the lifting of the
British tariff on American turpentine in 1846 accelerated the intensity of its
extraction in eastern North Carolina. By the eve of the Civil War, naval stores
had become the South's third largest export. At the height of the industry, ten
thousand enslaved men worked in the turpentine forests.[24]

The process of harvesting sap began in the winter, when slaves cut collection "boxes" into the tree bases, six inches from roots. Unlike maple sap
collection, these boxes were not attached to the exterior of the tree but were
"cavities dug in the trunk of the tree itself." Pocket-shaped, turpentine boxes
could hold approximately a quart of sap. Slave owners expected skilled hands
to cut seventy-five to a hundred boxes per day. At the height of the turpentine
boom, the largest longleaf pines hosted three or four boxes to expedite collection. As the weather warmed, sap began to flow into the boxes. Enslaved men
known as dippers collected sap from the boxes, using a paddle to scoop it into

FIGURE 3.3. Frederick Law Olmsted, *A Journey in the Seaboard Slave States* (New York: Dix and Edwards, 1856), 344.

buckets. The task left dippers' "hands and clothing . . . smeared with the gum," which was almost impossible to remove. Dippers accumulated layers of dried sap and dirt on their skin and clothes, an accumulation that they could only effectively remove in November when the harvest ended. They also suffered from the toxic cumulative effect of inhaling turpentine fumes, which left them dizzy and their throats raw. Sap only continued to flow into the boxes so long as the scars remained fresh. While dippers made their rounds collecting sap, a second band of enslaved lumbermen refreshed the wound. In a process known as chipping, they cut a new incision into the bark using a specially designed ax. As the gum crystalized, they returned every seven to ten days to add a new chip half an inch above the last one. Over weeks, months, and years, chipping left rows of gashes up a tree's trunk, leaving it, in Frederick Law Olmsted's terms, "scarified."[25]

Most visitors to North Carolina's longleaf pine forests saw the work of enslaved lumbermen inscribed on the tree trunks but rarely saw the workers themselves. Living in small camps deep in the woods, enslaved lumbermen had to cover a substantial territory: dippers might service twenty-five hundred trees per day, spread over a dozen acres. With enslaved lumbermen

FIGURE 3.4. "Dripping crude turpentine, Sampson County, N.C.," Commercial Museum (Philadelphia, Pa.) Collection of North Carolina Photographs, North Carolina Collection, University of North Carolina Library at Chapel Hill.

scattered throughout the forest, most enslavers found operating on the task system most efficient, setting a quota for each dipper or chipper to complete. Mounted overseers, known as "woodsriders," patrolled the forest, but the distances and visibility made close surveillance impossible. A guide to turpentine production in *DeBow's Review* warned that "the overseer of several hands cannot possibly inspect their work with any accuracy." Moreover, the forests provided enslaved lumbermen with many opportunities to disappear if they felt overburdened. "Can't press the hands—they won't have it," wrote one North Carolina overseer. "So I have to do the best I can to keep them here."[26]

Like most enslaved lumber camps, housing in the turpentine forests proved rudimentary, providing only moderate protection from the elements and little comfort. By the 1830s, most turpentine barons expected to exhaust their forests within a decade and saw little benefit in investing in permanent housing. Most enslaved lumbermen slept in shanties constructed from fallen timber. While providing scant rations of cornmeal, enslavers expected that lumberjacks would secure their own food through hunting and trapping.

While some turpentine barons employed women and children as dippers, men dominated enslaved turpentine camps, disconnected from families and broader social networks. Their numbers included many hired slaves, strangers thrown together in the woods for a season. Despite the isolation and autonomy, most enslavers believed that enslaved lumbermen preferred working in the forest to the alternatives; one quipped that "no set of hands have ever been known to willingly leave it and go back to cotton."[27]

Turpentine workers had more autonomy than most enslaved people. John Avirett enslaved 125 people at Rich Land, one of the largest turpentine plantations in North Carolina, producing thirty thousand barrels of turpentine per year. While some worked at the three-story mansion where Avirett lived with his family and on adjacent farmland, most of Avirett's slaves lived and labored in his vast holdings that extended over twenty thousand acres, stretching from White Oak and Angola swamps to the New River. In a post-emancipation memoir, Avirett's son noted that unlike tobacco or cotton plantations, commanding enslaved workers in a turpentine orchard required a different labor regime. Their enslaved lumbermen, he noted, worked in "large, wooded tracts of country, out of range of anything like close oversight and must be stimulated to their best work." Like many turpentine planters, Avirett tried to incentivize his enslaved workers by offering small financial rewards for exceeding their quotas. African American expertise undergirded the entire production process for turpentine at Rich Lands. Philip, a sixty-year-old enslaved man, managed chippers and dippers. He possessed an encyclopedic knowledge of the forest, and "without him the proprietor would have been sadly at sea." Another enslaved man, Harry, attended the distillery, where he processed the raw sap into turpentine. Distilling turpentine took both skill and nerves, as the flammable liquid often exploded in the still. Between them, Philip and Harry organized most of the labor on the plantation.[28]

During the colonial era, turpentine orchards could produce for nearly half a century before exhaustion. After 1830, however, more intensive extraction left most longleaf pine forests drained within a decade. Traveling through North Carolina in 1843, New York poet and journalist William Cullen

Bryant wrote, "We passed through extensive forests of pine, which had been boxed, as it is called for the collection of turpentine." He looked in horror at the "broad wound" that turpentine extraction had left in the trees. "This is the work of destruction; it strips acre after acre of the noble trees," he observed. "If it goes on, the time is not far distant when the long-leaved pine will become nearly extinct in this region." He was not optimistic about the future of this ecosystem, as he had seen "large tracts covered with the standing trunks of trees already killed by it." Enslaved lumberjacks cut down trees that no longer produced, using the lumber for barrels to transport the sap for refining.[29]

Some North Carolina planters recognized that the insatiable demand for turpentine would prove unsustainable. "Turpentine now being a good price, the labor you bestow on it is now richly compensated," wrote William Valentine in 1845. "The question [is] how to cultivate your pines to best advantage." Overzealous planters, Valentine thought, boxed their trees too often and too much. Rather than boxing "the same crop of pines" every year, "you should tend one year, then let them rest one year, and so on alternately as long as you choose. But if you think proper to let them rest [for] three years, the pines will be decidedly benefitted; they recover from the drains of its fluid which is its blood." He also advocated a conservative approach to how many boxes to cut into each tree. In their quest for quick profits, many turpentine planters had ordered "three or four boxes cut" into each tree. Valentine believed that over-boxing "exhaust[ed] the pine faster than it can supply the oil" and "deprive[d] the tree of so much bark at once that the tree soon dies." Despite Valentine's warnings about the perils of overtaxing the longleaf forests, most planters sought short-term profits over sustainability.[30]

Intensive extraction conspired with environmental factors to expedite the forests' destruction. Scarification caused by repeated chipping made the trees vulnerable to wood-boring insects such as the ips beetle, the turpentine borer, and the black turpentine beetle. Stripped of their bark, the pine trees stood defenseless against these insects. A turpentine-borer epidemic in 1848–1849 along the Cape Fear River devasted the heart of North Carolina's longleaf pine. Repeated tapping also so weakened trees so that a hurricane or heavy wind could level acres of woodlands. Traveling through the husk of a leached forest, one visitor recorded that he found "very dangerous riding in No. Carolina when the Winds blow hard, for you ride all the Way through the Pines, many of which have been 'boxed' to get Turpentine out . . . that a high Winds is a very apt to overset them."[31]

The most significant threat came from forest fires. While the longleaf pine's intact bark tended to protect the tree from the effects of naturally occurring forest fires, the exposed trunks of chipped trees, covered in combustible sap, lit up like a candle, turning the woods into an inferno. "No trees can be more flammable," warned Edmund Ruffin. A summer lightning strike could set a forest ablaze. "The evil consequence of getting a turpentine plantation on fire is so great," warned an article in *DeBow's Review*, that enslavers should take every precaution to prevent them. Abandoned turpentine forests proved particularly susceptible, as branches, pine straw, and hardened gum accumulated on the forest floor. Scarified trees were known to explode from the intense temperatures fueled by dry wood and highly flammable dried sap. The risk of fire proved so great that insurance companies often refused to insure turpentine plantations. Some turpentine plantation owners allowed poor white families to live in their woods "free of rent, with as much land as they choose to cultivate" to act as an emergency fire brigade.[32]

By the eve of the Civil War, intensive turpentine production had devastated the once expansive forests of longleaf pine in North Carolina. In the late 1850s, many turpentine barons began looking for alternatives in Florida, Georgia, Alabama, and Texas, forcibly relocating their enslaved lumberjacks in the process. "You don't know gloominess until you travel through that country," wrote one traveler in 1858; "even the pine trees look ghastly with their hearts scalped instead of their heads." In 1861, Edmund Ruffin lamented that because of "the great destruction of the trees, in tapping them for turpentine, these pines are rapidly diminishing in number, and if not protected, this noble species will almost disappear from the great region which it has heretofore almost exclusively covered and adorned. . . . Scarcely a good tree in North Carolina has escaped this operation." Ruffin concluded that "rapid destruction of the forests of long leaf pine" was "neither strange nor censurable" but was the inevitable result of the "great the profits of labor" in turpentine. During the Civil War, a soldier with the 44th Massachusetts stationed in New Bern noted, "The Country we passed was real N.C. . . . nothing but Pinewoods (hard Pines), on whose trees the process of gaining turpentine was visible." Patrols into the interior marched through "vast quantities of dry, dead pines standing, killed by 'chipping.'" Already dying when the war started, the turpentine industry in North Carolina never recovered; the once ubiquitous longleaf pine survived only in isolated and scattered patches.[33]

Some visitors to North Carolina's longleaf forests made connections between the environmental destruction there and elsewhere in the South. Touring the United States to raise funds for the Free Church of Scotland, Rev. George Lewis traveled through the region in 1844. "The only use made of these pine forests is in the preparation of turpentine," he noted. He saw the scars stretching up the trees' trunks and their roughly hacked collection boxes, learning that "a negro comes from time to time and removes what has accumulated." Lewis's travels cemented his opposition to slavery, and the sight of the wounded forest horrified him. He understood the profits of turpentine production "costs the tree its life, which thenceforth decays and disappears." Throughout his travels in the South, Lewis saw parallels between the experience of enslaved people and the environment around them. "Slave labour has entailed its usual curse upon Virginia," he wrote. "The soil became exhausted." In Georgia and Alabama, he also decried the "exhausted fields" wrought by the peculiar institution. Along the Mississippi, Lewis called the "high price of cotton" the "great enemy" of the environment, lamenting the destruction of "a beautiful old forest," replaced by "unsightly and savage" cotton fields.[34]

Forest Refuge

Enslaved Southerners saw forests not only as sites of labor but also as places of refuge. Forests provided the venue for a world beyond the watchful eyes of whites, part of what some historians have referred to as an alternate or "rival geography" of the plantation South. Forest byways allowed slaves to clandestinely visit family and friends on neighboring plantations. They knew the hidden paths through the trees that linked enslaved quarters. While white Southerners saw forests as boundaries delineating property and the border between wild and cultivated space, enslaved people saw the woods as liminal spaces that created opportunities for freedom. As a small child in eastern North Carolina, Moses Grandy recalled that his "mother often hid us all in the woods, to prevent master selling us. When we wanted water, she sought for it in any hole or puddle formed by falling trees or otherwise: it was often full of tadpoles and insects: she strained it, and gave it round to each of us in the hollow of her hand."[35]

During the Second Great Awakening, the forest provided the venue for the formation of independent Black religious communities, what historian Albert Raboteau called an "invisible institution." Enslaved preachers holding prayer meetings in the woods served as an alternative source of spiritual authority, outside of white supervision. While many enslaved people attended biracial church services in the antebellum South, they also sought unfettered spiritual enlightenment, where prayers of liberation could be uttered out loud. "Us could go to the white folk's church, but us wanter go whar us could sing all the way through," recalled Emily Dixon. They constructed "hush harbors" deep in the woods—secret places constructed from tree branches and brush to conceal worshippers. "We used to steal off to de woods and have church, like de spirit moved us—sing and pray to our own liking and soul satisfaction," noted Susan Rhodes, recalling her childhood in Jones County, North Carolina. "We had dem spirit-filled meetings at night on de bank of de river and God met us there. We was quiet 'nough so de white folks didn't know we was dere." Threatened by these clandestine prayer meetings, enslavers punished those discovered taking part. "Religious services among slaves were strictly forbidden," recalled one formerly enslaved Louisianan, "but the slaves would steal away into the woods at night and hold services." Enslaved in Florida, Charlotte Martin recalled that her brother was whipped to death for his role as a prayer leader. Enslaved people also retreated to the woods as a site for quiet reflection. "If any one wishes to be impressed with the soul-killing effects of slavery," observed Frederick Douglass, let him "place himself in the deep pine woods, and there let him, in silence, analyze the sounds that shall pass through the chambers of his soul."[36]

Enslaved people also used the forest as a foraging ground to supplement their meager diet. Charles Ball recalled hunting and trapping rabbits, turtles, opossums, and raccoons, which "abounded here, and were of a large size, and fat at all seasons." The woods held perils, however. Ball recalled that "serpents of various kinds swarmed in this country," including poisonous rattlesnakes, copperheads, and moccasins. On one occasion, Ball found himself stalked by "a huge panther creeping along the path after me." Despite the dangers, enslaved people often braved the forest depths in search of its hidden cornucopia. Enslaved midwives and healers relied on the roots, flowers, and leaves they found in the woods for a natural apothecary. "The old people," recalled a formerly enslaved Marylander, "could read the woods just like a book. Whenever you were sick, they could go out and pick you something, and you'd get well." Georgian Rhodus Walton recalled that enslaved people relied on "home remedies compounded of roots." Healers gathered "Queensy's light root, butterfly root, scurry root, red shank root, bull tongue root . . . all found in the woods" near his enslaved labor camp. In 1863, Confederate surgeon Francis Porcher published *Resources of the Southern Fields and Forests*, a handbook of remedies largely based on the herbal medicines used by "negroes on the plantations of South Carolina." Although enslaved people who ventured off the plantation always risked severe punishment, slave owners often tacitly tolerated using the woods adjacent to their plantation in this fashion.[37]

Slave owners recognized that enslaved people in the woods could engage in much more problematic activities than trapping turtles, religious meetings, or a nighttime rendezvous with family members on adjacent plantations. After all, Nat Turner plotted his slave revolt with his co-conspirators in the woods near Cabin Pond in Southampton County, Virginia, in 1831. Years earlier, Turner had first received his prophetic visions, seeing signs in the heavens and on "the leaves on the trees." For six months, Turner met with his lieutenants in the woods, "forming new schemes and rejecting them," believing that the trees would hide their bodies and the woodland noises would mask their conversations. In the revolt's aftermath, which left five dozen dead, Turner himself had managed to escape. For six weeks, anxious whites read newspaper reports indicating that Turner had been spotted "in the woods," before an extensive manhunt led to his capture.[38]

Only slightly less threatening to white Southerners, the woods served as a refuge for truant and runaway slaves. When Charles Ball sought to escape from bondage, he "took to the forest," knowing that it provided the most robust sanctuary and concealment from patrols. Like many runaways, Ball traveled primarily at night, making his way by moonlight. The darkness and density of the woods made his travel difficult, as he constantly became entangled in "the trees that grew . . . so tall, and stood so close together, that the interlocking of their boughs, and the deep foliage in which they were clad, preventing me from seeing the stars." Ball knew, however, that dense forests proved nearly impenetrable for slave patrols and negated the advantage that patrollers' horses offered. Runaway slaves assiduously avoided open spaces where slave owners and patrollers could take full advantage of mounted surveillance.[39]

While runaways used the woods to escape from bondage, truants lived among the trees. Six years before his rebellion, Nat Turner had fled an abusive overseer, "remaining in the woods thirty days" before returning to the plantation. While most truants absconded to the forests only briefly, some enslaved people managed to conceal themselves for extended periods. Chronic truants like Louisianan Sallie Smith "stayed in the woods one half of my time." Escaping an abusive overseer, fourteen-year-old Smith determined that a precarious life among the trees was preferable to life on the plantation. "I slept on logs. I had moss for a pillow," recalled Smith. "I could hear bears, wild-cats, panthers, and every thing. I would come across all kinds of snakes—moccasin, blue runner, and rattlesnakes—and got used to them." She also got used to living in the elements, taking shelter under a mat of dried moss. "One night while I was in the woods a mighty storm came up," she remembered, "the winds blowed, the rain poured down, the hail fell, the trees was torn up by the roots, and broken limbs fell in every direction." Scavenging for food, she often went to sleep hungry. Like many truants, Smith relied on her proximity

to the plantation to receive support from friends, who provided her with food
on occasion. Apprehended during one clandestine visit, Smith was brutally
tortured: suspended by ropes in a smoke house so that her toes barely touched
the ground and then rolled across the plantation inside a nail-studded barrel,
leaving her scarred and bruised. Sent back to work, Smith immediately determined to flee. "I did not stay more than a month before I ran away again. I tell
you, I could not stay there," she recalled. "I had got used to the woods, and the
overseer was so brutal to me."[40]

Deforestation both served slave owners' economic interests and enhanced
their control over the enslaved population. Not only did planters profit
from opening new fields for cotton production and from selling lumber to
steamboats, but clearing forests made escape more challenging. Few understood how deforestation transformed both the landscape and the enslaved
experience as well as John Parker, who liberated himself from bondage in
Alabama and helped hundreds of enslaved people escape across the Ohio
River to freedom. Born in Virginia, eight-year-old Parker was sold to a physician in Mobile at the height of the cotton boom. When he arrived, Alabama
was "covered with a dense woods, which was being cleared as rapidly as possible for cotton fields. . . . Cotton was in demand, each field was a gold mine,
so that Virginia, Kentucky, and Missouri, where cotton could not be raised,
were the new breeding places for the slaves, who were sold south like their
mules to clear away their forests. Consequently the slaves were driven hard,
early and late, to clearing the land for King Cotton." Parker watched as the
landscape changed, cotton fields supplanting woodlands. "There was no letting up in the driving," he recalled. "Whole forests were literally dragged out
by the roots."

Parker tried to escape on several occasions. Once he fled to the woods,
which he found forbidding and dangerous. "Knowing the forest was full of
wolves," he recalled "in dim twilight I broke down a branch, making a club for
my defense." At first, he "climbed up into the forks of one of the trees just like
Robinson Crusoe," but feared falling from that height and elected to sleep on
the ground, his back "against the trunk of a tree." Parker sustained himself on
wild blueberries but did not last long before he was captured and returned to
bondage.

Parker eventually raised enough money to purchase himself, left the
South, and settled in Ripley, Ohio, the site of a robust abolitionist network.
There Parker devoted himself to helping others escape bondage. "When I first
began my work among the slaves," Parker recalled, "all Northern Kentucky
was covered with virgin forest, broken here and there by clearings, with many

trails and few roads." By the 1850s, however, "the prime bluegrass regions were thickly settled and rich in money and slaves." The trees fell to erect fencing, build cabins, and feed the voracious appetite of steamboat engines, and "the forest gradually disappeared." Without the trees for concealment, it become much "more difficult for fugitives to pass through the country successfully, since there were many eyes and few hiding places."[41]

4

Breaches in the Levee

NOT LONG AFTER his abduction in Washington, DC, in 1841, Solomon Northup found himself on board the brig *Orleans,* alongside forty other enslaved people bound for New Orleans, the epicenter of the American slave trade. The voyage took them from Richmond down the James River, into the Chesapeake, and onto the open ocean. En route, they passed some of the oldest riverside plantations in Virginia—Shirley, Berkeley, and Westover—where for more than a century enslaved laborers rolled hogsheads of tobacco down the riverbank to be loaded onto ships. They were jostled by storms in the Atlantic, but the waters became placid as they passed the Bahamas and entered the Gulf of Mexico. When they arrived at New Orleans, Northup observed from the ship's deck enslaved men "at work on the levee," repairing the mighty wall that kept the city from flooding.[1]

Six years later, Scottish geologist Charles Lyell arrived in New Orleans from Mobile on board the steamer *James L. Day*. His fellow passengers included many "'movers' going to Texas with their slaves," intent on opening slavery's next frontier, and a Virginia slave trader, boasting about the prices his sixteen slaves would fetch. Not long after his arrival in the city, Lyell visited the levee to survey the Mississippi. Looking down at the "Father of Waters," he felt an initial disappointment—the "yellow muddy stream" appeared no wider than the Thames—but "after I had studied and contemplated the Mississippi for many weeks, it left on my mind an impression of grandeur and vastness far greater than I had conceived before seeing it." He also developed a greater appreciation of the levee, observing that "the greater part of New Orleans would be annually overflowed by the river, but for the 'levee,' an artificial embankment, eight or nine feet high, which protects the city." Visiting the site of Andrew Jackson's 1815 victory, Lyell saw enslaved men "strengthening the levee at this point, for the Mississippi is threatening to

Scars on the Land. David Silkenat, Oxford University Press. © Oxford University Press 2022.
DOI: 10.1093/oso/9780197564226.003.0005

pour its resistless current through this battle-ground." Traveling upriver, a steamboat captain pointed out a spot on the levee "through which the Mississippi burst [in 1844], inundating the low cultivated lands. . . . He had seen the water rush through the opening at the rate of ten miles an hour, sucking in several flat boats, and carrying them over a watery waste into a dense swamp forest." He also saw the "Carthage crevasse," where in May 1840 a breach in the levee remained open for eight weeks, flooding thousands of acres of the most valuable farmland in the country. Two years after Lyell's visit, these levees would fail in several locations, inundating the countryside and covering New Orleans in several feet of water.[2]

The South's waterways served as arteries for slavery's expansion. During the colonial era, slavery first established itself along rivers that fed into the Atlantic. In the Chesapeake, enslaved plantation labor followed the course of the James, Potomac, and Rappahannock, and in the Lowcountry, it progressed up the Pee Dee, Cooper, Ashley, Combahee, Stono, Altamaha, and Savannah. After the cotton boom, barges and steamboats laden with cotton picked by the enslaved connected the Black Belt to markets around the world. Along the Gulf Coast, global trade and domestic bondage flowed up and down the Apalachicola, Chattahoochee, Alabama, Tombigbee, and Pearl Rivers. For more than five hundred miles north of New Orleans, slaves worked on riverside plantations on the Mississippi. Fed by the Ohio, Missouri, Arkansas, and Red Rivers, Old Muddy not only created the continent's largest watershed but also enabled plantation slavery to flourish in the American heartland. These waterways—and thousands of smaller rivers, streams, and creeks—made slavery in the American South possible. Fed by fifty inches of rainfall per year, these rivers nourished Southern soil. Yet these same waterways that made enslaved agriculture possible also proved dangerously unpredictable. Droughts could cripple a harvest, and the risk of flooding kept slave owners awake at night. To control water's creative and destructive potential, planters used enslaved labor to alter the flow of Southern rivers, build levees, and dig canals.

Rivers served as diagnostic markers of the broader ecology. Travelers in the colonial backcountry marveled at the region's pristine waterways. Cataloging the wildlife of Georgia and the Carolinas in the 1720s, English naturalist Mark Catesby marveled at how the ecosystem was "replenished with brooks and rivulets of clear water." Cane lined the riverbanks, providing food for grazing bison herds of which he found "solacing in these limpid streams" to "enjoy a cool and secret retreat." Within these clear rivers, Catesby found an abundance of aquatic life: herring, bass, eel, and drum. Most impressive were the sturgeon, which swam upriver in the late spring to spawn. "The rivers abound with them," he wrote, "such large fish elated in the air, by their leaping some yards of the water." The local Indians, Catesby observed, harvested the sturgeon by stationing their canoes at sturgeon feeding spots and allowing the enormous fish to jump into them. Catesby's friend the Virginia planter William Byrd II found similar conditions when he surveyed the boundary between Virginia and North Carolina in 1728. Byrd observed that the waters of the Dan River flowed "as clear as crystal." Through the "perfectly clear" water, Byrd could see the river's gravel bottom, "spangled very thick" with flecks of mica "that almost dazzled the eye."[3]

Chronicling Southern flora and fauna on the eve of the American Revolution, naturalist William Bartram marveled at the purity of the region's waterways, which he described variously as "glittering," "crystal," and "salubrious." Exploring a tributary of Florida's St. Johns River, he remarked that because of the "unparalleled transparency of these waters," it should be renamed "the pellucid river. The waters are the clearest and purest of any river I ever saw, transmitting distinctly the natural form and appearance of the objects moving in the transparent floods, or reposing on the silvery bed, with the finny inhabitants sporting in its gently flowing stream." He attributed the region's ecological abundance and diversity to its pristine waterways. While Bartram waxed poetic on the rivers' unspoiled natural beauty, other explorers saw clear rivers as an indication that the land could support settlement. In 1752, August Spangenberg, a Moravian missionary, noted in his diary that the waters of North Carolina's Catawba River were "as clear and sweet as any one could possibly wish . . . clear as crystal." The pristine waters nourished the landscape "& keep them always fertile." A year later, the first Moravian settlers arrived.[4]

The clarity of colonial Southern waterways indicated that the upstream riverbanks remained intact. Tree roots, canebrakes, and native grasses slowly filtered rainwater before it entered the watershed. They also cemented the soil, preventing erosion and reducing the likelihood of flooding. Forest canopy shielded slow-moving rivers from direct sunlight, making them more hospitable to fish and inhibiting algae blooms. As the slave frontier expanded, deforestation, intensive plowing, and topsoil erosion transformed the region's waterways. By the 1840s, geologists recorded how most of the rivers flowing into the Atlantic had become muddied from agricultural runoff. During a visit to Lowcountry Georgia in 1846, Scottish geologist Charles Lyell heard from locals that rivers that had previously run clear had become cloudy because of upland cultivation, which sent "copious amounts of red mud" downriver.

One planter claimed that only five years earlier he could tell from which of Altamaha's two tributaries floodwaters originated: muddy waters meant that the freshet originated in the cleared and cultivated Oconee River basin, while clear waters indicated that they came from the untamed woodlands along the Ocmulgee. Intensive cotton cultivation along both tributaries rendered this diagnostic tool moot: by the time of Lyell's visit both tributaries yielded muddy water. Lyell saw the transformation of Southern waterways as evidence that plantation agriculture had remade the landscape. A decade later, Oscar Lieber, South Carolina's state geologist, noted, "It is often observed, that rivers which were clear and limpid, when first discovered, are now turbid and muddy." Lieber surmised that "increased cultivation in the interior" had changed the rivers' character. Many observers noted that the bottom-dwelling fish such as sturgeon, once ubiquitous in Southern waterways, had all but disappeared, as siltation had rendered conditions inhospitable.[5]

Rice Cultivation

In 1805, Charles Ball arrived at his new owner's South Carolina plantation on the Congaree River. Purchased by a slave trader in his birth state of Maryland, Ball had marched in chains to Columbia, where a local planter had purchased him at auction. Although he had grown up on the Chesapeake, Ball marveled at how water dominated the Lowcountry. "The country hereabout is very flat," he observed; "the banks of the river are low; and in wet season large tracts of country are flooded by the superabundant water of the river." Joining an enslaved community of 260, Ball ate his first meal at his new home: a bowl of Carolina rice. Ball arrived in South Carolina at the apex of rice production. More than a century earlier, Lowcountry planters discovered that the region's flat, swampy environment, initially considered worthless, could be converted into profitable rice fields.[6]

The earliest white settlers in Carolina favored high ground, which many believed could be transformed into wheat, tobacco, or cotton fields. Their first experiments with rice, a non-native crop, occurred in these settlements. When "upland rice" quickly exhausted the sandy loam, white settlers shifted their attention to previously marginal wetlands, which they had thought only useful for cattle and swine grazing. Freshwater inland swamps became the birthplace of Carolina's rice industry, fed by creeks whose periodic inundations nourished the water-hungry grain. The natural processes, however, proved unreliable: too much or too little water could ruin a harvest, as could a mistimed inundation. To maximize production, rice planters sought to manipulate these natural processes, constructing elaborate canals, dams, reservoirs, and floodgates to regulate when and how much water entered the fields.

From its earliest phases, Carolina planters recognized that successful rice cultivation required dominating both the environment and men. A 1711 letter expressed optimism about the prospects for those "men that can manage the Land and get a few slaves and can beat them well to make them work hard, [t]here is no living here without." Compared to the Chesapeake colonies, establishing a Lowcountry plantation required a substantial capital investment. While tobacco (and later cotton) could be profitably grown on a small scale, rice planting could only be successfully undertaken with an extensive enslaved workforce. Its robust labor demands meant that rice and slavery grew in tandem, prompting one visitor to observe that "rice is raised so as to buy more negroes, and negroes are bought so as to get more rice." By 1708, South Carolina had a Black majority, and Charlestown had become the largest embarkation site for enslaved Africans in the British mainland colonies. James Habersham argued that coastal lands "cannot be advantageously improved, but by people, who can purchase a number of Negroes, and many plantations from their peculiar situation require a large extent of land for reservoirs to water their fields." In 1769, one British official informed a prospective planter, "You'll never make yourself whole with less than thirty Negros."[7]

Inland rice cultivation relied on gravity and landscaping to manipulate water. Enslaved workers constructed earthen embankments around the field. On the high side, a dam held back water in a stream-fed reservoir. When needed, water could be released from the reservoir, flooding the field. To drain the field, slaves would open a channel at the low end of the field. One 1738 advertisement for unimproved swampland claimed that it could be transformed into a profitable rice plantation for "very moderate Charge of Labour, in raising Dams and Water stops, which would preserve Great Quantities of Water, sufficient to supply the same in the dryest Summer." This simple schema belies the hydraulic complexity of Lowcountry rice plantations, as subtle undulations in the topography necessitated the construction of elaborate secondary drainage canals and dams. One Santee River plantation boasted one hundred acres "ditched in, divided by cross dams, into small squares of about 10 acres into any of which, water may be let in, when necessary from a large reserve of back-water." Such systems, proponents argued, allowed "for the flowing of the Rice Land with Water, which may be let off again at pleasure."[8]

Inconsistent supplies of water plagued inland rice cultivation, as a dry season could imperil a harvest. During a drought in 1760, Elias Ball's rice crop failed because his plantation lacked a "suf[f]icent command of water." Such environmental volatility prompted planters to explore new ways to irrigate their fields. Starting in the 1730s planters experimented with using the tidal flow of coastal rivers, though the practice did not become common until after the Revolution. Because of the topography, ocean tides caused Lowcountry rivers to rise and fall diurnally more than thirty miles upriver. Where the ocean salt water met the river freshwater, it created a hydraulic wedge, with the lighter freshwater on top. Opening the floodgates at high tide allowed this freshwater to flow into the rice fields; opened at low tide, they allowed flooded fields to drain. Plantation records suggest that adopting tidal irrigation increased the yield of rice fields by half. Yet this method required careful calibration and entailed substantial risk. Salt water kills rice plants, so knowing when to open and close the floodgates required profound ecological knowledge not only of rice cultivation but also of the tides and how to distinguish brackish water from fresh. Enslaved trunk minders, who attended the floodgates, knew to look for the presence of wild rice and cattails as diagnostic measures of the water's salinity. Possessing irreplaceable local knowledge, cultivated over a lifetime, enslaved trunk minders held a position of privilege on rice plantations. So too did enslaved carpenters who built and repaired floodgates.[9]

Planters prided themselves on the quality of their hydraulic engineering. "Good Ditches and good Trunks," boasted one planter, "are absolutely necessary on a River Swamp plantation." For slaves living on rice plantations, building and maintaining these labyrinthine systems required herculean efforts. The largest rice plantation had miles of canals, ditches, and embankments that required constant maintenance. In the summer of 1765, naturalist John Bartram made his last Southern expedition, beginning in the Lowcountry before venturing into Florida. Near Charlestown, he marveled at plantations with "100 acres of rice growing as thick as it can stand & five or 6 foot high," worked by as many as three hundred enslaved men and women. Planters told him that the "best rice ground is where they have the command of water." On Gideon Dupont's plantation, Bartram inspected a twelve-foot-deep drainage ditch that stretched for half a mile from the rice field to the river. A series of recent storms (one of which Bartram described as a hurricane) had caused substantial damage to the region's hydrologic infrastructure, prompting frantic rebuilding. Only a few days earlier, Bartram had to make a substantial detour around fields flooded from a broken dam. Dupont had

FIGURE 4.1. A. R. Waud, "Rice Culture on the Ogeechee, near Savannah, Georgia," *Harper's Weekly* 11 (1867): 8.

ordered 130 enslaved men and women to repair the ditch, digging down to limestone in the August sun. Although enslaved women worked on canals in emergencies, like the one Bartram witnessed, enslaved men did most of labor on Lowcountry canals. Plantation records indicate that the strongest enslaved men had to dig ten feet of canal per day, wide and deep enough for a great flatboat.[10]

By 1800, most Lowcountry plantations had adopted a standard cycle of flooding. In early May, just after planting, the floodgates were opened, inundating the fields until the rice sprouted. This first flooding, known as the "spout flow," usually lasted for a few days to a week. After the fields drained, enslaved laborers hoed the muddy soil, careful not to disturb the fragile rice shoots. Then the fields were flooded a second time, completely submerging the immature crop. Intended to kill insects, weeds, and grasses, this inundation lasted for two or three days, after which the water level was lowered to half the plants' height, where it remained for three weeks. During the inundation, enslaved workers waded into the flooded fields, skimming off the detritus that floated to the surface. Over the summer, the rice fields received repeated inundations and hoeing, depending on how the crop progressed. The timing and length of these inundations required considerable expertise, as too much or too little water at the wrong time could doom a harvest.

Although the terminology varied slightly from plantation to plantation, the floods—the "sprout flow," the "point flow," the "stretch flow," and the "long water"—delineated the agricultural calendar.[11]

Enslaved rice workers toiled for much of the year in stagnant water. Charles Ball recalled that "water is sometimes let into the rice fields, and drawn off again, several times, according to the state of the weather." Working in shin-high water, enslaved men rolled their pants and enslaved women tied their skirts to keep them dry. They risked snake bites, particularly from water moccasins, which found a natural home in flooded fields, as did the occasional alligator. Even when drained, the rice fields remained waterlogged, the ground too muddy for draft animals. Slaves sent in the rice fields to hoe the soil and pick weeds emerged with thick mud caked over their bare feet.[12]

The enslaved and enslavers alike saw that the water that gave the rice life killed those working and living near it. In 1802, planter John Drayton remarked that South Carolina was "intersected by multitudes of swamps, bays, and low grounds." These "large reservoirs of water, and rice fields at particular times overflowed" made the Lowcountry deadly. "The waters," he noted, "spread over the face of the country, become unfriendly to health, and acquire some degree of mephitic influence." Charles Ball concurred, claiming that "watering and weeding the rice is considered one of the most unhealthy occupations on a southern plantation, as the people are obliged to live for several weeks in the mud and water, subject to all the unwholesome vapours that arise from stagnant pools, under the rays of a summer sun." Frederick Law Olmsted observed that the harvest, which took place "at the hottest season of the year, in the midst of the recently-exposed mire of the rice-fields, is acknowledged to be exceedingly severe, and must be very hazardous to the health, even of negroes." For many newly arrived slaves in the Lowcountry, this disease environment and labor regime proved fatal. One third of imported Africans died within a year after their arrival. Those brought from the Upper South, like Charles Ball, had a better survival rate, though they too found the region inhospitable.[13]

The combination of demanding physical labor and a hostile biological environment led many white South Carolinians to conclude that only people of African descent could survive in the rice fields. In 1775, Janet Schaw observed that "the labour required for [rice cultivation] is only fit for slaves, and I think the hardest work I have seen them engaged in." Embedded within this racist explanation was a begrudging admiration for the work that enslaved laborers performed. "Only the African race," wrote Elizabeth Allston Pringle, could build "a system of flooding the fields from the river by canals, ditches, or floodgates." Growing up on a rice plantation, Pringle claimed that only the enslaved could work in the Lowcountry's miasmas, "immune from the dread malaria fever." Many white Lowcountry residents expressed this notion that enslaved people of African descent had immunity to malaria and yellow fever, and by the nineteenth century this had become an article of faith among pro-slavery apologists. However, recent scholarship suggests that the effect of genetic immunity may be negligible, if it exists at all. Childhood exposure to yellow fever and malaria may have provided many enslaved adults with acquired immunity, but this came at a considerable cost: most enslaved children born in the Lowcountry did not live to see adulthood.[14]

Rice cultivation helped to create the Lowcountry's disease ecosystem. Although mosquitos had been present in the region prior to colonization, conversion of native swamps into rice fields created stagnant pools of water in direct sunlight, the mosquitoes' preferred breeding environment. Several species of mosquitoes spread diseases of both European and African origin, including two varieties of malaria (*Plasmodium vivax* from Africa and *Plasmodium falciparum* from Europe), yellow fever, dengue, and filariasis, which produces elephantiasis. Stagnant water also hosted invisible pathogens, amoebic parasites that spread cholera, whooping cough, diphtheria, and dysentery.[15] Without adequate latrines or wells, enslaved rice workers used the drainage ditches for both purposes. In the three decades prior to the Civil War, the enslaved population on Charles Manigault's Gowrie Plantation suffered from one of the highest mortality rates in the South, with twice as many slaves dying as being born. Cholera proved the most prolific killer at Gowrie, with outbreaks in 1834, 1852, and 1854. Caused by bacteria in contaminated food or water, cholera produces chronic diarrhea. Its victims suffer from dehydration and dry mucous membranes in the mouth, throat, and nose, creating an insatiable thirst. For the enslaved at Gowrie, the rice fields' stagnant water provided not just the venue for their labors but the conduit for killer pathogens. In 1848, an overseer on the Gowrie plantation attributed poor health among the enslaved to their reliance on ditch water. They "would come out of their houses at night, regardless of the weather (for it was constantly raining) & go even to the ditches & drink their fill." He concluded, "I look upon their deaths as suicide acts." Several years later, Robert, an enslaved driver, told Manigault that the chronic illnesses on the plantation could be traced to the drinking water. "The Negroes," he told him, "put all sorts of nasty things in the ditches & then dip up (I am Confident) the same water to drink." The disease ecosystem proved particularly deadly to children: of the 109 children born at Gowrie from 1833 to 1855, ninety-seven died before they reached the age of sixteen. Many of those who lived suffered from chronic illness brought on by repeated exposure to malaria and water-borne pathogens. Visitors noticed that many rice plantation slaves seemed shorter and punier than cotton or tobacco slaves, perhaps due to chronic illnesses during childhood. For his part, Charles Manigault did not seem overly concerned about the mortality among his Gowrie slaves. He made only scant effort to provide medical treatment or to improve the environment, despite the pleas of some of his overseers. Even in years when epidemics struck, the plantation remained profitable.[16]

Plantation owners found the rice fields especially noxious during the summer. Growing up on a Pee Dee River plantation, Elizabeth Allston Pringle recalled that "the cultivation of rice necessitated keeping the fields flooded with water until it became stagnant, and the whole atmosphere was polluted by the dreadful smell." Visitors to the Lowcountry commented on the nauseating stench emerging from the rice fields and "were obliged to apply a handkerchief to their noses, so noxious and intolerable was the effluvium." They knew that the summer months brought more than unpleasant odors, as the disease ecosystem made Carolina "a great charnel-house" in summer. William Gilmore Simms described Georgetown County, South Carolina, one of the epicenters of rice cultivation, as "moist, hot, and unhealthy; subject to fevers in summer and agues in autumn." White planters so feared the "marsh miasma" that most of them left the Lowcountry in the heat, retreating to healthier locales in the Piedmont or to Charleston.[17]

Built of mud, wood, and sweat, the elaborate infrastructure that made rice cultivation possible required constant maintenance. Wooden floodgates rotted, and canals became clogged with vegetation. Rogue livestock trampled drainage canals, and muskrats, alligators, turtles, and snakes burrowed into their walls, undermining calibrated hydraulic systems. Enslaved workers spent much of the winter maintaining this complex system: mending leaking embankments, clearing out debris from the canals, and replacing worn-out trunks. Enslaved people loathed and dreaded this "mudwork," because even in mild winters, it required them to work in wet and cold conditions. An itinerant carpenter working on a Carolina rice plantation recalled seeing slaves "driven into a ditch in a rice swamp to bail out the water, in order to put down a flood-gate, when they had to break the ice, and there stand in the water among the ice until it was bailed out."[18]

The greatest threats came from floods, known locally as freshets, which could overwhelm the carefully calibrated irrigation systems. Many Lowcountry planters believed that upriver development had made flooding more frequent and intense, as denuded riverbanks exacerbated the risk of flooding. Without trees and canebrakes to retard the waters' progress, heavy rains swelled waterways, overflowing their banks. In the decades after the Revolution, flooding wreaked havoc on Lowcountry plantations. In January 1796, the Great Yazoo Freshet—named for the Georgia land fraud case that year—caused many Lowcountry rivers to breach their banks. The *Charleston City Gazette* noted that "the Congaree and Wateree rivers have risen five feet higher than they were ever before known; the damage done by them is immense." The floodwaters destroyed the tobacco warehouse in Granby, taking with it 150 hogsheads of tobacco. Further downriver, the rising waters carried away "dwelling houses, corn houses, cattle, horses, &c." The worst flooding came where the two rivers converged to form the Santee, where "many negroes have perished at their settlements in the swamps," a reference to the maroon communities.[19]

After 1820, flooding in the Lowcountry became more intense, in large part because of increased development in the South Carolina and Georgia upcountry. The Congaree River, for instance, overtopped its banks in 1823, 1824, 1829, 1831, 1833, 1840, 1841, 1845, and 1852. Triggered by the Great Mobile Hurricane, which turned abruptly northeast after landfall, the 1852 flood caused nearly all of the rivers in Georgia and South Carolina to overflow. Along the Savannah River, water descended "like a wave," flooding the Manigault, Chisolm, King, Williamson, Daniell, and Hamilton plantations. On the Santee and Pee Dee Rivers, the flooding did "much damage to the rice crop: and especially to those who plant the most fruitful tide lands highest up." The flood destroyed wooden bridges and several sections of the South Carolina Railroad, effectively "cut[ting] off all communication entirely between Charleston and the interior." In 1854, a group of Savannah River rice planters, frustrated by the persistent flooding, formed the Freshet Bank Association to construct more than two miles of dikes.[20]

When flooding hit the Lowcountry, planters fretted about lost harvests. Yet the enslaved paid higher costs when floodwaters swept over rice plantations. When Charles Manigault's Gowrie Plantation flooded, as it did ten times between 1833 and 1864, the waters inundated slave quarters, making them inhospitable for a week or ten days and leaving behind a muddy film on everything when they receded. Charles Manigault's son Louis noted in March 1854 that after flooding, "every thing is nasty & dirty about the [slaves'] settlement. . . . We have no more time now this year to whitewash & all will remain dirty & dingy until next Fall. . . . Everything is Covered with the Freshet settlement." To protect them from flooding, some Lowcountry slaves erected their homes on brick stilts, elevating them above potential floodwaters.[21]

Mississippi

To fight the flooding, planters had their slaves construct levees. Nowhere did the growth of levees parallel the development of enslaved labor more visibly than along the Mississippi. From the earliest French settlements, white Louisianians depended on slave labor to hold back the river. Mississippi levees created an artificial boundary between wet and dry, one that became increasingly pronounced in the decades prior the Civil War.[22] While the precolonial Mississippi routinely slipped its banks, depositing centuries of alluvial nutrients that gave the soil its richness, planters sought to contain and tame its current, lest floodwaters destroy their sugar, cotton, and indigo fields. They loved and hated the river: it made the soil among the most productive and valuable anywhere in the world and provided an easy conduit for shipping their goods to market, but it also threatened to wash away their livelihood.

French colonists in Louisiana began an aggressive policy of levee construction shortly after New Orleans's establishment. In 1719, only a year after the city was founded, April floodwaters from the Mississippi inundated the nascent settlement, prompting many of the inhabitants to flee to Natchez. Even Jean-Baptiste Le Moyne de Bienville, the city's founder and greatest advocate, noted that "it may be difficult to maintain a town at New Orleans; the site is drowned under half a foot of water." Only by building levees along the river and digging a canal from the Mississippi to Lake Pontchartrain, he argued, could the settlement become sustainable. News of the flood and war with Spain prompted Parisian officials to temporarily halt settlement in New Orleans. In August 1720, one settler noted that "the Mississippi, overflowing more or less for six months of the year, renders New Orleans unpleasant as a place of sojourn. But at present, a great many slaves or negroes from Guinea are laboring to make it habitable." In the depth of summer heat, enslaved men shoveled dirt to build a "sound dike on the riverbank." With Louisiana's tiny enslaved population, the decision by slave owners and colonial officials to allocate scarce labor to flood prevention reveals how critical they saw mastering the Mississippi was to the colony's success. Slaves belonging to Joseph Villars Du Breuil constructed much of the initial levee system. Far from altruistic, Breuil knew that floodwaters would inundate his extensive holdings in Tchoupitoulas. Moreover, allocating his nearly fifty slaves to levee construction allowed him to profit from their labor during lulls in indigo production. These early artificial levees were built on alluvial ridges formed when the Mississippi left its banks.[23]

From the very beginning, French settlers assumed that only enslaved labor could secure the city from flooding. Levee construction in the 1720s was hampered by labor shortages. In 1724, colonists wrote to Paris officials that "all the colony is impatient to see some negroes," without whom they could not protect themselves from seasonal flooding. To expedite construction, the Company of the Indies required that newly imported slaves perform thirty days of digging drainage ditches and building levees upon their arrival. Backbreaking under the best of conditions, this intense labor proved deadly for enslaved Africans who had just survived the Middle Passage. Overworked and underfed, some of these new arrivals did not live to see their first winter. The small enslaved population, only 1,526 in all of Louisiana according to a 1726 census, limited levee construction and therefore constrained the colony's growth. Complaints from colonial officials that levee construction could not proceed without more slaves reached the highest level of the French imperial state: in 1732, King Louis XV observed that work on the flood walls "to enclose the city of New Orleans ceased more than two years ago because the settlers do not have a large enough number of negroes" to build it.[24]

Levee construction proved both labor intensive and slow going. In April 1722, French engineer Le Blond de La Tour reported on the progress. "To protect the town against river floods, the ground might be raised above high-water level by making a good earthen dike on the city-front by the river," he reported. "This has already begun, but is neither high enough nor wide enough." La Tour's assessment proved prescient, as a hurricane that September laid waste to the rudimentary and incomplete levee system. With the Mississippi cresting at eight feet above its banks, floodwaters washed away the earthen levees. In the hurricane's aftermath, French engineers planned for a more substantial system of flood control, ambitiously calling for a six-foot-thick dike on both sides of the river, reinforced by a timber palisade. A shortage of enslaved labor proved the greatest barrier to levee construction. After La Tour's death, engineer Franquet de Chaville had to scale back his predecessor's plans, complaining that he never had more than thirty-five enslaved men at his disposal. By January 1724, levees in New Orleans reached five hundred toises (nearly a kilometer) but failed due to a weak foundation, inundating a quarter of the town. In the autumn of 1727, Governor Étienne Boucher de Périer announced that New Orleans's levee—more than a mile long—was complete, protecting what is now called the French Quarter. This new levee served dual functions: it would both protect the city from flooding and provide docking facilities for vessels on the Mississippi, where cargo could be unloaded. Merchants established stalls on the levee where vendors hawked warm meals and trinkets. Commercial life in New Orleans began on its levees; its first slave markets emerged in its shadow. Moreover, the levees provided the first barrier of defense in case of attack.[25]

Completion of New Orleans's municipal levees did not eliminate the risk of flooding, however, as the lower Mississippi's topography made overland flooding just as threatening. Rising floodwaters miles above or below the city could traverse the low, flat terrain to New Orleans, causing as much destruction as if the breach happened in the city's levees. The city's future depended not just on maintaining its own flood protection infrastructure but on building levees all along the Mississippi. Outside of the city, French, then Spanish, then American administrations placed the responsibility for levee construction on riverside planters. After the 1722 flood, the French Superior Council passed the first in a series of local regulations requiring riverside landowners to construct levees; after 1744, they risked forfeiting their land if they failed to do so. This custom of shifting the burden of levee construction onto slave owners—and by extension to their slaves—continued during Spanish and American control. Philip Pittman, a British army captain and engineer, noted in 1770 that "the Levee before the town is repaired at public expense, [but] each inhabitant keeps that part in repair which is opposite his own plantation." In 1792, Spanish governor Hector de Carondelet declared that "the maintenance of the levees interests all the inhabitants where crevasses ruin in an instant the fruits of a year of labor." He prohibited livestock grazing near the levees and decreed that slave owners maintain "a deposit of pickets, planks, Spanish moss, and other articles necessary" to stop a breach, subject to a heavy fine. He empowered local overseers called syndics to police both levee maintenance and the enslaved population. Both slaves and levees, Carondelet believed, required constant surveillance, lest they threaten the colony's security: a slave revolt or a ruptured levee could cause enormous destruction unless those in power practiced constant vigilance. Syndics could fine planters for failing to maintain levees and requisition slaves from nearby plantations to work on levees (and further afield in an emergency). Moreover, Carondelet instructed syndics to "report to the Government the residents who are out of condition to keep up their levees for the want of negroes and means." Those who could not maintain their levees would be forced to sell their land to someone who could.[26]

Planters did not need much persuasion that secure and continuous levees provided the first requirement for a successful crop. They could see the disastrous effects that floodwaters could wreak on indigo or sugar plantations. Ironically, one of the first planters to lose a crop was engineer Le Blond de

La Tour, who had designed the city's levees. While his own levee held, those of his neighbors did not, and consequentially his indigo crop was "entirely destroyed by the flood which overflowed his lands from the rear." Inspired perhaps by La Tour's fate, planters pledged in an April 1725 "Declaration of Inhabitants" to build and maintain a continuous levee and "to employ the best and most considerable part of their strength in this common cause." Rural flooding threatened not just planters' livelihoods but the viability of the entire colonial enterprise. A spring flood in 1735 that breached the levees destroyed most of that year's rice crop and introduced caterpillars that ate their way through the growing corn fields. After the water subsided, four months of drought killed those food crops that had survived the flood and devastated the colony's cattle stock. Two years later, a series of levee breaches caused another round of crop failures. Planters recognized that their individual interests depended upon mutual policing and cooperation. Louisiana's planter class and levees grew in tandem: only they had the manpower to build and maintain the earthen barriers necessary to hold back the water.[27]

With slight modifications, Americans embraced the model of state-mandated public works through private enslaved labor chartered by the French and Spanish colonial administrations. On the eve of the Civil War, Louisiana law called for "riparian proprietors" to construct levees "throughout all that portion of the State watered by the Mississippi and the bayous running to and from the same . . . to protect the inhabitants against the inundation." Planters who neglected to maintain their section of the levee risked financial liability for damage and loss caused by breaching floodwaters. State law also authorized local inspectors to assess the levees every week and empowered them to "call out to work on the levees . . . all the male slaves above the age of fifteen years . . . within seven miles of the threatened land." Upriver states Arkansas, Mississippi, and Tennessee largely replicated Louisiana's system, placing the responsibility for levee maintenance on riverside plantation owners.[28]

The rural levee system grew in parallel with the enslaved population. By 1732, it stretched twelve miles south of New Orleans to thirty miles above, and for the rest of the eighteenth century it grew at a rate of a mile per year. The pace of levee construction accelerated after the Louisiana Purchase and the subsequent cotton boom. By 1828, enslaved labor had constructed levees to the Red River, 195 miles north of New Orleans, and 65 miles below the city; by 1844, they had reached Greenville, Mississippi. By 1850, enslaved labor had constructed 847 miles of levee along the Mississippi and its tributaries, stretching from the river's mouth to Memphis.[29] Levee construction techniques changed as well. Colonial French and Spanish levees allowed water to seep through, as river water permeated the mud walls and crayfish burrowed tunnels into them. Planters found that new levees, the dirt not yet compacted, suffered particularly from leakage. A traveler in 1810 described the rudimentary state of these early levees: "We should be much deceived if we were to form an idea of this from the dykes of Holland or the embankments of the Nile. . . . There is a ditch for the purpose of draining off the water which oozes through. . . . An immense quantity of water finds its way through the embankment, mostly through holes made by crawfish, which sometimes increase so rapidly, as to effect a breach. Several years are necessary for the levee to become perfectly solid and firm, previous to this, it is liable to be injured by rains." After 1820, planters increasingly sought to make their levees impermeable, creating a solid barrier between the river and the adjacent fields. They embedded thick cypress slabs into the levees, which not only held back the water but also impeded burrowing animals, and they covered their levees with sod to prevent erosion. Some planters carted in clay to form a waterproof barrier. By 1850, many planters had their enslaved laborers reinforce levees with wooden pickets, "closely driven and securely braced."[30]

Working on the levees proved physically taxing and dangerous even for the most robust slaves. In February 1817, a German merchant traveling along the Mississippi near Pointe Coupee witnessed "a poor negro, wheeling dirt to renew a ditch along the levee. The poor fellow had an iron with three hooks around his neck, working in the extreme cold weather." Although the enslaved man insisted that he had done nothing wrong, the merchant concluded that such backbreaking labor must have been punishment for running away. Two years later, architect Benjamin Latrobe observed slaves supervised by "an overseer directing the repair of the levee, with a long whip in his hand." He noted that Mississippi planters had a "reputation of working their slaves very hard and feeding them very badly."[31]

Mississippi planters allocated so much enslaved labor to levee maintenance because they dreaded the devastation a breach could cause. Their fears of flooding provoked the kind of anxiety usually reserved for rumors of slave conspiracies. They practiced a kind of hypervigilance, bordering on paranoia. They knew that "a few moments are sufficient to destroy the labor and industry of twenty years," such that "during the season of great floods, the levees require constant attention, they must be continually watched, and all hands are sometimes drawn from the fields to attend them for whole days and nights." Henry Brackenridge noted during his 1811 trip down the Mississippi that "in the season of high water," planters exuded "continual anxiety and apprehension; the hands withdrawn from the fields, and kept watching day and

night. . . . To one who has not seen this country it is almost impossible to
convey any idea of the terrors excited by a *crevasse* or breaking of the levees.
Like the breaking out of fire in a town, where no one knows when his own
dwelling might be assailed, it excites universal consternation; every employment is abandoned for miles above and below." Although mentioning it
only in passing, Brackenridge knew that only month earlier, hundreds of the
enslaved on the German Coast had engaged in the largest slave uprising in
American history. The revolt began on January 8, 1811, on Manuel Andry's
plantation, thirty miles upriver from New Orleans, and gained momentum
as it moved toward the city. Led by Charles Deslondes, the rebels marched
quickly, burning plantations and killing whites who refused to give ground.
A swift military response, however, crushed the rebellion, killing dozens of
the conspirators. After capturing Deslondes, incensed whites slowly tortured
him to death; twenty-nine others faced trial and summary execution. To dissuade other slaves from following their example, planters erected more than
one hundred decapitated heads of rebellious slaves on pikes on the levee, silent, haunting sentinels on the Mississippi stretching from Andry's plantation
to New Orleans. If the heads remained in situ when Brackenridge traveled
down the Mississippi, he chose not to share that sight with his readers.[32]

Despite the herculean efforts to prevent flooding, the Mississippi repeatedly breached its banks over the coming decades. Although enslaved workers
built thicker, higher, and more robust levees, flooding became more common
in the years prior to the Civil War. Indeed, levee construction may have
exacerbated the flood risk: artificially constricting the river prompted higher
water levels, especially during spring rains. Moreover, forcing the Mississippi
into a single channel prevented the natural deposit of river sediment on adjacent fields. Instead, it settled on the riverbed, especially in areas where the river
bent. Longtime residents observed that the Mississippi's bed rose in tandem
with the levees. By 1850, more than a century of levee construction along the
lower Mississippi had contributed to a riverbed that was substantially higher
than the surrounding fields. The elevated riverbed placed additional pressure
on the levees and resulted in more intense flooding when they breached.[33]

Every generation of New Orleanians recorded a time when their mighty
levees failed to hold back the muddy water. The Flood of 1735 kept parts of
city submerged for six months, while floods in 1770, 1782, 1785, 1791, and 1799
caused substantial damage to parts of the city. On May 6, 1816, a fissure in the
levee at Barthelemy Macarty's plantation inundated much of the city. With
floodwaters covering low-lying areas in five feet of water, "one could travel in a
skiff from the corner of Chartres and Canal streets to Dauphin," local tradition

recounted, "down Dauphin to Bienville, down Bienville to Burgundy, thus to St. Louis Street, from St. Louis to Rampart, and so throughout the rear suburbs." The Carrollton Crevasse Flood was New Orleans's first major inundation after the United States purchased Louisiana. The city remained only a kernel of what it would become over the next forty years, though its population had doubled since 1803. Its wealthiest inhabitants resided in the Vieux Carré, while the city's free Black and poor white population lived in the low-lying neighborhoods closer to Lake Pontchartrain. When the city flooded, they experienced the worst of it. "The distress is dreadful," one resident observed; "all the poor people turn'd out of their houses, and many have no place to go to."[34] Even after the crevasse was closed, much of the city remained underwater. To drain the city, Mayor Augustin Macarty authorized the hiring of enslaved trenching crews to channel the water into Bayou St. John. Drum-beating recruiters scoured the city for those with "negroes to hire" to "apply to the Mayor's office within the shortest delay."[35]

After a serious flood in 1828 threatened to halt New Orleans's phenomenal growth, city fathers decided that levees alone could not protect the city. Under the direction of state engineer George T. Dunbar, the New Orleans Drainage Company extended the street gutters to the outlying swamps and constructed drainage canals, the largest of which, the Orleans Canal, ran along Orleans Avenue into Bayou St. John. A large steam-powered paddlewheel known as the Bienville Drainage Machine drove the canal's current toward Lake Pontchartrain. Despite initial funding of a million dollars (much of it in public money) and a twenty-year charter, the New Orleans Drainage Company fell victim to the Panic of 1837, leaving many of its projects unfinished.[36]

Riverside residents watched the river closely for early signs of potential flooding. Heavy rains during the winter of 1848I–1849 alarmed many along the lower Mississippi. When he saw the Mississippi's level rising in December 1848, Issaquena county planter Stephen Duncan began to plan for the worst. "We are threatened with a flood in the Miss[issipp]i equal to that of '28," he wrote. He immediately assigned more than two hundred enslaved men to work on a hundred-yard segment of the levee that had partially broken the year before. Despite their efforts, floodwaters covered three thousand acres of Duncan's cotton fields. By April 1849, he had "abandoned all hope of being able to plant [his] overflowed lands." He estimated that his extensive holdings—Duncan was one of the largest cotton planters in the country—would produce only 350 bales that year. The rural flooding in 1849 hit sugar planters even worse, destroying two years' worth of crop. One planter estimated that the flooding had destroyed fifty thousand hogsheads worth of sugar.[37]

The Mississippi levees breached at several spots that spring, most significantly on May 3, 1849, at Pierre Sauvé's Jefferson Parish sugar plantation,
seventeen miles north of the city. A journalist marveled at the "mighty river
rushing out of its banks and flooding thousands of acres with its turbid waters." By the morning of May 13, the water had reached the city, flooding everything north of the French Quarter, including most of the 7th Ward. The
slow-moving floodwaters rose a foot every thirty-six hours, giving residents
time to evacuate. At its greatest expanse, the flood filled 220 city blocks
and displaced twelve thousand residents. Water on Canal Street stood four
feet deep.

With much of New Orleans lying below the level of the riverbed, the
flooding would only stop once the breach in the levee had been repaired.
After the severity of the breach became apparent, "neighboring planters
[were] requested to send their negroes to aid in prosecuting the undertaking."
During the month after the breach, enslaved men and women worked fran-
tically to keep the crevasse from getting worse but failed to close the fissure.
By early June, the breach had expanded to three hundred feet. Only when the
Mississippi's level dropped did the enslaved engineering corps begin to make
progress. More than five hundred strong, they spent six weeks sinking timber
piles into the soft mud at the crevasse, throwing in thousands of hastily-filled
sandbags—made from coffee and manure sacks—to fill the breach. Ships
passing the crevasse claimed that "from the hundreds of spiles now driven
in front, [it] represents an enormous mouth of some great monster, showing
his numerous teeth." The enslaved repair crew's prodigious effort came at a
cost: at least one man died, and many fell ill. Only after forty-eight days did
the floodwater recede.[38]

The flooding along the Mississippi became progressively worse in the
1850s. In the decade prior the Civil War, the levees broke nearly twenty
times in the stretch between the Red River and New Orleans, inundating
in the neighboring cotton and sugar fields. Unfortunate riverside planters
often went bankrupt when they lost a year's crop, but enslaved families
paid a much higher price. In 1851, floodwaters destroyed a year's sugar crop
on Judah P. Benjamin's Bellechase Plantation, sixteen miles south of New
Orleans. Burdened by debts, Benjamin decided to abandon sugar planting for
law and politics. He hired a well-known slave auction house to liquidate his
holdings. At noon on January 12, 1852, interested parties gathered in the St.
Louis Hotel's ornate rotunda, which had hosted slave auctions for more than
a decade and had become notorious among abolitionists for its juxtaposition
of luxury and human degradation: published later that year, Harriet Beecher

Stowe's *Uncle Tom's Cabin* featured a New Orleans slave auction modeled on the site. For sale that day was not only the land, buildings, agricultural equipment, and livestock but also 129 enslaved men, women, and children, each listed by name, age, and occupation on an advertising broadside. Auctioned individually and in small lots, Bellechase's enslaved community fragmented, dispersed to plantations up and down the Mississippi. The historical record remains silent on the eventual fate of Syphax, a thirty-five-year-old bricklayer; Armstead, a forty-year-old stable hand; fifty-five-year-old Maria Cooper and her twenty-three-year-old daughter Harriet; and the 125 other enslaved people auctioned that day. It does reveal, however, that Judah Benjamin was elected to the US Senate later that year. He would go on to serve the Confederacy as Jefferson Davis's attorney general, secretary of war, and secretary of state.[39]

The dramatic environmental changes brought about in the Lowcountry and along the Mississippi were replicated on a smaller scale along riverbanks across the enslaved South. In subtle but profound ways, enslaved agriculture transformed Southern waterways, creating rivers that flooded more often and proved increasingly inhospitable to native aquatic life. This metamorphosis followed the enslaved frontier, traveling upriver as the institution expanded. Three years before the Yazoo Freshet inundated the Lowcountry, heavy spring rains in 1793 prompted the Potomac and Monocacy rivers to overflow, flooding Chesapeake plantations for miles around. Planter Charles Carroll of Carrollton, a signer of the Declaration of Independence, noted in his journal that the rising waters had "done much damage to low grounds; the floods have washed away all of the Tob[acc]o hill[s]." Carroll's own agricultural practices contributed to the flood's destruction. One of Maryland's largest slaveowners, Carroll embraced progressive farming techniques that emphasized the use of the plow, fully cleared and tilled fields, and continuous cultivation. Although these techniques helped Carroll successfully shift much of his holdings to grain cultivation from tobacco (which the soil would no longer support), the resulting erosion silted the adjacent river, raised its bed, and increased the chance of flooding. To mitigate the risk of inundation, Carroll adopted two strategies, both of which relied on enslaved labor. First, he tasked his slaves with constructing a series of levees and drainage ditches to prevent flooding and carry away excess water. Second, he ordered them to dredge and straighten the river in a vain attempt to remove silt deposits. Despite the toil and sweat, neither effort did much to reduce flooding on Carroll's plantation.[40]

The hydraulic techniques used to construct rice plantations and levees also built thousands of mill ponds across the South. Transforming riparian power into friction to grind grain and cut lumber, mills became ubiquitous across the plantation South, spreading westward and upriver with settlement. Large planters often built gristmills on their slave labor camps to grind grain for their neighbors. The diversion of Southern waterways and the creation of mill ponds, however, had profound effects on the local environment. One Georgia surveyor observed in the early 1760s that the construction of mill ponds disrupted the entire ecosystem, through "Destruction proceeding from Stagnant water." Acres of forestland became barren, as root systems became inundated. Moreover, he claimed that the damming process caused the water's source to dry up or choose a different course. "Rivulets have disappeared two or three years after being chosen," he noted, "and left the mills dry." In 1837, Edmund Ruffin claimed that mill ponds proved an ecological disaster. Except on swiftly moving rivers, they presented "enormous evils" in "covering much land of great value for cultivation" and "producing disease." Although the role of mosquitoes as a disease vector did not become clear until decades later, Ruffin surmised that slow-moving water, full of "decaying and putrefying vegetable matter," was "productive of little else than malaria and disease."[41]

Bondage on the Water

Many enslaved people brought a lifetime of experience in and around water. Born near Tuckahoe Creek on Maryland's Eastern Shore, Frederick Douglass grew up in a landscape shaped by the Chesapeake and its many tributaries. As a very small child, before he knew about his own enslavement, Douglass caught fish in a millpond and, for amusement, would "plunge into the river or the pond." When he could swim competently, Douglass swam in the "Long Green," a nearby creek where other children congregated. Douglass probably inherited some of his affinity for water from his grandmother, Betsey Baily, who made fishing nets for catching shad and herring; Douglass recalled, "I have known her to be in the water half the day."[42]

Many enslaved people swam well. West African cultures valued swimming as an important skill, and European explorers marveled at West Africans' aptitude in the water. For the enslaved, swimming served several roles: for recreation, to demonstrate mastery, and as a practical ability than enabled them to live in an environment dominated by water. In Georgia and the Carolinas, slaves waded into rivers to wrestle alligators, a sport that attracted both enslaved and free spectators. "Some Negro's" in Carolina, wrote English naturalist John Lawson, "that can swim and dive well, go naked into the Water, with a Knife in their Hand, and fight the Shark, and very commonly kill him."

South Carolinian John Andrew Jackson drew upon his aquatic experience to avoid punishment. About to receive a beating from an overseer, Jackson "swam across a mill pond, which was full of alligators, and so escaped the whipping."[43]

Chronicling the experience of fugitives who made it to Canada, abolitionist Benjamin Drew found that many runaways had used their swimming skills in their flight. One noted that they "meet many rivers and streams where there were no bridges; some we could wade over, and some we crossed by swimming." For those enslaved people who could not swim, however, rivers could prove a profound but not unsurmountable barrier. "A man and his wife came to the Ohio River at night," John Parker recalled. "Neither could swim a stroke. Still they were so determined, he placed his wife astride a log, while he placed his hand on the other side and literally kicked his way across that deep and dangerous river." Francis Fedric grew up on a plantation in Virginia near a thirty-yard-wide Potomac tributary, which overflowed during the rainy season and inundated the adjacent fields. "But although near so fine a body of water," Fedric recalled, "unlike most slaves, I never learned to swim." Relocated to Kentucky as a teenager, Fedric found his inability to swim a hindrance when he tried to escape. After his owner drunkenly whipped him for attending a prayer meeting, Fedric ran away, taking shelter in a swamp and a cave. Pursued by bloodhounds, he "tried to plan out some way of escape, over the Ohio River. . . . But I could not swim; and I was well aware that my master would set a watch upon every ferry or ford, and that the whole country would be put on the alert, to catch me." Unable to cross the river and weakened by six weeks as a fugitive, Fedric turned himself in to a local preacher he hoped would intercede on his behalf. Returned to his owner, Fedric received more than one hundred lashes, wounds that would pain him for the rest of his life. Despite his proximity to free territory, Fedric felt trapped in bondage, until a traveling abolitionist ferried him across the Ohio River.[44]

Enslaved people associated the water with freedom, even as many of them lived and worked on the water. As a boy on the Chesapeake, Frederick Douglass often marveled at the passing ships, such "beautiful vessels, robed in white . . . freedom's swift-winged angels." Thousands of enslaved people worked in maritime trades, laboring as pilots, fishermen, ferrymen, flatboat men, and sailors, employing their understanding of the region's waterways to escape the drudgery of plantation labor. Riverine commerce depended on enslaved Black men, which white authorities recognized posed a security threat. Black watermen, both enslaved and free, ferried stowaways to freedom. As heralds of the greater Black Atlantic, they disseminated knowledge of abolitionist networks, news of enslaved uprisings, and visions of alternatives to bondage. Seaport cities like Charleston, Savannah, Wilmington, Mobile, and New Orleans—where rivers met the ocean—became nexus points for the slave trade and Atlantic commerce, but they also became sites of institutional vulnerability, places where enslaved people built connections that could help them become free.[45]

Working on the water gave enslaved people access to information about geography and the wider world that enabled some to escape bondage. Laboring as a rented slave on a Mississippi steamboat, William Wells Brown immediately saw the potential for escape. Work on the *Patriot* "opened to me a new life, and gave me an opportunity to see different phases of slave life," he wrote, "and to learn something more of the world. . . . To escape from slavery and become my own master, was now the ruling passion of my life." Although they benefited from their labor, enslavers understood the danger posed by enslaved watermen to the broader institution. "Don't let the boat Negroes go amongst the Plantation Negroes," Henry Laurens warned his plantation overseers.[46]

Southern officials took active measures to curtail interactions between Black seamen and the enslaved population and to limit Black access to watercraft. In 1696, South Carolina passed "An Act to Prevent the Stealing and Taking Away of Boats and Canoes," which punished enslaved people who "shall take away or let loose any boat, perriager or canoe" with thirty-nine lashes. In the aftermath of the Denmark Vesey conspiracy, South Carolina passed the first Negro Seamen Act. The 1822 law required that free Black sailors arriving in Charleston be held in jail for the duration of their vessel's time in port. Other Southern states followed suit, with North Carolina, Georgia, Mississippi, Louisiana, and Texas passing similar legislation in the coming decades. Some inland riverside cities passed local ordinances modeled on the Negro Seamen Acts, including Memphis, which in 1849 prohibited Northern steamboats with free Black workers from docking at the city's levee for longer than three hours. Challenged in the courts, Southern legislators vigorously defended their right to police their maritime commerce. Branding Black steamboat workers a "dangerous body of incendiaries" and "fomenters of disturbance," Southern newspapers frequently complained of "no evil . . . more dangerous to the institutions of the South" than "the employment of free blacks on steamboats whereby the free negro and the slave are brought frequently together."[47]

Despite white vigilance, some enslaved people evaded patrols to stow away on North-bound vessels. An 1831 advertisement for a New Orleans runaway noted that as "he has been bred to the seas it is to be presumed that he will endeavor to get on board of some vessel or steamboat." In 1849, the *Wilmington Journal* complained, "It is almost an every day occurrence for our negro slaves to take passage [aboard ships] and go North." To expose fugitives hidden among the cargo, North Carolina required the smoking of shipboard holds. Hidden among barrels of "tar, rosin, and spirits of turpentine," Abraham Galloway constructed a rudimentary gas mask out of damp towels and silk oilskins to breathe during the smoking. Luckily for Galloway, his ship left Wilmington uninspected, though the turpentine fumes nearly overcame him on the voyage to Philadelphia.[48]

Enslaved people saw rivers as both sites of labor and avenues for freedom. John Parker recalled, "[The] Mississippi River attracted me like a magnet, for as soon as I was free to move in my own selected direction I made straight for the river." Even while enslaved, Parker saw the river as a route to liberation. He eventually bought his freedom and secured passage on "an upriver Mississippi River packet." En route, he passed by cotton plantations and levees, watching for familiar sights from his life in bondage. In freedom, Parker established himself in Ripley, Ohio, his house overlooking the Ohio River. From his front steps, he could look across the water into the slave state of Kentucky. Over the next two decades, Parker rowed across the river dozens of times, ferrying fugitives to freedom—more than 315 individuals by his count. Reflecting on his work decades later, he observed, "The Ohio River still remains a thing of real beauty to me." Other enslaved people saw rivers as barriers to freedom. "Sometimes standing on the Ohio River bluff, looking over on a free State, and as far north as my eyes could see," Henry Bibb recalled, "I have eagerly gazed upon the blue sky of the free North, which at times constrained me to cry out from the depths of my soul." Across the river he imagined a land with "no slavery; no clanking of chains, no captives, no lacerating of backs, no parting of husbands and wives; and where man ceases to be the property of his fellow man." From bondage in Kentucky, Bibb gazed in awe "upon the splendid steamboats, wafted with all their magnificence up and down the river, and I thought of the fishes of the water, the fowls of the air, the wild beasts of the forest, all appeared to be free, to go just where they pleased, and I was an unhappy slave!"[49]

5

A Southern Cyclone

IN AUGUST 1800, a rebellion nearly overthrew Virginia's slave regime.
Orchestrated by twenty-four-year-old Gabriel, a literate blacksmith owned
by Thomas Prosser, the revolt had over the course of months recruited hundreds of enslaved people across eastern Virginia. Gabriel's plan called for the
conspirators to assemble on Prosser's Brookfield Plantation, six miles north of
Virginia's capital, and from there march on Richmond, seizing weapons and
taking Governor James Monroe hostage. At the same time, allies in Norfolk
and Petersburg, upon hearing of Richmond's fall, would rise up. With the
governor and Virginia's three largest cities under his control, Gabriel would
proclaim slavery's demise. Despite the complexity and scale of the conspiracy,
most white Virginians went to sleep on August 30, 1800, completely unaware
that a revolution loomed.[1]

After months of clandestine planning, Gabriel's plot ultimately failed not
because of the vigilance of Virginia's slave owners but because a torrential late
summer storm made travel impossible. Journalist James Callender wrote to
his friend and patron Thomas Jefferson that "just about Sunset, there came
on the most terrible thunder Storm, accompanied with an enormous rain,
that I ever witnessed in this State." The storm washed out the road between
Prosser's plantation and Richmond, including a bridge over the Brook Swamp.
Recognizing that the plot could not proceed under such conditions, Gabriel
tried to postpone the revolt for one night. In the intervening day, however, at
least two conspirators got cold feet and revealed the details to their owners.
The alarm sounded, Governor Monroe dispatched patrols to round up the
conspirators, twenty-six of whom received death sentences.[2]

Storms like the one that doomed Gabriel's rebellion typified the South's
capricious and violent weather. Throughout the South, sudden summer
thunderstorms could quickly inundate fields, swell rivers and streams over

Scars on the Land. David Silkenat, Oxford University Press. © Oxford University Press 2022.
DOI: 10.1093/oso/9780197564226.003.0006

their banks, and wash away roads and bridges. Along both the Atlantic and Gulf coasts, hurricane season could bring devastation, while inland regions experienced frequent tornadoes. In the Upper South, sudden winter ice storms could descend without warning. In an era without meaningful forecasting, the South's violent and unpredictable weather could cause profound devastation. European visitors complained of a "climate so disorderly" that the skies could appear "one minute serene, the next cloudy and tempestuous."[3] While all Southerners could suffer from inclement weather, enslaved people often felt its effects most acutely. Working outside and living in vulnerable housing, they suffered disproportionately when violent weather struck. Human choices made capricious weather events into "natural" disasters. The ways in which white and Black Southerners prepared for and responded to them shaped their human consequences. Hurricanes and tornadoes that spared robustly constructed plantation mansions (and their inhabitants) were less kind to the slave quarters. To be sure, slavery in the American South did not cause an eighteenth- and nineteenth-century version of climate change. It did, however, exacerbate the effects that severe weather had on the ecosystem and on the human geography.

Storms

With a Black majority from its inception, the South Carolina Lowcountry witnessed repeatedly how hurricanes wrought devastation on enslaved people. The same factors that made rice cultivation flourish—a flat topography and river tides that stretched for miles inland—made the region vulnerable to intense storms. Constructed of wattle and daub and thatched with palmetto fronds, colonial slave cabins in the Lowcountry provided little protection from intense winds and rising floodwaters.[4] When in quick succession two hurricanes hit in 1752, they destroyed nearly all of the slave housing within thirty miles of Charles Town but left plantation houses intact. The first hurricane hit at high tide, sending a seventeen-foot storm surge to subsume rice and cotton fields and filling Charles Town with several feet of water. Two weeks later, the second storm scattered the detritus everywhere, sending "wrecks of boats, masts, yards, barrel staves, &c. floating and driving with great violence through the town." Amid the debris, bodies of human and animal victims of the storm washed ashore for weeks afterward. In October 1797, a hurricane nearly leveled Allard Belin's Belmont plantation, a storm he described as "a most violent and destructive tornado." Belin himself weathered the storm from the safety of "the house in which I live, seated on a high

hill, and elevated on brick work 5 feet high," a structure that suffered only
superficial damage. The enslaved people who labored and lived in the rice
flats below did not fare as well, as the storm tore "up by the roots trees of the
largest size" and tossed their homes and other outbuildings "nearly 100 yards
before they fell, and were thrown down with such violence that they were
shivered to pieces." Several of them died in the storm, "their bodies much
mangled."[5]

    An 1804 storm caused the greatest loss of life, killing more than five hun-
dred people, an estimated 90 percent of them enslaved. Sea Island slaves
suffered from the highest death toll. On Broughton Island, the storm swept
over the low-lying rice plantations, carrying eighty-five enslaved men, women,
and children out to sea, "never to be seen again." On Sullivan Island, one
planter noted that the "tide rose to an alarming height. Many hands [slaves]
were pulled into the sea. . . . There was a great loss of crops and buildings . . . and
negroes." A similar story unfolded on Hutchinson Island, where more than
one hundred slaves died in the storm, most of them lost in the rising waters.
On the lam since murdering Alexander Hamilton two months earlier, Vice
President Aaron Burr had taken refuge in South Carolina when the hurricane
hit. In a letter to his daughter Theodosia, Burr recounted a "scene of confusion and dismay." Burr and his host, John Couper, remained safe inside the
plantation house but watched in horror as the waters rose "about seven feet
above the height of an ordinary high tide . . . sufficient to inundate a great part
of the coast; to destroy all the rice; to carry off most of the buildings which
were on low lands, and to destroy the lives of many blacks."[6]

    In the aftermath of the 1804 storm, Sea Island planters recognized the
threat that hurricanes posed to their investment in human property. Some
of these coastal planters began to construct their slave quarters out of tabby,
a concrete of lime, oyster shells, and sand. With eight-inch-thick walls, these
masonry structures proved strong enough to survive a hurricane, with the
added benefit of remaining cool in the summer heat. Local tradition attributes
the innovation either to sugar planter Thomas Spaulding or John Couper's
son James, and other planters quickly emulated their example. In many cases,
these tabby structures reflected an amalgam of cultural practices: the enslaved
people who built the structures used indigenous materials but constructed
them using West African building techniques and arranged in arc and horse-
shoe configurations, layouts reminiscent of West African villages. They are
among the best-preserved slave quarters, and modern visitors often mistake
their quality as a manifestation of slave owner's paternalistic benevolence
rather than a calculated investment to protect their human property.[7]

The height of hurricane season, August through October, fell precisely at the moment in the agricultural cycle when crops were most vulnerable. Early in the season, a sudden storm surge of salt water onto coastal rice plantations could ruin crops nearly ready for harvesting. Later in the season, storms often destroyed rice barns storing the staple for export. Either way, hurricanes brought economic devastation to planters, although enslaved people often paid the highest price. Having lost their crop, Lowcountry planters balanced their books by liquidating their slave property. When John Couper lost the harvest from his rice and cotton plantations on St. Simon's Island in an 1824 hurricane, he found himself "without a dollar to support my people or family." To pay off his debts, he sold 380 slaves, breaking up families and communities in the process.[8]

Of course, the Lowcountry did not have a monopoly on hurricanes. Storms could cause devastation all along the Atlantic and Gulf coasts. In 1842 a pair of hurricanes devasted the plantation belt in eastern North Carolina and Virginia. The first hit in mid-July, destroying much of that year's tobacco, wheat, and corn crop. "I have not been down to the Lake since the storm," Ebenezer Pettigrew wrote to fellow planter James C. Johnston, "but I learn today by my Jim [enslaved man] that the field is yet under water and that the corn is nearly all dead." In its aftermath, planters rushed to plant a second crop, only to have that ruined by a second hurricane in August. Pettigrew heard from his son that "times are hard in Scuppernong, and the prospect is that they will be worse." Some neighboring planters decided to abandon their worn-out fields for better prospects in Alabama and Mississippi, relocating hundreds of enslaved people. Amid "talk of famine in the neighbor," Pettigrew wrote, "all is darkness & uncertainty." The effects of the twin hurricanes lasted into 1843, prompting some planters to reduce rations and sell off enslaved people to purchase corn. "The Storm last year," wrote one, "did more damage than ever has been known."[9]

Enslaved people laboring on Louisiana sugar and cotton plantations proved particularly vulnerable to tropical storms. Hurricanes impeded the development of slave-based plantation agriculture in Louisiana under both French and Spanish rule. The first major hurricane hit in 1722, three years after the first slave ship arrived. Although only a few individuals died, it destroyed thirty-four houses, all the ships moored at port, and the year's entire harvest. One survivor described it as "the most terrible tempest and hurricane that could ever be seen." A decade later, another devastating hurricane hit New Orleans, followed by months of drought, and in July 1733 another hurricane. After facing two major hurricanes in eleven months, many settlers believed that the colony could not succeed and returned to France. Another pair of hurricanes hit New Orleans in 1779 and 1780. After the first of these storms, Governor Bernardo de Gálvez wrote to his superior in Cuba that "the city is the most deplorable spectacle ever seen. There is a hardly a house which wasn't destroyed . . . the fields razed, the surrounding plantations . . . are all downed." Facing financial ruin, many planters abandoned the colony, selling their land and slaves at discount prices. The boom in sugar cultivation during the 1790s rejuvenated the Louisiana plantation economy, but the devastation wrought by three hurricanes in 1793 and 1794 tempered undue enthusiasm. Interpreting the hurricanes in light of the Haitian Revolution and the 1791 Pointe Coupee slave conspiracy, some planters believed that their Gulf Coast colony had been doomed to failure. A letter from panicked white residents described "the many calamities which they have endured since the year of 1779 up to the present year during which time we experienced five hurricanes, many floods, and two great fires." They expected "the emigration of several useful residents" and that "the population will decrease instead of increasing." When white Louisianans uncovered a much larger planned rebellion among Pointe Coupee slaves in 1795, only a few months after a hurricane had hit the colony, many concluded that the locale could not sustain a profitable and secure plantation economy. Although many factors contributed to the persistent failure of French and Spanish settlers to establish a slave society, the financial and social devastation caused by successive hurricanes undermined their efforts.[10]

Thomas Jefferson knew about the persistent threat of hurricanes to New Orleans before the Louisiana Purchase. In his 1803 pamphlet *An Account of Louisiana* (based on reports from Dr. John Sibley), Jefferson noted that "the whole lower part of the country . . . is subject to overflowing in hurricanes . . . whereby many lives were lost, horses and cattle swept away, and a scene of destruction laid." He tried to reassure prospective settlers that the last such storm happened in 1794 and that "fortunately they are not frequent." During its territorial phase (1803–1812), Louisiana was spared from the impact of a significant hurricane; indeed, the entire Gulf Coast seems to have escaped a major storm during that decade. In 1812, however, the same year that Louisiana received statehood, a devastating hurricane hit New Orleans, the first of many storms that would batter the Gulf Coast during the heyday of the sugar and cotton boom.[11]

Local accounts indicate that the August 1812 hurricane passed west of Jamaica and Cuba before entering the Gulf of Mexico. With the outbreak of the War of 1812 a few months earlier, the British Royal Navy had begun blockading American ports, including Mobile and New Orleans, reducing shipping traffic in the Gulf. About an hour before sunset on August 19, the storm made landfall near the northern shore of Black Bay, less than forty miles from New Orleans. Over the next two hours, it quickly made its way over St. Bernard and Plaquemines Parishes, home to more than one thousand enslaved people. The storm surge, "fifteen feet in some places," subsumed the low-lying sugar plantations, making "all the country into a temporary sea for about eighty miles." Survivors described climbing onto rooftops to escape the floodwaters, ten feet deep.

When the hurricane hit New Orleans, it laid waste to the levee, flooding the city with water from the Mississippi. River vessels broke free from their moorings and were pushed miles upriver by the storm surge. High winds tore the roofs from many of the buildings in the city. When the waters receded, survivors found "only death and ruin." The storm had left nearly all commercial river vessels "splintered to atoms." The worst destruction, however, lay south of the city, where the storm had left "mostly all the Sugar estates . . . wholly or partly destroyed, and the cane leveled with the earth." Fatality estimates varied widely, ranging from a few dozen to hundreds. The highest death toll appears to have been in rural Plaquemines Parish, where "very few homes [were] left standing," the plantations "swept away & every living soul with them." Major General James Wilkinson reported that most naval vessels in the region had been seriously damaged in the storm, including the USS *Enterprise*, famed for its performance in the Barbary Wars and recently refitted as a brig. Moreover, the storm had drowned or driven off the federal garrison at Fort St. Philip, the major masonry fort guarding the approach to New Orleans. In the storm's wake, British soldiers had occupied the fort, jeopardizing the city's security.

Under threat from a British invasion, rumors spread among southern Louisiana's white residents of a looming slave insurrection. When alarm bells rang on the night the hurricane hit, some residents interpreted them as "news of an intended Insurrection of the Negroes." Panicked white New Orleanians whispered that "the Negroes were to fire the city and murder its white inhabitants." One shopkeeper spent the nights following the storm cowering in his shop, as "our minds were filled with the images of negroes and assassins, each noise we heard startled us." His "great fear" was that "a band of blacks" would see the chaos as an opportunity to loot and revolt. In response to the panic, local militia patrolled New Orleans, imprisoning "many persons" suspected of participation. A contingent of the militia marched south from the city to contain the slave insurrection and reclaim Fort St. Philip. Many worried that General Wilkinson could not contain the dual threats posed by the British military and a hostile slave population.

Suspicions that the region's Black majority would use the hurricane as an opportunity to rebel grew out of a recent history of slave insurgency. Only a year earlier, hundreds of enslaved people from the sugar fields north of New Orleans had revolted and marched on the city, burning many of the plantations en route. White authorities, led by Governor William C. C. Claiborne and General Wade Hampton, quickly repressed the German Coast Uprising, executed its leaders, and impaled their heads on pikes along the levee as a visual deterrent. As with most rumors of slave conspiracy, little evidence indicates whether Louisiana slaves saw the 1812 hurricane as an opportunity to revolt. Nonetheless, for slave owners, it triggered fears that they would use the chaos created by the storm to find cracks in the plantation police state. For weeks after the storm, white Louisianans lived in a state of heightened alert. New Orleans mayor Charles Trudeau implemented a sundown curfew and ordered nightly patrols of the city in response to the "vivid fears that criminals are trying to set fire to the city." More than one resident feared that the hurricane would provide the impetus to "have the scenes of Ste Domingue [Haiti] renew themselves here." In the aftermath of the 1812 hurricane, Louisiana slave owners adjusted their plantation management to accommodate the threat posed by hurricanes. Increasingly, they constructed slave quarters out of brick, so they could withstand severe wind.[12]

The most destructive hurricane to hit the Gulf Coast struck on August 10, 1856, devastating Isle Dernière, Louisiana. It was more than twenty miles long, with only a mile of sand dunes dividing the island's northern and southern shore. By 1850, the island had become a popular resort destination for Louisiana planters, as the breezes off the Gulf of Mexico made summers on the island more bearable than on the mainland. Boasting a modest hotel and twenty-odd cottages, Isle Dernière (or Last Island) had a full complement of tourists and attending slaves when the hurricane struck. When the storm's outer edges hit the island, the first indication of its strength came when winds destroyed the slave quarters, "blown down" due to their flimsy construction. The slow-moving storm lingered for four hours over the narrow islet, reaching its apex in the early afternoon. One survivor described the sea waters rapidly advancing on both sides of the island, and "fiery lightning almost constantly illumined the heavens." Flying debris and a thirteen-foot storm surge destroyed nearly all of the buildings on the island. More than two hundred people died, half of them enslaved. Survivors weathered the storm aboard rafts or by clinging to debris, fearful that they would drown or be eaten by sharks. Battered and dehydrated, survivors found that the storm surge had permanently cleaved the sandy island in half.[13]

The Last Island hurricane passed west of New Orleans, making landfall in St. Mary's Parish. Barreling northward parallel to the Mississippi River, the storm struck the heartland of Louisiana's plantation belt. An overseer recorded that the storm surge raised the Mississippi one foot over the levees, "destroying nearly in toto the entire rice crop." One newspaper noted that everywhere in the storm's path, "sugar houses and dwellings, negro houses and barns, were all blown down and strewn about the fields." In Iberville, "every house in the village was leveled to the ground; trees were torn up by the roots and thrown great distances; even the tomb stones in the grave yard were thrown down and broken up."[14] William Walker provides the only account of the hurricane's destructive force from an enslaved person's perspective. Born in Virginia, Walker had been sold as a young man to an enormous cotton plantation twenty miles north of New Orleans. When the Last Island hurricane hit, Walker observed the gathering storm with awe. "The twisting and circling of the clouds and blue flashes of lightning mingling with a thousand confusing noises and the thunder peals plainly predicted the re-appearance of a Southern cyclone, the king of storms, which for years have been more destructive to Southern property and is more dreaded by the inhabitants than all the combined epidemical diseases inherent to Southern clime," he noted.

> It left death and destruction in its wake. Only those who have witnessed a Southern cyclone can form any adequate idea of its destructive power. Its awful fury was not more than one-half mile in width and everything within its path was forced to disappear. The air was filled with flying debris, and huge trees that had resisted the storms of centuries were wrenched from their places and lifted high in the air; and many of them were reduced to kindling wood. Many slave huts were raised to a dizzy height and then hurled back to the earth again with a tremendous force, and the lifeless forms of forty slaves were buried in the wreck.[15]

Although enslaved African Americans disproportionally suffered the effects of natural disasters, some slaves did seize the opportunities that the ensuing chaos provided. In the aftermath of violent storms, hurricanes, and tornadoes, they collected debris, enriching themselves from the scattered wreckage. Worried local authorities routinely called out slave patrols in the aftermath of major storms. After the 1752 hurricane, South Carolina governor James Glen pledged that any "wicked and evil disposed Person" found looting would be subject to harsh punishment. Enslaved people sometimes took advantage of sudden storms to escape, knowing that their absence would not be immediately noticed or that they would be counted among the dead.[16]

Heat

"Work in the burning sun," recalled William Wells Brown, "was very hard." Laboring from sunup to sundown, enslaved men and women found the relentless and debilitating heat nearly as oppressive as the lash. Indeed, one British visitor to Tennessee in 1820 saw the sun's inescapable rays as part of the torture inflicted upon enslaved people. He became "frequently sickened at the sight of large gangs . . . broiling under the vertical sun, and goaded to preternatural labour by the brutish lash." No amount of pleading, cajoling, or guile could spare them from the Southern summer sun.[17]

The South's heat and sunshine made plantation agriculture and the formation of a slave society possible. The major cash crops—tobacco, sugar, rice, and cotton—all require direct sunlight and long, hot summers to flourish. Both Sea Island cotton and Louisiana sugar need at least 250 frost-free days. Short-staple cotton proved more forgiving, requiring (depending on the variety) only two hundred frost-free days to harvest, while tobacco can be cultivated with a minimum of 120 days, though most planters preferred a longer season. Yet these same conditions made agricultural labor in the South onerous, if not torturous. Enslaved workers toiling in open fields experienced the worst of the Southern heat. Moses Roper remembered the torture of having to "work without any shirt, in the cotton field, in a very hot sun, in the month of July." He had just been whipped for failing to meet his quota, the wounds still fresh on his shoulders.[18]

Visitors to the plantation South marveled that anyone could live in such heat. Trekking through the swamps of Georgia and Florida in 1774, naturalist William Bartram complained repeatedly about the region's "sultry heat," which he deemed "intolerable." Overcome by the "scorching heat of the meridian sun," Bartram often sought a "desirable retreat from the sun's heat." Six decades later, British zoologist Philip Gosse found "the fierce heat of the high sun" in Alabama almost unbearable. He restricted his observations to the early mornings and late evenings, the only times he believed human and animal life could tolerate the heat. "Even by the time the sun is two hours high," Gosse noted, "his rays are oppressively hot, scorching one's back and head like a fire." After eight months, Gosse left Alabama, disgusted by slavery and convinced that the region was unfit for human habitation.[19]

Both the enslaved and enslavers knew that the sun's rays could inflict a form of torture. When he displeased a new owner, Solomon Northup had his wrists and ankles bound, leaving him unable to move. Dissuaded from his original plan of hanging Northup, the owner abandoned him in the open piazza to roast. "As the sun approached the meridian that day it became insufferably warm. Its hot rays scorched the ground. The earth almost blistered the foot that stood upon it. I was without coat or hat, standing bareheaded, exposed to its burning blaze," Northup recalled. "Great drops of perspiration rolled down my face, drenching the scanty apparel wherewith I was clothed. Over the fence, a very little way off, the peach trees cast their cool, delicious shadows on the grass. I would gladly have given a long year of service to have been enabled to exchange the heated oven, as it were, wherein I stood, for a seat beneath their branches."[20]

Slave owners argued that only Black laborers could toil in the Southern heat. The idea had deep roots in European racial thought but increased in currency as climate science and racial pseudoscience matured in tandem. By the 1840s Southern physicians such as Samuel Henry Dickson, Edward Barton, Samuel Cartwright, and Josiah Nott had crafted a defense of slavery built on the premise that black skin made those of African descent immune to the ill effects of working under the intense Southern sun. Slaves' capacity to "expose their bare heads and backs . . . to the rays of a sun hot enough to blister the skin of a white man," argued Cartwright, demonstrated that they were uniquely suited to toil in the cotton, rice, and sugar fields. Both science and divine sanction made racial slavery imperative where "no other kind of laborers can do the required drudgery-work in the sun *and live*." Professor Samuel Henry Dickson, an instructor at the Medical University of the State of South Carolina, taught his students that Blacks could be healthy nowhere "except under the hot sun of the South." Like many of his contemporaries, Dickson advocated polygenesis, a theory of human origins that postulated that races amounted to distinct species, created separately. Polygenesis helped to justify not only slavery and imperialism but also distinct medical treatment for white and Black Southerners. While whites might suffer in the Southern sun and heat, polygenists argued that intense heat prompted Blacks to flourish. "God has adapted him," wrote one pro-slavery physician, "both in his physical and mental structure, to the tropics." He is "wholly impervious to its fiercest heats." In 1853, a Scottish visitor to the South learned from one of his guides that slavery was "absolutely necessary, in the hot southern states, where no negro would work but on compulsion, and where free white labourers could not work at all without falling a sacrifice to the climate." By the eve of the Civil War, this idea had become so embedded in Southern racial thought that it found its way into Mississippi's official justification for secession, which noted that "none but the black race can bear exposure to the tropical sun."[21]

Although Southern racial thought claimed that Black slaves were immune to the ill effects of intense heat, slave owners knew that even the most robust enslaved people could succumb to heatstroke and dehydration. One Virginia planter noted in 1825 that the harvest brought the "hotest day ever felt—men gave out & some fainted." Charlotte Foster, a formerly enslaved person in upcountry South Carolina, recalled that she and her mother "used to plow, hoe, and dig and do anything the men did on the plantation." Working "in the hot sun" caused her periodically to get a "sick headache," an early symptom of heatstroke.[22]

Enslaved people working on rice plantations proved particularly susceptible to heatstroke. One man noted that among the many factors that made life unbearable in the Lowcountry was constant direct sunlight. "The heat," he noted, "from the sun over-head, reflected back into your face from the water, is intolerably painful, frequently bringing on giddiness and sun-stroke." After one particularly brutal July day in 1851, an overseer on a South Carolina rice plantation recorded that two slaves, "Cotta and Sarey[,] received a stroke of the sun" and that "many of the other negroes staggered about considerably." Visiting a South Carolina plantation during the harvest, Frederick Law Olmsted learned from his host that "this work, at the hottest season of the year, in the midst of the recently-exposed mire of the rice-fields, is acknowledged to be exceedingly severe, and must be very hazardous to the health, even of negroes."[23]

Prolonged heat and sun exposure contributed to many of the chronic health problems slaves faced. Dehydration exacerbated underlying medical conditions, including malaria, yellow fever, cholera, dysentery, hookworm, and tapeworm. A lifetime of excessive sunlight can also contribute to vision loss and blindness, very common disabilities among the enslaved. Pregnant slaves risked miscarriage from prolonged heat exposure. The torrid temperatures in the fields and slave quarters contributed to lower birthrates among the enslaved in the Deep South than those who lived in milder climates.[24]

The domestic slave trade often brought enslaved people into hotter, more humid climates, as approximately one million slaves were sold from the Upper

South to the Deep South between 1790 and 1860. Many of them found that the adjustment from the milder temperatures of the Chesapeake to the intense heat of the Gulf Coast sapped their strength, difficulties compounded by the more intense labor regime and the challenges of adapting to a new crop. One Alabama slave noted that slaves brought from Virginia "suffered greatly from the extreme heat and the severity of the toil." Enslavers in the Deep South complained that slaves born in the Upper South could not adjust to working in the heat. "The loss by *death* in bringing slaves from a northern climate," complained one Louisiana sugar planter, made buying slaves from Virginia or Kentucky a risky proposition: one in four died not long after arrival. Advertisements for slave auctions in New Orleans, Mobile, and Natchez mentioned if the people for sale had been born in the Gulf region or had been "seasoned" by years of labor under the sun.[25]

Field slaves sought whatever pretense they could to escape from the heat. For those laboring under the task system, escaping the worst of the summer heat provided an extra incentive to complete their task before the hottest part of the day. However, for the vast majority who worked in a gang system, the only respite from the heat came at the midday meal, when they could seek shade. Charles Ball praised the Southern magnolia not only for its beauty and fragrant flowers but for its foliage, which proved "as impervious as a brick wall to the rays of the sun, and its coolness, in the heat of a summer day, affords one of the greatest luxuries of a cotton plantation." Some enslaved people sought work assignments that would allow them to escape the unrelenting heat and backbreaking labor of the fields for the relative comfort of alternate employment indoors. Georgian Lindsey Moore learned soap making, which allowed him "to spend many hours in the shade pouring water over oak ashes while other young slaves picked cotton in the hot sun."[26]

For enslaved people who could not escape the fields, the intermittent water bucket was a rare relief from the intense heat. The task of bringing water to those working in the fields often fell to children. Tom Baker grew up on a plantation in Alabama's Black Belt, where summer temperatures regularly exceeded 90 degrees. He recalled that the plantation's fifty field slaves "worked in de sun all day long." Carrying water buckets from the springhouse to the slaves in the field, Baker relished the relief provided by the shade. The route from the springhouse to one field took him "between some willow trees an' it was powerful cool down dere in de shade." The spring house provided even more relief, as Baker "us' to lie on de moss an' let my bare belly git cool an' put my face in de outlet of de spring an' let de water trickle over my haid."

Baker's escape from the heat proved only temporary, as he heard the plaintive calls from the adult slaves: "Water Boy! Bring dat bucket!"[27]

To minimize exposure, some planters advocated allowing enslaved people to escape the sun during the hottest part of the day. One Alabama planter noted in *DeBow's Review* that he varied the length of the midday meal break depending on the heat. "In the winter they have one hour," he said, "and summer three to rest, in the heat of the day." Commentary from the formerly enslaved suggests that some slave owners followed this practice. Louisianan Clara Brim noted that they "didn't work in de heat of the day." Some of them framed these heat allowances as an indicator of an owner's kindness and paternalism. One Tennessee woman concluded that her owner "was pretty good to his slaves" because he allowed his field slaves to take a midday break "in the heat of the day" and "rest in the shade"[28]

Yet for every admonition to protect slaves from the excessive heat came demands to extract more labor, regardless of the toll upon enslaved bodies. Jourden Banks recalled an Alabama overseer who would "drive men until they fell exhausted from the effects of heat and labour upon the ground, and then manifest not the slightest feelings of regard for their condition. He would simply order others to take a man in that state and lay him under the shade of a tree until he recovered." Banks dubbed this man "one of the regular nigger killers" for his cruelty. One fugitive from bondage in South Carolina recalled, "They used to drive us so hard that some of the hands could not stand it. They would faint away and drop down in the fields." Seeking relief, "some of them would go to the brook to drink, and after stooping down they could not get up again, but died there with their faces in the water. A great many died in that way."[29]

Some enslavers sought dietary and medical advice to enable their slaves to work despite the heat. Dr. Thomas Hamilton, a physician, politician, and planter in Jones County, Georgia, tested various remedies for heatstroke. He borrowed an enslaved man from a neighbor, ostensibly as payment for medical treatment, for experimentation. The unwilling subject, a man called Fed, who would adopt the name John Brown when he escaped slavery, believed that he had been selected because as a healthy man, he would probably survive the experiments. Every few days, after Fed had finished his labor in the fields, Dr. Hamilton forced him to sit in a three-and-a-half-foot-deep pit that had been heated with burning red oak bark "like an oven." With only Fed's head above ground and the pit's opening sealed off with wet blankets, Dr. Hamilton administered various remedies to assess their effectiveness. Although Fed "tried hard to keep up against its effects," he usually succumbed to the heat after half an hour, when Hamilton would extract Fed's unconscious body from the pit. After a half dozen trials, Hamilton concluded that he had discovered a treatment for heatstroke: cayenne-pepper tea. According to Brown, Hamilton marketed the remedy and "realized a large fortune."[30]

Southern planters created a built environment to make themselves comfortable in the summer heat. They adopted Mediterranean architectural styles not only to demonstrate their wealth and familiarity with classical modes but also because the designs encouraged cooling breezes. They constructed elaborate shutter systems to provide shade or trap heat as weather dictated and capped their mansions with cupolas to allow hot air to escape. They planted shade trees—oaks, hickory, and magnolia—to keep their houses out of the direct sun. Some plantation houses featured punkahs, ceiling-mounted fans, designed to cool the room and dissuade flies from settling on food. Enslaved boys, including a young Booker T. Washington, operated the punkahs via ropes or chains, creating a gentle breeze. Many planters and their families found the heat so oppressive and unhealthy that they abandoned their plantations during the summer months for cooler locales. For South Carolina rice magnates, their preferred destination became Flat Rock, a small town in the North Carolina mountains, which garnered the nickname "Little Charleston" because of its summertime residents. Mississippi and Louisiana gentry flocked to Bay St. Louis on the Gulf Coast, where the sea breezes made the heat and humidity tolerable.[31]

While slave owners tried to minimize the effects of the heat and maximize their own comfort, the designs of slave quarters often added to the misery and ill health of their tenants. By their own admission, planters recognized that slave housing often compounded rather than ameliorated the effects of the region's subtropical climate. An 1856 *Southern Cultivator* article claimed, "That negroes are not, as a general thing, as well provided for in the way of comfortable dwellings as they might be is simply a well known fact," identifying the main culprits as poor "ventilation and shading." Although some construction material, including brick and tabby, could provide a cool shelter, most slave quarters had wooden log or plank walls that trapped the sun's heat. Indeed, the temperature in unshaded slave quarters often exceeded that of the air outside. Frederick Law Olmsted described slave quarters in South Carolina that seemed almost designed to suffocate their inhabitants: "The negro-cabins, here, were the smallest I had ever see—I thought not more than twelve feet square, inside. . . . They were built of logs, with no windows—no opening at all, except the doorway, with a chimney of sticks and mud; with no trees about them, no porches, or shades, of any kind." Olmsted concluded that the buildings were unfit even "for an animal to sleep in."[32]

Cold

"Ole Boss he send us niggahs out in any kine ob weathah," recalled Sarah Gudger. "Rain o' snow, it nebbah mattah." Enslaved on a plantation in western North Carolina's Swannanoa Valley, deep in the Appalachians, Gudger had to hike up the nearby mountains, "cut wood an' drag it down t' de house." During the winter, this often meant trekking barefoot through snow, across frozen creeks, and down muddy slopes. Gudger's toes and fingers went numb from cold, and "many de time we come in wif ouh cloes stuck t' ouh pah ole cold bodies." After depositing a load of wood in the pile, she received no respite from the cold before another trip up the mountain, "else we git de lash." Gudger also recalled waiting until after her owners had fallen asleep to "walk barfoot in de snow" the two miles to her aunt's house, where she would enjoy a warm meal before the bitter slog home. She slept beneath a pile of rags, "ha'dly 'nuf t' keep us from freezin.'"[33]

Although not as infamous as its oppressive summer heat, the slave South could experience bitterly cold winters. Indeed, winter weather in the antebellum South was probably colder than the region today. Historical climatologists have described the several centuries ending in 1850s as the little ice age, when winter temperatures in the Northern Hemisphere often dipped substantially below current levels. Colonists in Jamestown noted that the James River sometimes froze over; John Smith complained that Virginia winters were so miserable that "a dogge would scarce have indured it." Freak weather events could also make bitterly cold temperatures descend on the South. In 1815, the volcanic eruption of Mount Tambora in the Dutch East Indies (modern Indonesia) sent tons of ash into the atmosphere that produced global cooling over the next couple of years. In 1816, the "year without a summer," some enslaved Virginians awoke in late August to find frost on the tobacco leaves. Corn crops in the Upper South came up short that year, prompting a financial crisis for some planters. Former president Thomas Jefferson fell even deeper into debt as a consequence, forced to borrow more than a thousand dollars from his agent.[34]

Starting in 1776, Jefferson kept detailed records of the weather at Monticello. In 1818, near the end of his life, he summarized the data he had collected. He noted that the average "extreme of cold in ordinary winter [was] 16°," but that in "extraordinary" years temperatures could reach 5°. Monticello experienced on average "50 freezing nights in the year, and 10 freezing days." Summer temperatures, by comparison, could reach 92°. In deference to these temperature fluctuations and the dictates of fashion, Jefferson acquired an extensive wardrobe, which allowed him to dress comfortably regardless of the weather. In comparison to some of his neighbors, Jefferson provided a relatively generous enslaved clothing allowance. His household slaves (some of whom were also his children) received the most generous provision. His field slaves received enough coarse fabric to fashion two sets of clothes: a lighter flax-hemp textile known as osnaburg for summer and woven wool for winter. Laboring men and women received one pair of leather shoes per year, while enslaved children went barefoot and elderly slaves shod themselves with the remnants of previous years.[35]

Jefferson knew that poorly clad slaves could suffer permanent disability from exposure to inclement weather. In 1810, he hired three enslaved men and one enslaved woman from a neighbor, one of whom, Tom Buck, arrived with both feet "frost-bitten and extremely bad." Jefferson sent Buck to Charlottesville for medical treatment, where he had his big toe amputated, but after months of convalescence, Buck "still continues unable to walk, except about the house." For enslaved people on Jefferson's plantations in the Virginia Piedmont, it was the first of a series of bitterly cold winters. The following year, Jefferson wrote to his neighbor, President James Madison, "We have had a wretched winter."[36]

Like many enslaved people in the Upper South, Charles Ball found the clothing provided by his owner inadequate for winter weather. His yearly allocation—"one pair of shoes, one pair of stockings, one hat, one jacket of coarse cloth, two coarse shirts, and two pair of trousers"—had to suffice regardless of the weather. With January temperatures often dipping below freezing, Ball found himself shivering as he trudged home late at night, having delivered his master's tobacco to market. "In the winter time," he recalled, "I often suffered very much from the cold." Frederick Douglass, who grew up on a plantation not far from Charles Ball, recalled that enslaved children received even less clothing, such that even in the "coldest winter, I was kept almost naked—no shoes, no stockings, no jacket, no trousers, nothing on but a coarse tow linen shirt, reaching only to my knees." Douglass tried to keep warm at night by sleeping in a stolen cornmeal bag, but his exposed feet became "so cracked with the frost, that the pen with which I am writing might be laid in the gashes."[37]

Across the Border South, enslaved people often felt that the clothing allowance was inadequate for the region's winter. "We didden have much

clothes, nevah no undahweah, no shoes, old ovahalls and a tattahed shirt,
wintah and summah," recalled John Eubanks from Barron County, Kentucky.
"Come de wintah, it be so cold mah feet weah plumb numb mos' o' de time
and manya time—when we git a chanct—we druve the hogs from outin the
bogs an' put ouah feet in the wahmed wet mud. They was cracked and the
skin on the bottoms and in de toes weah cracked and bleedin' mos' o' time,
wit bloody scabs but de summah healed them agin." Many enslaved people
in the Border South shared Eubanks's complaint of inadequate footwear. As
with other regions of the South, only adults received shoes, with children and
adolescents remaining barefoot. Emma Knight recalled of her childhood,
"We went barefoot until it got real cold. Our feet would crack open from
de cold and bleed. We would sit down and bawl and cry because it hurt so."
Since her owner refused to purchase shoes for children, Knight wore rude
moccasins her mother crafted from old pants.[38]

Inadequate clothing caused more than temporary discomfort; for some it
led to permanent disfigurement. An enslaved woman in Maryland, forced by
her owner to leave her fourteen-month-old infant alone, returned to find his
"feet frozen stiff as stones." The panicked mother applied warm bandages to
the child's feet, but when she removed them the next morning, his "toes all
came off in the poultices." Never able to walk properly, Lewis Charlton found
Maryland's cold winters defined his life in bondage. As a teenager, he was
sent with other slaves to gather wood. "It was a bitter cold day in the winter
and the snow was deep," he recalled. "My feet were very cold . . . and when we
started for home my feet and legs were frozen to the knees." He spent that
night lying on the farmhouse kitchen floor "with no one to help me or pity."
When his owner saw him the next morning, he concluded that frostbite had
made this young slave worthless. Fifty years later, Charlton vividly recalled,
"My pain was dreadful to think of, and to this hour I have continued to suffer.
These old limbs all shrunken, pitted and scarred are the homes of pain."[39]

Despite the profound challenges that cold weather posed for the poorly
clad, some enslaved people welcomed winter. "Generally winter is the easiest
time for the slaves," recalled Francis Fedric, who escaped from a plantation
bordering the Ohio River in Mason County, Kentucky. A blanket of snow
generally precluded work in the fields and facilitated a temporary respite and,
at least on Fedric's plantation, the occasion for a dance in the quarters. More
significantly, some enslaved people took advantage of the rare occasions when
the Ohio River froze solid to escape. Abolitionist attorney and future president Rutherford B. Hayes noted that during the 1850s "when the Ohio River
was frozen for several weeks, it was terror to the slaveholders. . . . The slaves

who had been punished anywhere were considering the question of how to cross." According to abolitionist Levi Coffin, the character of Eliza in Harriet Beecher Stowe's *Uncle Tom's Cabin* drew from a runaway he assisted. When her owner went into debt and planned to sell her child, the enslaved woman tried to cross the frozen Ohio River. "She knew that it was frozen over, at that season of the year, and hoped to cross without difficulty on the ice," only to find that "the ice had broken up and was slowly drifting in large cakes." Pursued by slave catchers, she scampered across the ice floes, babe in arms, narrowly escaping drowning. Runaway slaves faced better conditions in 1856 when the river froze solid. According to the editor of the *Louisville Courier*, during the deep freeze in January and February 1856, more than 250 enslaved people escaped across the ice. Fleeing with seventeen members of her extended family, Margaret Garner made it safely to Ohio before slave catchers caught up with her. Unwilling to return her children to bondage, Garner slit her two-year-old daughter's throat and attempted to kill her other children and herself before she was overpowered.[40]

Winter also provided other advantages to runaway slaves. Cold weather kept white Southerners inside, allowing fugitive slaves to flee with a reduced chance of raising an alarm. Moreover, long winter nights provided added cover for fugitives. According to one associate, Harriet Tubman "always came in the winter, when the nights are long and dark, and the people who have homes stay in them." Yet escaping in the middle of winter posed significant challenges when the temperature dropped. In 1857, Elizabeth Williams managed to escape from her Maryland plantation, but "four days and nights out in the bitter cold weather without the chance of fire" resulted in her losing her toes to frostbite and left her unable to walk for seven months.[41]

Slave coffles suffered some of the worst exposure to cold weather. The interregional slave trade followed seasonal patterns, with Upper South slave owners selling surplus chattel after the autumn harvest. Thus, the overland slave-trading routes to the west and south became clogged with slaves during the coldest months of the year. In November 1826, a slave trader in Richmond, Virginia bound William Anderson's wrists in shackles for the six-hundred-mile trek to Nashville, Tennessee. "Chained together, two by two," Anderson marched with sixty other bondspeople. Their route took them through the Appalachian Mountains, traversing the Cumberland Gap in the depths of winter. Bereft over the forced separation from his mother, Anderson tramped on, as "The snow and rain came down in torrents, but we had to rest out in the open air every night; sometimes we would have to scrape away the snow, make our pallets on the cold ground, or in the rain, with a bunch of leaves and a chunk of wood for our pillow, and so we would have to rest the best we could, with our chains on. . . . We were driven with whip and curses through the cold and rain." W. L. Bost recalled that just prior to the Civil War, slave traders came through his western North Carolina plantation, arriving every year in December "so that the niggers would be ready for sale on the first day of January." With temperatures regularly dipping below freezing, Bost noted that "the poor critters nearly froze to death." Chained together and barefoot, "they never had enough clothes on to keep a cat warm. The women never wore anything but a thin dress and a petticoat and one underwear. I've seen the ice balls hangin' on to the bottom of their dresses." From horseback, the slave traders ordered the manacled slaves to run to keep warm.[42]

As a corollary to their claims about heat, pro-slavery writers argued that people of African descent did not tolerate cold as well as whites did. Many scientific authorities agreed, including Benjamin Franklin, who noted, "They do not bear cold weather so well as the whites; they will perish when exposed to a less degree of it, and are more apt to have their limbs frost-bitten." Runaway slaves themselves, however, dismissed this notion that they could not tolerate cold weather, arguing that excessive exposure and inadequate clothing were to blame for their suffering in the cold rather than inherent racial susceptibility. Interviewed by the American Freedmen's Inquiry Commission during the Civil War, runaway slaves who had taken refuge in Canada commented that while the cold weather north of the border proved a challenge for newcomers, black skin did not preclude living in a cold climate. One of the commissioners was surprised to discover that "the refugees are not generally conscious of the great disadvantage of the climate. Indeed, to hear them talk, one would suppose they were 'to the artic born.' They have a bravado way about, and say, 'We can stand the climate just as well as white men.' "[43]

The South's violent and unpredictable weather mirrored slavery's capricious brutality. Indeed, slaves often drew upon meteorological metaphors to describe how their lives could be overturned by a mercurial owner. Mississippi slave Henry Watson recalled mild treatment from a new owner, but "soon the cloud grew black, the storm commenced, . . . her temper soon burst forth in all its fury," such that Watson and his fellow slaves suffered from nearly daily whippings. A sudden tempest's destructive power on the landscape mirrored the psychological impact of the auction block and the lash. When slaves and former slaves sang "Been in Storm So Long," they recalled the profound uncertainty and brutality that defined their lives.[44]

6

An Inhospitable Refuge

IN 1806, CHARLES BALL ventured into a Lowcountry swamp in search of turtles. Three miles from his labor camp "in a very solitary part of the swamps," he heard wagon bells, which alarmed him so far from the nearest road. Hearing the bells get closer, he "crouched down upon the ground, under cover of a cluster of small bushes that were near me," paralyzed by "a feeling of horror." His courage nearly failing him, Ball heard approaching footsteps on the dry leaves and saw emerging through the trees "a brawny, famished-looking black man, entirely naked, with his hair matted and shaggy, his eyes wild and rolling, and bearing over his head something in the form of an arch, elevated three feet above his hair, beneath the top of which were suspended the bells, three in number, whose sound had first attracted my attention." Ball initially mistook the figure as "an inhabitant of a nether fiery world" before recognizing him as "only a poor destitute African negro, still more wretched and helpless than myself." He learned that the man's name was Paul, he had been born in Congo, and he had been enslaved for four years. He had escaped from a cruel, alcoholic owner who took pleasure in whipping his slaves, leaving Paul's back "seamed and ridged with scars of the whip." Paul revealed that he had "been wandering in the woods, more than three weeks, with no other subsistence than the land tortoises, frogs, and other reptiles that he had taken in the woods, and along the shores of the ponds, with the aid of his spear." Without fire, he had eaten this prey raw, and his bells had scared away most animals. Without hesitation, Ball shared his food with the famished and emaciated man.

Using flint, moss, and the iron on Paul's collar, Ball built a fire so that the fugitive could cook his food. Paul recounted that he had fled to the swamp multiple times since surviving the Middle Passage. Two years earlier, he had fled after a beating and taken refuge in the swamp for six months before

Scars on the Land. David Silkenat, Oxford University Press. © Oxford University Press 2022.
DOI: 10.1093/oso/9780197564226.003.0007

being recaptured. As punishment, he had labored for three months with a
heavy wooden block chained to his leg. Finding an old file, he liberated himself from this manacle and took to the swamp for a second time, only to be
recaptured a week later. Unable to remove Paul's iron collar and bells, Ball
pledged to return with tools as soon as he could. When he returned a week
later, Ball found the campfire abandoned, surrounded by the terrapin and
frog skeletons. Ball initially supposed that Paul had either freed himself from
his collar and had fled or had been apprehended. Alerted by a swarm of buz-
zards and an overwhelming stench, Ball found "the lifeless and putrid body
of the unhappy Paul hung suspended by a cord made of twisted hickory bark,
passed in the form of a halter round the neck, and firmly bound to a limb
of the tree." Looking on in horror, Ball watched as a crow pecked at Paul's
face, making the still-attached bells ring deathly tones. "The body of Paul was
never taken down," Ball recalled, "but remained hanging where I had seen it
until the flesh fell from the bones, or was torn off by the birds. I saw the bones
hanging in the sassafras tree more than two months afterwards, and the last
time that I was ever in these swamps."[1]

Charles Ball's account reveals the twin uses of swamps among the enslaved.
For Ball, the swamp served as a larder, a site where he could supplement his
meager rations with the meat of turtles, fish, and birds. For the fugitive Paul,
the swamp was a refuge, an inhospitable landscape that he saw as preferable to a life in bondage. While the enslaved often ventured into the swamp,
white Southerners viewed them with fear and disgust, the abode of beasts

FIGURE 6.1. Nathaniel Southard, ed., *American Anti-Slavery Almanac for 1838*
(Boston: Isaac Knapp, 1838), 13. This image appeared alongside an excerpt from Ball's
narrative.

that slithered in the mud and swam in the murky waters. They elided easy categorization: neither land nor water, swamps did not fit into the schemas white Southerners used to divide the environment. They saw swamps as unruly slaves, requiring discipline before they would submit to cultivation and mastery. "Another great resource," noted Virginia planter Edmund Ruffin, "is presented in your great inland swamps, now only wide-spread seed-beds of disease, pestilence, and death; and which, by drainage, with certainty and great profit, might be converted to dry fields of exuberant fertility."[2]

Forbidding and menacing, swamps across the South hosted dozens of maroon communities. Ranging in size from less than a dozen individuals to settlements numbering in the hundreds, these communities took advantage of the ecological defenses that swamps created. The terrain made searching the swamp upon horseback nearly impossible, and the density of vegetation hid maroons from interlopers and provided defensible positions in case of attack. These maroon communities demonstrated an alternative to chattel bondage: African American communities living apart, but not entirely divorced, from the broader slave society. Some maroon communities survived for generations, shielded and nurtured by the swamp.

Not all maroons lived in large settlements hidden deep within the swamp. Throughout the South, enslaved people saw swamps as havens where they could escape from bondage. Some maroons sought sanctuary in swamps adjacent to enslaved labor camps, relying on this proximity and social connections to sustain themselves, while others took refuge in more secluded parts of the swamp.[3] Maroons included both those who left temporarily (sometimes called "petit marronage") and those who sought a permanent home in the swamp ("grand marronage"). Enslaved on a Georgia plantation, Samson experienced both. "Too much of a man to be flogged," Samson "would frequently make his escape when he was to be whipped." He relied on an encyclopedic knowledge of the local geography and ecosystem to escape and survive. "Perfectly acquainted with the surrounding country, woods, creeks, rivers, and swamps," Samson could "outwit both dogs and hunters. If closely pushed, he could cross a stream, or float himself down it upon a log, or in a skiff, or plunge into the depths of miry swamp, where pursuit would be impossible." If necessary, he would rub himself with jimson weed, a toxic member of the nightshade family, to disguise his scent. Samson's periodic flights to the swamp rarely lasted very long, and he returned to the plantation when his enslaver pledged not to whip him. In 1844, however, after a lifetime of abuse, Samson asserted he would "not be a beast" but would "have my liberty" and elected to live permanently in the swamp. "Those not acquainted with southern life

will think this strange," noted Lewis Paine, a teacher and Rhode Island trans-
plant in Georgia who spent six years in prison for assisting Samson. "It not
unfrequently happens that they stay out for years." Fugitives from bondage
concealed themselves in "large tracts of land, covered with heavy timber" and
"deep and almost impenetrable swamps," emerging at night to steal potatoes,
corn, and bacon from nearby plantations.[4]

The largest and best documented maroon communities in the American
South were in the Great Dismal Swamp, the Lowcountry swamps of South
Carolina and Georgia, and the cypress swamps of Louisiana. All established
prior the American Revolution, these wetland sanctuaries from slavery came
under attack in the decades that followed. White authorities wanted not only
to exploit the swamps' resources but to root out maroon communities that
they saw as a threat to the broader institution of slavery. To this end, they
paired armed patrols and military intervention with hydraulic engineering
to make swamps inhospitable to maroon communities. Using enslaved labor,
white authorities built canals to drain the swamps, shrinking their ecological footprint. The varying geography of these swamps determined in large
measure which maroon communities survived and which fell victim to white
conquest.[5]

Lowcountry

Maroon communities formed in the swamps along Lowcountry rivers in the
early eighteenth century. Dominated by tupelo and cypress trees, these back
swamps proved too far upriver for tidal rice cultivation. The earliest reference
to them in colonial records appears in 1711, in which a band of "several Negroes
runaway from their masters & keep out, arm'd, robbing & plundering houses
& Plantations." Led by Sebastian, "the Spanish Negroe," these maroons put
the "Inhabitants of this province in great fear and terrour." Over the next half
century, periodic references to maroons appear in government papers, noting
that they always lived close to white settlement. In 1733, the governor called
out the militia to apprehend maroons who had "committed many Outrages
and Robberys and lye in the Swamp at the Head of the Wando River."[6]

Maroons living in the Stono Swamp may also have participated the largest
enslaved uprising in the British mainland colonies. In September 1739, a core
of twenty-three rebels began a march southward, flying a banner that read
"Liberty!," bound for Spanish Florida, which promised sanctuary for Black
refugees from British colonies. Led by a literate Kongolese man named Jemmy
and accumulating followers en route, the rebels burned six plantations and

killed two dozen whites, leaving the countryside "full of Flames." Confronted by a white militia at the Edisto River, the rebels fought fiercely but took heavy casualties. The survivors scattered, fleeing to the swamps. In the weeks that followed, Carolina authorities engaged in concerted efforts to round up the rebels, employing Chickasaw and Catawba scouts and enslaved men in the hunt. However, colonial records suggest that at least half of those who survived the battle at the Edisto River eluded capture, either making it successfully to Spanish Florida or taking up refuge in the swamp. One rebel remained in the swamp for three years before he was apprehended and executed. While the extant source material makes documenting their role impossible, the presence of maroons in the Stono Rebellion would help to explain how the rebels coalesced so quickly, navigated their route to Florida, and evaded capture in its aftermath.[7]

In the decades that followed, colonial authorities grew increasingly concerned about the presence of maroons in the swamps. At the height of the Stamp Act crisis, fears of a maroon community in swamps along the Savannah River sent officials in Georgia and South Carolina into a panic. Georgia legislators heard alarming reports of "a number of fugitive slaves . . . in the River Swamp" who "Committed several robberies and depredations" in nearby plantations." Georgia governor James Wright sent "partys of Rangers & of the Militia" into the swamp "to search every suspected place," but turned up empty-handed. They did, however, find evidence of a substantial settlement four miles into the swamp: a "Town . . . totally deserted" with "a Square Consisting of four Houses seventeen feet long and fourteen feet wide." Well-supplied, the maroons had stockpiled rice, shoes, blankets, and axes. One enslaved man who had visited the camp testified that its inhabitants included "many Negroe men, some Women & Children and at least thirty Guns."[8]

To colonial officials, the well-supplied and armed settlement suggested that an attack might be imminent. Prior to Christmas 1765, rumors spread that "Plots are forming & some attempts of Insurrection to be made during these Holydays." Reports indicated that more than a hundred enslaved men had recently fled the plantations to join maroons in the Colleton swamps. Intensified slave patrols searched swamps and byways, on high alert. To supplement slave patrols and militias, South Carolina officials enlisted "Catawbas, as Indians strike terrour into the Negroes and the Indians manner of hunting render them more sagacious in tracking and expert in finding out the hidden recesses, where the runaways conceal themselves." When the initial panic passed, they remained concerned that the swamp maroons presented an existential threat to the colonial project. "The large number of negroes,

said to be run'd away and assembled in the great Swamps," wrote South
Carolina lieutenant governor William Bull, "may give some kind of encour-
agement to others badly or idly inclined to think of a General Insurrection."
With enslaved Africans significantly outnumbering the white population,
some colonial officials contemplated closing the Atlantic slave trade, if only
temporarily.[9]

A decade later, many enslaved people in the Lowcountry took advantage of the chaos and uncertainty generated by the Revolution to create
opportunities for freedom. At times, they shared their environmental knowledge with British soldiers when they thought it advantageous. In December
1778, an enslaved man named Quamino Dolly lead Col. Archibald Campbell's
troops through the swamps, enabling them to circumvent Savannah's defenses
and capture the city. The following October, enslaved men guided British
reinforcements from Beaufort, South Carolina, to Savannah "through
swamps, creeks, and bogs which had never been attempted before by bears,
wolves, and run-away negroes." Occupied by the British from 1778 to 1782,
Savannah attracted thousands of enslaved people who saw the Redcoats as
liberators. While three to six thousand bondspeople managed to depart with
Crown forces at the war's conclusion, most were forced back onto the plantation. In the chaos during the British departure, many fled to the swamps
eighteen miles upriver of the city, where on a series of densely forested islands they built fortified settlements on the highlands. The environmental
conditions aided in their defense: accessible only by boat, the swamp islands
provided a natural refuge, with only the initiated able to navigate their boggy
interiors. The presence of rattlesnakes, water moccasins, and alligators provided an added deterrent to interlopers. Yet their size—roughly thirty square
miles—allowed them to support a robust maroon population. Sitting on the
border between South Carolina and Georgia, the Savannah River swamp islands occupied a no man's land.[10]

Lowcountry maroons continued to raid neighboring plantations after
British troops had abandoned the region. In 1786 and 1787, a maroon band
calling themselves the "King of England's Soldiers" conducted a series of raids
on Savannah River plantations. State officials believed that more than one
hundred armed men were encamped in the riverine swamp. "Their leaders,"
noted one Georgia militia officer, "are the very fellows that fought, and
maintained their ground against the brave Lancers at the siege of Charleston."
One of them called himself "Captain Cudjoe," possibly a reference to the famous Jamaican maroon leader. Newspapers reported that they were "strongly
fortified in the midst of an almost impenetrable swamp" and "had been

employed in arms by the British in the late war" and had been in a "state of rebellion ever since the peace."

State officials saw these maroon communities as a fundamental threat to the re-establishment of a slave society after the Revolution. Aware that maroons in Jamaica and Dutch Surinam had become so entrenched and powerful that they had negotiated for quasi-independence, they sought to root out the problem before it was too late. They targeted a maroon community on Belleisle, an island in the Savannah River located seventeen miles upriver from Savannah, where they believed "large gangs of runaway Negroes are allowed to remain quietly within a short distance of this town." Militia raids on the settlement in October 1786 discovered that the maroons were more numerous, better armed, and well-supplied than they expected. The first militia incursion had to "retreat for want of ammunition"; the second fled when "the Negroes came down in such numbers that it was judged advisable to retire to their boats." When a larger militia force arrived two days later, they found the site abandoned. General James Jackson, a Revolutionary War hero and future senator and governor of Georgia, reported that the maroons had left in a hurry, leaving behind two tons of unprocessed rice, sixty bushels of corn, and "14 or 15 boats and canoes." Unable to locate the maroons, Jackson and his men stayed at the site overnight, leaving after they had "burnt a number of their houses and huts, and destroyed about four acres of green rice." The site suggested a large, stable maroon population that planned to make the island their permanent home.

Jackson hoped that destroying their supplies would force the maroons "to disperse about the country," making it easier for the militia to capture them. The next two months, however, demonstrated that the Belleisle maroon community would not be easily broken. They increased raids on nearby Savannah River plantations, "from whence they carry off whole stacks of rice at a time to compensate, as they term it, for their incredible magazine of provisions destroyed at their camp." Their raids also liberated dozens of enslaved people. "Their numbers are daily increasing," Jackson wrote to South Carolina governor Thomas Pinckney, as "the freebooty they reap, and the independent [state] they are in" were "strong charms of allurement" for the enslaved to flee the plantation.

In the autumn of 1786 through the spring of 1787, Georgia and South Carolina militias launched repeated raids into the swamp, burning fields and settlements and executing a few captured maroons, displaying their heads on roadside poles as a deterrent. The militia incursions had the effect of bringing the maroon raids on nearby plantations to a halt. Yet they managed to kill and capture only a small number of those runaway slaves they believed lived in the swamp. The rest vanished, retreating farther from white settlement.[11]

Lowcountry maroons responded by fortifying their swamp enclaves. At Bear Creek, they erected breastworks and felled trees across the creek to limit boat traffic. With twenty-one houses and a population exceeding one hundred, Bear Creek maroons posted sentries to guard their community. In May 1787, South Carolina and Georgia militiamen, supported by twenty Catawba mercenaries, overwhelmed the Bear Creek settlement, burning the houses, killing some of the maroons, and capturing others. The rest vanished amid the confusion. Some made their way to Spanish Florida, while others appear to have found new homes in the swamp.[12]

The slow demise of the Lowcountry's maroon settlements owed as much to man-made environmental change as military action. As techniques for inland cultivation improved at the end of the eighteenth century, land-hungry planters sought to convert swamps into rice fields. They envisioned a transformed landscape, with worthless wetlands giving way to acres of profitable rice plantations, worked by enslaved laborers. Just prior to the Revolution, one South Carolina colonial official reported that "many large swamps, otherwise useless and affording inaccessible shelter for deserting slaves and wild beasts, have been drained and cultivated." While the Revolution temporarily disrupted this ecological transformation, it resumed with vigor afterwards. "While there remain[s] one acre of swamp-land un-cleared in South Carolina," remarked Charles Cotesworth Pinckney in 1788 during the ratification debates, "I would raise my voice against restricting the importation of negroes." Maps of the Lowcountry chronicled the dis-appearance of the region's swamps. James Cook's 1773 map includes dozens of swamps scattered across coastal South Carolina and Georgia: Hell Hole, Wambaw, Great Bay, Sockestee, Lake, Buck, Megerts, and Sparrow. A half century later, they left a smaller footprint, replaced with hundreds of acres of rice plantations. Even with this ecological transformation, swamps continued to dominate the Lowcountry. In 1819, one British visitor observed, "About one-third of this plain consists of immense swamps, which, interlocking with each other, form part of long chain, which stretches for several hundred miles along the coast of Georgia and the Carolinas."[13]

Runaway slave advertisements document Lowcountry enslavers' belief that fugitives had found sanctuary in the swamp, and slave patrols and militias routinely scoured the swamps in search of runaways. In 1816, South Carolina Governor David Williams ordered the militia to apprehend "a few runaway negroes, concealing themselves in the swamps and marshes contiguous to

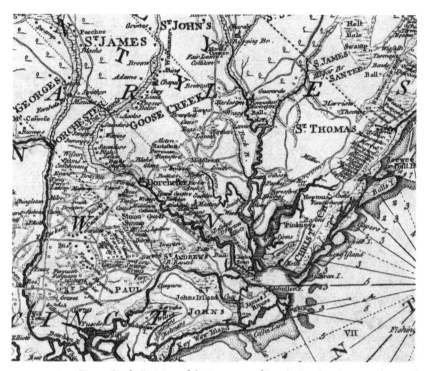

FIGURE 6.2. James Cook, "A Map of the Province of South Carolina," 1773. Library of Congress. https://www.loc.gov/item/74692124/.

the Combahee and Ashepoo river." Well-armed, the maroons used the environment to disguise their movements, enabling them to raid plantations and inland river commerce. Rarely successful in capturing or engaging swamp maroons, white patrols frequently uncovered their camps. "Situated on small elevations, surrounding by extensive arrears of marsh," these "places of retreat" proved well supplied, including wells for drinking water and "relics of ducks, turkeys, vegetables, and beef." Patrollers marveled that, buried deep in the swamp, these camps had "every necessary preparation for a long residence."[14]

After a flurry of activity in the 1820s, references to maroons in the Lowcountry swamps declined significantly after 1830. White settlement above the fall line had encroached on even the most remote swampland, leaving maroon communities vulnerable. A century of intensive hydraulic engineering had transformed swampland into rice plantations, and Jacksonian-era canal building simultaneously drained wetlands and opened up thousands of acres for development, both of which endangered maroon communities. The large, fortified maroon settlements of the eighteenth century gave way to smaller enclaves in the nineteenth. They increasingly lived in the shadow of the plantation, requiring them to build economic ties with the enslaved population.[15]

After 1830, Lowcountry maroons only attracted the attention of white authorities when their numbers appeared to grow. In 1846, South Carolina planters along the Savannah River complained of "serious crimes by desperate gangs of runaways, who are becoming more numerous, more reckless and are almost entirely secure from apprehension in our swamps." Two years later, South Carolina governor Whitemarsh Seabrook made "reclamation of the swamps" one of the state's top agricultural priorities. He deemed them "utterly valueless in their present state . . . poisonous property . . . a perpetual source of disease and death." Draining the swamps, he argued, would open up thousands of acres to cultivation, and canals through the Biggin and Wassamasaw swamps would connect the Cooper, Ashley, and Edisto Rivers, greatly improving transportation networks in the state. The construction of this extensive canal network, of course, depended upon the enslaved labor of thousands of men.[16]

Even after the maroon threat had passed, few Lowcountry whites braved the swamps, viewing them as both worthless for agriculture and dangerous, infested by alligators and poisonous snakes. Married to rice planter Pierce Butler, British actress Fanny Kemble spent the winter of 1837–1838 on his Georgia slave labor camp. "Upon this swamp island of ours," Fanny Kemble came to loathe both human bondage and the ecosystem where enslaved people worked, lived, and died. "Amphibious creatures, alligators, serpents, and wild-fowl haunt these yet but half-formed regions," she wrote, "where land and water are of the consistency of hasty-pudding." Enslaved people, however, often ventured into the swamps, either to hunt and fish or escape the looming surveillance of the slave labor camp, if only for a few hours. Some like Charles Ball found a kind of quasi-freedom in the swamp, hidden among the trees and the cacophony of frogs, birds, and insects.[17]

Louisiana

From the arrival of the first cargo of enslaved Africans in 1719, Louisiana's swamps proved an irresistible lure. Drawn mainly from Senegambia, the Africans understood how to navigate the region's wetlands better than their French enslavers. This first generation constructed maroon settlements in swamps that resembled those built by Bambara rebels along the Senegal River. Confronting hostile European rivals, powerful Native nations in the Lower Mississippi, and a staggering mortality rate, French authorities in

Louisiana faced an uphill battle to control their enslaved African majority. Louisiana's 1723 Code Noir established an escalating series of punishments for maroons: enslaved people away for one month were to have both ears cut off and be branded on the shoulders with a fleur-de-lis; those away for two months could be hamstrung and branded on both shoulders; and those absent for three months warranted execution.

Ensconced in the swamp, maroons developed economic and military partnerships with Native Americans. In 1726, the Louisiana attorney general called for "prompt and sweeping action against runaway slaves, lest soon the community be raided by whole gangs." Hoping to pit enslaved Africans against Native Americans, he argued that French authorities should hire "neighboring Indians" as runaway hunters. Fearing their combined power, Governor Étienne Boucher de Périer urged the end of Native enslavement, claiming that "these Indian slaves being mixed with our negroes may induce them to desert with them." Attempts to navigate the intricacies of Native politics, however, failed more often than not. Recognizing the threat posed by the expanding plantation frontier, Natchez Indians allied themselves with African maroons. In November 1729, their combined forces massacred 230 French colonists, one-eighth of Louisiana's European population.

Maroons remained a persistent irritant in the development of a slave society in colonial Louisiana. French and Spanish court records reveal that a steady stream of enslaved Louisianans took flight, though these records only offer hints at the size and scope of maroon communities. They lived on the fringes of the plantation landscape, opportunistically hunting cattle and pigs. These fragmentary glimpses suggest small maroon settlements, usually no more than a half dozen individuals, with deep personal and economic relationships with the enslaved population. Cypress logging gave unsupervised slaves and maroons opportunities to trade and socialize in the swamp, and sometimes they also developed strategic partnerships with white Louisianans, exchanging their labor in the swamp for food and other supplies. Far from being isolated within the depths of the swamp, maroons were embedded in complex social, economic, and political networks.[18]

Environmental factors constrained the size of maroon communities in colonial Louisiana. The topography of Louisiana swamps limited the amount of arable land that maroons could farm. While Lowcountry maroons established robust gardens in the swamp, Louisiana maroons had more limited options. Pierre-Louis Berquin-Duvallon, a French refugee who fled to Spanish Louisiana during the Haitian Revolution, described the region as "low and swampy . . . drowned by the river, uninhabited and uninhabitable, where only a wild and misshapen vegetation subsists; wet rushes, or trees whose trunks stand in the mud, and are covered with divers reptiles, and troublesome insects." Rather than in fortified settlements, like in the Lowcountry or in the Great Dismal Swamp, the environment forced Louisiana maroons to live in small camps, dispersed among acres of bayou.[19]

Louisiana's largest documented maroon community lived in the swamps between New Orleans and the mouth of the Mississippi in a region they called Terre Gaillarde—"land full of life." Access to Terre Gaillarde required wading through chest-high water, in reedy marshes, and through dense woods, rendering the maroon landscape invisible to the uninitiated. With its population only slightly upwards of one hundred people, this maroon community used the environment's inhospitality as its primary defensive strategy. Spread thinly over a vast territory, Terre Gaillarde maroons remained highly mobile, disappearing at the sign of interlopers, while still able to leave the swamp when opportunities for trade presented themselves. Indeed, they sometimes visited New Orleans at night to barter for ammunition, food, and other supplies. During the 1770s, this vast maroon community fell under the leadership of a mysterious figure whose name in Spanish records appears variously as St. Malo, Juan Malo, and San Malo.

Starting in March 1783, Spanish authorities began a series of raids into Terre Gaillarde. Over the next two months, they captured forty-three maroons, but St. Malo remained at large. Recognizing the indefensibility of the swamp, he relocated the remaining maroons to the outskirts of a plantation at the English Turn, twelve miles southeast of New Orleans, where they spent the winter. There they traded with enslaved people, acquiring sufficient ammunition and supplies to return to the swamp. In the meantime, Spanish authorities in New Orleans prepared for a second set of raids into the swamp. Governor Miró issued a series of regulations to isolate maroons from the enslaved and free people of color. Over the next several months, Spanish forces attempted to capture St. Malo and his small band, while the maroons successfully raided plantation warehouses with impunity. "All these swamps are so terrible and so vast that it is impossible to attack all the maroon settlements which are spread out in the swamps," complained one Spanish official. The maroons' luck would not hold out, however. In June 1784, Spanish militiamen tracked down St. Malo's band in the swamp, fired on them, and pursued them through waist-deep water. They captured seventeen maroons, including St. Malo himself. Along with three of his lieutenants, St. Malo was executed after a brief trial, while the other captured maroons received brandings and as many as three hundred lashes.[20]

Some Spanish officials heralded St. Malo's capture as the end of the maroon problem. Yet within a decade there were renewed calls for action against runaway slaves in the swamps. In 1798, Governor Manuel Gayoso de Lemos pledged military action to purge "any district of lower Louisiana a large number of fugitives, either hidden in the wilderness or in a fortified settlement." Yet, like his predecessors, Gayoso did not have the resources necessary to patrol the swamps for maroons or the understanding of the local environment needed to find them. Indeed, Berquin-Duvallon observed that after nearly a century of French and Spanish occupation, no adequate map of the lower Mississippi existed, a failure he attributed to "the careless of the government, and the indifference of the colonists." Beyond the riverside plantation belt lay only terra incognito.[21]

The situation did not change significantly with American administration. In 1804, Governor William C. C. Claiborne attempted to entice maroons to leave the swamp and return to the plantation. He believed that "fear of punishment" kept them "in the woods and swamps, where they are necessarily subjected to inquietude, and compelled to seek a livelihood by plundering, to the great injury and terror of the good inhabitants." Claiborne offered a general amnesty to all maroons "who have no other offence, but that of running away" who returned to their purported owners, promising they "shall receive no punishment of any kind." He gave them a two-month deadline, after which they would "be pursued, and may receive such punishment as their owner or owners, may under the Law, choose to inflict." Claiborne's proclamation had little effect. Although he posted the offer of amnesty in French and English in public locations and in the newspaper, maroons in the swamp had little incentive to believe the promises of this new administrator or his ability to dictate to slave owners how they should treat returning maroons. Moreover, Claiborne did not have the military resources needed to effectively drive them out of the swamps, as his proclamation claimed.[22]

Demographic and environmental change ultimately did more to suppress Louisiana's maroon population than military action. After 1820, the state's booming enslaved population provided the labor force to build and maintain not only robust levees to restrain the Mississippi but also a series of canals that drained millions of acres of swamp, opening them up for cultivation. Cypress swamps gave way to sugar and rice plantations. American occupation imposed upon a wet Mississippi valley the image of a dry agricultural landscape. By 1860, Louisiana had lost a significant amount of its wetlands. Even against this environmental transformation, enslaved people continued to flee to the swamp. In 1836, newspapers reported that "a band of runaway negroes in the Cypress Swamp" near New Orleans "had been committing depredations." In 1854, a French-language newspaper reported that many "nègres maroons" were found living in cabins in the woods and swamps along the German Coast. Antebellum Louisiana newspapers treated maroons more as a curiosity than an existential threat to slavery. While maroons continued to prey upon livestock, their numbers dwindled on the fringes of a robust slave society.[23]

Those who ventured deep into Louisiana's swamps still encountered maroons. In the 1820s, ornithologist John James Audubon frequently explored the remote corners of the bayou, miles from the nearest plantation. Traveling with his dog, Audubon worried about encountering alligators but rarely saw other people. During one sweltering summer day, "laden with a pack consisting of five or six Wood Ibises, and a heavy gun," he heard "a stentorial voice [that] commanded me to 'stand still, or die!'" Startled, Audubon raised and cocked his gun when "a tall firmbuilt Negro emerged from the bushy underwood," armed with a rusty firearm. Cautiously, both men lowered their weapons, perhaps recognizing that neither wanted a violent confrontation. "I am a runaway," admitted the maroon, pleading, "Do not kill me." Incredulous that anyone could live in the swamp, Audubon asked, "Why . . . have you left your quarters, where certainly you must have fared better than in these un-wholesome swamps?" In Audubon's retelling, his interlocutor didn't answer directly, claiming, "My story is a short, but a sorrowful one," before making Audubon an offer: "My camp is close by, and as I know you cannot reach home this night, if you will follow me there, depend upon *my honour* you shall be safe until the morning, when I will carry your birds, if you choose, to the great road." Audubon accepted the unexpected offer, and the pair headed deeper among the trees. No stranger to the swamp, Audubon marveled at the maroon's ability to maneuver through the environment. Just before they arrived at the camp, the maroon "emitted a loud shriek, not unlike that of an owl" to alert his family to their approach.

"There, in the heart of the cane-brake," Audubon recalled, "I found a regular camp." Nestled in the swamp, the maroon family had "various articles of household furniture" and a pile of bear and deer skins that served as a communal bed. Venison and sweet potatoes roasted on the fire. While his wife and their three children eyed Audubon suspiciously, the Runaway (as Audubon called him) provided him with hearty portions of venison, arranged his clothes to dry by the fire, and offered to oil his musket. Only then did he reveal the circumstances that led him to live in the swamp. Eighteen months prior, their owner had gone into debt, prompting an auction of his human property. To his horror, the Runaway saw each member of his family purchased by a different planter. Shortly thereafter, "on a stormy night, when the elements raged with all the fury of a hurricane," he had run away to the swamp and established the camp in the cane break. In the weeks that followed, he managed to find his wife and children and bring them back with him "until at last the whole objects of his love were under his care."

Despite the remoteness of their camp, the maroon family had never been cut off from broader enslaved social networks. At night, the Runaway had frequently returned to his previous owner's plantation, where enslaved friends provided him with supplies, including ammunition. During the day, he hunted deer and gathered berries in the swamp. Yet he did not see the swamp as a permanent home for himself and his family. The Runaway begged Audubon to intercede on their behalf with their previous owner. According to Audubon's account, the following morning the party of six left the swamp, and Audubon arranged for their previous owner to repurchase the family and "treated them with his former kindness; so that they were rendered as happy as slaves generally are in that country." While Audubon may have exaggerated or embellished this episode for dramatic effect, the plight of the maroon family in his narrative reflected the daunting choices that enslaved people had in antebellum Louisiana. "To provide for five individuals was no easy task in those wilds," Audubon observed. While the swamp served as a sanctuary for many enslaved people, it was rarely a paradise.[24]

While running away to the swamp became increasingly difficult, enslaved people in Louisiana continued to use the wetlands. Scant rations compelled Solomon Northup "to hunt in the swamps for coon and opossum." He observed, "There are planters whose slaves, for months at a time, have no other meat than such that is attained in this manner." Yet Northup only entered the swamp with apprehension. The "interminable swamps," he warned, were "alive with aligators, rendering it unsafe for swine, or unthinking slave children to stroll along its banks." Northup only entered the swamp when he had no other choice. Fleeing from an enraged overseer, he elected "to be a wanderer among the swamps, a fugitive and a vagabond on the face of the earth." Pursued by bloodhounds, he entered the "Great Pacoudrie Swamp." Among the "immense trees—the sycamore, the gum, the cotton wood and cypress," Northup believed he had escaped his hunters into a world "without inhabitants, save wild beasts." He expressed justified fears at the ubiquitous water moccasins and alligators. Yet his previous time in the swamp and knowledge he acquired from other enslaved people had prepared him. He understood what to do if he came "directly upon a monster before observing it": by running in a zigzag, he emerged from alligator attacks unharmed. "Straight forward, they will run a short distance rapidly, but do not possess the power of turning," he noted. "In a crooked race, there is no difficulty in evading them."[25]

Many enslaved people in Louisiana shared Northup's aversion to the swamps. After he was apprehended trying to escape through the swamp with his wife and child, Henry Bibb described the experience as horrifying. "What would induce me to take my family and go into the Red river swamps of Louisiana among the snakes and alligators, with all the liabilities of being destroyed by them, hunted down with blood hounds, or lay myself liable to be shot down like the wild beasts of the forest? Nothing I say, nothing but the strongest love of liberty, humanity, and justice to myself and family, would induce me to run such a risk again."[26]

Great Dismal Swamp

The most successful maroon community in the American South lived in a swamp whose forbidding name belied a rich ecosystem. Straddling the border between North Carolina and Virginia, the Great Dismal Swamp covered some two thousand square miles. At its heart lay Lake Drummond, an enormous circular basin stretching over more than three thousand acres. Tannin-rich peat stained the water a deep walnut brown, disguising perch, catfish, and longnose gar in its shallow depths. Along the lake's edge and throughout the swamp stood enormous bald cypress, some more than a thousand years old. Dense forests of white cedar and black gum grew in acidic black peat, the product of several millennia of decaying vegetation. Maroons shared the swamp with black bears, beavers, bobcats, bald eagles, panthers, white-tailed deer, and warblers. Dense swarms of mosquitoes fed on everything that moved. Impenetrable on horseback, much of the swamp sat under several inches of water, with more than two hundred hillocks forming inhabitable islands.

Compared to those in the Lowcountry and Louisiana, the Dismal Swamp maroon communities were more populated and more durable. While the earliest textual references to maroons in the Great Dismal Swamp date from the 1720s, archaeological evidence indicates maroon occupation from 1660 onwards. Maroons lived in the Great Dismal continuously until the Civil War, two hundred years later. The maroon community included not only enslaved people who fled to the swamp but several generations born and raised there. At its apex, hundreds, possibly thousands, of maroons lived in the swamp.[27]

Their presence was no secret. White Southerners knew about the Dismal Swamp maroons and made regular reference to their existence. By the mid-nineteenth century, the Dismal Swamp maroons had become common knowledge and featured in popular poetry and literature. In 1842, Henry Wadsworth Longfellow composed "The Slave in the Dismal Swamp." The poem described an elderly maroon, dressed in rags, heavily scarred, and living like an animal:

> *In dark fens of the Dismal Swamp*
> *The hunted Negro lay;*
> *He saw the fire of the midnight camp,*
> *And heard at times a horse's tramp*
> *And a bloodhound's distant bay.*

The Dismal Swamp also served as a venue for Frederick Douglass's 1853 novella *The Heroic Slave*. The protagonist, Madison Washington (named for the two Virginia statesmen–slave owners), had escaped from a plantation to find sanctuary in the swamp. "In the dismal swamps I lived, sir, five old years," he reveals, "a cave for my home during the day. I wandered about at night with the wolf and the bear." In 1856, Harriet Beecher Stowe's follow-up to *Uncle Tom's Cabin* saw the swamp as a site of revolutionary politics among the maroons. The titular character in *Dred: A Tale of the Dismal Swamp*, based on Denmark Vesey and Nat Turner, escaped from the plantation to come a messianic leader in the swamp, with a divine mission to assist fugitive slaves.[28]

One of the earliest references to maroons in the Great Dismal Swamp came from Virginia planter William Byrd II, who chronicled his experience as part of a 1728 expedition surveying the border between Virginia and North Carolina. Locals warned Byrd away, claiming the entire region "full of bogs, of marshes and swamps, not fit for human creatures." Few whites had ventured into the swamp, which was dark and foreboding. "How little the bordering inhabitants were acquainted with this mighty swamp," Byrd noted, "notwithstanding they had lived their whole lives within smell of it." In the swamp's depths, the survey party came across "a family of mullatoes that called themselves free," though Byrd surmised based on their skittishness that "their freedom seemed a little doubtful." While the survey party did not encounter any other maroons, he believed that many more fugitives lived in the swamp. "It is certain many slaves shelter themselves in this obscure part of the world," Byrd noted. Without the introduction of regular patrols of the swamp, he expected that their numbers would grow over time.[29]

Byrd loathed his time in the Dismal Swamp. "Never was rum," he wrote, "that cordial of life, found more necessary than it was in this dirty place." However, after he returned to his Westover plantation, he hatched a plan for transforming the swamp into an agricultural paradise. While "the ground of this swamp is a meer [*sic*] quagmire, trembling under the feet of those that walk upon it," Byrd wrote, "if any way could be found to drain it," the swamp would become "the fittest soil in the world." He proposed constructing a canal that ran through the swamp "betwixt Virginia and North Carolina," which would have the twin benefits of draining the swamp and improving commerce between the neighboring colonies. His proposal fell on deaf ears, and the Great Dismal Swamp remained largely closed to outsiders for a generation.[30]

In 1763, a dozen Virginia planters decided to put Byrd's plans into action, forming the Adventurers to Drain the Great Dismal Swamp, a corporation dedicated to "draining Improving and Saving the Land." Later rebranded the Dismal Swamp Company, it purchased forty thousand acres of wetlands, intending to convert them into productive farmland. Having surveyed the swamp, proprietor George Washington took command of the company's ground operations the following year. Working from a farm on the edge of the swamp (Dismal Plantation), fifty enslaved people commenced digging a ditch through the black peat. Three feet deep, ten feet wide, and nearly five miles long, the Washington Ditch ran from Dismal Plantation to Lake Drummond and was intended to drain the adjoining wetlands. Work on the ditch proved slower, more labor intensive, and more expensive than the proprietors expected. To defray costs, enslaved workers cut roofing shingles from the swamp's white cedar. After a decade of work, the company had little to show for its efforts.[31]

The Revolution brought a temporary halt to work in the swamp. In 1775, one visitor to the Great Dismal Swamp noted that its depths were "in a great degree inaccessible, and harbour prodigious multitudes of every kind of wild beast." The swamp's maroon community was an open secret, as even visitors had heard of the "run-away negroes, who in these horrible swamps are perfectly safe, and with the greatest facility elude the most diligent search of their pursuers." Within the swamp's recesses, they had established a permanent settlement, where "run-away Negroes have resided in these places for twelve, twenty, or thirty years and upwards," living "on some of the spots not perpetually under water, nor subject to be flooded, as forty-nine parts of fifty of it are; and on such spots they have erected habitations, and cleared small fields around them; yet these have always been perfectly impenetrable to any of the inhabitants of the country around, even to those nearest to and best acquainted with the swamps." Two years later, another visitor noted that "the Great Dismal Swamp . . . was infested with concealed royalists, and runaway negroes, who could not be approached with safety."[32]

In the Revolution's aftermath, Washington and other land speculators began planning for a more extensive intervention. They envisioned a canal running through the swamp connecting the Elizabeth River in Virginia to the Pasquotank in North Carolina, thereby creating a water route between the Chesapeake and the Albemarle Sound. After twelve years of construction, the Dismal Swamp Canal opened in 1805. Twenty-two miles long, the canal ran north-south along the eastern edge of the swamp. By 1820, several other adjoining canals crisscrossed the swamp. In 1830, a hotel opened where the canal crossed the Virginia–North Carolina border, "furnished with the choicest wines and liquors of every description." By the time of Nat Turner's rebellion in nearby Southampton County, these canals carried a robust commerce: barrels of turpentine, bushels of potatoes and peas, crates of candles and nails. The heaviest traffic, however, came from timber extracted from the swamp itself, as enslaved labor converted white cedar and cypress into barrel staves, shingles, mast timber, and fence rails.[33]

Enslaved workers built the canals through the Great Dismal Swamp under brutal conditions. "The labour there is very severe," recalled Moses Grandy, an enslaved North Carolinian who piloted canal boats through the swamp. "The ground is often very boggy: the negroes are up to the middle or much deeper in mud and water, cutting away roots and baling out mud: if they can keep their heads above water, they work on." Those who failed to work to the overseer's demanding pace received floggings that Grandy characterized as "extreme torture." Living in camps, enslaved workers had only rudimentary shelter "made of shingles or boards. They lie down in the mud which has adhered to them, making a great fire to dry themselves, and keep off the cold. No bedding whatever is allowed them; it is only by work done over his task, that any of them can get a blanket." High mortality rates among canal workers prompted planters to charge a premium before agreeing to rental agreements in the swamp.[34]

Even after the canal's construction, most of the Great Dismal remained a mystery to outsiders—dark, forbidding, and unmapped. Few white Southerners ventured into the swamp's interior if they could help it. One canal passenger noted that "travelling here without pistols is considered very dangerous, owing to the great number of runaway negroes. They conceal themselves in the woods & swamps by day and frequently plunder at night."[35] According to Edmund Ruffin, "Few strangers would ever have been induced

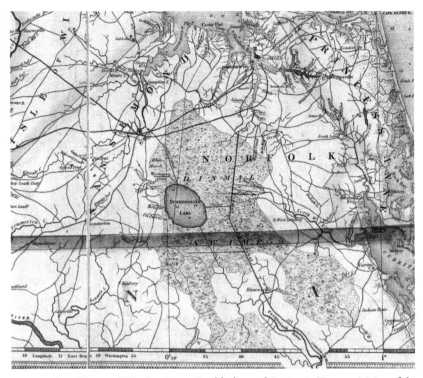

FIGURE 6.3. Herman Böÿe, Lewis von Buchholtz, and Benjamin Tanner, A Map of the
State of Virginia (1859). Library of Congress.

by curiosity to attempt the great labors necessary for even a slight investigation." In late 1836, Ruffin ventured into this "unknown land," chronicling his
observations for the readers of *The Farmers' Register*. With the swamp covering more than a million acres, Ruffin claimed, "The whole of this extensive
region is one great morass, or quagmire" such that "the swamp furnishes very
difficult ground to travel upon. . . . It is difficult to imagine a sufficient motive to have induced any man to penetrate a mile into the swamp." Ruffin
saw in the swamp a record of a lost nature; animals that had been driven to
extinction in the rest of Virginia over the past two centuries lived on in the
swamp: bears, wild cats, and wolves.

Yet the swamp was not uninhabited. "The only sign of life was seen at
intervals in a 'camp' of a pair of shingle-getters," Ruffin wrote. "Their houses,
or shanties, are barely wide enough for five or six men to lie in, closely packed
side by side—their heads to the back wall, and their feet stretched to the
open front, close by a fire kept up through the night." He estimated that five
hundred enslaved men labored in the Great Dismal in the shingle industry.

If Ruffin saw any evidence of the maroon population in the swamp, he made no mention of it. He closed the essay by assessing "the feasibility and policy of draining this immense body of swamp." He argued that a new canal could effectively bring thousands of acres of "fertile land . . . into cultivation," though he had doubts about how realistic this was. To add historical gravitas to his article, Ruffin appended William Byrd's essay from the previous century.[36]

Lumbering in the swamp fell into seasonal patterns. In early February, enslaved men entered the swamp and erected camps on high ground, usually near a canal. They constructed elevated huts built on piers or the wood shavings from the previous season. Lumbering continued until June, when the enslaved workers had a brief respite from the swamp to resupply, and they resumed for another five months, sometimes in a new part of the swamp. Lumbering offered enslaved men more liberty than plantation life. If he met his shingle quota, "the slave lumberman then lives measurably as a free man," noted one visitor. He "hunts, fishes, eats, drinks, smokes and sleeps, plays and works, each when and as much as he pleases." Lumbermen also received better rations than plantation slaves and often received small payments if they exceeded their quota. Work in the swamp, however, required enslaved men to spend most of the year away from their families.[37]

Enslaved lumbermen often worked and traded with Great Dismal maroons. In many lumber camps, maroons contributed significantly to the production of shingles, exchanging them for cloth, tobacco, salted meat, whiskey, and ammunition. White overseers often turned a blind eye to the work that maroons performed in the swamp, benefiting from the increased shingle production that maroons enabled. Some maroons passed themselves off as free, receiving two dollars a month for their work in the swamp. "The runaways were the hardest workers of his gang," admitted one overseer. A North Carolinian observed that "men have made fortunes from the labour of fugitive slaves whom they would not question." Archaeological excavations of a maroon camp not far from one of the canals revealed machine-cut nails, gun flints, lead glass bottles, and a cobalt-blue glazed bowl, indicative of the robust trade between maroons there and the outside world. Maroons benefited from this arrangement not only in securing material goods but also in the knowledge they acquired from enslaved lumbermen about their families and friends still in bondage.[38]

While some white Southerners profited from working with Dismal Swamp maroons, the planter elite decried this elicit commerce. In 1816, a Virginia slave owner offered one hundred dollars reward for the return of

enslaved man named George Hicks, whom he believed was employed in the
Great Dismal Swamp by "a *White Person* in procuring Shingles and other
Lumber." In 1822, the North Carolina General Assembly passed a bill to encourage slave catchers to hunt down fugitives who had fled to the swamp.
Recognizing that it proved "dangerous and difficult to apprehend runaway
slaves who have secreted themselves in the great dismal swamp," the bill provided that slave catchers would receive a quarter of the runaway's value as
a bounty, ten times the going rate. Repealed a year later, probably because
the compensation proved too generous, the bill was not the last time North
Carolina's legislature tried to crack down on the swamp's maroon population.
In 1847, it passed "An Act to Provide for the Apprehension of Runaway Slaves
in the Great Dismal Swamp and for Other Purposes." The presence of such a
large Black population outside of white authority, they argued, posed a fundamental threat to the integrity of the peculiar institution. "Consorting with
such white men and free persons of color," the law claimed, maroons "remain
setting at defiance the power of their masters, corrupting and reducing their
slaves, and by their evil example and evil practices, lessening their due sub-
ordination and greatly impairing the value of the slaves in the district of the
country bordering on the said dismall [*sic*] swamp." The law established a reg-
istry of enslaved and free Black workers in the swamp, providing "an exact
description," including name, height, "complexion, and every peculiar mark."
It dictated that undocumented lumbermen would receive thirty-nine lashes,
as would documented workers found working alongside maroons, while the
white men employing them faced a $100 fine.[39]

Conditions in the swamp deteriorated in the decades prior to the Civil
War. Archaeological evidence suggests that maroon camps supported smaller
populations after 1830. In the aftermath of Nat Turner's revolt, many whites
living near the swamp feared that armed maroons would be at the vanguard
of an enslaved uprising. They believed that Nat Turner planned to "con-
quer Southampton County . . . , and then retreat, if necessary, to the Dismal
Swamp." In the rebellion's aftermath, Federal soldiers stationed in Old Point
Comfort, Virginia, "were ordered to scour the Dismal Swamp, where it was
believed that two or three thousand fugitives were preparing to join the
insurgents." In the years that followed, slave patrols in and near the swamp became more common, requiring maroons to take further precautions. Fugitive
hunters sometimes braved the swamp to reclaim runaway slaves. Knowing
that the maroons were often armed, they only ventured into the Great
Dismal in force and proved quick to violence. "Dreadful scenes, I tell ye,
'sperienced in de Dismal Swamp," recalled one maroon who eventually made

it to freedom in Canada. "When de masters comes dar," he remembered, "dey shoot down runaways, and tink no more sendin' a ball t'rough dar hearts." In 1848, Frederick Douglass's *North Star* reported that "parties of young men, with dogs, have hunted out these poor creatures; and, to use the expression of my informant, have 'shot them down like partridges.'" The maroons fought back, "armed with pistols," but the better equipped "man-hunters, with their longer and heavier guns," prevailed, shooting several maroons and returning several of the wounded to their purported owners. Slave patrols made farming within the swamp more challenging, compelling maroons to trade with enslaved people and poor whites. Born in 1854 on a Virginia plantation just north of the Great Dismal, Sis Shackleford recalled, "The runaway slaves used to come out from the Dismal Swamp and beg us for food. At first we was scared to death of them and just fly, but after while we used to steal bread and fresh meat and give it to 'em. But they never would let you follow 'em. They hide in the Dismal Swamp in holes in the ground so hidden they stay there years and white folks, dogs, or nothin' else could find 'em."[40]

While some Dismal Swamp maroons lived and worked in close proximity to the canal and lumber camps, others did everything in their power to isolate themselves in the swamp's hinterland. Especially for maroon women and children, remote corners of the swamp proved the safest. "Dar is families growed up in dat ar Dismal Swamp dat never seed a white man," recalled one former maroon, "an' would be skeered most to def to see one." Generations of maroons lived with little contact with the outside world. While seclusion within the swamp provided a modicum of safety, their isolation had material consequences. Archaeological excavations of a maroon camp deep within the swamp, dubbed "the nameless site" by archaeologist Daniel Sayers because the name that maroons called it remains a mystery, reveals that hinterland maroons had a much more modest existence than those who lived closer to the lumber camps. Manufactured goods proved extremely rare, and those that did make their way into the depths of the swamp were reused and reworked extensively: glass and metal items that began as bottles and saws became trinkets and jewelry. Residents of the nameless site relied on what they could make in the swamp. They lived in cabins and on elevated platforms built between cypress trees. Deep within the swamp, they grew corn and sweet potatoes, trapped turtles and opossums, and hunted deer and bear. They also feasted upon domesticated cattle and hogs that farmers allowed to wander in the swamp. For clothing, they relied on racoon and deer skins. Cut off from the broader world in the swamp's interior, maroons built self-sustaining communities that maintained themselves for generations.[41]

When Frederick Olmsted visited the Great Dismal in 1853, he witnessed the effects of several decades of intensive logging. "Nearly all the valuable trees have now been cut off from the swamp," he observed. "The whole ground has been frequently gone over, the best timber selected and removed at each time." He envisioned that shingle production in the Great Dismal would come to a close in the near future, as timber barons plotted to relocate their enslaved labor force to the Everglades. In its aftermath, Olmsted foresaw "some extensive scheme of draining and reclaiming" the swamp, as the ground seemed "suitable for rice culture." On the swamp's fringes, he had witnessed drained swampland converted to profitable corn fields.

The intensive shingle extraction had a significant impact on the swamp's maroon population. "The Dismal Swamps are noted places of refuge for runaway negroes," he observed, but "they were formerly peopled in this way much more than at present; a systematic hunting of them with dogs and guns" ten years ago had reduced their numbers. The persistence of the maroon community in the swamp amazed Olmsted. "There are people in the swamps now," he wrote, "that are the children of fugitives and fugitives themselves all their lives." Yet the encroachment of white Southerners into the swamp had made even the most remote corners vulnerable. The canal network, intensive timber extraction, and plantation development on the swamp's edges all created vulnerabilities for Dismal Swamp maroons. "They cannot obtain the means of supporting life without coming often either to the outskirts to steal from the plantations, or to the neighborhood of the camps of the lumbermen," Olmsted observed. "They depend much upon the charity or the wages given them by the latter."[42]

A few years after Olmsted's visit, another New York–based journalist visited the Great Dismal. Writing under the name Porte Crayon, *Harper's Monthly* author and illustrator David Hunter Strother had read about its maroon population. "The Swamp is said to be inhabited by a number of escaped slaves, who spend their lives, and even raise families, in its impenetrable fastnesses," Strother wrote. "I had long nurtured a wish to see one of those sable outlaws who dwell in the fastness of the Swamp; who, from impatience of servitude, or to escape the consequences of crime, have fled from society, and take up their abode among the wild beasts of the wilderness." Traveling from the town of Suffolk, Virginia, to Lake Drummond on a canal barge, Strother could not see far into the swamp, his view blocked by the "thick undergrowth" lining the canal. Locals warned him against wandering too far into the swamp. The maroons, they cautioned, were dangerous. He heard, however, that maroons often worked with enslaved lumbermen, so "although

I have been told there would danger in any attempt to gratify this fancy, I determined to visit the spot where the shingle-makers were at work." Along the canal, they stopped at a logging camp. Its residents away at work, Strother saw the "accommodation for a number of men and mules." His inspection was interrupted by the arrival of mule carts, laden with shingles and driven by enslaved boys.

Eager to see a maroon if he could, Strother left the camp and "made [his] way with the greatest difficulty through the tangled undergrowth." Exhausted after crawling and scampering through the swamp, Strother stopped cold when he heard footsteps. He then caught a glimpse of what he presumed was a maroon:

FIGURE 6.4. Osman. *Harper's New Monthly Magazine* 13 (1856): 452.

About thirty paces from me I saw a gigantic negro, with a tattered blanket wrapped about his shoulders, and a gun in his hand. He head was bare, and he had little other clothing than a pair of ragged breeches and boots. His hair and beard were tipped with gray, and his purely African features were cast in a mould betokening, in the highest degree, strength and energy. The expression of the face was of mingled fear and ferocity, and every movement betrayed a life of habitual caution and watchfulness. He reached forward his iron hand to clear away the briery screen that half concealed him while it interrupted his scrutinizing glance.

Strother only exhaled when the sound of the maroon's footsteps faded, believing that his presence had gone undetected during their brief encounter. He quickly returned to the lumber camp, where he drew "a hasty sketch of the remarkable figure," which he intentionally left out in the open, in case anyone recognized him. Some of the enslaved workers congregated around the drawing, whispering excitedly, and Strother distinctly heard them utter the name Osman, but when he questioned them directly, they feigned ignorance.[43]

Local folklore suggests that Osman had escaped slavery in North Carolina and fled to the Great Dismal Swamp, where he led an armed maroon band. Known as the "king of the swamp," Osman was rumored to possess supernatural powers, including "the power of speech with snakes and animals of the forest and cypress swamps." Yet the swamp also proved his undoing: tradition indicates that he died from a cottonmouth bite. As part of the last generation of Dismal Swamp maroons, Osman drew upon two centuries of local knowledge about how to live in a hostile environment. Dismal Swamp maroons managed to survive in part because they learned how use the swamp's size and natural obstacles to their advantage. Despite efforts to drain the swamp and exploit its resources, maroons created an ecological niche for themselves, adapting to profoundly challenging circumstances.[44]

7

Landscape of Freedom

ENVIRONMENTAL DESTRUCTION UNDERGIRDED the argument for Southern secession and the formation of the Confederacy. For more than a century, the planter class had relied upon the expanding slavery frontier, replacing worn-out soils and denuded landscapes with fresh western lands. This constant pressure shaped Southern politics throughout the antebellum era, driving Indian removal, territorial expansion, and military policy. The Republican Party's call for restricting the spread of slavery into the territories threatened the peculiar institution's expansion, which many fire-eaters saw as an existential threat. "The security and honor of the South demands that she should maintain her equal rights in the Territories," concluded a December 1856 resolution at the Savannah Southern Convention. "She should resist at every cost any attempt, whenever made, to exclude her" from those lands. "The system of slave labor requires more space," Virginia fire-eater Edmund Ruffin proclaimed in 1857. Recent efforts to restrict its growth, he argued, demonstrated that Northern states could not be trusted and that the only option remaining to preserve a social and economic order built on enslaved labor was secession and the formation of a Southern Confederacy. Any military efforts by the North to defeat this new slave-holding republic, Ruffin predicted, were doomed to failure.[1]

Some Southern nationalists concluded that only an independent slave-holding republic could save the region from ruin. The economic prosperity of the early 1850s that enriched the planter class had left many non-slave-owning white Southerners behind. "The wealth and strength of the South lie in its agricultural resources," Georgia journalist James Gardner wrote in January 1858, but that success had come at a great cost. "No thoughtful, intelligent man can survey the old fields from the Chesapeake to the Mississippi," he observed, "and not bear witness to the fact that there is something fundamentally wrong

Scars on the Land. David Silkenat, Oxford University Press. © Oxford University Press 2022.
DOI: 10.1093/oso/9780197564226.003.0008

in Southern agriculture." As the cotton frontier stretched westward, "our present practice of skinning and bleeding the soil" had left behind "millions of
acres of impoverished lands." Gardner blamed this crisis on the closing of the
Atlantic slave trade in 1808, which had created "great demand for negro labor
in all cotton, sugar and rice-growing districts, with the unavoidable high price
of slaves." As a consequence, Gardner argued, "planters have been placed in
that unnatural and unwise position which renders it more profitable to wear
out the very cheap lands of the sunny South, than to maintain their virgin
fertility." Doubling during the 1850s, high slave prices had created a significant barrier for entry into the slaveholding classes. While nearly a third of
white families owned slaves at the start of the decade, only a quarter did so at
its conclusion. Gardner envisioned an alternative past in which the Atlantic
slave trade had remained open. "Had labor, during the last fifty years, been
approximately as cheap as farming lands, or were slaves now as cheap as plantations," he claimed, "they could be bought at prices that would enable every
enterprising man to improve his soil, and thus soon double the wealth and
every kind of business connect therewith, in the slaveholding States." The solution to its environmental crisis and the future of the South, he concluded,
depended on reopening the Atlantic slave trade. Gardner's voice joined a
chorus of fire-eaters and pro-slavery zealots who envisioned fleets of slave
ships arriving in Charleston and New Orleans.[2]

On the eve of secession, the environmental barriers to freedom remained
as daunting as they had ever been. In the aftermath of Harpers Ferry, white
Southerners embraced a hypervigilant paranoia, ramping up slave patrols
and on the constant lookout for Black insurgency. Yet many fugitive slaves
found the environmental obstacles to freedom more onerous than the human
barriers. "Late in the fall of the year 1860," Louisianan William Mallory saw
"the opportunity of escaping." Along with three other slaves, Mallory bolted
from his sugar plantation, avoiding roads and populated areas and keeping to
the woods. Fearful of recapture, they made slow progress, traveling mostly at
night. Hunted throughout by slave catchers and bloodhounds, the band fled
"from swamp to swamp and bush to bush, and frequently being compelled
to ford and swim streams in our efforts to throw the dogs off our tracks."
When their pursuers caught up with them, Mallory and his companions fled
in different directions, and he was "now forced to continue my way alone."
His route took him through the Appalachians, a land he described as "the
most dismal on the face of the earth." His journey north presented Mallory
with new environmental challenges. "To add to my sufferings and discomfort
I had to encounter the rigors of winter weather," he wrote. "The ice, sleet and

snow were unknown quantities to the slave, who had never before ventured so far north from the place of his birth, and the experience was by no means a pleasant one, unprovided as I was with clothing suitable for cold weather." Despite several close calls, Mallory successfully overcame the environmental and human barriers to freedom, arriving in Canada in time to hear the news of Abraham Lincoln's election and South Carolina's secession.[3]

In their debates over secession that winter, white Southerners drew upon well-established ideas about the relationship between enslaved Black labor and the environment. Only people of African descent, secessionists argued, could pick cotton, plant rice, or cut sugarcane under the Southern sun, and only slavery provided the discipline necessary to extract value from the soil. They articulated a national vision built on perpetuating slavery and the destructive land use patterns it engendered. One delegate to Alabama's January 1861 secession convention envisioned a united Southern confederacy that would boast "a salubrious climate, fertile soil, and nearly nine hundred thousand square miles of slave territory." Another delegate argued that their new slaveholding republic needed to expand, or it would suffer an environmental collapse. If constrained to its current borders, "much of our best soil would become exhausted" within a generation, and "slaves would become a charge upon their owner, and soon we would be compelled to emancipate them." The only alternative, he argued, was an aggressive policy of territorial acquisition. "Arizona and Mexico, Central America and Cuba," he noted, "all may yet be embraced within the limits of our Southern Republic." To remain vibrant, he argued, enslaved agriculture always needed its frontier of virgin soils, as "expansion seems to be the law and destiny and necessity of our institutions." Mississippi's convention embedded this link between slavery and the environment in its Declaration of Immediate Causes. "Our position is thoroughly identified with the institution of slavery—the greatest material interest of the world," the declaration asserted. King Cotton demanded a "climate verging on the tropical regions, and by an imperious law of nature, none but the black race can bear exposure to the tropical sun." A Republican administration, they argued, fundamentally threated this foundational premise, leaving them no choice but disunion.[4]

Intended to preserve the peculiar institution, the Confederacy sowed the seeds of its own demise. Drawing upon the long history of Southern land use, proponents of this new slaveholding republic articulated an environmental vision predicated on territorial expansion and enslaved Black labor. The grinding forces of civil war, however, accelerated both the destruction of slavery and an environmental revolution. Whenever the opportunity presented itself, enslaved African Americans fled to Union lines, drawing upon generations of environmental knowledge about how to navigate through the woods and swamps, how to nourish themselves on wild foods, and how to survive in inclement weather. This expertise not only proved invaluable in helping them escape from slavery but also contributed to national emancipation, as the Union military used Black knowledge and labor to bend the landscape to their advantage. Working as scouts and soldiers, African Americans guided Union forces through swamps and forest byways. As Union pioneers, African Americans rerouted rivers, constructed enormous earthworks, and felled forests for firewood and fortifications, backbreaking work that contributed to Confederate defeat and remade the landscape. The transition from enslaved labor to free labor had significant environmental consequences. Wartime destruction and slavery's demise prompted white and Black Southerners to reevaluate their relationship to the land, changes that would have profound consequences for generations to come.[5]

While Confederates celebrated the foundation of their new nation, many enslaved Southerners interpreted secession as a signal that the revolution against slavery had entered a new phase. This General Strike, as W. E. B. Du Bois dubbed it, took many forms: resisting the demands of enslavers, working less, stealing, and running away at unprecedented levels. When enslaved people fled bondage during the Civil War, they did so against a dynamic landscape. The environmentally destructive forces of Union and Confederate armies exacted a heavy toll on the Southern countryside. They left an enormous ecological footprint, stretching for miles in every direction, as soldiers voraciously consumed local timber, water, crops, and livestock. Millions of acres of forest fell to build fortifications, shelter, corduroy roads, and campfires. "The forest is fast disappearing before the axe of the stalwart solider," noted one Southern newspaper. The conflict also devastated the livestock that enslaved people relied upon prior to the war and freed people desperately needed in its aftermath. In many parts of the South, the war resulted in the disappearance of half of the hog population. While Confederate and Union armies confiscated and consumed millions of tons of pork, a hog cholera epidemic proved the real killer. Largely unknown in the antebellum South, the disease spread along roads, rails, and supply depots, as provost marshals channeled thousands of animals to hungry armies. While the war created the hog cholera epidemic, the disease devasted Southern swine populations for decades to come.[6]

Capricious Southern weather shaped both the movement of armies and the flight of enslaved people seeking freedom. Between 1856 and 1865, a sustained drought across much of the South baked fields and drained streambeds.

Influenced by the La Niña weather pattern, the "Civil War Drought" raised alarms about famine "as crops shriveled and cattle died from lack of water." The drought did not preclude fast-moving storms and heavy rains, and the conflict witnessed its fair share of flooding and muddy roads, as McClellan's soldiers discovered during the Peninsula Campaign in 1862 and Burnside's men found after Fredericksburg in January 1863.[7]

For enslaved people trying to escape to Union lines, the specific weather conditions during the war had significant consequences. A heatwave and a drought in the summer of 1862, for instance, lowered river levels in Virginia, prompting one Union officer to comment that "the hot sun of July was scorching... transforming the turbid mountain streams into sluggish currents." Low water levels and exposed riverbeds made fording easier for thousands of African Americans who crossed the Rappahannock River that summer. Taken shortly before Second Bull Run, Timothy O'Sullivan's photograph of five Black refugees in a wagon and on horseback crossing the Rappahannock in August 1862 shows the effects of the drought. The water at the cow ford where they crossed usually reached the knee or, during a freshet, the waist, but on that day the river had been reduced to a slow-moving creek, only half its normal span. No more than a few inches deep, it barely covered the hooves of the emaciated horse ridden by a barefoot Black adolescent. Atop the wagon, one of the women shaded her face with a bonnet to protect her from the heat and glare of the midday sun. The four oxen pulling the wagon showed signs of malnourishment, the drought parching Virginia's grasses. Nearby, a detachment of Union cavalrymen allowed their thirsty horses to drink. Without the drought, O'Sullivan's picture would have shown a very different scene, possibly one in which the self-emancipating African Americans remained stranded on the other side of the river.[8]

While La Niña cycles usually produce stronger and more frequent Atlantic hurricanes, this trend did not hold during the Civil War, one of the quietest periods in recorded storm history. Nonetheless, two hurricanes in 1861 shaped the early progress of emancipation. On September 27–29, a swift-moving hurricane hit North Carolina's Outer Banks and hugged the coast up into the Chesapeake Bay, inundating the nascent contraband community established a few months earlier at Fortress Monroe.[9] A little over a month later, a much larger hurricane nearly destroyed Flag Officer Samuel F. DuPont's fleet bound from Hampton Roads for Port Royal, South Carolina, causing even the largest ships to "twist, roll and writhe." DuPont lost several ships to the storm, though most of the soldiers and sailors were rescued. Severely battered and waterlogged, the crippled fleet managed to take the poorly defended

FIGURE 7.1. Timothy H. O'Sullivan, "Rappahannock River, Va. Fugitive African Americans fording the Rappahannock." Library of Congress.

Confederate fortifications. When both Confederate soldiers and plantation owners took flight, more than eight thousand African Americans cheered the victorious Union soldiers and sailors. At the epicenter of the long-staple cotton kingdom, Port Royal became one of the first wartime experiments in free Black labor.[10]

The only other hurricane to make landfall in the United States during the conflict struck during the last week of May 1863. Modern climatologists have dubbed it Hurricane Amanda, after the USS *Amanda*, part of the blockade fleet that was driven ashore on Dog Island, Florida. The storm hit near Apalachicola on the morning of May 28, well before the traditional hurricane season. At least 110 people died in the storm, including "some forty white men and negroes" at Confederate salt works near St. Marks and Bayport. Many of these sites had been bombarded by Union naval artillery the previous September but were quickly rebuilt. In the aftermath of the hurricane, enslaved laborers again reconstructed the damaged salt works.[11]

Enslaved people drew upon their prewar knowledge of the environment to help them reach Union lines. Their intimate familiarity with the local geography enabled them to evade slave patrols and Confederate pickets. "They know every road and swamp and creek and plantation in the country," noted Georgia planter Rev. Charles Colcock Jones in 1862. Their geographic knowledge enabled them not only to escape but also to aid the enemy, making them "the worst of spies." Jones believed that they would return, leading Union soldiers to kill him and his family. However, environmental barriers also shaped who could reach Union lines. Enslaved in North Carolina, Hattie Rogers observed that "all who could swim the [White Oak] river and get to the Yankees were free." Rogers recalled that "lots of slaves" managed to escape from Onslow County to Union-occupied New Bern, but that many more, including herself and her mother, remained enslaved throughout the war.[12]

Enslaved accounts of escape during the Civil War reveal how fugitives used their environmental and geographic knowledge to secure their own freedom. Sold from Virginia to Alabama in 1860, fourteen-year-old Wallace Turnage immediately decided to run away, claiming that he intended to "go in the woods and go back to where I come from." The repeated sight of enslaved men and women stripped naked and whipped horrified him. During an overseer's daily torture session that followed the cotton weighing, Turnage "saw my chance while he was whiping [*sic*] to make my escape . . . in the woods with the wild animals." Overtaken with hunger, he returned to the plantation shortly thereafter on a false promise of clemency. Ove the next two years, Turnage became a chronic truant, venturing dozens of miles from his plantation. As a fugitive, Turnage ran from pursuing hounds, hid in forests and swamps, and foraged what food he could. Repeated whippings upon recapture did not lessen his determination. As Union forces penetrated the Deep South, Turnage became increasingly aware of how he could use military developments to secure his freedom. After Admiral David Farragut's incursion in August 1864, he said, "I could see the warships of the Union lying way off in the pass and in Mobile Bay." Environmental barriers and Confederate encampments sat between him and freedom: to reach Union lines he had to cross "a dreadful looking river, called Foul river and a rebel picket line." With twelve thousand Confederate soldiers in Mobile, Turnage knew he had to "try to get from that side of the river; it was death to go back and it was death to stay there and freedom was before me." Navigating the "swamps south of Mobile," he had "many snakes to contend with" as "I was bare footed and therefore greatly exposed to their venom." The swamp gave way to an "old open Piny woods," where only waist-high broom sage hid his movements from mounted Confederate patrols. Without food or fresh water and assaulted by mosquitoes, Turnage hid among the reeds, carefully plotting his way across the landscape. Only his mastery of the local ecosystem enabled him to reach Union lines.[13]

Northern soldiers and aid workers marveled at Black refugees' determination to escape bondage and their capacity to navigate environmental barriers. According to Elizabeth Botume, a white teacher and missionary in South Carolina, Jack Flowers had fled from a life of brutal labor and physical torture on a rice plantation. His "incredible efforts to get out of bondage" impressed her:

> He secretly took leave of his family, and ran away, first hiding in the rice-swamps during the day, and creeping along at night, until he reached the woods. Here he hid in the bushes until dark, and then crawled down the banks of the creeks and marshes to elude the dogs, which were out in hot pursuit. At one time he stood in the water up to his chin all day, the hounds were so near. At another time he was "bogged," and sunk so deep in the black mud, he despaired of ever getting out. Finally, he made a basket-boat, woven of the reeds cut in the swamps, and calked with bits of cotton picked up in the fields, and smeared with the pitch from the pine-trees near by.

Flowers managed to float downriver on his reed boat, using a barrel stave as a paddle, sneaking past Confederate pickets to freedom. Impressed by his efforts, Massachusetts missionaries sent his boat north to Governor Andrew.[14]

For some Civil War fugitives, their exodus from slave labor camps entailed extensive time in the wilderness before they reached Union lines. In February 1864, Octave Johnson testified before a representative of the American Freedman's Inquiry Commission about how he obtained his freedom. Born in New Orleans in 1840, Johnson had trained as a cooper. Sold in 1861 for $2,400 to a planter fifty miles upriver, Johnson ran away when an overseer threatened to whip him for not rising with the predawn bell. He fled to the woods, where he hid for eighteen months in a swamp four miles from the riverside labor camp. Other fugitives joined him, and the community eventually grew to twenty men and ten women. They relied upon their knowledge of the geography and environment to prevent capture. They commandeered animals from the plantation and traded with the enslaved who had not yet escaped. "We slept on logs," Johnson recalled, "and burned cypress leaves to make a smoke and keep away mosquitoes." Pursued by a pack of twenty bloodhounds, the maroon band killed eight of them, leading the rest into a bayou, where the remainder fell victim to alligators. "The alligators preferred dog flesh to personal flesh," Johnson noted wryly.

Johnson and his maroon compatriots only survived in their Bayou Faupron refuge because they understood how to transform the inhospitable landscape into a sanctuary. They knew how to evade and kill bloodhounds, how to gather wild food and steal livestock, how to build rudimentary shelters, and how to mitigate mosquitoes. During the year and a half that Johnson created an asylum in the swamp, the Union military occupied New Orleans and its environs. Having escaped the bloodhounds, Johnson's band made its way to Union lines, where he found work in the commissary, before enlisting in the Corps d'Afrique under Colonel George Hanks.[15]

Johnson's journey from slavery to freedom came through his under-standing and use of the environment as much as it did from an executive order or the advancement of the Union military. Like Johnson, many enslaved people relied upon their knowledge of the local swamps, forests, and rivers to secure their liberty. In June 1861, two months after the firing on Fort Sumter, enslavers near Marion, South Carolina, discovered in the swamp a hidden trail "winding about much" that led them "to a knoll in the swamp on which corn, squashes, and peas were growing and a camp had been burnt." Further investigation yielded "another patch of corn . . . and a camp from which several negroes fled, leaving two small negro children, each about a year old." They found the maroon camp prepared for sustained resistance, if not open revolt: "well-provided with meal, cooking utensils, blankets, etc." Most trou-bling from their perspective were twelve rifles left behind. South Carolina's Black majority understood what the war meant.[16]

For maroons living in the Great Dismal Swamp, the Civil War presented an opportunity and a turning point. After the Union invasion of eastern North Carolina in early 1862, many maroons elected to leave the swamp. In March 1862, General Ambrose Burnside reported that among the refugees arriving in New Bern were two men "who have been in the swamps for five years." A few months later, a Union company sent to patrol the Dismal Swamp Canal encountered five men who "presented themselves fearlessly and asked to be permitted to join the party." According to one New York soldier, they "evidently had full information regarding the situation by that unexplained and mysterious system used for spreading information, known only to them and which no white man has yet been able to discover." Some maroons used their knowledge of the swamp to aid the Union military efforts. A Dismal Swamp inhabitant since 1857, William Kinnegy did not live in one of the large maroon settlements in the interior but on the swamp's edge, in "the woods in

a close jungle, so thick that you could not penetrate it, except with the axe."
His location enabled him to visit his enslaved wife and children on a nearby
plantation but also made him vulnerable to slave patrols and hounds sent in
search of runaways. For five years, he lived in a rudimentary hut constructed
from tree branches and fence boards, hunting pigs and cattle allowed to roam
in the swamp. After the occupation of New Bern, Kinnegy abandoned the
swamp and worked as a Union spy, venturing deep into Confederate territory,
land of which he "knew every inch." He returned not just with information
but with his family, whom he rescued from bondage. Although some African
Americans continued to live in the swamp, the maroon sanctuaries in the
Great Dismal disappeared with emancipation.[17]

Some enslaved people traveled extraordinary distances through swamps
and forests to secure their freedom. In Union-occupied New Bern, North
Carolina, Christian Commission volunteer Vincent Colyer witnessed hundreds of black refugees arriving every week, using hidden paths through the
"woods and swamps." While most Black refugees had come from the plantations nearby, Colyer noted that two men had trekked "through the woods
and bye-paths" all the way from northern Alabama, a distance of 750 miles,
"avoiding white men all the way." In September 1864, an enslaved man
named Jack fled from Wylie Boddy's plantation six miles north of Jackson,
Mississippi, to Union lines at Vicksburg, a distance of fifty miles, making
"my way thrgh the woods & cane breaks. swam Big Black River." Although
he encountered "rebel scouts" during his flight, Jack "dodged them through
the woods," drawing upon his knowledge of both the landscape and rebel
troop movements, knowledge that he shared with Union military officials in
Vicksburg.[18]

Life in contraband refugee camps posed its own environmental
challenges. Often located in the shadow of Union army encampments, refugee settlements suffered from chronic overcrowding, poor sanitation, and
frequent disease outbreaks. After their victory at the Battle of Pea Ridge in
March 1862, General Samuel Curtis's Army of the Southwest marched across
northern Arkansas. Enslaved people saw them as agents of liberation, "flocking
to the army from every direction" and "every day bring[ing] in information"
about nearby Confederate forces and local resources. Curtis's march ended
at Helena on the Mississippi, where "a perfect cloud of negroes" greeted the
army. Curtis immediately put the able-bodied men to work as "teamsters and
laborers, driving mules, unloading steamboats and performing any service
required of them." Yet, as one reporter observed, "Besides those employed,
there are many more who cannot be employed, some infirm and disabled, and

FIGURE 7.2. "Wm. Kinnegy Returning to the Union Army with His Family, from Whom He Had Been Separated by Slavery for Five Years." Vincent Colyer, *Brief Report of the Services Rendered by the Freed People to the United States Army* (New York: V. Colyer, 1864), 21.

many women and children, only a few of whom can do anything for themselves. These have come to us in midsummer, with thin clothing, leaving everything behind them." Numbering in the thousands, Black refugees found shelter where they could, including "huddling together in huts," "cast-off tents," caves, and "shelters of brush." With Curtis's soldiers occupying the elevated parts of town, many refugees congregated in what became known as Camp Ethiopia, a flat low-lying settlement next to the Mississippi, which "frequently rises in the Spring to the height of three or four feet above the level of the ground where the camp is." Outside of flood season, poor drainage left the ground muddy, polluted with "putrid matter" and "effluvia." As more refugees arrived in 1863, the camp became increasing overcrowded. Outbreaks of cholera, dysentery, and other water-borne diseases added to their suffering. "This is a terrible hole for niggers," wrote one Union officer. "They are sickening and dying very rapidly."[19]

In early 1864, the Union military relocated many of the Helena refugees to a nearby island in the Mississippi. Known as Island 63, the site was "selected by the Secretary of War for a contraband camp, where it is hoped, by cutting and sale of wood, they may be self supporting." Military officials cited several reasons for the relocation: refugees would be safer from Confederate attack on an island; they could provide fuel for military and commercial traffic on the Mississippi; and they would be isolated from white Union soldiers, who often expressed hostility to Black refugees. Probably most importantly, Federal officials wanted to prevent refugees from becoming dependent upon the government: self-sufficiency lay at the heart of Republican free labor ideology and Union emancipation policy. By the end of the year, over one thousand refugees were relocated to six additional islands, producing sixty thousand cords of wood. Yet the island colonies proved short-lived experiments. Flooding in early 1865 had left Island 63 "completely under water," forcing the evacuation of its 250 residents, and a similar fate befell the other island colonies. Rapid deforestation had left the sites vulnerable to erosion, forcing the refugees to flee from the environmentally untenable locations.[20]

The vulnerability of contraband camps exposed Black refugees to a variety of environmental threats. Diseases spread quickly in the crowded conditions, leading to high mortality rates. Even compared to the drafty conditions of most slave quarters, housing in contraband camps offered little protection from the elements. At Camp Nelson in Kentucky, Black refugees suffered through a painfully bitter winter. "In warm weather we got along tolerably well," noted an American Missionary Association teacher, but conditions became unbearable "when it was cold." Because Kentucky had not seceded from the Union, both Lincoln and Congress had exempted it from protections afforded to Black refugees elsewhere, and slave owners, professing loyalty to the Union, repeatedly made demands upon military officials to have their enslaved property returned to them. In November 1864, with the temperature well below freezing, General Speed Smith Fry expelled four hundred Black refugees, including the families of United States Colored Troops (USCT). "The morning was bitter cold. It was freezing hard," recalled Joseph Miller, a Black refugee who had recently arrived at Camp Nelson with his wife and children. "I was certain that it would kill my sick child to take him out in the cold. I told the man in charge of the guard that it would be the death of my boy. I told him that my wife and children had no place to go and I told him that I was a soldier of the United States." The soldier replied that his orders required him to escort all Black civilian refugees out of Camp Nelson, threatening to shoot them if they did not comply. "When they left the tent," Miller recalled, "the wind was blowing hard and cold and having had to leave much of our clothing when we left our master, my wife with her little one was poorly clad. I followed them as far as the lines." That night, he went out in search of his family, finding them six miles away, huddled together around a fire with other Black refugees in an old meetinghouse, "shivering with cold and famished with hunger." His initial relief at finding his family quickly turned to grief. "My boy was dead. He died directly after getting down from the wagon. I Know he was Killed by exposure to the inclement weather." Miller had to walk back to Camp Nelson that night, leaving his family behind. Several weeks later, after a wellspring of public outrage, Union officials allowed Black refugees to return to Camp Nelson, but three months after their expulsion, a quarter of them had died, including all of Joseph Miller's family. Consumed by grief, he did not live to see the spring.[21]

Even before they served officially in uniform, freedpeople provided the Union military with information about the location, strength, and disposition of Confederates, as well as crucial knowledge about the environmental geography. In April 1862, General Abner Doubleday instructed the men under his command along the Potomac "that all negroes coming into the lines . . . are to be treated as persons and not as chattels." He justified this policy by citing their military utility, as "they are acquainted with all the roads, paths[,] fords and other natural features of the country, and they make excellent guides." In North Carolina, Vincent Colyer observed that "upwards of fifty volunteers of the best and most courageous, were kept constantly employed on the perilous but important duty of spies, scouts, and guides. . . . They frequently went from thirty to three hundred miles within the enemy's lines; visiting his principal camps and most important posts, and bringing us back important and reliable information." These journeys into Confederate territory drew upon decades and generations of experience navigating up rivers and through swamps and forests and evading bloodhounds. In testimony before the American Freedmen's Inquiry Commission, Colonel Thomas Wentworth Higginson observed that enslaved people "had been spies all their lives. You cannot teach them anything in that respect. I should not attempt to give them instruction; they would be better able to teach me." Higginson testified that enslaved people in South Carolina possessed an encyclopedic knowledge of the local waterways that Union forces could exploit.[22]

White Union soldiers disregarded their guides' local knowledge at their peril. In 1862, a formerly enslaved North Carolinian named Sam Williams persuaded Union military officials that he could lead an expedition to "catch several hundred of the rebel soldiers." Using a map, Williams described "the location of the enemy, and the character of the country, pointed out a bye-road through the swamps, by which, he said, they could readily be approached and surrounded." Alongside twenty cavalrymen, Williams rode ahead of three Union regiments. At a crucial juncture, however, the white officer in command overrode Williams's guidance and "decided to take another road," upon which Confederate forces ambushed the expedition's vanguard. In the chaos, Williams, the only unarmed member of the party, "escaped to the woods," using his knowledge of the local geography to avoid Confederate patrols looking for him and returned to Union lines twenty-four hours later. In his report, the white officer admitted his error, claiming that "if he had followed Samuel William's [sic] advice, as he should have done, they would have been entirely successful."[23]

For much of the war, the Union relied upon African Americans' labor, knowledge of local ecosystems, and experience in manipulating it. In 1862 and 1863, Union military officials tried to use Black labor to circumvent Vicksburg. Located on a bluff at a bend in the Mississippi, the Confederate stronghold occupied a strategically important and defensible position. Hoping to avoid a lengthy siege and assault on the city, Union engineers devised a plan to dig a canal that would leave Vicksburg dry and thereby give the Union unfettered control of the Mississippi. The project started in June 1862 under General Thomas Williams, who relied on the labor of white soldiers and more than a thousand African American men recently "gathered from the neighboring plantations," many of whom brought prior experience building levees along the Mississippi. In the intense summer heat, they dug through heavy clay soils and dense vegetation. Plagued by mosquitoes, lacking adequate shelter, and fed rations of hardtack, hundreds died building the three-quarter-mile-long canal. One Union soldier noted that "the Negroes died off like a disease infected flock of sheep," and a nearby plantation owner observed that they were "worked to death on the canal with no shelter at night and not much to eat."

The working conditions on the canal reflected Williams's hostility to African Americans. Ever since his regiment arrived in Louisiana, he had predicted that slavery's demise would prompt a "a servile war." On June 5, prior to his starting work on the canal, Williams had ordered the expulsion of African Americans refugees from Union camps and had permitted enslavers into Union lines to kidnap the refugees. He had turned to Black labor for the canal only after his soldiers, most of whom came from Connecticut and Wisconsin, fell ill from the heat and humidity. Yet he found African Americans' determination impressive: "The negroes are flying from their masters in all directions," he wrote, "and have become thoroughly impressed with the idea of being free. Old, decrepit men and women, even, come into our lines, whose old age and infirmities were probably well provided for. Yet they leave the comforts their age and infirmities require, for freedom, which, may be, has been the dream of all their lives. That idea of being free, how can they ever be dispossessed of it? Never. The doom of slavery is already written." Williams saw this determination for freedom in the enthusiasm with which they attacked the canal project. "They work and shout as they work, thinking they're working for their freedom," he wrote his wife, "and if the canal is a success will deserve it and shall have it."

Unfortunately for both the Union war effort and for the Black laborers, the canal proved a failure. From the very beginning, the project seemed doomed, with cave-ins and engineering miscalculations. After a month's work, Williams announced that he needed three thousand African American laborers to dig a canal thirty-five to forty feet deep, a task he thought could be completed in an additional three months. However, by the end of July, Williams was ordered to stop construction, as his command was needed at Baton Rouge. On July 21, Williams directed African Americans from plantations below Vicksburg to board the steamer *Ceres* to be returned to their enslavers. As the *Ceres* traveled south, Confederate artillery bombarded the vessel, killing several on board. For those who originated north of Vicksburg, Williams distributed three days' rations, instructing them to return to their owners. Fearing torture at the hands of their enslavers and Confederate soldiers, they attempted to board Union troop ships, only to be beaten back. "As means of acquiring information, as guides and as laborers," noted one Union soldier in Louisiana, African Americans "have been found eminently useful, conferring great benefits on the cause of the Union, and at the same time drawing upon their own devoted heads the bottled-up wrath of rebeldom to be forced out as soon as the protecting presence of the Federal guard is withdrawn."[24]

In January 1863, General Ulysses S. Grant resumed work on the abandoned canal project and commenced work on two others, each intended to bypass Vicksburg. Like Williams, Grant relied on a combination of white military labor and labor provided by African Americans who had been enslaved on

FIGURE 7.3. Theodore R. Davis, "Cutting the Canal Opposite Vicksburg," *Harpers Weekly* 6 (1862): 481.

nearby plantations. Grant authorized subordinates to "collect as many able bodied Negro men as you can conveniently carry on your transports, and send them here to be employed on the canals." Changing federal policy, including the Emancipation Proclamation, however, had transformed the status of African Americans within Union lines. "It is the policy of the government to withdraw from the enemy as much productive labor as possible," General-in-Chief Henry W. Halleck wrote Grant in March 1863. "Every slave withdrawn from the enemy, is equivalent to a white man put hors de combat." Black men who worked on Grant's canals would, in Lincoln's words, be "henceforth and forever free."[25]

Their new status did nothing to improve working conditions, as Grant's hydraulic mission proved as doomed as Williams's efforts. "Poor creatures[,] these contrabands," noted Iowa soldier Cyrus Boyd. "They fly for their freedom to the union army and we are not able to do much for them as it is all we can do to take care of ourselves." Many of Grant's soldiers expressed outright hostility to their presence. "The men in our camp treat them worse than *brutes*," Boyd claimed; "when they come into camp cries of 'Kill him', 'drown him' &c are heard on every hand." Heavy rains and cold weather added to their misery, leaving both white soldiers and Black laborers coated in thick mud. Heading the US Sanitary Commission, Frederick Law Olmsted marveled at "the most dismal place and the most dismal prospect upon which an army could be put." Disease exacted a heavy toll, with hundreds dying from dysentery and typhoid. "The levee itself was lined with graves," Olmsted noted, "there being no other place where the dead could be buried, on account of the water, which at once fills every cavity."[26]

New Confederate batteries made daytime work on the Williams Canal impossible and would have limited its utility once completed. Grant tasked more than four thousand freedmen and white soldiers to work mostly at night to minimize the effectiveness of rebel guns. However, after more than a month of work, in early March 1863, the rising Mississippi destroyed a cofferdam, flooding the canal and filling it with silt. At the same time, Grant had started work on several other hydraulic projects intended to neutralize Vicksburg, projects that included digging canals and dismantling levees. Near Helena, Arkansas, for instance, Grant had formerly enslaved men cut through levees that enslaved men had constructed and maintained for decades. "The river being high the rush of water through the cut was so great that in a very short time the entire obstruction was washed away," Grant wrote. "The bayous were soon filled and much of the country was overflowed," leaving the adjacent plantations submerged. By the end of March, Grant abandoned these schemes. Even the labor of ten thousand men could not sufficiently reroute the Mississippi to circumvent Vicksburg. William Tecumseh Sherman noted in his memoirs, "The Mississippi River was very high and rising, and we began that system of canals on which were expended so much hard work fruitlessly."[27]

Grant's hydraulic engineering during the Vicksburg campaign contributed to widespread flooding along the Mississippi River. As the institutional structures of slavery crumbled with the advances of Union forces, so too did the systems of levee maintenance built upon enslaved labor. Crevasses opened at several spots along the Mississippi, flooding thousands of acres of riverside cotton fields. "The war had suspended the peaceful pursuits in the South," noted Union general Ulysses S. Grant; "in consequences the levees were neglected and broken in many places and the whole country was covered in water." Confederate guerrillas also breached Mississippi levees to slow Union advances. Four years of war devasted a century and half's worth of enslaved levee construction, damage that took decades to repair.[28]

Union officials recognized that formerly enslaved African Americans brought robust environmental knowledge that could prove useful in military service, not only as scouts and spies but also as soldiers. Tasked with raising Black regiments in the Mississippi valley, General Lorenzo Thomas told an assembled crowd at Lake Providence, Louisiana, in April 1863 that formerly enslaved men brought a particular set of skills. "Knowing the country well, and familiar with all the roads and swamps," he said, "they will be able to track out the accursed guerilla and run them from the land." Leading Black soldiers through Georgia "swamps . . . numerous and almost impassable," Captain Charles Trowbridge benefited from their local knowledge, as "his Negro troops were familiar with the country." His soldiers, most of whom had run away from nearby plantations, knew how to traverse the swamp undetected, enabling them to attack and destroy Confederate salt works. African American soldiers also relied upon their environmental knowledge in more prosaic ways. One white USCT officer from Vermont noted in January 1865 how the men of his regiment supplemented their meager rations with "fish, oysters and alligators." Stationed on Cat Island, Mississippi, most of the 74th USCT had escaped from enslavement along the Lower Mississippi and knew the local flora and fauna. When inclement weather prevented fishing, they had to "resort to rats," which, to the Vermonter's surprise, tasted "very good."[29]

The mass exodus of enslaved peoples from Confederate plantations prompted widespread land abandonment, especially in regions of the South closest to Union lines. Cotton went unpicked and tobacco plants became subsumed in weeds. Without crops to protect the remaining topsoil, abandoned fields in the Piedmont eroded at an even faster pace. In some areas, abandoned cotton and tobacco fields became reforested. Traveling though the South in the aftermath of Confederate defeat, journalist and abolitionist John Trowbridge observed that "old fields" were now "covered with briers, weeds, and broom-sedge—often with a thick growth of infant pines coming up like grass." Another touring journalist, John Dennett, observed in September 1865 that in the North Carolina Piedmont, "much of the hilly land has lost almost all its soil by the action of the rain-water torrents, and the hard clay beneath is scantily covered by thin grass, or stands out bare and barren, refusing to sup-port vegetable life."[30]

Newly emancipated African Americans saw connections between their freedom and the land. In January 1865, a delegation of Black ministers met with General William Tecumseh Sherman and Secretary of War Edwin Stanton in recently liberated Savannah, Georgia. "The way we can best take care of ourselves is to have land," the ministers told them, "and turn it and till it by our own labor." At freedmen's conventions across the South in 1865 and 1866, African Americans articulated an economic agenda rooted in an envi-ronmental vision. They had worked the land for generations, transforming it in the process. Their labor gave them a moral claim that superseded that of their former owners. "We intend to live and die on the soil which gave us birth," noted one delegate to the North Carolina convention. In December 1866, African Americans in Yorktown, Virginia, rejected a recommendation by Freedman's Bureau officials that they find new homes elsewhere. Speaking on their behalf, Bayley Wyat argued, "We has a right to the land where we are located." Their claim was not based in law but on the unpaid wages of brutal labor, torture, and separation. "Our wives, our children, our husbands, has been sold over and over again to purchase the lands we now locates on," which gave them "a divine right to the land." Those who were once "bought and sold like horses" stood as freedpeople, ready to claim their due. Located a day's walk from Point Comfort, where Virginia's first documented African slaves arrived in 1619, Wyat reflected on more than two centuries of bondage: "We clear the land, and raise de crops of corn, ob cotton, ob tobacco, ob rice, ob sugar, ob ebery ting." Now, he argued, without land of their own, he argued, African Americans would be driven "into de woods, or into de ribber."[31]

Conclusion

ON THE EVENING of June 1, 1863, three Union gunboats steamed up the Combahee River, carrying three hundred soldiers with the 2nd South Carolina, one of the first Black regiments raised during the war. Commanded by Colonel James Montgomery and guided by Harriet Tubman, the expedition sought to strike the slaveholder's rebellion at its heart, destroying plantations and liberating those held in bondage. "We broke the sluice gates," noted one participant, "and flooded the fields so that the present crop, which was growing beautifully, will be a total loss." The raid freed scores of enslaved people, including two hundred who lived and worked on Titus Bissell's Green Pond Plantation. The rice plantation remained largely abandoned until the war's conclusion, two years later.

When Bissell returned, he found the levees breached and the irrigation canals and ditches silted and clogged with weeds. In 1873, a decade after the Combahee River Raid, Massachusetts journalist Edward King toured the ruins of South Carolina's rice plantations, including Green Pond. "The injury done to all the plantations in these lowland counties, by the neglect consequent on the war," he wrote, "is incalculable." When South Carolina seceded from the Union in December 1860, the state claimed more than a million productive acres committed to rice cultivation; by the time of King's visit, only a quarter of that remained. Without constant maintenance, the "whole apparatus of levels, floodgates, trunks, canals, banks, and ditches" had collapsed. A rice plantation, he concluded, was "a huge hydraulic machine, maintained by constant warring against the rivers." For more than a century, rice plantation owners had fought this war using enslaved Black labor. Like generations of planters before him, Titus Bissell knew that "the slightest leak in the banks or dikes may end in the ruin of the whole plantation," prompting him to keep his enslaved workers "ready at a moment's notice for the most exhausting

Scars on the Land. David Silkenat, Oxford University Press. © Oxford University Press 2022.
DOI: 10.1093/oso/9780197564226.003.0009

efforts." Without slaves to man the barricades, the river had reclaimed the land and won the war.[1]

Two centuries of brutal enslaved labor had transformed the American South. The expanding slave frontier had caused a cascade of ecological change that left soils eroded, waterways polluted, and habitats denuded. Driven by the lash, enslaved African Americans had cut down forests, rerouted rivers, and mined toxic elements from the earth. Enslavers saw the environment as disposable, a resource that could be exploited and replaced as needed. Although some of them professed devotion to the land, their individual and collective choices exposed their environmental stewardship as a fraud, a willful self-deception that mirrored the paternalistic ethos they used to justify dominating and torturing the people they held in bondage. Committed to an economic and social order built on enslaved labor and racial superiority, most white Southerners cast their lots with the Confederacy, believing that only a war for independence could preserve their peculiar institution.

For Black Southerners, freedom presented a new set of environmental opportunities and challenges. Most African Americans understood that their futures could not be disconnected from the land. In claiming control over their own labor, they refused to engage in the environmentally destructive processes that had defined the enslaved frontier. They balked at landowners' demands to perform work not directly connected to the planting and harvesting of the crop. "Men who are free will not clear land," observed an Alabama Freedmen's Bureau agent, "while the breadth of land annually thrown out of cultivation is about the same as formerly." Without new farmland, he worried, the entire project would be doomed to failure. "The country itself seems to be fast retrograding," he wrote, "difficult to sustain livelihoods." The reconstruction of Southern agriculture transformed extensive enslaved agriculture into intensive tenant farming. As sharecropping and tenancy became the dominant land-labor models in the Cotton South, they exacerbated soil-killing agricultural practices. Black farmers became trapped in cycles of debt built upon agricultural practices that exhausted the land and their bodies.[2]

Emancipation also transformed how white Southern landowners related to the soil. Former planters could no longer avail themselves of an expanding slave frontier. They needed to make the same soil productive year after year. During Reconstruction, they enthusiastically embraced chemical fertilizers that Northern and European farmers had been using since the 1840s. Chemical fertilizer proponents, like Georgia's David Dickson, argued that this was the solution to the region's postwar economic crisis. With formerly enslaved African Americans claiming control over their own labor, the chemical mixture in "Dickson's Compound," an advertisement promised, "enables you to work freedmen when they would bring you into debt without it." Drawing upon the robust phosphate deposits near Charleston, chemically enhanced Southern agriculture grew bumper crops without enslaved labor, with cotton production surpassing prewar levels by 1870. The combination of free Black labor and fertilizers prompted white Southerners to look at the land in new ways. "Old fields nearly exhausted will now bring more per acre than rich wood land," noted one Georgia land baron in 1870, "because it is cheaper to buy fertilizers and make cotton on them than to clear new land without slave labor." The resulting chemically enhanced agricultural system transformed the relationship between labor and land. "More than gold was to California, diamonds to Brazil and the Cape, or silks to France," opined the *New York Times* in 1881, "commercial fertilizers are to the South." As the South became the most chemically dependent region in the country, the costs became increasingly apparent. By the 1880s, fertilizer expenses contributed to the chronic indebtedness that plagued Southern farmers, both white and Black. With more than 75 percent of fertilizer purchases made on credit, farmers bet that the resulting harvest would pay off the debt, bets that they lost more often than not. By the end of the nineteenth century, these debts helped to fuel agrarian unrest that culminated in the Populist movement.[3]

Some African Americans came to believe that emancipation had transformed their relationship with the environment. In September 1873, Frederick Douglass stood before a crowd of five thousand people at Nashville's Colored Fairgrounds to deliver an address to the third annual meeting of the Tennessee Colored Agricultural Association. Summer drought had left a thick cloud of dust in the air, and midday sun produced "great drops of perspiration" on Douglass's face as he spoke. He praised the organizers and audience for their accomplishments in the eight years since the Civil War's conclusion. He felt pride in seeing "so vast a concourse of newly emancipated people" who were once "ranked by the laws of the land with horses, sheep and swine, and like these subject to be bought and sold."

Douglass admitted that he knew less about farming than most in the audience, since "the last thirty-five years I have been actively employed in a work which left me no time to study either the theory or the practice of farming." He took the opportunity to reflect on African Americans' relationship to the land in slavery and freedom. He touted agriculture as "the grand refuge of our oppressed and persecuted people," as "the brave old earth has no prejudice against 'race, color, or previous condition of servitude' but flings open her ample breast to all who will come to her for succor and relief." Success in agriculture required more than hard work, as "beside land, labor, and skill there must be heat, moisture, and manure." Tennessee, he argued, offered the right environment for African Americans to succeed, providing "mountain, valley, river, and plain, heat and moisture, and a beautifully temperate climate."

Despite its natural riches, however, Douglass warned that "the very soil of your State was cursed with a burning sense of injustice. Slavery was the parent of anger and hate. Your fields could not be lovingly planted nor faithfully cultivated in its presence." Slavery's cruelty had left scars in the soil, as erosion stripped Tennessee's tobacco fields, leaving them gullied and worn. Slavery polluted everything it touched, infecting the environment with cruelty and malice. "There is no denying that slavery had a direct and positive tendency to produce coarseness and brutality in the treatment and management of domestic animals, especially those most useful to agricultural industry," Douglass argued. "Not only to the slave, but the horse, the ox and the mule shared the general feeling of indifference to the rights naturally engendered by a state of slavery. The master blamed the overseer; the overseer the slave, and the slave the horses, oxen and mules, and violence and brutality fell upon the animals as a consequence." The rot went deep.

Freedom offered an opportunity for rebirth and regeneration. "There need be no such thing in the world as worn-out land," Douglass claimed. With sufficient care and ample fertilizer, even the most degraded soil could be made productive. "Feed the land and it will feed you!" he said. Douglass saw emancipation as an environmental milestone: "Emancipation has liberated the land as well as the people." Without the cruelty of slavery, a new kind of Black ecology could flourish. Free Black farmers would nurture the tortured land, enriching themselves and renewing the ecosystem. Douglass envisioned an entwined future for African Americans and the Southern environment: slavery's wounds would heal, though the scars would remain.[4]

Some scars fade but never fully disappear. In 1898, a quarter century after Douglass's speech, W. E. B. Du Bois toured southwest Georgia's Dougherty County, what he called the "heart of the Black Belt." The area had once been a "Land of Canaan," with "pendent gray moss and brackish waters" and "forests filled with wildfowl," until whites drove Creeks from the land. "Then came the black slaves," Du Bois observed. "Day after day the clank of chained feet marching from Virginia and Carolina to Georgia was heard in these rich swamp lands" to create the "richest slave kingdom the modern world ever knew." By the time of Du Bois's visit, this was all a memory. He found abandoned plantations and scrub oak, a barren landscape "all dilapidated and half ruined." He attributed this poverty to the legacy of slavery. Well before secession, he argued, "the hard ruthless rape of the land began to tell. The red-clay sub-soil already had begun to peer above the loam. The harder the slaves were driven the more careless and fatal was their farming." After the "revolution of war and Emancipation" turned the world upside down, the renewal that Frederick Douglass had predicted failed to come to pass, at least in Dougherty County. "The poor land groans with its birth-pains," Du Bois observed, "and brings forth scarcely a hundred pounds of cotton to the acre, where fifty years ago it yielded eight times as much." Lynching, convict labor, and sharecropping left the Black community in Dougherty County "hopelessly in debt, disappointed, and embittered." Du Bois left dispirited. "Here lies the Negro problem in its naked dirt and penury," he observed, in a land scarred by the "memory of forced human toil."[5]

More than a century and a half after the legal end of slavery in the United States, its scars remain on the landscape. Faded and worn, these scars have been overlaid with more recent wounds, as the sites of former slave labor camps have become venues for some of the most egregious examples of environmental racism anywhere in America. The profound transformations in the Southern economy, politics, and demography have not changed the underlying racial and environmental disparities as much as some of us might have hoped. As the destruction of Hurricane Katrina so vividly demonstrated, those that had the least often suffered the most. Today's environmental challenges, the climate crisis foremost among them, cannot be disentangled from the long histories of the land and the people who lived there. As Americans continue to grapple with the legacies of slavery, we also need to see the scars on the land.[6]

Acknowledgments

I HAVE ALWAYS found writing acknowledgments the hardest part of completing a book. No matter how many times I rewrite them, my words always seem inadequate for the task. I accrued tremendous debts in writing this book, and words alone cannot repay them.

This has been a difficult book to write. Researching and writing amid the Black Lives Matter Movement and a global environmental crisis has meant that the questions undergirding this volume have never been far from my mind. My work has always been shaped (both consciously and unconsciously) by contemporary issues. While that may make me guilty of presentism, I am convinced that historians can and should use their knowledge of the past to help explain the present and their understanding of the present to shape the questions they ask about the past.

This book would not have been possible without substantial support from those who saw promise in my ideas. I benefitted from the generosity of Nau Center at the University of Virginia and the Swem Library at the College of William and Mary, which enabled me to use their archival collections. I was lucky to present some early thoughts at the British American Nineteenth Century Historians (BrANCH) conference in Cambridge and at the University of Glasgow's American Studies seminar. The feedback I received at both venues proved immensely valuable. I felt very lucky to work with Susan Ferber at Oxford University Press. She guided this book through its development with a critical eye, tempered by patience and kindness. Three anonymous reviewers provided insightful comments for which I am very grateful. This book is substantially better because of their input.

My colleagues at the University of Edinburgh have supported my research and helped me to become a better historian. More importantly, they have been good friends during a few particularly challenging years. Special thanks goes out to Celeste-Marie Bernier, Frank Cogliano, Fabian Hilfrich, Megan Hunt, Robert Mason, and Di Paton. I am also grateful to the School of History, Classics, and Archaeology at the University of Edinburgh, which has given me the resources and time necessary to bring this project to completion.

Conversations with friends and colleagues over the past few years have shaped this project in large and small ways. A radically incomplete list of those whose influence can be found in these pages includes Ana Lucia Araujo, Bruce Baker, Catherine Bateson, Amanda Bellows, Steve Berry, Jim Broomall, Thomas Brown, Judkin Browning, Fitz Brundage, Pete Carmichael, Catherine Clinton, Karen Cox, Adam Domby, Greg Downs, Jim Downs, Doug Egerton, Carole Emberton, Leigh Fought, Elaine Frantz, Joanne Freeman, Sarah Gardner, David Gleeson, Becky Goetz, Lesley Gordon, Susan-Mary Grant, Hilary Green, Mick Gusinde-Duffy, Emma Hart, Laura Hart, Christy Hyman, Carrie Janney, Martha Jones, William Kurtz, Tim Lockley, James Mackay, Kate Masur, Erin Mauldin, Hannah-Rose Murray, Barton Myers, Megan Kate Nelson, Scott Nelson, Holly Pinheiro, Manisha Sinha, Mark Smith, Jewel Spangler, Amy Murrell Taylor, George Toth, Frank Towers, Kevin Waite, Jon Wells, Emily West, Tim Williams, and Karin Wulf.

My family has provided tremendous solace in writing this volume. After twenty-five years of marriage, Ida is probably tired of me saying how important she is to my work, but her influence is on every page. Our three children are all adults now, but they have continued to be the most wonderful reason to step away from the keyboard. As always, my father has encouraged me, support for which I am perennially grateful. My wife's parents, Willis and Leona Whichard, have championed my work from the very start. I have benefited tremendously from their support, guidance, wisdom, kindness, and love. This book is dedicated to them.

Notes

1. William J. Anderson, *Life and Narrative of William J. Anderson* (Chicago: Daily Tribune Book and Job Printing Office, 1857), 26.

2. L. W. Spratt, *The Philosophy of Secession* (Charleston, SC: n.p., 1861), 1; Alexander H. Stephens, "Cornerstone Address, March 21, 1861," in *The Rebellion Record*, ed. Frank Moore (New York: Putnam, 1862), 1:44–46; "The Importance of Agricultural Education," *Southern Federal Union* (Milledgeville, Georgia), April 16, 1861; Karen Fritz, *Voices in the Storm: Confederate Rhetoric, 1861–1865* (Denton: University of North Texas Press, 1999), 53–77; Ira Berlin, *Many Thousands Gone: The First Two Centuries of Slavery in North America* (Cambridge, MA: Harvard University Press, 1998), 8–9.

3. Ulrich Bonnell Phillips, *Life and Labor in the Old South* (Boston: Little Brown, 1929), 3; Avery Craven, *Soil Exhaustion as a Factor in the Agricultural History of Virginia and Maryland, 1606–1860* (Urbana: University of Illinois Press, 1926). Also see Cecil Lewis Gray, *A History of Agriculture in the Southern United States to 1860* (Washington, DC: Carnegie, 1933); Paul W. Gates, *The Farmer's Age: Agriculture, 1815–1860* (New York: Holt, Rinehart & Winston, 1960).

4. Mart A. Stewart, "If John Muir Had Been an Agrarian: American Environmental History West and South," *Environmental History* 11 (2005): 139–162; Albert E. Cowdrey, *This Land, This South: An Environmental History*, rev. ed. (Lexington: University of Kentucky Press, 1996); Drew A. Swanson, *Remaking Wormsloe Plantation: An Environmental History of a Lowcountry Landscape* (Athens, GA: University of Georgia Press, 2012); Lynn A. Nelson, *Pharsalia: An Environmental Biography of a Southern Plantation, 1780–1880* (Athens, GA: University of Georgia Press, 2012); Mikko Saikku, *This Delta, This Land: An Environmental History of the Yazoo-Mississippi Floodplain* (Athens, GA: University of Georgia Press, 2005); Mart A. Stewart, *"What Nature Suffers to Groe": Life, Labor, and Landscape on the Georgia Coast, 1680–1920* (Athens,

GA: University of Georgia, 1996); Christopher Morris, "A More Southern Environmental History," *Journal of Southern History* 75 (2009): 581–598.

5. John W. Blassingame, "Using the Testimony of Ex-Slaves: Approaches and Problems," *Journal of Southern History* 41 (1975): 473–492; Norman R. Yetman, "Ex-Slave Interviews and the Historiography of Slavery," *American Quarterly* 36 (1984): 181–210; Catherine A. Stewart, *Long Past Slavery: Representing Race in the Federal Writers' Project* (Chapel Hill: University of North Carolina Press, 2016); Paul D. Escott, *Slavery Remembered: A Record of Twentieth Century Slave Narratives* (Chapel Hill: University of North Carolina Press, 1979); Carl N. Degler, "Why Historians Change Their Minds," *Pacific Historical Review* 45 (1976): 167–184; Kimberly K. Smith, "Environmental Criticism and the Slave Narratives," in *The Oxford Handbook of the African American Slave Narrative*, ed. John Ernest (New York: Oxford University Press, 2014), 315–327.

6. Sven Beckert and Seth Rockman, eds., *Slavery's Capitalism: A New History of American Economic Development* (Philadelphia: University of Pennsylvania Press, 2016); Walter Johnson, *River of Dark Dreams: Slavery and Empire in the Cotton Kingdom* (Cambridge, MA: Harvard University Press, 2013); Sven Beckert, *Empire of Cotton: A Global History* (New York: Knopf, 2013); Scott Reynolds Nelson, "Who Put Their Capitalism in My Slavery?" *Journal of the Civil War Era* 5 (2015): 289–310; Matthew Pratt Guterl, "Slavery and Capitalism: A Review Essay," *Journal of Southern History* 81 (2015): 405–420; Edward Baptist, *The Half Has Never Been Told: Slavery and the Making of American Capitalism* (New York: Basic Books, 2014); Joshua Rothman, *Flush Times and Fever Dreams: A Story of Capitalism and Slavery in the Age of Jackson* (Athens, GA: University of Georgia Press, 2012).

7. Teresa Singleton, "Archaeology and Slavery," in *The Oxford Handbook of Slavery in the Americas*, ed. Mark M. Smith and Robert L. Paquette (New York: Oxford University Press, 2012), 702–724.

8. Donald Edward Davis, *Where There Are Mountains: An Environmental History of the Southern Appalachians* (Athens, GA: University of Georgia Press, 2003), 1–34; Cowdrey, *This Land, This South,* 11–24; David Rich Lewis, "American Indian Environmental Relations," in *A Companion to American Environmental History*, ed. Douglas Sackman (Hoboken, NJ: Wiley-Blackwell, 2010), 191–213; Jack Temple Kirby, *Mockingbird Song: Ecological Landscapes of the South* (Chapel Hill: University of North Carolina Press, 2006), 38–74.

CHAPTER 1

1. Charles Ball, *Slavery in the United States* (New York: John S. Taylor, 1837), 37–48.

2. Matthew Karp, *This Vast Southern Empire: Slaveholders at the Helm of American Foreign Policy* (Cambridge, MA: Harvard University Press, 2016); Rothman, *Flush Times and Fever Dreams,* 18–19; Christina Snyder, *Slavery in Indian Country: The Changing Face of Captivity in Early America* (Cambridge, MA: Harvard University

Press, 2012), 209; Steven Hahn, *A Nation Without Borders: The United States and Its World in the Age of Civil Wars, 1830–1910* (New York: Penguin, 2017), 30; Adam Rothman, *Slave Country: American Expansion and the Origins of the Deep South* (Athens, GA: University of Georgia Press, 2012), 166–169, 182–184.

3. Craven, *Soil Exhaustion*; Gray, *History of Agriculture in the Southern United States*; Eugene D. Genovese, *The Political Economy of Slavery* (New York: Pantheon, 1965), 85–105.

4. Timothy Silver, "Learning to Live with Nature: Colonial Historians and the Southern Environment," *Journal of Southern History* 73 (2007): 546–548; Carville Earle, "The Myth of the Southern Soil Miner: Macrohistory, Agricultural Innovation, and Environmental Change," in *The Ends of the Earth: Perspectives on Modern Environmental History*, ed. Donald Worster (New York: Cambridge University Press, 1989), 175–178; Douglas Helms, "Soil and Southern History," *Agricultural History* 74 (2000): 723–731.

5. Silver, "Learning to Live with Nature," 546–548; Erin Mauldin, *Unredeemed Land: An Environmental History of Civil War and Emancipation* (New York: Oxford University Press, 2018), 15; David S. Hardin, "'The Same Sort of Seed in Different Earths': Tobacco Types and Their Regional Variation in Colonia Virginia," *Historical Geography* 34 (2006): 147–148; Craven, *Soil Exhaustion*, 32; Gates, *The Farmer's Age*, 100; Allan Kulikoff, *Tobacco and Slaves: The Development of Southern Cultures in the Chesapeake, 1680–1800* (Chapel Hill: University of North Carolina Press, 1988), 47–48; Lorena S. Walsh, "Plantation Management in the Chesapeake, 1620–1820," *Journal of Economic History* 49 (1989): 393; Lorena S. Walsh, *Motives of Honor, Pleasure and Profit: Plantation Managements in the Colonial Chesapeake, 1607–1763* (Chapel Hill: University of North Carolina Press, 2010), 153, 224; Gavin Wright, *Slavery and American Economic Development* (Baton Rouge: Louisiana State University Press, 2013), 50, 122.

6. Walsh, *Motives of Honor*, 363–368; Anthony S. Parent Jr., *Foul Means: The Formation of a Slave Society in Virginia, 1660–1740* (Chapel Hill: University of North Carolina Press, 2003), 55–101; William J. Hinke, "Report of the Journey of Francis Louis Michel from Berne, Switzerland to Virginia," *Virginia Magazine of History and Biography* 24 (1916): 30–1, 116; Kulikoff, *Tobacco and Slaves*, 48; Philip Vickers Fithian, *Journals and Letters of Philip Vickers Fithian, 1773–1774: A Plantation Tutor of the Old Dominion* (Williamsburg, VA: Colonial Williamsburg, 1943), 140.

7. Gray, *History of Agriculture*, 2:602–608; Craven, *Soil Exhaustion*, 67–70; Richard Lyman Bushman, *The American Farmer in the Eighteenth Century: A Social and Cultural History* (New Haven, CT: Yale University Press, 2018), 52; Claudia L. Bushman, *In Old Virginia: Slavery, Farming, and Society in the Journal of John Walker* (Baltimore: Johns Hopkins University Press, 2001), 44–55; George Washington to George William Fairfax, November 10, 1785, *Founders Online*, https://founders.archives.gov/documents/Washington/04-03-02-0317; Lucia Stanton, *Those Who Labor for My Happiness: Slavery at Thomas Jefferson's Monticello* (Charlottesville: University of Virginia Press, 2012), 63.

8. Lorena S. Walsh, "Land Use, Settlement Patterns, and the Impact of European Agriculture, 1620–1820," in *Discovering the Chesapeake: The History of an Ecosystem*, ed. Philip D. Curtin, Grace S. Brush, and George W. Fisher (Baltimore: Johns Hopkins University Press, 2001), 242; David O. Percy, "Ax or Plow? Significant Colonial Landscape Alteration Rates in the Maryland and Virginia Tidewater," *Agricultural History* 66 (1992): 72–73.

9. Cowdrey, *This Land, This South*, 2–3; Mauldin, *Unredeemed Land*, 4, 16–17; Thomas Anburey, *Travels through the Interior Parts of America* (London: W. Lane, 1789), 2:405–406; Arthur R. Hall, *Early Erosion-Control Practices in Virginia* (Washington, DC: GPO, 1938), 5. Scholars have demonstrated that Anburey plagiarized significant sections of his account from other sources. This particular passage appears to be original. See Whitfield J. Bell Jr., "Thomas Anburey's 'Travels Through America': A Note on Eighteenth Century Plagiarism," *Papers of the Bibliographical Society of America* 37 (1943): 23–36.

10. Thomas Jefferson to Tristram Dalton, May 2, 1817, *Founders Online*, https:// founders.archives.gov/documents/Jefferson/03-11-02-0270-0001; Stanton, *Those Who Labor for My Happiness*, 144; "On Ploughing," *Southern Agriculturalist* 4 (1831): 275–276.

11. T. H. Breen, *Tobacco Culture: The Mentality of the Great Tidewater Planters on the Eve of the Revolution* (Princeton, NJ: Princeton University Press, 1985), 57–58; *American Husbandry: Containing an Account of the Soil, Climate, Production and Agriculture of the British Colonies in North-America and the West-Indies* (London: J. Bew, 1775), 1:229–230; Alan Taylor, *Internal Enemy: Slavery and War in Virginia, 1772–1832* (New York: Norton, 2013), 23–29; Woody Holton, *Forced Founders: Indians, Debtors, Slaves, and the Making of the American Revolution in Virginia* (Chapel Hill: University of North Carolina Press, 1999), 156–161; Johann David Schoepf, *Travels in the Confederation*, trans. Alfred J. Morrison (Philadelphia: W. J. Campbell, 1911), 2:32.

12. James M. Garnett, "Defects in Agriculture," in *Memoirs of the Society of Virginia for Promoting Agriculture* (Richmond, VA: Shepard & Pollard, 1818), 54; James M. Garnett, "Address," *Farmers' Register* 3 (1836): 615–619; Agricola [George W. Jeffreys], *Series of Essays on Agriculture & Rural Affairs* (Raleigh, NC: Joseph Gales, 1819), 5; Joan Cashin, "Landscape and Memory in Antebellum Virginia," *Virginia Magazine of History and Biography* 102 (1994): 477–500; Steven Stoll, *Larding the Lean Earth: Soil and Society in Nineteenth-Century America* (New York: Hill & Wang, 2003), 34, 45–46, 128–131.

13. Thomas Jefferson Farm Book, 194, Thomas Jefferson Papers, Massachusetts Historical Society; Jefferson to Joel Yancey, January 17, 1819, *Founders Online*, https://founders.archives.gov/documents/Jefferson/03-13-02-0522; Jefferson to Richard Peters, March 6, 1816, *Founders Online,* https://founders.archives.gov/documents/Jefferson/03-09-02-0371.

14. Frederick Law Olmsted, *A Journey in the Seaboard Slave States* (New York: Dix & Edwards, 1856), 90; Wayne Trimble, *Man-Induced Soil Erosion on the Southern Piedmont, 1700–1970* (Ankeny, IA: Soil Conservation Society of America, 1974), 17, 41–47; John Hartwell Cocke, "Tobacco the Bane of Virginia Husbandry," *Southern Planter* 19 (August 1859): 482.

15. Edmund Ruffin Farm Journal, College of William & Mary Special Collections (hereafter W&M); Edmund Ruffin, *Agricultural, Geological, and Descriptive Sketches of Lower North Carolina, and Similar Adjacent Lands* (Raleigh, NC: Institution for the Deaf & Dumb & the Blind, 1861), 83; William M. Mathew, *Edmund Ruffin and the Crisis of Slavery in the Old South: The Failure of Agricultural Reform* (Athens, GA: University of Georgia Press, 1988), 42–48, 86–90, 93–126, 132–139; Craven, *Soil Exhaustion*, 93, 135; John Majewski, *Modernizing a Slave Economy: The Economic Vision of the Confederate Nation* (Chapel Hill: University of North Carolina Press, 2009), 53–57.

16. *American Farmer* 9 (1854): 310, 347; *Fredericksburg News*, January 15, 1855; *American Farmer* 11 (1855): 147; Weymouth Jordan, "Peruvian Guano Gospel in the Old South," *Agricultural History* 24 (1950): 216; Mauldin, *Unredeemed Land*, 39; Gregory T. Cushman, *Guano and the Opening of the Pacific World: A Global Ecological History* (New York: Cambridge University Press, 2013), 81–84; Stoll, *Larding the Lean Earth*, 49–68, 187–194.

17. Mauldin, *Unredeemed Land*, 39; *Arator*, April 1855, 15; Ebenezzer Emmons, *Report of the North-Carolina Geological Survey* (Raleigh, NC: H. D. Turner, 1858), 124.

18. William B. Smith, "Can the Culture of Tobacco Be Dispensed with in Eastern Virginia," *Farmer's Register* 6 (1838): 748; Edward Strutt Abdy, *Journal of a Residence and Tour in the United States of North America* (London: G. Woodfall, 1835), 2:183.

19. Johnson, *River of Dark Dreams*, 153–157; Anthony E. Kaye, *Joining Places: Slave Neighborhoods in the Old South* (Chapel Hill: University of North Carolina Press, 2009), 97–98; Gates, *The Farmer's Age*, 137.

20. Joseph Holt Ingraham, *The South-West: By a Yankee* (New York: Harpers, 1835), 86–87.

21. *Georgia Courier* (Augusta), October 11, 1827; William Chandler Bagley Jr., *Soil Exhaustion and the Civil War* (Washington, DC: American Council on Public Affairs, 1942), 20–22; James Silk Buckingham, *The Slave States of America* (London: Fisher, 1845), 1:173; Mauldin, *Unredeemed Land*, 36; James Oakes, *Ruling Race: A History of American Slaveholders* (New York: Knopf, 1982), 77–78; J. D. B. DeBow, *Industrial Resources, Etc. of the Southern and Western States* (Charleston, SC: DeBow's, 1853), 1:73; William L. Barney, *Rebels in the Making: The Secession Crisis and the Birth of the Confederacy* (New York: Oxford University Press, 2020), 14–16.

22. P. Phillips, "Alabama Railroad Enterprise," *DeBow's Review* 8 (1850): 181; David T. Morgan, "Philip Phillips and Internal Improvements in Mid-Nineteenth-Century

Alabama," *Alabama Review* 34 (1981): 83–93; Barney, *Rebels in the Making*, 14–17; Majewski, *Modernizing a Slave Society*, 72–75.

23. John Thompson, *Life of John Thompson, a Fugitive Slave* (Worcester, MA: John Thompson, 1843), 43; Ball, *Slavery in the United States*, 56, 82–83; Lewis Clarke, *Narrative of the Sufferings of Lewis Clarke* (Boston: David G. Ela, 1845), 62.

24. Philip R. P. Coelho and Robert A. McGuire, "Biology, Diseases, and Economics: An Epidemiological History of Slavery in the American South," *Journal of Bioeconomics* 1 (1999): 158–168; Todd L. Savitt, *Medicine and Slavery: The Diseases and Heath Care of Blacks in Antebellum Virginia* (Champaign: University of Illinois Press, 2002), 69–71; Alan I. Marcus, "The South's Native Foreigners: Hookworm as a Factor in Southern Distinctiveness," in *Disease and Distinctiveness in the American South*, ed. Todd L. Savitt and James Harvey Young (Knoxville: University of Tennessee Press, 1988), 79–99.

25. Marli F. Weiner and Mazie Hough, *Sex, Sickness, and Slavery: Illness in the Antebellum South* (Champaign: University of Illinois Press, 2012), 25–28; Stephen M. Stowe, *Doctoring the South: Southern Physicians and Everyday Medicine in the Mid-Nineteenth Century* (Chapel Hill: University of North Carolina Press, 2004), 50; Robert W. Twyman, "The Clay-Eater: A New Look at an Old Southern Enigma," *Journal of Southern History* 37 (1971): 439–448; Deanne Stephens Nuwar, "'I'll be blame ef I hanker after making my bowels a brick-yard': Dirt Eating in the Antebellum and Early Modern South," *Southern Quarterly* 53 (2016): 141–155; Weiner and Hough, *Sex, Sickness, and Slavery*, 25–27.

26. Kenneth F. Kiple and Virginia H. King, *Another Dimension to the Black Diaspora: Diet, Disease, and Racism* (New York: Cambridge University Press, 1981), 76, 113–114; Savitt, *Medicine and Slavery*, 64–71. Medical historians debate whether enslaved peoples in the North America had guinea worm, which was endemic among enslaved populations in the Caribbean and parts of South America. See Herbert C. Covey, *African American Slave Medicine: Herbal and Non-Herbal Treatments* (Lanham, MD: Lexington, 2007), 10; Peter McCandless, *Slavery, Disease, and Suffering in the Southern Lowcountry* (New York: Cambridge University Press, 2011), 6–7; Susan J. Watts, "Population Mobility and Disease Transmission: The Example of the Guinea Worm," *Social Science Medicine* 25 (1987): 1073–1081; Watts, "Dracunculiasis in the Caribbean and South America: A Contribution to the History of Dracunculiasis Eradication," *Medical History* 45 (2000): 227–250.

27. Jack P. Greene, *Diary of Colonel Landon Carter of Sabine Hall* (Charlottesville: Virginia Historical Society, 1965), 1:205–206; Larkin Stanard to Carmichael, June 4, 1823, George Banks to Carmichael, August 10 and 16, 1823, William Herndon to Carmichael, February 16, 1820, M. Jones to Carmichael, April 27, 1821, Dr. James Carmichael Papers, University of Virginia Special Collections. Also see Bennett H. Wall, "Medical Care of Ebenezer Pettigrew's Slaves," *Journal of American History* 37 (1950): 467.

28. Adeline Cunningham, *Federal Writers' Project: Slave Narrative Project*, vol. 16, *Texas*, pt. 1:268; Charlie Davenport, *Federal Writers' Project: Slave Narrative Project*, vol. 9, *Mississippi*, pt. 1, 37–38.

29. Henry Barnard, "The South Atlantic States in 1833, as Seen by a New Englander," *Maryland Historical Magazine* 13 (1918): 346–347.

30. Drew A. Swanson, *Beyond the Mountains: Commodifying Appalachian Environments* (Athens, GA: University of Georgia Press, 2018), 64; Wilma A. Dunaway, *Slavery in the American Mountain South* (New York: Cambridge University Press, 2003), 119; Davis, *Where There Are Mountains*, 155–156; Porte Crayon [David Hunter Strother], "North Carolina Illustrated," *Harper's New Monthly Magazine* 87 (August 1857): 298.

31. Jason L. Hauser, "Agrarianism, Industry, the Environment, and Change: Gold Mining in Antebellum North Carolina" (master's thesis, Appalachian State University, 2012), 14–15; William Thornton, *North Carolina Gold-Mine Company* (Washington, DC: np, 1806), 10; Jason Hauser, "'A Golden Harvest': Gold Mining and Agricultural Reform in North Carolina, 1799–1842," *Agricultural History* 91 (2017): 473–474; Dennison Olmsted, "Geology and Mineralogy of North-Carolina," *Southern Review* 1 (1828): 251–252; Richard F. Knapp, "Golden Promise in the Piedmont: The Story of John Reed's Mine," *North Carolina Historical Review* 52 (1975): 4–5; Elizabeth Hines and Michael S. Smith, "Gold Is Where You Find It: Placer Miner in North Carolina, 1799–1849," *Earth Sciences History* 21 (2002): 121; Dunaway, *Slavery in the American Mountain South*, 120; Fletcher Melvin Green, "Gold Mining: A Forgotten Industry of Ante-Bellum North Carolina," *North Carolina Historical Review* 14 (1937): 9.

32. Hauser, "Agrarianism, Industry, the Environment, and Change," 43–44; Jeff Forret, "Slave Labor in North Carolina's Antebellum Gold Mines," *North Carolina Historical Review* 76 (1999): 142–143.

33. David Williams, *The Georgia Gold Rush: Twenty-Niners, Cherokees, and Gold Fever* (Columbia: University of South Carolina Press, 1993), 25–30; Jonathan Dean Sarris, *A Separate Civil War: Communities in Conflict in the Mountain South* (Charlottesville: University of Virginia Press, 2006), 13; H. David Williams, "Gambling Away the Inheritance: The Cherokee Nation and Georgia's Gold and Land Lotteries of 1832–33," *Georgia Historical Quarterly* 73 (1989): 519–539; E. Merton Coulter, *Auraria: The Story of a Georgia Gold Mining Town* (Athens, GA: University of Georgia Press, 1956); Claudio Saunt, *Unworthy Republic: The Dispossession of Native Americans and the Road to Indian Territory* (New York: Norton, 2020), 271–273.

34. Forret, "Slave Labor in North Carolina's Antebellum Gold Mines," 138–144; Dunaway, *Slavery in the American Mountain South*, 120–124; Williams, "Georgia's Forgotten Miners," 42; John C. Inscoe, *Mountain Masters: Slavery and the Sectional Crisis in Western North Carolina* (Knoxville: University of Tennessee Press, 1989), 72–73; Hauser, "Agrarianism, Industry, the Environment, and Change," 25–26;

H. B. C. Nitze and H. A. J. Wilkens, "The Present Condition of Gold-Mining in the Southern Appalachian States," *Transactions of the American Institute of Mining Engineers* 25 (1896): 681. Also see Charles E. Rothe, "Remarks on the Gold Mines of North Carolina," *American Journal of Science and Arts* 13 (1826): 208.

35. Isaac T. Avery to Samuel P. Carson, Report 39, *Reports of the Committees of the House of Representatives, Twenty-Second Congress*, First Session, 22; Edward W. Phifer, "Champagne at Brindletown: The Story of the Burke County Gold Rush, 1829–1833," *North Carolina Historical Review* 40 (1963): 492; Jane Turner Censer, *North Carolina Planters and Their Children* (Baton Rouge: Louisiana State University Press, 1990), 12; "Deed of Conveyance from David C Gibson to John C Calhoun and John E Colhoun of a Gold Mine" (1833), Thomas Green Clemson Papers, Clemson University; Sheri L. Boatright, *John C. Calhoun Gold Mine: An Introductory Report on Its Historical Significance* (Atlanta: Georgia Department of Natural Resources, 1974), 11–13, 20; John C. Calhoun to James Edward Colhoun, September 23, 1835, in *The Papers of John C. Calhoun*, ed. Clyde N. Wilson (Columbia: University of South Carolina Press, 1979), 12:554–555; David Williams, "Georgia's Forgotten Miners: African-Americans and the Georgia Gold Rush," *Georgia Historical Quarterly* 75 (1991): 80; George Washington Paschal, *Ninety-Four Years: Agnes Paschal* (Washington, DC: M'Gill & Witherow, 1871), 238, 241–242; Thomas G. Clemson, "Gold and the Gold Region," *Orion* 4 (1844): 65.

36. Green, "Gold Mining," 13; Barnard, "South Atlantic States," 340; *Western Democrat*, August 30, 1859; Williams, "Georgia's Forgotten Miners," 82; Forret, "Slave Labor," 145; Robert S. Starobin, *Industrial Slavery in the Old South* (New York: Oxford University Press, 1970), 47; James G. Scott to John Scott; November 12, 1833, Dr. John Scott Papers, Southern Historical Collection, University of North Carolina—Chapel Hill (SHC hereafter); Inscoe, *Mountain Masters*, 72, 92.

37. Elizabeth Hines, "McCulloch's Rock Engine House: An Antebellum Cornish-Style Gold Ore Mill near Jamestown, North Carolina," *Material Culture* 27 (1995): 1–28; Knapp, "Golden Promise," 12–14; Hines and Smith, "Gold Is Where You Find It," 136–138; Alasdair Bland, "The Environmental Disaster That Is the Gold Industry," *Smithsonian*, February 14, 2014, https://www.smithsonianmag.com/science-nature/environmental-disaster-gold-industry-180949762/. Mercury poisoning remains a major health risk for miners in developing countries. Louisa J. Esdaile and Justin M. Chalker, "The Mercury Problem in Artisanal and Small-Scale Gold Mining," *Chemistry* 24 (2018): 6905–6916; Suzanne Daley, "Peru Scrambles to Drive Out Illegal Gold Mining and Save Precious Land," *New York Times*, July 25, 2016.

38. "Dahlonega, or Georgia Gold Region," *Merchants' Magazine and Commercial Review* 19 (1848): 112–113; Swanson, *Beyond the Mountains*, 63; George Cooke, "Sketches of Georgia," *Southern Literary Messenger* 6 (November 1840): 775–777; Francis M. Goddard Diary, November 14, 1833, University of Kentucky; Dunaway, *Slavery in the American Mountain South*, 120.

39. Dunaway, *Slavery in the American Mountain South*, 122.

40. George William Featherstonhaugh, *A Canoe Voyage Up the Minnay Sotor* (London: R. Bentley, 1847), 2:333; *Niles' Register*, August 7, 1830; Williams, "Georgia's Forgotten Miners," 81; *Adams Centennial* (Gettysburg, PA), November 22, 1826; Green, "Gold Mining," 15; Forest C. Wade, *Cry of the Eagle* (Cumming, GA: np., 1969), 79; Jennifer Oast, *Institutional Slavery: Slaveholding Churches, Schools, Colleges, and Businesses in Virginia, 1680–1860* (New York: Cambridge University Press, 2016), 224–225.

41. August Partz, "Gold-Bearing Belts of the Atlantic States," *Mining Magazine* 3 (1843): 165; Williams, "Georgia's Forgotten Miners," 79–82; Forret, "Slave Labor," 150.

42. Williams, "Georgia's Forgotten Miners," 82; John Hope Franklin and Loren Schweninger, *Runaway Slaves: Rebels on the Plantation* (New York: Oxford University Press, 2000), 80–82; Forret, "Slave Labor," 150–151; Williams, "Georgia's Forgotten Miners," 82–84; Wash Ingram, *Federal Writers' Project: Slave Narrative Project*, vol. 16, *Texas*, pt. 2, 177.

43. Forret, "Slave Labor," 153.

44. *Carolina Spectator*, October 1, 1831; Forret, "Slave Labor," 154; Hauser, "Agrarianism, Industry, the Environment, and Change," 44–45.

45. Isaac T. Avery to Selina Lenoir, September 26, 1831, Lenoir Family Papers, SHC; Forret, "Slave Labor," 155; Dunaway, *Slavery in the American Mountain South*, 120; Edward W. Phifer, "Slavery in Microcosm: Burke County, North Carolina," *Journal of Southern History* 28 (1962): 150–151.

46. Inscoe, *Mountain Masters*, 79; Swanson, *Beyond the Mountains*, 64–65; Stephen P. Leeds, "Notes on the Gold Region of North and South Carolina," *Mining Magazine* 2 (1854): 367.

47. William P. Blake and Charles T. Jackson, *Gold Placers of the Vicinity of Dahlonega* (Boston: n.p., 1859), 10–14; Swanson, *Beyond the Mountains*, 65–71; William Smith Yeates, S. W. McCallie, and Francis P. King, *Preliminary Report on a Part of the Gold Deposits* (Atlanta: G. W. Harrison, 1896), 276.

48. Crayon, "North Carolina Illustrated," 289–294.

49. Featherstonhaugh, *A Canoe Voyage*, 255.

50. Davis, *Where There Are Mountains*, 147–160; Starobin, *Industrial Slavery*, 14–24

51. Ronald L. Lewis, *Black Coal Miners in America: Race, Class, and Community Conflict, 1780–1980* (Lexington: University Press of Kentucky, 1987), 12; Jonathan Daniel Wells, *Origins of the Southern Middle Class, 1800–1861* (Chapel Hill: University of North Carolina Press, 2005), 188; Starobin, *Industrial Slavery*, 23; *Richmond Enquirer*, March 23, 1839; Charles Lyell, "On the Structure and Probable Age of the Coal-Field of the James River," *Quarterly Journal of the Geological Society* 3 (1847): 270; "Explosion at the Midlothian Coal Pits," *Mining Magazine* 4 (1855): 316–317; Oswald J. Heinrich, "The Midlothian, Virginia, Colliery in 1876," *Transactions of the American Institute of Mining Engineers* 4

(1875–1876): 310; *Richmond Daily Dispatch*, December 16–17, 1856; Ronald L. Lewis, "'Darkest Abode of Man': Black Miners in the First Southern Coal Field, 1780–1865," *Virginia Magazine of History and Biography* 87 (1979): 197–199; Todd L. Savitt, "Slave Life Insurance in Virginia and North Carolina," *Journal of Southern History* 43 (1977): 592.

52. Lynn Rainville, *Hidden History: African American Cemeteries in Central Virginia* (Charlottesville: University of Virginia Press, 2014); Joseph A. Downer, "Hallowed Ground, Sacred Space: The Slave Cemetery at George Washington's Mount Vernon and the Cultural Landscapes of the Enslaved" (master's thesis, George Washington University, 2015); Dan Summer Allen, "'Yea, Though I Walk Through the Valley of the Shadow of Death': Mortuary and Material Culture Patterning at the Donelson Slave Cemetery" (master's thesis, Middle Tennessee State University, 2013); David R. Roediger, "And Die in Dixie: Funerals, Death, and Heaven in the Slave Community, 1700–1865," *Massachusetts Review* 22 (1981): 163–183; Allen Parker, *Recollections of Slavery Times* (Worcester, MA: Charles W. Burbank, 1895), 80–81.

CHAPTER 2

1. Stuart Seeley Sprague, *His Promised Land: The Autobiography of John P. Parker, Former Slave and Conductor on the Underground Railroad* (New York: Norton, 1988), 26, 29–30, 47, 49, 61.

2. Stephanie H. M. Camp, *Closer to Freedom: Enslaved Women and Everyday Resistance in the Plantation South* (Chapel Hill: University of North Carolina Press, 2004), 4–34.

3. Abraham Gibson, *Feral Animals in the American South: An Evolutionary History* (New York: Cambridge University Press, 2016), 66. On the colonial practice of open husbandry, see Virginia DeJohn Anderson, *Creatures of Empire: How Domestic Animals Transformed Early America* (New York: Oxford University Press, 2006), 114, 158–163.

4. Sam Bowers Hilliard, *Hog Meat and Hoecake: Food Supply in the Old South, 1840–1860* (Carbondale: Southern Illinois University Press, 1972), 25.

5. Hilliard, *Hog Meat and Hoecake*, 125–126; Reuben Gold Thwaites, *Early Western Travels* (Cleveland: A. H. Clark, 1904), 3:257; Wilma A. Dunaway, *The First American Frontier: Transition to Capitalism in Southern Appalachia, 1700–1860* (Chapel Hill: University of North Carolina Press, 1996), 280; Elisha Mitchell, *Diary of a Geological Tour*, James Sprunt Historical Monograph 6 (Chapel Hill: University of North Carolina Press, 1905), 40.

6. Frederick Douglass, *Narrative of the Life of Frederick Douglass, an American Slave* (Boston: Anti-Slavery Office, 1845), 26; Ball, *Slavery in the United States*, 195–198; Thomas G. Andrews, "Beasts of the Southern Wild: Slaveholders, Slaves, and Other Animals in Charles Ball's *Slavery in the United States*," in *Rendering*

Nature: Animals, Bodies, Places, Politics, ed. Marguerite S. Schaffer and Phoebe S. K. Young (Philadelphia: University of Pennsylvania Press, 2015), 21–47.

7. J. H. Easterby, "South Carolina through New England Eyes: Almira Coffin's Visit to the Low Country in 1851," *South Carolina Historical and Genealogical Magazine* 45 (1944): 133–134; B. R. Carroll, *Historical Collections of South Carolina* (New York: Harper & Brothers, 1836), 2:132; Hilliard, *Hog Meat and Hoecake*, 129–133.

8. Buckingham, *The Slave States of America*, 2:234; Sam B. Hilliard, "Pork in the Ante-Bellum South: The Geography of Self-Sufficiency," *Annals of the Association of American Geographers* 59 (1969): 464; Hilliard, *Hog Meat and Hoecake*, 92–99.

9. St. George Cocke, "Management of Negroes," *DeBow's Review* 14 (1853): 177; Shade Richards, *Federal Writers' Project: Slave Narrative Project*, vol. 4, *Georgia*, pt. 3, 22.

10. Philip Henry Gosse, *Letters from Alabama* (London: Morgan & Chase, 1859), 63; Olmsted, *A Journey in the Seaboard Slave States*, 65–66, 76.

11. Henry Clay Bruce, *New Man: Twenty-Nine Years a Slave, Twenty-Nine Years a Free Man* (York, PA: F. Anstadt & Sons, 1895), 19–20.

12. Kurt C. VerCauteren et al., *Invasive Wild Pigs in North America: Ecology, Impacts, and Management* (Boca Raton, FL: CRC, 2019).

13. Jack Temple Kirby, *Poquosin: A Study of Rural Landscape and Society* (Chapel Hill: University of North Carolina Press, 1995), 100; Gibson, *Feral Animals*, 69–70; Drew A. Swanson, "Fighting Over Fencing: Agricultural Reform and Antebellum Efforts to Close the Virginia Open Range," *Virginia Magazine of History and Biography* 117 (2009): 104–139.

14. Dylan C. Penningroth, *Claims of Kinfolk: African American Property and Community in the Nineteenth-Century South* (Chapel Hill: University of North Carolina Press, 2003), 94; Olmsted, *A Journey in the Seaboard Slave States*, 422, 439; Charles W. Joyner, *Down by the Riverside: A South Carolina Slave Community* (Urbana: University of Illinois Press, 1985), 52; Philip D. Morgan, "The Ownership of Property by Slaves in the Mid-Nineteenth Century Low Country," *Journal of Southern History* 49 (1983): 399–420; Jeff Forret, *Race Relations at the Margins: Slaves and Poor Whites in the Antebellum Southern Countryside* (Baton Rouge: Louisiana State University Press, 2006), 81–82; Loren Schweninger, "Slave Independence and Enterprise in South Carolina, 1780–1865," *South Carolina Historical Magazine* 93 (1992): 101–125.

15. John Smyth, *A Tour in the United States* (London: G. Robinson, 1784), 2:102; Schoepf, *Travels in the Confederation*, 100; Sylviane A. Diouf, *Slavery's Exiles: The Story of the American Maroons* (New York: New York University Press, 2014), 145, 223; Ted Maris-Wolf, "Hidden in Plain Sight: Maroon Life and Labor in Virginia's Dismal Swamp," *Slavery and Abolition* 34 (2013): 447–8.

16. William A. Smith, *Lectures on the Philosophy and Practice of Slavery, as Exhibited in the Institution of Domestic Slavery in the United States, with the Duties of Masters to Slaves* (Nashville: Stevenson & Evans, 1856), 297–298; Jeff Calhoun, *Federal Writers'*

Project: Slave Narrative Project, vol. 16, *Texas*, pt. 1, 188; Nicholas W. Proctor, *Bathed in Blood: Hunting and Mastery in the Old South* (Charlottesville: University of Virginia Press, 2002), 150.

17. Eugene D. Genovese, *Roll, Jordan, Roll: The World the Slaves Made* (New York: Vintage, 1976), 62–63; Philip D. Morgan, *Slave Counterpoint: Black Culture in the Eighteenth-Century Chesapeake and Lowcountry* (Chapel Hill: University of North Carolina Press, 1988), 92–93, 102–103, 134–145; Elizabeth J. Reitz, Tyson Gibbs, and Ted A. Rathbun, "Archaeological Evidence for Subsistence on Coastal Plantations," in *The Archaeology of Slavery and Plantation Life*, ed. Theresa A. Singleton (Orlando, FL: Academic Press, 1985), 163–191; Tyson Gibbs, Kathleen Cargill, Leslie Sue Lieberman, and Elizabeth J. Reitz, "Nutrition in a Slave Population: An Anthropological Examination," *Medical Anthropology* 4 (1980): 175–262; Daniel L. Fountain, "Historians and Historical Archaeology: Slave Sites," *Journal of Interdisciplinary History* 26 (1995): 67–77; William L. McKee, "Plantation Food Supply in Nineteenth Century Tidewater Virginia" (PhD diss,, University of California, Berkeley, 1988), 98; Amy L. Young, Michael Tuma, and Cliff Jenkins, "The Role of Hunting to Cope with Risk at Saragossa Plantation, Natchez, Mississippi," *American Anthropologist* 103 (2001): 697–699.

18. Solomon Northup, *Twelve Years a Slave* (Auburn, NY: Derby & Miller, 1853), 200; Scott Giltner, "Slave Hunting and Fishing in the Antebellum South," in *"To Love the Wind and the Rain": African Americans and Environmental History*, ed. Dianne D. Glave and Mark Stoll (Pittsburgh: University of Pittsburgh Press, 2006), 23.

19. Betty Wood, *Women's Work, Men's Work: The Informal Slave Economies of Lowcountry Georgia* (Athens, GA: University of Georgia Press, 1995), 44–46; Ball, *Slavery in the United States*, 43; Ira Berlin and Philip D. Morgan, eds., *The Slaves' Economy: Independent Production by Slaves in the Americas* (London: Frank Cass, 1991); Loren Schweninger, "The Underside of Slavery: The Internal Economy, Self-Hire, and Quasi-freedom in Virginia, 1780–1865," *Slavery and Abolition* 12 (1991): 1–22; Forret, *Race Relations at the Margins*; Timothy J. Lockley, "Trading Encounters Between Non-Elite Whites and African Americans in Savannah, 1790–1860," *Journal of Southern History* 66 (2000): 25–48; David E. Paterson, "Slavery, Slaves, and Cash in a Georgia Village, 1825–1865," *Journal of Southern History* 75 (2009): 879–930; Giltner, "Slave Hunting and Fishing," 33; Thomas Cole, *Federal Writers' Project: Slave Narrative Project*, vol. 16, *Texas*, pt. 1, 229.

20. Jenny Proctor, *Federal Writers' Project: Slave Narrative Project*, vol. 16, *Texas*, pt. 3, 210; James Bolton, *Federal Writers' Project: Slave Narrative Project*, vol. 4, *Georgia*, pt. 1, 93.

21. Stewart, *What Nature Suffers*, 161; Alex Woods, *Federal Writers' Project: Slave Narrative Project*, vol. 11, *North Carolina*, pt. 2, 418; Giltner, "Slave Hunting and Fishing," 23; Ball, *Slavery in the United States*, 352.

22. Giltner, "Slave Hunting and Fishing," 30; Ball, *Slavery in the United States*, 230–231, 262–263, 324–325.

23. Amos Lincoln, *Federal Writers' Project: Slave Narrative Project*, vol. 16, *Texas*, pt. 3, 18; Julius Nelson, *Federal Writers' Project: Slave Narrative Project*, vol. 11, *North Carolina*, pt. 2, 145; Proctor, *Bathed in Blood*, 149–151.

24. Julia Rush, *Federal Writers' Project: Slave Narrative Project*, vol. 4, *Georgia*, pt. 3, 229; Stewart, *What Nature Suffers*, 136; Midge Burnett, *Federal Writers' Project: Slave Narrative Project*, vol. 11, *North Carolina*, pt. 1, 137; Giltner, "Slave Hunting and Fishing in the Antebellum South," 27–28.

25. George Rogers, *Federal Writers' Project: Slave Narrative Project*, vol. 11, *North Carolina*, pt. 2, 222; Ball, *Slavery in the United States*, 43, 278–279, 292, 298, 301; Giltner, "Slave Hunting and Fishing in the Antebellum South," 28.

26. Frances Anne Kemble, *Journal of a Residence on a Georgian Plantation in 1838–1839* (New York: Harpers & Brothers, 1863), 48, 165, 168–169, 201.

27. Ball, *Slavery in the United States*, 150–151, 352–353, 355–357.

28. Savitt, *Medicine and Slavery*, 71–72; William Dusinberre, *Them Dark Days: Slavery in American Rice Swamps* (New York: Oxford University Press, 1996), 61; Timothy Silver, *New Face on the Countryside: Indians, Colonists, and Slaves in South Atlantic Forests, 1500–1800* (New York: Cambridge University Press, 1990), 153; Harriet A. Jacobs, *Incidents in the Life of a Slave Girl* (Boston: published for the author, 1861), 76; John Andrew Jackson, *Experience of a Slave in South Carolina* (London: Passmore & Alabaster, 1862), 29; Irving E. Lowery, *Life on the Old Plantation in Ante-Bellum Days* (Columbia, SC: State Co. Printers, 1911), 50.

29. Northup, *Twelve Years a Slave*, 139–140; Ball, *Slavery in the United States*, 392–393.

30. Wes Brady, *Federal Writers' Project: Slave Narrative Project*, vol. 16, *Texas*, pt. 1, 134; Johnson, *River of Dark Dreams*, 222–224; Rhys Isaac, *The Transformation of Virginia, 1740–1790* (Chapel Hill: University of North Carolina Press, 1982), 52–57; Sally E. Hadden, *Slave Patrols: Law and Violence in Virginia and the Carolinas* (Cambridge, MA: Harvard University Press, 2003), 43–44, 49–52, 85, 121; Northup, *Twelve Years a Slave*, 165; Henry Bibb, *Narrative of Life and Adventures of Henry Bibb, An American Slave* (New York: published by the author, 1849), 130; Frederick Douglass, *Life and Times of Frederick Douglass* (Boston: De Wolfe & Fiske, 1892), 214

31. Katherine C. Mooney, *Race Horse Men: How Slavery and Freedom Were Made at the Racetrack* (Cambridge, MA: Harvard University Press, 2014); Robert Lee Meriwether, *The Expansion of South Carolina, 1729–1765* (Kingsport, TN: Southern Publishers, 1940), 12; Carroll, *Historical Collections of South Carolina*, 2:133; Edward A. Pearson, "A Countryside Full of Flames: A Reconsideration of the Stono Rebellion and Slave Rebelliousness in the Early Eighteenth-Century South Carolina Lowcountry," *Slavery and Abolition* 17 (1996): 25–28.

32. Sam Jones Washington, *Federal Writers' Project: Slave Narrative Project*, vol. 16, *Texas*, pt. 4: 139, Kyle Ainsworth, "Field Hands, Cowboys, and Runaways: Enslaved People on Horseback in Texas's Planter-Herder Economy, 1835–1865," *Journal of Southern History* 86 (2020): 557–600.

33. Jacob D. Green, *Narrative of the Life of J. D. Green, a Runaway Slave* (Huddersfield, UK: Henry Fielding, 1864), 11–12; "Rules in the Management of a Southern Estate," *DeBow's Review* 22 (April 1857): 378.

34. Charles Perret, "Letter to *Moniteur de la Louisiane*," January 17, 1811, in *Slavery*, ed. Stanley L. Engerman, Seymour Drescher, and Robert L. Paquette (New York: Oxford University Press, 2001), 324–326; Nathan A. Buman, "To Kill Whites: The 1811 Louisiana Slave Insurrection" (master's thesis, Louisiana State University Press, 2008), 71–73; Franklin and Schweninger, *Runaway Slaves*, 81–82; William Wells Brown, *Narrative of William W. Brown, a Fugitive Slave* (Boston: Anti-Slavery Office, 1847), 150.

35. George B. Ellenberg, *Mule South to Tractor South: Mules, Machines, and the Transformation of the Cotton South* (Tuscaloosa: University of Alabama Press, 2007), 3–21; Gibson, *Feral Animals*, 59–62; Robert Byron Lamb, *The Mule in Southern Agriculture* (Berkeley: University of California Press, 1963), 28; *Southern Planter*, November 1858, 693; Genovese, *Political Economy of Slavery*, 113; Olmsted, *Journey in the Seaboard Slave States*, 47; James Redpath, *Roving Editor* (New York: A. B. Burdick, 1859), 241.

36. Gibson, *Feral Animals*, 60; Lamb, *Mule in Southern Agriculture*, 5–6; Ellenberg, *Mule South*, 24.

37. T. Lindsay Baker and Julie P. Baker, *The WPA Oklahoma Slave Narratives* (Norman: University of Oklahoma Press, 1996), 484; Lula Jackson, *Federal Writers' Project: Slave Narrative Project*, vol. 2, *Arkansas*, pt. 4, 14; Kate E. R. Pickard, *The Kidnapped and the Ransomed* (Syracuse, NY: William T. Hamilton, 1856), 358–359.

38. Genovese, *Political Economy of Slavery*, 112; Franklin and Schweninger, *Runaway Slaves*, 2; Dusinberre, *Them Dark Days*, 137; Marshal Butler, *Federal Writers' Project: Slave Narrative Project*, vol. 4, *Georgia*, pt. 1, 162–163.

39. Ball, *Slavery in the United States*, 82.

40. John Campbell, "'My Constant Companion': Slaves and their Dogs in the Antebellum South," in *Working toward Freedom: Slave Society and Domestic Economy in the American South*, ed. Larry E. Hudson Jr. (Rochester, NY: University of Rochester Press, 1994), 54; Gibson, *Feral Animals*, 56–57; S. Charles Bolton, *Fugitivism: Escaping Slavery in the Lower Mississippi Valley, 1820–1860* (Fayetteville: University of Arkansas Press, 2019), 26–27; Tyler D. Parry and Charlton W. Yingling, "Slave Hounds and Abolition in the Americans," *Past and Present* 246 (2020): 69–108.

41. John Dixon Long, *Pictures of Slavery in Church and State* (Philadelphia: published by the author, 1857), 17; Ball, *Slavery in the United States*, 354–355.

42. Campbell, "My Constant Companion," 60; Northup, *Twelve Years a Slave*, 200; Allen Parker, *Recollections of Slavery Times* (Worcester, MA: Chas. W. Burbank, 1895), 52–53; Isaac D. Williams, *Sunshine and Shadow of Slave Life* (East Saginaw, MI: Evening News, 1885), 71.

43. Penningroth, *Claims of Kinfolk*, 47, 93–97.

44. Ball, *Slavery in the United States*, 389–393.

45. George Washington to Anthony Whitting, December 16, 1792, *Founders Online*, https://founders.archives.gov/documents/Washington/05-11-02-0315; Thomas Jefferson to Edmund Bacon, December 26, 1808, *Founders Online*, https://founders.archives.gov/documents/Jefferson/99-01-02-9403.

46. Edwin Adams Davis, *Plantation Life in the Florida Parishes of Louisiana, 1836–1846* (New York: Columbia University Press, 1943), 373; Campbell, "My Constant Companion," 63–68; Gibson, *Feral Animals*, 56–57.

47. Franklin and Schweninger, *Runaway Slaves*, 160–164; Johnson, *River of Dark Dreams*, 234–238; Northup, *Twelve Years a Slave*, 140.

48. "Recollections of Slavery by a Runaway Slave," *Emancipator*, September 13, 1838; Olmsted, *Journey in the Seaboard Slave States*, 161; Bibb, *Narrative*, 128; Anderson, *Life and Narrative*, 48; Pickard, *The Kidnapped and the Ransomed*, 188–192; Jacob Stroyer, *My Life in the South* (Salem, MA: Salem Observer, 1885), 64; Hadden, *Slave Patrols*, 80; Larry H. Spruill, "Slave Patrols, 'Packs of Negro Dogs' and Policing Black Communities," *Phylon* 53 (2016): 53.

49. Anderson, *Life and Narrative*, 48; Franklin and Schweninger, *Runaway Slaves*, 164; Davis, *Plantation Life in the Florida Parishes of Louisiana*, 369–376; Williams, *Sunshine and Shadow of Slave Life*, 10; Ferebe Rogers, *Federal Writers' Project: Slave Narrative Project*, vol. 4, *Georgia*, pt. 3, 214.

50. Williams, *Sunshine and Shadow of Slave Life*, 10; Octavia V. Rogers Albert, *House of Bondage* (New York: Hunt & Eaton, 1890), 22; Louis Hughes, *Thirty Years a Slave* (Milwaukee: South Side, 1897), 143–144; Sarah Ford, *Federal Writers' Project: Slave Narrative Project*, vol. 16, *Texas*, pt. 2, 45; Andrew Jackson, *Narrative and Writings of Andrew Jackson, of Kentucky* (Syracuse, NY: Daily & Weekly Star Office, 1847), 11.

51. Williams, *Sunshine and Shadow*, 16–17.

52. Karl Jacoby, "Slaves by Nature? Domestic Animals and Human Slaves," *Slavery and Abolition* 15 (1994): 89–99. Also see David Brion Davis, *Inhuman Bondage: The Rise and Fall of Slavery in the New World* (New York: Oxford University Press, 2006), 32; Floyd, "Management of Servants," *Southern Cultivator* 11 (1853): 301; George B. Ellenberg, "African Americans, Mules, and the Southern Mindscape, 1850–1950," *Agricultural History* 72 (1998): 381–398; Frederick Law Olmsted, *The Cotton Kingdom* (New York: Mason Brothers, 1861), 2:203.

53. Robert Falls, *Federal Writers' Project: Slave Narrative Project*, vol. 15, *Tennessee*, 12–13; Bibb, *Narrative*, 18; Anderson, *Life and Narrative*, 12; Leonard Black, *Life and Sufferings of Leonard Black, a Fugitive from Slavery* (New Bedford, MA: Benjamin Lindsey, 1847), 5, 19; Thomas Cole, *Federal Writers' Project: Slave Narrative Project*, vol. 16, *Texas*, pt. 1, 229; Charles Thompson, *Biography of a Slave* (Dayton, OH: United Brethren, 1875), 29; Theodore Dwight Weld, *American Slavery As It Is: Testimony of a Thousand Witnesses* (New York: Anti-Slavery Office, 1839), 159; Interview with Fountain Hughes, Archive of Folk Culture, American Folklife Center, Library of Congress.

54. Joyner, *Down by the Riverside*, 172–195; Sergio Lussana, "Reassessing Brer Rabbit: Friendship, Altruism, and Community in the Folklore of Enslaved African-Americans," *Slavery and Abolition* 38 (2018): 123–146.

CHAPTER 3

1. Olmsted, *A Journey in the Seaboard Slave States*, 338–347; Natalie P. Adams, "A Pattern of Living: A View of the African American Slave Experience in the Pine Forests of the Lower Cape Fear," in *Another's Country: Archaeological and Historical Perspectives on Cultural Interactions in the Southern Colonies*, ed. J. W. Joseph and Martha Zierden (Tuscaloosa: University of Alabama Press, 2002), 67; Louis Masur, "Olmsted's Southern Landscapes.," *New York Times*, July 9, 2011, https://opiniona tor.blogs.nytimes.com/2011/07/09/olmsteds-southern-landscapes.

2. John A. Eisterhold, "Colonial Beginnings in the Southern Lumber Industry: 1607–1800," *Southern Lumberman* 223 (1971): 150–153; John A. Eisterhold, "Charleston: Lumber and Trade in a Declining Southern Port," *South Carolina Historical Magazine* 74 (1972): 61–72; Joseph A. Goldenberg, *Shipbuilding in Colonial America* (Charlottesville: University Press of Virginia, 1976), 117–122; Lynn B. Harris, *Patroons and Periaguas: Enslaved Watermen and Watercraft of the Lowcountry* (Columbia: University of South Carolina Press, 2014), 30–31.

3. Vanessa E. Patrick, "Partitioning the Landscape: The Fence in Eighteenth-Century Virginia," *Colonial Williamsburg Foundation Library Research Report Series* 134 (1983): 32–36; Greene, *Diary of Colonel Landon Carter*, 1:382; Walsh, *Motives of Honor*, 252, 534; Rhys Isaac, *Landon Carter's Uneasy Kingdom: Revolution and Rebellion on a Virginia Plantation* (New York: Oxford University Press, 2004), 59–60.

4. William Bartram, *Travels Through North and South Carolina, Georgia, East and West Florida, the Cherokee County, the Extensive Territories of the Muscogulges, or Creek Confederacy, and the Country of the Chactaws* (Philadelphia: James & Johnson, 1791), 197–198; Janet Schaw, *Journal of a Lady of Quality: Being the Narrative of a Journey from Scotland to the West Indies, North Carolina, and Portugal, in the Years 1774 to 1776* (New Haven, CT: Yale University Press, 1921), 184–185.

5. *De Brahm's Report of the General Survey in the Southern District of North America* (Columbia: University of South Carolina Press, 1971), 94.

6. William Eddis, *Letters from America* (London: printed for the author, 1792), 34; Silver, *A New Face*, 132; David Ramsay, *The History of South Carolina* (Charleston: David Longworth, 1809), 2:341.

7. William Darby, *The Emigrant's Guide to the Western and Southwestern States and Territories* (New York: Kirk & Mercein, 1818), 132–133; Weymouth Jordan, "Early Ante-Bellum Marion, Alabama," *Alabama Historical Quarterly* 5

(1943): 27; Clanton W. Williams, "Early Ante-Bellum Montgomery: A Black Belt Constituency," *Journal of Southern History* 7 (1941): 495–525; Erhard Rostlund, "The Myth of a Natural Prairie Belt in Alabama: An Interpretation of Historical Records," *Annals of the Association of American Geographers* 47 (1947): 392–411; John Barone, "Historical Presence and Distribution of Prairies in the Black Belt of Mississippi and Alabama," *Castanea* 70 (2005): 170–183; Alice Simms Jones and E. Gibbes Patton, "Forest, 'Prairie,' and the Soils in the Black Belt of Sumter County, Alabama, in 1832," *Ecology* 47 (1966): 75–80.

8. Olmsted, *A Journey in the Seaboard Slave States*, 574–577; Roger G. Kennedy, *Mr. Jefferson's Lost Cause: Land, Farmers, Slavery, and the Louisiana Purchase* (New York: Oxford University Press, 2003), 22–23.

9. Silver, *A New Face*, 134; William Cronon, *Changes in the Land: Indians, Colonists, and the Ecology of New England* (New York: Hill & Wang, 1983), 122–126; John Jerdone to his father Francis Jerdone, March 4, 1830, March 28, 1830, March 1, 1831, March 6, 1831, Francis Jerdone to William Jerdone, June 13, 1833, Jerdone Family Papers, W&M.

10. Saikku, *This Delta, This Land*, 49–50; Philip Drennon Thomas, "Endangered Species," in *The New Encyclopaedia of Southern Culture*, vol. 8: *Environment*, ed. Martin Melosi (Chapel Hill: University of North Carolina Press, 2007), 47–54.

11. Gwendolyn Midlo Hall, *Africans in Colonial Louisiana: The Development of Afro-Creole Culture in the Eighteenth-Century* (Baton Rouge: Louisiana State University Press, 1995), 202; John Hebron Moore, "The Cypress Lumber Industry of the Lower Mississippi Valley during the Colonial Period," *Louisiana History* 24 (1983): 25–47; John Hebron Moore, *Andrew Brown and Cypress Lumbering in the Old Southwest* (Baton Rouge: Louisiana State University Press, 1967), 4–11; Jerame Joseph Cramer, "Logs, Labor, and Living: An Archaeological Investigation of African-American Laborers at the Upper and Middle Landing Sawmills at Natchez-Under-the-Hill" (master's thesis, Louisiana State University, 2003), 6.

12. Hall, *Africans in Colonial Louisiana*, 202; Moore, "Cypress Lumber Industry," 29.

13. Hall, *Africans in Colonial Louisiana*, 202–211; Diouf, *Slavery's Exiles*, 121–124.

14. Antoine Simon Le Page du Pratz, *History of Louisiana* (London: T. Becket, 1774), 239; Moore, "Cypress Lumber Industry," 39, 46–47.

15. David J. Libby, *Slavery and Frontier Mississippi, 1720–1835* (Jackson: University Press of Mississippi, 2004), 23–24; Eron Rowland, *Life, Letters and Papers of William Dunbar of Elgin, Morayshire, Scotland and Natchez, Mississippi* (Jackson: Mississippi Historical Society, 1930), 23–26; Arthur H. DeRosier Jr., *William Dunbar: Scientific Pioneer of the Old Southwest* (Lexington: University Press of Kentucky, 2007), 34–35; William Dunbar Account Book, SHC.

16. Johnson, *River of Dark Dreams*, 154; Hughes, *Thirty Years a Slave*, 36; James Paulding, "The Mississippi," *Graham's American Monthly* 22 (1843): 217.

17. Thompson, *Life of John Thompson*, 26–27; Thompson, *Biography of a Slave*, 72; Ronald L. Lewis, *Transforming the Appalachian Countryside: Railroads, Deforestation, and Social Change in West Virginia, 1880–1920* (Chapel Hill: University of North Carolina Press, 1998), 36.

18. Cramer, "Logs, Labor, and Living," 72; Dunaway, *Slavery in the Mountain South*, 134–137.

19. Northup, *Twelve Years a Slave*, 92–94, 97, 154–156. Tibaut's name is spelled Tibeats in Northup's narrative.

20. Johnson, *River of Dark Dreams*, 90, 94; Ari Kelman, "Forests and Other River Perils," in *Transforming New Orleans and Its Environs: Centuries of Change*, ed. Craig E. Colton (Pittsburgh: University of Pittsburgh Press, 2000), 45–63; David E. Schob, "Woodhawks & Cordwood: Steamboat Fuel on the Ohio and Mississippi Rivers, 1820–1860," *Journal of Forest History* 21 (1977): 124–132; Charles Mackay, *Life and Liberty in America* (New York: Harper & Bros., 1859), 155.

21. Zora Neale Hurston, *Barracoon: The Story of the Last "Black Cargo"* (New York: Harper Collins, 2018), 60–61.

22. Joseph Holt Ingraham, *The Sunny South* (Philadelphia: G. G. Evans, 1860), 298; John W. Oldmixon, *Transatlantic Wanderings* (London: Routledge, 1855), 140.

23. Dunaway, *The First American Frontier*, 173–174, 281; Raymond F. Hunt, "The Patrolus Ironworks," *Tennessee Historical Quarterly* 25 (1966): 176–196; J. Peter Lesley, *The Iron Manufacturer's Guide to the Furnaces, Forges, and Rolling Mills of the United States* (New York: J. Wiley, 1859), 63–86, 122–137; Chris Bolgiano, *The Appalachian Forest* (Mechanicsburg, PA: Stackpole, 1998), 68; Sean Patrick Adams, *Iron from the Wilderness: The History of Virginia's Catharine Furnace* (Fredericksburg, VA: National Park Service, 2011), 40–62; James Larry Smith, "Historical Geography of the Southern Charcoal Iron Industry, 1800–1860" (PhD diss., University of Tennessee, 1982); Lester J. Cappon, "Lucy Selina's Charcoal Era," *Virginia Cavalcade* 7 (1957): 31–39; Ernest M. Lander, "The Iron Industry in Ante-Bellum South Carolina," *Journal of Southern History* 20 (1954): 354–355; Davis, *Where There Are Mountains*, 147–154; S. Sydney Bradford, "The Negro Ironworker in Ante-Bellum Virginia," *Journal of Southern History* 25 (1959): 194–195; Starobin, *Industrial Slavery in the Old South*, 14–15; Drew A. Swanson, *A Golden Weed: Tobacco and Environment in the Piedmont South* (New Haven, CT: Yale University Press, 2014), 46–48, 57, 113; Barbara M. Hahn, *Making Tobacco Bright: Creating an American Commodity, 1617–1937* (Baltimore: Johns Hopkins University Press, 2011), 123.

24. Robert B. Outland III, "Slavery, Work, and the Geography of the North Carolina Naval Stores Industry, 1835–1860," *Journal of Southern History* 62 (1998): 30–32; Starobin, *Industrial Slavery*, 26; David S. Cecelski, "Oldest Living Confederate Chaplain Tells All?" *Southern Cultures* 3 (1997): 8.

25. Robert B. Outland III, "Suicidal Harvest: The Self-Destruction of North Carolina's Naval Stores Industry," *North Carolina Historical Review* 78 (2001): 320; Outland,

"Slavery, Work, and the Geography of the North Carolina Naval Stores Industry," 34–38; Adams, "A Pattern of Living," 65–67.

26. "Turpentine: Hints for Those About to Engage in its Manufacture," *DeBow's Review* 19 (October 1855): 487; Gloria Vollmers, "Industrial Slavery in the United States: The North Carolina Turpentine Industry, 1849–61," *Accounting, Business and Financial History* 13 (2003): 379.

27. Vollmers, "Industrial Slavery in the United States," 376–379; Outland, "Slavery, Work, and the Geography of the North Carolina Naval Stores Industry," 45.

28. James Battle Avirett, *The Old Plantation: How We Lived in Great House and Cabin before the War* (New York: F. Tennyson Neeley, 1901), 62–71; Cecelski, "Oldest Living," 14–17; Outland, "Slavery, Work, and the Geography of North Carolina's Naval Stores Industry," 46–47; Vollmers, "Industrial Slavery in the United States," 388.

29. William Cullen Bryant, *Letters of a Traveller* (New York: Putnam, 1850), 79.

30. William D. Valentine Diary, December 23, 1845, SHC; Kirby, *Poquosin*, 33.

31. Perceval Perry, "The Naval-Stores Industry in the Old South, 1790–1860," *Journal of Southern History* 34 (1968): 521–522; Hugh Buckner Johnston, "The Journal of Ebenezer Hazard in North Carolina, 1777 and 1778," *North Carolina Historical Review* 36 (1959): 375–376; Outland, "Suicidal Harvest," 309–344.

32. "Turpentine," 188; Edmund Ruffin, "Notes of a Steam Journey," *Farmers' Register* 8 (April 30, 1840): 250; William Kauffman Scarborough, ed., *Diary of Edmund Ruffin* (Baton Rouge: Louisiana State University Press, 1972), 1:52; Silver, *A New Face on the Countryside*, 126–127; Outland, "Suicidal Harvest," 322–323; Cecelski, "Oldest Living," 20; Avirett, *The Old Plantation*, 70.

33. Outland, "Suicidal Harvest," 309–344; Silver, *A New Face on the Countryside*, 129; Perry, "The Naval-Stores Industry," 523; Ruffin, *Agricultural, Geological, and Descriptive Sketches*, 255–256; Union soldier letter, November 16, 1862, Federal Soldiers' Letters, SHC; Cecelski, "Oldest Living," 8, 19; Lawrence S. Earley, *Looking for Longleaf: The Rise and Fall of an American Forest* (Chapel Hill: University of North Carolina Press, 2004), 1–4.

34. George Lewis, *Impressions of America and the American Churches* (Edinburgh: W. P. Kennedy, 1845), 106–107, 119, 231.

35. Camp, *Closer to Freedom*, 7; Stephanie McCurry, *Confederate Reckoning: Power and Politics in the Civil War South* (Cambridge, MA: Harvard University Press, 2010), 229; Kaye, *Joining Places*, 44; Franklin and Schweninger, *Runaway Slaves*, 98; Emily West, "He come sometime widout de pass: Rethinking Cross-Plantation Marriages and Enslaved Families in Antebellum South Carolina," in *Family Values in the Old South*, ed. Craig Thompson Friend and Anya Jabour (Gainesville: University of Florida Press, 2010), 42–61; Moses Grandy, *Narrative of the Life of Moses Grandy* (London: C. Gilpin, 1843), 8.

36. Albert J. Raboteau, *Slave Religion: The "Invisible Institution" in the Antebellum South* (New York: Oxford University Press, 1978), 212–219; Janet Duitsman Cornelius,

Slave Missions and the Black Church in the Antebellum South (Columbia: University of South Carolina Press, 1999), 8–12; Susan Rhodes, *Federal Writers' Project: Slave Narrative Project*, vol. 10, *Missouri*, 288–289; Peter Randolph, *From Slave Cabin to the Pulpit* (Boston: James H. Earle, 1893), 202–203; John B. Cade, "Out of the Mouths of Ex-Slaves," *Journal of Negro History* 20 (1935): 331; Michael A. Gomez, *Exchanging Our Country Marks: The Transformation of African Identities in the Colonial and Antebellum South* (Chapel Hill: University of North Carolina Press, 1998), 259; Douglass, *Narrative*, 14.

37. Ball, *Slavery in the United States*, 230–231, 262–263, 324–325, 352–353; Sharla M. Fett, *Working Cures: Healing, Health, and Power on Southern Slave Plantations* (Chapel Hill: University of North Carolina Press, 2002), 60–83; Camp, *Closer to Freedom*, 46; Rhodus Walton, *Federal Writers' Project: Slave Narrative Project*, vol. 4, *Georgia*, pt. 4, 124–125; Francis P. Porcher, *Resources of Southern Fields and Forests* (Charleston: Evans & Cogswell, 1863), 90.

38. Gray, *Confessions of Nat Turner*, 10–11; Patrick H. Breen, *The Land Shall Be Deluged in Blood: A New History of the Nat Turner Revolt* (New York: Oxford University Press, 2015), 17, 29, 140–141; Anthony E. Kaye, "Neighborhoods and Nat Turner: The Making of a Slave Rebel and the Unmaking of a Slave Rebellion," *Journal of the Early Republic* 27 (2007): 705–720.

39. Ball, *Slavery in the United States*, 420.

40. Thomas R. Gray, *Confessions of Nat Turner* (Baltimore: T. R. Gray, 1831), 9; Breen, *The Land Shall Be Deluged in Blood*, 19; Franklin and Schweninger, *Runaway Slaves*, 101; Albert, *House of Bondage*, 88–100; Camp, *Closer to Freedom*, 35, 50–51.

41. Sprague, *His Promised Land*, 29–30, 47, 137.

CHAPTER 4

1. Northup, *Twelve Years a Slave*, 65–76.

2. Charles Lyell, *A Second Visit to the United States of North America* (New York: Harper & Brothers, 1849), 2:109, 131, 142–143, 155, 168–169.

3. Trimble, *Man-Induced Soil Erosion on the Southern Piedmont*, 22–25; Alan J. Feduccia, *Catesby's Birds of Colonial America* (Chapel Hill: University of North Carolina Press, 1985), 142, 161; Christopher John Manganiello, "Dam Crazy with Wild Consequences: Artificial Lakes and Natural Rivers in the American South, 1845–1990" (PhD diss., University of Georgia, 2010), 36–37; William Byrd, *Westover Manuscripts: Containing the History of the Dividing Line Betwixt Virginia and North Carolina* (Petersburg, VA: Edmund & Julian C. Ruffin, 1841), 112–113.

4. Bartram, *Travels*, 224–225; Trimble, *Man-Induced Soil Erosion*, 23; William L. Saunders, *Colonial Records of North Carolina* (Raleigh, NC: Hale, 1887), 5:7.

5. Lyell, *Second Visit*, 1:256; Robert H. Dott Jr., "Charles Lyell's Debt to North America: His Lectures and Travels from 1841 to 1853," in *Lyell: The Past is the Key to the Present*, ed. D. J. Blundell and A. C. Scott (London: Geological Society,

1998), 53–69; Oscar M. Lieber, *Report of the Survey of South Carolina* (Columbia, SC: Gibbes, 1856), 106; Walsh, "Land Use, Settlement Patterns, and the Impact of European Agriculture," 242.

6. Ball, *Slavery in the United States*, 136. The origins of rice cultivation in colonial Georgia and South Carolina have divided historians since the 1970s. Noting the similarities between rice cultivation on both sides of the Atlantic, proponents of the "Black rice thesis" argue that enslaved Africans brought extensive knowledge about rice agriculture from Upper Guinea with them to the Lowcountry. First articulated by Peter Wood, and expanded by Daniel Littlefield and Judith Carney, the "Black rice thesis" places the roots of colonial rice firmly in Africa. As skilled agricultural workers, enslaved rice farmers used their expertise for leverage, extracting meaningful concessions from white planters who depended upon their knowledge to cultivate the fickle crop. More recent scholarship has questioned the African origins of Carolina rice, noting that the archival evidence from the formative period in Carolina rice production (1670–1700) suggests that the founding generation of slaves did not come from rice planting regions of Africa and that many of the water management techniques had European origins. Peter H. Wood, *Black Majority: Negroes in Colonial South Carolina from 1650 through the Stono Rebellion* (New York: Knopf, 1974); Daniel C. Littlefield, *Rice and Slaves: Ethnicity and the Slave Trade in Colonial South Carolina* (Champaign: University of Illinois, 1991); Judith A. Carney, *Black Rice: The African Origin of Rice Cultivation in the Americas* (Cambridge, MA: Harvard University Press, 2002); S. Max Edelson, *Plantation Enterprise in Colonial South Carolina* (Cambridge, MA: Harvard University Press, 2011), 53–91; Joyce E. Chaplin, *An Anxious Pursuit: Agricultural Innovation and Modernity in the Lower South, 1730–1815* (Chapel Hill: University of North Carolina Press, 1996), 231–251, 262–275; Robert Olwell, *Masters, Slaves, and Subjects: The Culture of Power in the South Carolina Low Country, 1740–1790* (Ithaca, NY: Cornell University Press, 1998), 43–44; S. Max Edelson, "Beyond 'Black Rice': Reconstructing Material and Cultural Contexts for Early Plantation Agriculture," *American Historical Review* 115 (2010): 125–135; David Eltis, Philip Morgan, and David Richardson, "Agency and Diaspora in Atlantic History: Reassessing the African Contribution to Rice Cultivation in the Americas," *American Historical Review* 112 (2007): 1329–1358; Walter Hawthorne, *Planting Rice and Harvesting Slaves: Transformations along the Guinea-Bissau Coast* (Portsmouth, NH: Heinemann, 2003); Walter Hawthorne, "Black Rice Reconsidered," in *Rice: Global Networks and New Histories*, ed. Francesca Bray, Peter A. Coclanis, Edda Fields-Black, and Dagmar Schaefer (Cambridge, MA: Cambridge University Press, 2015), 279–290.

7. St. Julien R. Childs, "A Letter Written in 1711 by Mary Stafford to Her Kinswoman in England," *South Carolina Historical Magazine* 81 (1980): 4; Schoepf, *Travels in the Confederation*, 2:182; James Habersham to Earl of Hillsborough, April 24, 1772, James Habersham, *The Letters of Hon. James Habersham, 1756–1775* (Savannah, GA: Savannah Morning News, 1904), 171–173; Watson W. Jennison, *Cultivating*

Race: The Expansion of Slavery in Georgia, 1750–1860 (Lexington: University Press of Kentucky, 2012), 21; Morgan, *Slave Counterpart*, 35.

8. Hayden Ros Smith, "Rich Swamps and Rice Grounds: The Specialization of Inland Rice Culture in the South Carolina Lowcountry, 1670–1861" (PhD diss., University of Georgia, 2012), 50; Edelson, *Plantation Enterprise*, 104–106.

9. Edelson, *Plantation Enterprise*, 107–108; Matthew Mulcahy, "'Miserably Scorched': Drought in the Plantation Colonies of the British Great Caribbean," in *Atlantic Environments and the American South*, ed. Thomas Blake Earle and D. Andrew Johnson (Athens, GA: University of Georgia Press, 2020), 70–71; Chaplin, *Anxious Pursuit*, 228–276; Stewart, *What Nature Suffers*, 97–104; Peter A. Coclanis, *Shadow of a Dream: Economic Life and Death in the South Carolina Low Country, 1670–1920* (New York: Oxford University Press, 1991), 97.

10. John Channing to Edward Telfair, October 31, 1787, Telfair Papers, Duke University Special Collections; John Bartram, "Diary of a Journey through the Carolinas, Georgia, and Florida, from July 1, 1765 to April 10, 1766," ed. Frances Harper, *Transactions of the American Philosophical Society* 33 (1942): 22; J. H. Easterby, *The South Carolina Rice Plantation as Revealed in the Papers of R. W. Allston* (Chicago: University of Chicago Press, 1945), 346; Dusinberre, *Them Dark Days*, 71.

11. Joyner, *Down by the Riverside*, 46–48; Charles W. Joyner, *Remember Me: Slave Life in Colonial Georgia* (Athens, GA: University of Georgia Press, 2011), 11–13; Erskine Clarke, *Dwelling Place: A Plantation Epic* (New Haven, CT: Yale University Press, 2007), 194–195; Julia Floyd Smith, *Slavery and Rice Culture in Low Country Georgia, 1750–1860* (Knoxville: University of Tennessee Press, 1985), 48–49; Olmsted, *Journey in the Seaboard Slave States*, 471–472; James H. Tuten, *Lowcountry Time and Tide: The Fall of the South Carolina Rice Kingdom* (Columbia: University of South Carolina Press, 2010), 16–19; Duncan Clinch Heyward, *Seed from Madagascar* (Chapel Hill: University of North Carolina Press, 1937), 36–39.

12. Dusinberre, *Them Dark Days*, 143; Silver, *New Face*, 148; Smith, *Slavery and Rice Culture*, 49–50.

13. Ball, *Slavery in the United States*, 204; John Drayton, *A View of South Carolina as Respects Her Natural and Civil Concerns* (Charleston: W. P. Young, 1802), 16; Olmsted, *Journey in the Seaboard Slave States*, 474; Morgan, *Slave Counterpoint*, 445.

14. Schaw, *Journal of a Lady of Quality*, 194; Elizabeth W. Allston Pringle, *Chronicles of Chicora Wood* (New York: Scribner's, 1922), 15; Savitt, *Medicine and Slavery*, 8–35; Maria Espinoza, "The Question of Racial Immunity to Yellow Fever in History and Historiography," *Social Science History* 38 (2014): 437–453; J. R. McNeill, *Mosquito Empires: Ecology and War in the Greater Caribbean, 1620–1914* (New York: Cambridge University Press, 2012), 45–46. On mortality on rice plantations, see Dusinberre, *Them Dark Days*, 50–55, 70–75, 80, 236–245; Jeffrey R. Young, "Ideology and Death on a Savannah River Rice Plantation: Paternalism

amidst 'a Good Supply of Disease and Pain,'" *Journal of Southern History* 59 (1993): 673–706; Karen Cook Bell, *Claiming Freedom: Race Kinship, and Land in Nineteenth-Century Georgia* (Columbia: University of South Carolina Press, 2018), 11–15.

15. McCandless, *Slavery, Disease, and Suffering*, 8; McNeill, *Mosquito Empires*, 205; Kiple and King, *Another Dimension to the Black Diaspora*, 152–56; Stewart, *What Nature Suffers*, 140; Leslie Howard Owens, *This Species of Property: Slave Life and Culture in the Old South* (New York: Oxford University Press, 1976), 21.

16. Dusinberre, *Them Dark Days*, 50–62.

17. Pringle, *Chronicles of Chicora Wood*, 67; *Life and Adventures of Zamba, an African Negro King* (London: Smith, Elder, 1847), 221; Coclanis, *Shadow of a Dream*, 38; William Gilmore Simms, *Geography of South Carolina* (Charleston, SC: Babcock, 1843), 81.

18. Weld, *American Slavery As It Is*, 14; Dusinberre, *Them Dark Days*, 7–8; Silver, *New Face*, 148; Smith, *Slavery and Rice Culture*, 50; Heyward, *Seed from Madagascar*, 27–40; Donald G. Niemann, *From Slavery to Sharecropping: White Land and Black Labor in the Rural South, 1865–1900* (New York: Garland, 1994), 293; Leslie A. Schwalm, *A Hard Fight for We: Women's Transition from Slavery to Freedom in South Carolina* (Urbana: University of Illinois Press, 1997), 22.

19. Mark Kinzer, *Nature's Return: An Environmental History of Congaree National Park* (Columbia: University of South Carolina Press, 2017), 87; John Belton O'Neall, *Annals of Newberry* (Newberry, SC: Aull & Houseal, 1892), 185; Stewart, *What Nature Suffers*, 155

20. Kinzer, *Nature's Return*, 88; Lawrence S. Rowland, Alexander Moore, and George C. Rogers, *History of Beaufort County, South Carolina*, vol. 1: *1514–1861* (Columbia: University of South Carolina Press, 1996), 325; *Winyah Observer*, September 8, 1852; Aaron W. Marrs, *Railroads in the Old South: Pursuing Progress in a Slave Society* (Baltimore: Johns Hopkins University Press, 2009), 125; *Report of the Secretary of War*, vol. 2, pt. 2, 1283; Freshet Bank Association, Smith Family Papers, South Carolina Historical Society.

21. Dusinberre, *Them Dark Days*, 8, 61, 185–186.

22. Christopher Morris, *The Big Muddy: An Environmental History of the Mississippi and Its People, from Hernando de Soto to Hurricane Katrina* (New York: Oxford University Press, 2012), 3.

23. Marc De Villiers, "A History of the Foundation of New Orleans (1717–1722)," *Louisiana Historical Quarterly* 3 (1920): 158, 189–195; Ari Kelman, *A River and Its City: The Nature of Landscape in New Orleans* (Berkeley: University of California Press, 2006), 20; Jeffrey Alan Owens, "Holding Back the Waters: Land Development and the Origins of Levees on the Mississippi, 1720–1845" (PhD diss., Louisiana State University, 1999), 27, 36–37; Morris, *Big Muddy*, 58–59.

24. Richard Campanella, *Bienville's Dilemma: A Historical Geography of New Orleans* (Lafayette: Center for Louisiana Studies, 2008), 125, 204; Marion Stange,

"Governing the Swamp: Health and the Environment in Eighteenth-Century Nouvelle-Orléans," *French Colonial History* 11 (2010): 8–11; Hall, *Africans in Colonial Louisiana*, 127–128.

25. De Villiers, "A History of the Foundation of New Orleans," 233–240; Christopher Morris, "Impenetrable but Easy: The French Transformation of the Lower Mississippi Valley and the Founding of New Orleans," in *Transforming New Orleans and Its Environs: Centuries of Change*, ed. Craig E. Colten (Pittsburgh: University of Pittsburgh Press, 2000), 34–35; Marcel Giraud, *History of French Louisiana: The Company of the Indies, 1723–1731* (Baton Rouge: Louisiana State University Press, 1991), 5:192–194, 207–215; Campanella, *Bienville's Dilemma*, 123, 203–204, 303–308; Richard Campanella, *Delta Urbanism: New Orleans* (Chicago: American Planning Association, 2010), 27–31; Owens, "Holding Back the Waters," 39–40.

26. Shannon Lee Dawdy, *Building the Devil's Empire: French Colonial New Orleans* (Chicago: University of Chicago Press, 2008), 82; Morris, "Impenetrable but Easy," 34–38; Samuel Wilson, *The Vieux Carré: Its Plan, Its Growth, Its Architecture* (New Orleans: Bureau of Government Research, 1968), 15–20, 30–32, 38; Owens, "Holding Back the Waters," 66–67, 81, 175–178; Philip Pittman, *The Present State of the European Settlements on the Mississippi* (London: J. Nourse, 1770), 41; Campanella, *Bienville's Dilemma*, 204; Laura L. Porteous, "Governor Carondelet's Levee Ordinance of 1792," *Louisiana Historical Quarterly* 10 (1927): 513–514.

27. Owens, "Holding Back the Waters," 77.

28. A. A. Humphreys and H. L. Abbot, *Report on the Physics and Hydraulics of the Mississippi River* (Washington, DC: GPO, 1914), 80–95; Elizabeth Fussell, "Constructing New Orleans, Constructing Race: A Population History of New Orleans," *Journal of American History* 94 (2007): 846–855.

29. Owens, "Holding Back the Waters," 56–57; Morris, "Impenetrable but Easy," 34; George S. Pabis, "Subduing Nature through Engineering: Caleb G. Forshey and the Levees-Only Policy, 1851–1881," in *Transforming New Orleans and Its Environment: Centuries of Change*, ed. Craig E. Colten (Pittsburgh: University of Pittsburgh Press, 2000), 68; Humphreys and Abbot, *Report*, 82–83; Campanella, *Bienville's Dilemma*, 205; E. W. Gould, *Fifty Years on the Mississippi* (St. Louis: Nixon-Jones, 1889), 224–226.

30. Henry M. Brackenridge, *Views of Louisiana* (Pittsburgh: Cramer, Spear, & Eichbaum, 1814), 176–177; Humphreys and Abbot, *Report*, 94.

31. Lyle Saxon, *Father Mississippi* (New York: Century, 1927), 188; Benjamin Henry Latrobe, *The Journal of Latrobe* (New York: Appleton, 1905), 160.

32. Brackenridge, *Views of Louisiana*, 177–180; Robert L. Paquette, "'A Horde of Brigands?': The Great Louisiana Slave Revolt of 1811 Reconsidered," *Historical Reflections / Réflexions Historiques* 35 (Spring 2009): 72–96.

33. Morris, "Impenetrable but Easy," 35; Pabis, "Subduing Nature through Engineering," 65–66; Donald W. Davis, "Historical Perspective on Crevasses, Levees, and the Mississippi River," in *Transforming New Orleans and Its*

Environment: Centuries of Change, ed. Craig E. Colten (Pittsburgh: University of Pittsburgh Press, 2000), 86–90; Giraud, *History of French Louisiana*, 5: 195.

34. Owens, "Holding Back the Waters," 418.

35. *Louisiana Gazette and New Orleans Mercantile Advertiser*, May 24, 1816; Owens, "Holding Back the Waters," 420.

36. Humphreys and Abbot, *Report on the Physics and Hydraulics of the Mississippi River*, 95–97; Davis, "Historical Perspective," 85–90; Richard Campanella, "Disaster and Response in an Experiment Called New Orleans, 1700s–2000s," in *Oxford Research Encyclopedia of Natural Hazard Science*, ed. Susan L. Cutter (New York: Oxford University Press, 2016), 1–41; W. H. Coleman, *Historical Sketch Book and Guide to New Orleans* (New York: W. H. Coleman, 1885), 277–279; John Kendall, *History of New Orleans* (Chicago: Lewis 1922), 565.

37. William Kauffman Scarborough, *Masters of the Big House: Elite Slaveholders of the Mid-Nineteenth-Century South* (Baton Rouge: Louisiana State University Press, 2003), 144–145; P. A. Champomier, *Statement of the Sugar Crop Made in Louisiana, 1849–1850* (New Orleans: Cook, Young, 1850), 52–53.

38. *New Orleans Picayune*, May 9, 1849; *Daily Crescent* (New Orleans), May 14, 1849; May 18, 1849; May 24, 1849; May 28, 1849; June 2, 1849; June 11, 1849; Greg O'Brien, "Satire and Politics in the New Orleans Flood of 1849," in *Environmental Disaster in the Gulf South*, ed. Cindy Ermus (Baton Rouge: Louisiana State University Press, 2018), 14–36; J. D. Rogers, "Development of the New Orleans Flood Protection System prior to Hurricane Katrina," *Journal of Geotechnical and Geoenvironmental Engineering* 134 (2008): 602–604; Morris, *Big Muddy*, 106–107.

39. Scarborough, *Masters of the Big House*, 143–148; Eli N. Evans, *Judah P. Benjamin: The Jewish Confederate* (New York: Free Press of Macmillan, 1988), 47; Rollin G. Osterweis, *Judah P. Benjamin: Statesman of the Lost Cause* (New York: G. P. Putnam, 1933), 62; William C. Gilmore, *The Confederate Jurist: The Legal Life of Judah P. Benjamin* (Edinburgh: Edinburgh University Press, 2021), 26–30; "Sale of sugar plantation & slaves, to effect a partition between joint owners . . . January 12th, 1852," National Library of Scotland; Maurie D. McInnis, *Slaves Waiting for Sale: Abolitionist Art and the American Slave Trade* (Chicago: University of Chicago Press, 2011), 171; Frederick Bancroft, *Slave Trading in the Old South* (Baltimore: J. H. Furst, 1931), 324–326; Walter Johnson, *Soul by Soul: Life Inside the Antebellum Slave Trade* (Cambridge, MA: Harvard University Press, 2001), 55.

40. Carville Earle and Ronald Hoffman, "Genteel Erosion: The Ecological Consequences of Agrarian Reform in the Chesapeake," in *Discovering the Chesapeake: The History of an Ecosystem*, ed. Philip D. Curtin, Grace S. Brush, and George W. Fisher (Baltimore: Johns Hopkins University Press, 2001), 295.

41. Daniel Rood, "Bogs of Death: Slavery, the Brazilian Flour Trade, and the Mystery of the Vanishing Millpond in Antebellum Virginia," *Journal of American History* 101 (2014): 19–20; Tom Downey, "Riparian Rights and Manufacturing in

Antebellum South Carolina: William Gregg and the Origins of the 'Industrial Mind,'" *Journal of Southern History* 65 (1999): 102; *De Brahm's Report*, 165; Kirby, *Poquosin*, 138–139; Edmund Ruffin, "On the Sources of Malaria," *Farmers' Register* 6 (1838): 216–228.

42. Frederick Douglass, *My Bondage and My Freedom* (New York: Miller, Orton, & Mulligan, 1855), 36, 41, 45, 65.

43. Kevin Dawson, "Enslaved Swimmers and Divers in the Atlantic World," *Journal of American History* 92 (2006): 1327–1355; Kevin Dawson, *Undercurrents of Power: Aquatic Culture in the African Diaspora* (Philadelphia: University of Pennsylvania Press, 2018), 16–25; Ambrose E. Gonzales, *The Black Border: Gullah Stories of the Carolina Coast* (Columbia, SC: States Company, 1922), 121–124; John Lawson, *New Voyage to Carolina* (London: n.p., 1709), 155; Jackson, *The Experience of a Slave in South Carolina*, 24; Harris, *Patroons and Periaguas*, 64–65.

44. Benjamin Drew, *North-Side View of Slavery* (Boston: Jewett, 1856), 25, 221; Sprague, *His Promised Land*, 73; Francis Fedric, *Slave Life in Virginia and Kentucky* (London: Wertheim, Macintosh, & Hunt, 1863), 1–2, 78.

45. Douglass, *Life and Times*, 152–153; David S. Cecelski, *Waterman's Song: Slavery and Freedom in Maritime North Carolina* (Chapel Hill: University of North Carolina Press, 2001), 121–151; Paul A. Gilje, *Liberty on the Waterfront: American Maritime Culture in the Age of Revolution* (Philadelphia: University of Pennsylvania Press, 2004), 25–26, 135–139; Whittington B. Johnson, *Black Savannah, 1788–1864* (Fayetteville: University of Arkansas Press, 1996), 93–94; Julius S. Scott, *The Common Wind: Afro-American Currents in the Age of the Haitian Revolution* (New York: Verso, 2018), 38–40, 121–126; Harris, *Patroons and Periaguas*, 54–72; Michael D. Thompson, *Working on the Dock of the Bay: Labor and Enterprise in an Antebellum Southern Port* (Columbia: University of South Carolina Press, 2015), 57–63, 75–85.

46. William Wells Brown, *The Black Man: Twenty-Nine Years a Slave, Twenty-Nine Years a Free Man* (Boston: Anti-Slavery Office, 1847), 20–23; Henry Laurens to Timothy Creamer, June 26, 1794, in *Papers of Henry Laurens*, ed. George C. Rogers (Columbia: University of South Carolina Press, 1974), 4:319.

47. Harris, *Patroons and Periaguas*, vii; Michael Shoeppner, "Peculiar Quarantines: The Seaman Acts and Regulatory Authority in the Antebellum South," *Law and History Review* 31 (2013): 559–586; Edlie L. Wong, *Neither Fugitive nor Free: Atlantic Slavery, Freedom Suits, and the Legal Culture of Travel* (New York: New York University Press, 2009), 183–239; Lacy K. Ford, *Deliver Us from Evil: The Slavery Question in the Old South* (New York: Oxford University Press, 2009), 279–293; Manisha Sinha, *The Counter-Revolution of Slavery: Politics and Ideology in Antebellum South Carolina* (Chapel Hill: University of North Carolina Press, 2000), 15; Thompson, *Working on the Dock of the Bay*, 64–70; Thomas C. Buchanan, "Levees of Hope: African American Steamboat Workers, Cities, and Slave

Escapes on the Antebellum Mississippi," *Journal of Urban History* 30 (2004): 360; Thomas C. Buchanan, "Rascals on the Antebellum Mississippi: African American Steamboat Workers and the St. Louis Hangings of 1841," *Journal of Social History* 34 (2001): 797.

48. Franklin and Schweninger, *Runaway Slaves*, 26–27, 118–119, 133–134, 144, 229; Harris, *Patroons and Periaguas*, 62–63; *New Orleans Bee*, May 13, 1831; David S. Cecelski, "The Shores of Freedom: The Maritime Underground Railroad in North Carolina, 1800–1861," *North Carolina Historical Review* 71 (1994): 174; William Still, *The Underground Rail Road* (Philadelphia: Porter & Coates, 1872), 151–152; David S. Cecelski, *Fire of Freedom: Abraham Galloway and the Slaves' Civil War* (Chapel Hill: University of North Carolina Press, 2012), 17–18.

49. Sprague, *His Promised Land*, 63, 70, 99–100; Bibb, *Narrative*, 29–30; Matthew Salafia, *Slavery's Borderland: Freedom and Bondage along the Ohio River* (Philadelphia: University of Pennsylvania, 2013), 187.

CHAPTER 5

1. Douglas R. Egerton, *Gabriel's Rebellion: The Virginia Slave Conspiracy of 1800 to 1802* (Chapel Hill: University of North Carolina Press, 1993), 50–68.

2. James Thomson Callender to Thomas Jefferson, September 13, 1800," *Founders Online*, https://founders.archives.gov/documents/Jefferson/01-32-02-0090; Egerton, *Gabriel's Rebellion*, 69–115.

3. Carroll, *Historical Collections of South Carolina*, 2:471; Edmund Berkeley Jr. and Dorothy Smith Berkeley, eds., *Correspondence of John Bartram, 1734–1777* (Gainesville: University Press of Florida, 1992), 694; Edelson, *Plantation Enterprise*, 99.

4. On the architecture of colonial Lowcountry slave cabins, see Leland Ferguson, *Uncommon Ground: Archaeology and Early African America, 1650–1800* (Washington, DC: Smithsonian Institution Press, 1992), 67, 74–79; Fitz Hamer and Michael Trinkley, "African Architectural Transference to the South Carolina Low Country, 1700–1880," *Tennessee Anthropologist* 22 (1997): 9–23.

5. David M. Ludlum, *Early American Hurricanes, 1492–1870* (Boston: American Meteorological Society, 1963), 45, 54; Walter J. Fraser, *Lowcountry Hurricanes: Three Centuries of Storms at Sea and Ashore* (Athens, GA: University of Georgia Press, 2006), 16–20; Carroll, *Historical Collections of South Carolina*, 2: 474–476; *Georgia Gazette*, November 10, 1797.

6. Fraser, *Lowcountry Hurricanes*, 53; Caroline Couper Lovell, *Golden Isles of Georgia* (Boston: Little, Brown, 1932), 185; Frederick Rutledge to John Rutledge, September 22, 1804, John Rutledge Papers, SHC; Francis Butler Leigh, *Ten Years on a Georgia Plantation Since the War* (London: Richard Bentley & Son, 1883), 183–185; Ludlum, *Early American Hurricanes*, 117; Mark Van Doren, *Correspondence of Aaron Burr and His Daughter Theodora* (New York: Covici-Friede, 1929), 181–184.

7. John Michael Vlach, *Back of the Big House: The Architecture of Plantation Slavery* (Chapel Hill: University of North Carolina Press, 1993), 111; E. Merton Coulter, *Georgia's Disputed Ruins* (Chapel Hill: University of North Carolina Press, 1937), 72–73, 82–83, 128–131; Margaret Davis Cate, *Early Days of Coastal Georgia* (St. Simons Island, GA: Fort Frederica Association, 1955), 65; Morgan, *Slave Counterpoint*, 118; Janet Bigbee Gritzner, "Tabby in the Coastal Southeast: The Cultural History of an American Building Material" (PhD diss., Louisiana State University Press, 1978), 75–130.

8. Fraser, *Lowcountry Hurricanes*, 95; John Couper to brother, May 24, 1828, Couper Family Papers, SHC.

9. Sarah McCulloh Lemmon, *The Pettigrew Papers* (Raleigh, NC: State Department of Archives and History, 1971), 2:521, 530, 540, 560; Roy T. Sawyer, *America's Wetland: An Environmental and Cultural History of Tidewater Virginia and North Carolina* (Charlottesville: University of Virginia Press, 2010), 62–66.

10. Eleonora Rohland, "Hurricanes in New Orleans: Disaster Migration and Adoption, 1718–1794," in *Cultural Dynamic of Climate Change and the Environment in Northern America*, ed. Bernd Sommer (Leiden: Brill, 2015), 137–158; Dawdy, *Building the Devil's Empire*, 81. On the early history of slavery in Louisiana, see Hall, *Africans in Colonial Louisiana*; Berlin, *Many Thousands Gone*, 77–92, 195–216, 325–357.

11. Thomas Jefferson, *An Account of Louisiana* (Providence, RI: Heaton & Williams, 1803), 14–15; Ludlum, *Early American Hurricanes*, 60.

12. *Federal Republican* (Washington, DC), September 25, 1812; *Spooner's Vermont Journal*, September 28, 1812; *Connecticut Herald*, September 29, 1812; *Albany Gazette*, September 28, 1812; Robert Stevens Jr., Letter to Parents, August 23, 1812, W&M; Eleonora Rohland, *Changes in the Air: Hurricanes in New Orleans from 1718 to the Present* (New York: Berghahn, 2018), 122–143; Ludlum, *Early American Hurricanes*, 75–76; Cary J. Mock, Michael Chenoweth, Isabel Altamirano, Matthew D. Rodgers, and Ricardo Garcia-Herrera, "The Great Louisiana Hurricane of August 1812," *Bulletin of the American Meteorological Society* (2010): 1653–1663. On the German Coast Uprising, see Rothman, *Slave Country*, 106–116; Nathan A. Buman, "Two Histories, One Future: Louisiana Sugar Planters, Their Slaves, and the Anglo-Creole Schism, 1815–1865" (PhD diss., Louisiana State University, 2013), 170–171.

13. Jams Pritchard, "The Last Island Disaster of August 10, 1856," *Louisiana Historical Quarterly* 20 (1937): 690–737.

14. Plantation diary, August 10, 1856, Andrew McCollum Papers, SHC; "Account of the Hurricane which Destroyed Last Island," Magnolia Plantation journal, Henry Clay Warmoth Papers, SHC; Ludlum, *Early American Hurricanes*, 165–171; Pritchard, "The Last Island Disaster," 690–737; J. Carlyle Sitterson, "Magnolia Plantation, 1852–1862: A Decade of a Louisiana Sugar Estate," *Mississippi Valley Historical Review* 25 (1938): 205.

15. William Walker, *Buried Alive (Behind Prison Walls) for a Quarter of a Century* (Saginaw, MI: Freidman & Hynan, 1892), 36–37.

16. Matthew Mulcahy, *Hurricanes and Society in the British Greater Caribbean* (Baltimore: Johns Hopkins University Press, 2005), 97–99; Jonathan Mercantini, "The Great Carolina Hurricane of 1752," *South Carolina Historical Magazine* 103 (2002): 357.

17. Brown, *Narrative*, 35; "Letters Written during a Journey Through North America," *Christian Observer* 23 (1823): 154.

18. Stewart, *What Natures Suffers*, 118; Richard J. Follett, *Sugar Masters: Planters and Slaves in Louisiana's Cane World, 1820–1860* (Baton Rouge: Louisiana State University Press, 2005), 10; Moses Roper, *Narrative of the Adventures and Escape of Moses Roper, from American Slavery* (Berwick-upon-Tweed, UK: Warder Office, 1848), 10; Jason L. Hauser, "By Degree: A History of Heat in the Subtropical American South" (PhD diss., Mississippi State University Press, 2017), 165–169.

19. Bartram, *Travels*, 107, 134–137; Gosse, *Letters from Alabama*, 59.

20. Northup, *Twelve Years a Slave*, 118.

21. William Chambers, *Things as They Are in America* (Edinburgh: William & Robert Chambers, 1854), 255; Samuel A. Cartwright, "How to Save the Republic, and the Position of the South in the Union," *DeBow's Review* 11 (1851): 184–197; John Van Evrie, *Negroes and Negro "Slavery"* (New York: Van Evrie, Horton, 1863), 251, 256; Savitt, *Medicine and Slavery*, 39; *A Declaration of the Immediate Causes Which Induce and Justify the Secession of the State of Mississippi from the Federal Union* (Jackson: Barksdale, 1861), 4; Hauser, "By Degree," 179–186; Christopher D. Willoughby, "'His Native, Hot Country': Racial Science and Environment in Antebellum American Medical Thought," *Journal of the History of Medicine and Allied Sciences* 72 (2017): 328–351; Rona A. Hogarth, *Medicalizing Blackness: Making Racial Differences in the Atlantic World, 1780–1840* (Chapel Hill: University of North Carolina Press, 2017), 34–36; Weiner and Hough, *Sex, Sickness, and Slavery*, 72.

22. Savitt, *Medicine and Slavery*, 104; Charlotte Foster, *Federal Writers' Project: Slave Narrative Project*, vol. 14, *South Carolina*, pt. 2, 80.

23. John Brown, *Slave Life in Georgia* (London: n.p., 1855), 186; James M. Clifton, ed., *Life and Labor on Argyle Island: Letters and Documents of a Savannah River Rice Plantation, 1833–1867* (Savannah, GA: Beehive, 1978), 83; Olmsted, *Journey in the Seaboard Slave States*, 474–475.

24. Dea H. Boster, *African American Slavery and Disability: Bodies, Property, and Power in the Antebellum South, 1800–1860* (New York: Routledge, 2013), 41–42; Jeff Forret, "Deaf & Dumb, Blind, Insane, or Idiotic," *Journal of Southern History* 82 (2016): 503–548; Richard Follett, "Heat, Sex, and Sugar: Pregnancy and Childbearing in the Slave Quarters," *Journal of Family History* 28 (2003): 510–539.

25. Johnson, *Soul by Soul*, 6–8; Steven Deyle, *Carry Me Back: The Domestic Slave Trade in American Life* (New York: Oxford University Press, 2006), 4; Damian

Alan Pargas, "In the Fields of a 'Strange Land': Enslaved Newcomers and the Adjustment to Cotton Cultivation in the Antebellum South," *Slavery and Abolition* 34 (2013): 562–578; Damian A. Pargas, *Slavery and Forced Migration in the Antebellum South* (New York: Cambridge, 2014), 123–124; James Williams, *Narrative of James Williams* (New York: American Anti-Slavery Society, 1838), 48; Weld, *American Slavery As It Is*, 161–162.

26. Joyner, *Down by the Riverside*, 43–44; Morgan, *Slave Counterpoint*, 185–186; Ball, *Slavery in the United States*, 134; Lindsey Moore, *Federal Writers' Project: Slave Narrative Project*, vol. 3, *Florida*, 230–231; Hauser, "By Degree," 166.

27. Tom Baker, *Federal Writers' Project: Slave Narrative Project*, vol. 1, *Alabama*, 17–18; Josiah Henson, *Uncle Tom's Story of His Life: An Autobiography of the Rev. Josiah Henson* (London: Christian Age Office, 1876), 22.

28. "Department of Agriculture," *DeBow's Review* 13 (1852): 193; Mark M. Smith, *Mastered by the Clock: Time, Slavery, and Freedom in the American South* (Chapel Hill: University of North Carolina Press, 1997), 112; Daina Ramey Berry, *Swing the Sickle for the Harvest is Ripe: Gender and Slavery in Antebellum Georgia* (Champaign: University of Illinois Press, 2007), 27; Hauser, "By Degree," 165.

29. Jourden H. Banks, *A Narrative of Events of the Life of J. H. Banks, an Escaped Slave* (Liverpool: M. Rourke, 1861), 53; "Recollections of Slavery by a Runaway Slave," *Emancipator*, September 13, 1838.

30. Brown, *Slave Life in Georgia*, 45–48; F. N. Boney, "Doctor Thomas Hamilton: Two Views of a Gentleman of the Old South," *Phylon* 28 (1967): 288–292; Fett, *Working Cures*, 152.

31. Hauser, "By Degree," 170–172; Dana E. Byrd, "Motive Power: Fans, Punkah, and Fly Brushes in the Antebellum South," *Buildings and Landscapes* 23 (2016): 29–51; Elaine LaFay, "The Wind Can Blow Through and Through: Ventilation, Public Health, and the Regulation of Fresh Air on Antebellum Southern Plantations," in *Atlantic Environments and the American South*, ed. Thomas Blake Earle and D. Andrew Johnson (Athens, GA: University of Georgia Press, 2020), 38–43. On Flat Rock, see David Silkenat, *Driven from Home: North Carolina's Civil War Refugee Crisis* (Athens, GA: University of Georgia Press, 2016), 186–187; Lawrence Fay Brewster, *Summer Migrations and Resorts of South Carolina Low-Country Planters* (Durham, NC: Duke University Press, 1947), 63–66; Edward Read Memminger, *Historical Sketch of Flat Rock* (Flat Rock, NC: Stephen, 1954), 8–12. On Bay St. Louis, see Mary Carol Miller, *Lost Mansions of the Mississippi* (Jackson: University of Mississippi Press, 2010), 2:87–88.

32. Hauser, "By Degree," 175; Vlach, *Back of the Big House*, 154–169; Follett, "Heat, Sex, and Sugar," 518; LaFay, "The Wind Can Blow Through and Through," 43–55; Olmsted, *Journey in the Seaboard Slave States*, 386.

33. Sarah Gudger, *Federal Writers' Project: Slave Narrative Project*, vol. 11, *North Carolina*, pt. 1. 352–354.

34. While there is some scientific consensus that the little ice age ended circa 1850, considerable debate remains about when this climatic period began. Current estimates range from 1250 to 1600. Climatologists also hotly debate the driving forces for climate change during this era. John E. Kutzbach and Thompson Webb III, "Climate and Climate History in the Chesapeake Bay Region," in *Discovering the Chesapeake: The History of an Ecosystem*, ed. Philip D. Curtin, Grace S. Brush, and George W. Fisher (Baltimore: Johns Hopkins University Press, 2001), 19–23; H. H. Lamb, *Climate, History, and the Modern World* (London: Routledge, 1982), 211–241; Karen Ordahl Kupperman, *The Jamestown Project* (Cambridge, MA: Harvard University Press, 2007), 163–170; Sean Michael Munger, "1816: 'The Mighty Scourge of Nature': An Environmental History of the Year without a Summer" (master's thesis, University of Oregon, 2012), 22–24; Brian Fagan, *The Little Ice Age: How Climate Made History, 1300–1850* (New York: Basic Books, 2000), 167–177.

35. Weather Record, 1776–1818, Thomas Jefferson Papers, Library of Congress; Stanton, *Those Who Labor for My Happiness*, 61, 114, 171; Linda Baumgarten, "'Clothes for the People': Slave Clothing in Early Virginia," *Journal of Early Southern Decorative Arts* 14 (1988): 27–70.

36. Thomas Jefferson to William Chamberlayne, August 17, 1810, *Founders Online*. https://founders.archives.gov/documents/Jefferson/03-03-02-0009; Thomas Jefferson to James Madison, March 8, 1811, *Founders Online*. https://founders.archives.gov/documents/Jefferson/03-03-02-0323.

37. Ball, *Slavery in the United States*, 26–27; Douglass, *Narrative*, 26–27.

38. John Eubanks, *Federal Writers' Project: Slave Narrative Project*, vol. 5, *Indiana*, 73; Diane Mutti Burke, *On Slavery's Border: Missouri's Small Slaveholding Households, 1815–1865* (Athens, GA: University of Georgia Press, 2010), 153–154.

39. Lewis Charlton, *Sketch of the Life of Mr. Lewis Charlton and Reminiscences of Slavery* (Portland, ME: Daily Press, n.d.), 6.

40. Fedric, *Slave Life in Virginia and Kentucky*, 90–91; Rutherford B. Hayes Interview, 1893, Wilbur Siebert Papers, Ohio History Connection; Levi Coffin, *Reminiscences of Levi Coffin* (Cincinnati: Robert Clarke, 1880), 147–149, 557–560; J. Blaine Hudson, *Fugitive Slaves and the Underground Railroad in the Kentucky Borderland* (Jefferson, NC: McFarland, 2002), 64. Toni Morrison used Garner as a model for her novel *Beloved*.

41. Tony C. Perry, "In Bondage When Cold was King: The Frigid Terrain of Slavery in Antebellum Maryland," *Slavery and Abolition* 38 (2017): 31, 36; Catherine Clinton, *Harriet Tubman: The Road to Freedom* (New York: Little, Brown, 2004), 85; Still, *Underground Rail Road*, 429–430.

42. Johnson, *Soul by Soul*, 48–49; Anderson, *Life and Narrative*, 12; W. L. Bost, *Federal Writers' Project: Slave Narrative Project*, vol. 9, *North Carolina*, pt. 1, 140–141.

43. Van Evrie, *Negroes and Negro "Slavery"*, 25; Benjamin Franklin to John Lining, June 17, 1758, *Founders Online*, https://founders.archives.gov/documents/Franklin/

01-08-02-0023; Savitt, *Medicine and Slavery*, 37; S. G. Howe, *Refugees from Slavery in Canada West: Report to the Freedmen's Inquiry Commission* (Boston: Wright & Potter, 1864), 36.

44. Henry Watson, *Narrative of Henry Watson, a Fugitive Slave* (Boston: Bela Marsh, 1848), 23.

CHAPTER 6

1. Ball, *Slavery in the United States*, 325–337.

2. Anthony Wilson, *Shadow and Shelter: The Swamp in Southern Culture* (Jackson: University Press of Mississippi, 2006), 10–11, 44–46; David C. Miller, *Dark Eden: The Swamp in Nineteenth-Century American Culture* (New York: Cambridge University Press, 1989), 78; Edmund Ruffin, *Exhausting and Fertilizing Systems of Agriculture* (Charleston, SC: Walker & James, 1853), 18.

3. Diouf, *Slavery's Exiles*, 5.

4. Lewis W. Paine, *Six Years in a Georgia Prison* (New York: printed for the author, 1851), 22–23, 28–31.

5. Adam Bledsoe, "Marronage as a Past and Present Geography in the Americas," *Southern Geographer* 57 (2017): 38–41.

6. Timothy J. Lockley, *Maroon Communities in South Carolina: A Documentary Record* (Columbia: University of South Carolina Press, 2009), 8–11.

7. Lockley, *Maroon Communities*, 12–13; Mark M. Smith, *Stono: Documenting and Interpreting a Southern Slave Revolt* (Columbia: University of South Carolina Press, 2005), 4–6; Wood, *Black Majority*, 308–320; John K. Thornton, "African Dimension of the Stono Rebellion," *American Historical Review* 96 (1991): 1101–1113.

8. Lockley, *Maroon Communities*, 17–23; Sylvia R. Frey, *Water from the Rock: Black Resistance in a Revolutionary Age* (Princeton, NJ: Princeton University Press, 1991), 51–52.

9. Lockley, *Maroon Communities*, 24–33; Frey, *Water from the Rock*, 52–53.

10. Benjamin Quarles, *The Negro in the American Revolution* (Chapel Hill: University of North Carolina Press, 1961), 144–145; David K. Wilson, *The Southern Strategy: Britain's Conquest of South Carolina and Georgia, 1775–1780* (Columbia: University of South Carolina Press, 2005), 74–75; Douglas K. Egerton, *Death or Liberty: African Americans and Revolutionary America* (New York: Oxford University Press, 2009), 150–151; Timothy J. Lockley, "'The King of England's Soldiers': Armed Blacks in Savannah and Its Hinterlands during the Revolutionary War Era, 1778–1787," in *Slavery and Freedom in Savannah*, ed. Leslie M. Harris and Daina Ramey Berry (Athens, GA: University of Georgia Press, 2014), 26–32; Olwell, *Masters, Slaves and Subjects*, 229–270; Karen Cook Bell, *Running from Bondage: Enslaved Women and Their Remarkable Fight for Freedom in Revolutionary America* (New York: Cambridge University Press, 2021), 137.

11. *Georgia State Gazette*, October 28, 1786; Diouf, *Slavery's Exiles*, 188–197; Alan Taylor, *American Revolutions: A Continental History, 1750–1804* (New York: Norton, 2016), 314; Frey, *Water from the Rock*, 227; Lockley, "The King of England's Soldiers," 32–41; Lockley, *Maroon Communities*, 39–71; Bell, *Running from Bondage*, 137, 150.

12. Diouf, *Slavery's Exiles*, 197–208.

13. Tom Hatley, *The Dividing Paths: Cherokees and South Carolinians through the Era of the Revolution* (New York: Oxford University Press 1998), 73; Jonathan Elliot, *Debates, Resolutions, and Other Proceedings in Convention on the Adoption of the Federal Constitution* (Washington, DC: Elliot, 1830), 3:357; James Cook, "A Map of the Province of South Carolina," Library of Congress; Adam Hodgson, *Letter from North America* (London: Hurst, Robinson, 1824), 104.

14. Lockley, *Maroon Communities*, 86–87, 121–122.

15. Lockley, *Marron Communities*, 128–134; Robert J. Kapsch, *Historic Canals and Waterways of South Carolina* (Columbia: University of South Carolina Press, 2010); Ryan A. Quintana, "The Plantation All in Disorder: Black Carolinians' Spatial Practices and the Construction of the Lowcountry Landscape, 1739–1830" (PhD diss., Louisiana State University, 1999), 36–37, 116–118, 148–155.

16. Lockley, *Maroon Communities*, 129; Whitemarsh B. Seabrook, *Agricultural Capabilities of S. Carolina* (Columbia, SC: Bowman, 1848), 40–9.

17. Kemble, *Journal of a Residence*, 46, 51; Timothy J. Lockley and David Doddington, "Maroon and Slave Communities in South Carolina before 1865," *South Carolina Historical Magazine* 113 (2012): 129–130; Edelson, *Plantation Enterprise*, 67.

18. Diouf, *Slavery's Exiles*, 32; Daniel H. Usner Jr., "From African Captivity to American Slavery: The Introduction of Black Laborers to Colonial Louisiana," *Louisiana History* 20 (1979): 41–45; "Records of the Superior Council of Louisiana," *Louisiana Historical Quarterly* 3 (1920): 414; James Thomas McGowan, "Creation of a Slave Society: Louisiana Plantations in the Eighteenth Century" (PhD diss., University of Rochester, 1976), 53–57; Daniel H. Usner Jr., *Indians, Settlers, and Slaves in a Frontier Exchange Economy: The Lower Mississippi Valley before 1783* (Chapel Hill: University of North Carolina Press, 1992), 58–59, 65–75; Berlin, *Many Thousand Gone*, 87–89; Hall, *Africans in Louisiana*, 143–144, 202–203; Thomas N. Ingersoll, *Mammon and Manon in Early New Orleans: The First Slave Society in the Deep South, 1718–1819* (Knoxville: University of Tennessee Press, 1999), 86–90; Gilbert C. Din, *Spaniards, Planters, and Slaves: The Spanish Regulation of Slavery in Louisiana, 1763–1803* (College Station: Texas A&M Press, 1999), 11, 22–29; Bolton, *Fugitivism*, 35–41

19. Pierre-Louis Berquin-Duvallon, *Travels in Louisiana and the Floridas* (New York: I. Riley, 1806), 19.

20. Diouf, *Slavery's Exiles*, 157–185; Din, *Spaniards, Planters, and Slaves*, 89–115; Hall, *Africans in Louisiana*, 205–236.

21. Din, *Spaniards, Planters, and Slaves*, 194–219; Berquin-Duvallon, *Travels in Louisiana*, 5–6.

22. Dunbar Rowland, *Official Letter Books of W. C. C. Claiborne, 1801–1816* (Jackson, MS: State Department of Archives and History, 1917), 1: 379–381; Diouf, *Slavery's Exiles*, 32–33; Buman, "To Kill Whites," 49–50.

23. Morris, *The Big Muddy*, 3; *Liberator*, July 2, 1837; "Nègres Maroons," *Le Meschacebe*, December 3, 1854; Bolton, *Fugitivism*, 80.

24. John James Audubon, *Ornithological Biography* (Edinburgh: Black, 1834), 2:27–32; Gregory Nobles, *John James Audubon: The Nature of the American Woodsman* (Philadelphia: University of Pennsylvania Press, 2017), 203–208; William M. Souder, *Under a Wild Sky: John James Audubon and the Making of the Birds of America* (New York: North Point, 2004), 261–262; Ben Forkner, *Audubon on Louisiana* (Baton Rouge: Louisiana State University Press, 2018), 39–40; Albert Boime, "John James Audubon: A Birdwatcher's Fanciful Flights," *Art History* 22 (1999): 750–751.

25. Northup, *Twelve Years*, 106, 135–140, 200.

26. Bibb, *Narrative*, 123–4.

27. Daniel O. Sayers, P. Brendan Burke, and Aaron M. Henry, "The Political Economy of Exile in the Great Dismal Swamp," *International Journal of Historical Archaeology* 11 (2007): 60–97; Diouf, *Slavery's Exiles*, 210–212.

28. Henry Wadsworth Longfellow, *Poems on Slavery* (Cambridge, MA: John Owen, 1842), 18–20; Frederick Douglass, *The Heroic Slave* (Boston: John P. Jewett, 1853), 158; Harriet Beecher Stowe, *Dred: A Tale of the Great Dismal Swamp* (Boston: Philips, Sampson, 1856); Wilson, *Shadow and Shelter*, 18; William Tynes Cowan, "The Slave in the Swamp: Disrupting the Plantation Narrative" (PhD diss., College of William and Mary, 2001), 183–208; Megan Kate Nelson, *Trembling Earth: A Cultural History of the Okefenokee Swamp* (Athens, GA: University of Georgia Press, 2005), 37.

29. Byrd, *Westover Manuscripts*, 11, 17–18; Marcus P. Nevius, *City of Refuge: Slavery and Petit Marronage in the Great Dismal Swamp, 1763–1856* (Athens, GA: University of Georgia Press, 2020), 16.

30. Byrd, *Westover Manuscripts*, 20; William Byrd, "Proposal to Drain the Dismal Swamp," *Farmers' Register* 4 (January 1, 1837): 521–524.

31. Charles Royster, *The Fabulous History of the Dismal Swamp Company: A Story of George Washington's Times* (New York: Knopf, 1999), 82–99, 217.

32. Smyth, *A Tour of the United States of America*, 2:64–65; Maris-Wolf, "Hidden in Plain Sight," 447–448; Elkanah Watson, *Men and Times of the Revolution* (New York: Dana, 1856), 44.

33. Royster, *Fabulous History*, 423; Daniel O. Sayers, *A Desolate Place: The Archaeology of Maroons, Indigenous Americans, and Enslaved Laborers in the Great Dismal Swamp* (Gainesville: University Press of Florida, 2014), 90–94.

34. Grandy, *Narrative*, 35; Cecelski, *Waterman's Song*, 106–113.

35. Robert C. McLean, "A Yankee Tutor in the Old South," *North Carolina Historical Review* 47 (1970): 56.

36. Edmund Ruffin, "Observations Made During An Excursion to the Dismal Swamp," *Farmers' Register* 4 (January 1 ,1837): 513–521.

37. Diouf, *Slavery's Exiles*, 212–213; Olmsted, *Seaboard Slave States*, 153–155; McLean, "Yankee Tutor," 56–58; Grandy, *Narrative*, 11.

38. Diouf, *Slavery's Exiles*, 213–216; Redpath, *Roving Editor*, 289–295; Calvin H. Wiley, *Adventures of Old Dan Tucker and His Son Walter: A Tale of North Carolina* (London: Willoughby, 1851), 95; Sayers, *A Desolate Place*, 176–199.

39. Diouf, *Slavery's Exiles*, 214–216, 227–228; Kathryn Elise Benjamin Golden, "Through the Muck and Mire: Marronage, Representation, and Memory in the Great Dismal Swamp" (PhD diss., University of California, Berkeley, 2018), 74–76; *Laws of the State of North Carolina, Passed by the General Assembly at the Session of 1846–1847* (Raleigh, NC: Thomas J. Lemay, 1847), 109–113.

40. Thomas Wentworth Higginson, "Nat Turner's Insurrection," *Atlantic Monthly* 8 (August 1861): 173–187; Frank Roy Johnson, *Tales from Old Carolina* (Murfreesboro, NC: Johnson, 1965), 159; Nevius, *City of Refuge*, 79; Redpath, *Roving Editor*, 294–295; "Slaves in the Dismal Swamp," *North Star*, March 31, 1848; Charles L. Perdue Jr., Thomas E. Barden, and Robert K. Phillips, *Weevils in the Wheat: Interviews with Virginia Ex-Slaves* (Charlottesville: University of Virginia Press, 1976), 252; Golden, "Through the Muck and the Mire," 73–78.

41. Redpath, *Roving Editor*, 294; Diouf, *Slavery's Exiles*, 216–220; Sayers, *A Desolate Place*, 116–134; Golden, "Through the Muck and the Mire," 82–88.

42. Olmsted, *Seaboard Slave States*, 157–160.

43. Porte Crayon [David Hunter Strother], "Dismal Swamp," *Harper's New Monthly Magazine* 13 (1856): 441–455.

44. Some scholars have suggested that Strother's account and image of Osman inspired Harriet Beecher Stowe's *Dred*. Thomas C. Parramore, "Muslim Slave Aristocrats in North Carolina," *North Carolina Historical Review* 77 (2000): 131; Nevius, *City of Refuge*, 96–98.

CHAPTER 7

1. "Southern Convention at Savannah," *DeBow's Review* 22 (January 1857), 101; Mauldin, *Unredeemed Land*, 32–34, 38; Bagley, *Soil Erosion and the Civil War*, 8, 78–81; Adam Wesley Dean, *An Agrarian Republic: Farming, Antislavery Politics, and Nature Parks in the Civil War Era* (Chapel Hill: University of North Carolina Press, 2015), 1–70; Edmund Ruffin, "Consequences of Abolition Agitation," *DeBow's Review* 23 (December 1857): 598; Adrian Brettle, *Colossal Ambitions: Confederate Planning for a Post–Civil War World* (Charlottesville: University of Virginia Press, 2020), 1–6, 9, 12–18.

2. Barney, *Rebels in the Making*, 13, 34–35; "What the South Most Needs," *Augusta Daily Constitutionalist*, January 23, 1858. Later reprinted as "The South Cries, More Labor," *DeBow's Review* 24 (March 1858): 201–203. Barney mistakenly attributes the article in *DeBow's* to George Fitzhugh.

3. Susan Eva O'Donovan, *Becoming Free in the Cotton South* (Cambridge, MA: Harvard University Press, 2010), 61; William Mallory, *Old Plantation Days* (Hamilton, ON: n.p., 1902), 5–11.

4. William R. Smith, *History and Debates of the Convention of the People of Alabama* (Montgomery, AL: White, Pfister, 1861), 87, 236–237; Mauldin, *Unredeemed Land*, 38; *Secession of Mississippi from the Federal Union* (Jackson: Mississippian Book and Job Printing Office, 1861).

5. Edward L. Ayers and Scott Nesbit, "Seeing Emancipation: Scale and Freedom in the American South," *Journal of the Civil War Era* 1 (2011): 3–24; Joseph P. Reidy, *Illusions of Emancipation: The Pursuit of Freedom and Equality in the Twilight of Slavery* (Chapel Hill: University of North Carolina Press, 2019), 131–139; Yael A. Sternhell, "Emancipation," in *A Companion to the U.S. Civil War*, ed. Aaron Sheehan-Dean (Malden, MA: Wiley Blackwell, 2014), 965–968; Steven Hahn, *Political Worlds of Slavery and Freedom* (Cambridge, MA: Harvard University Press, 2009), 55–114; Chandra Manning, *Troubled Refuge: Struggling for Freedom in the Civil War* (New York: Knopf, 2016); Amy Murrell Taylor, *Embattled Freedom: Journeys through the Civil War's Slave Refugee Camps* (Chapel Hill: University of North Carolina Press, 2018); Silkenat, *Driven from Home*; Jim Downs, *Sick from Freedom: African-American Illness and Suffering during the Civil War and Reconstruction* (New York: Oxford University Press, 2012); Lisa M. Brady, "Environmental Histories," *Journal of the Civil War Era*, https://www.journalo fthecivilwarera.org/forum-the-future-of-civil-war-era-studies/the-future-of-civil-war-era-studies-environmental-histories/; Judkin Browning and Timothy Silver, "Nature and Human Nature: Environmental Influences on the Union's Failed Peninsula Campaign, 1862," *Journal of the Civil War Era* 8 (2018): 388–415; Judkin Browning and Timothy Silver, *An Environmental History of the Civil War* (Chapel Hill: University of North Carolina Press, 2020); Megan Kate Nelson, "Looking at Landscapes of War," *Journal of the Civil War Era* 3 (2013): 439–449; Matthew M. Stith, "'The Deplorable Condition of the Country': Nature, Society, and War on the Trans-Mississippi Frontier," *Civil War History* 58 (2012): 322–347; Brian Allen Drake, ed., *The Blue, the Gray, and the Green: Toward an Environmental History of the Civil War* (Athens, GA: University of Georgia Press, 2015); Lisa M. Brady, *War Upon the Land: Military Strategy and the Transformation of Southern Landscapes during the American Civil War* (Athens, GA: University of Georgia Press, 2012); Joan E. Cashin, *War Stuff: The Struggle for Human and Environmental Resources in the American Civil War* (New York: Cambridge University Press, 2018); Mauldin, *Unredeemed Land*; Kathryn Shively Meier, *Nature's Civil War: Common Soldiers and the Environment in 1862 Virginia* (Chapel Hill: University of North Carolina

Press, 2013); Megan Kate Nelson, *Ruin Nation: Destruction and the American Civil War* (Athens, GA: University of Georgia Press, 2012); Kelby Ouchley, *Flora and Fauna of the Civil War: An Environmental Reference Guide* (Baton Rouge: Louisiana State University Press, 2010); Matthew M. Stith, *Extreme Civil War: Guerrilla Warfare, Environment, and Race on the Trans-Mississippi Frontier* (Baton Rouge: Louisiana State University Press, 2016); Mark Fiege, "Gettysburg and the Organic Nature of the American Civil War," in *Natural Enemy, Natural Ally: Toward an Environmental History of War*, ed. Edmund Russell and Richard Tucker (Corvallis: Oregon State University Press, 2004), 93–109; Andrew McIlwaine Bell, *Mosquito Soldiers: Malaria, Yellow Fever, and the Course of the American Civil War* (Baton Rouge: Louisiana State University Press, 2010).

6. W. E. B. Du Bois, *Black Reconstruction in America* (New York: Free Press, 1998), 55–83; Cashin, *War Stuff*, 82–107, 141–145; Nelson, *Ruin Nation*, 103–159; *Charleston Mercury*, November 18, 1863; R. Douglas Hurt, *Agriculture and the Confederacy: Policy, Productivity, and Power in the Civil War South* (Chapel Hill: University of North Carolina Press, 2015), 245; Mauldin, *Unredeemed Land*, 90–93; Browning and Silver, *Environmental History*, 125–126.

7. Browning and Silver, "Nature and Human Nature," 391; Barney, *Rebels in the Making*, 91–95; Kenneth W. Noe, *The Howling Storm: Weather, Climate, and the American Civil War* (Baton Rouge: Louisiana State University Press, 2020), 7–9, 162–166.

8. Noe, *Howling Storm*, 166; Susan Eva O'Donovan, "Finding a New War in an Old Image," in *Lens of War: Exploring Iconic Photographs of the Civil War*, ed. J. Matthew Gallman and Gary W. Gallagher (Athens, GA: University of Georgia Press, 2015), 143–148.

9. Ludlum, *Early American Hurricanes*, 194; Jose F. Partagas and Henry F. Diaz, *A Reconstruction of Historical Tropical Cyclone Frequency* (Boulder, CO: NOAA, 1995), 35–37. On Fortress Monroe, see Reidy, *Illusions of Emancipation*, 39; Kate Masur, "'Rare Phenomenon of Philological Vegetation': The Word 'Contraband' and the Meanings of Emancipation in the United States," *Journal of American History* 93 (2007): 1050–1084.

10. Willie Lee Rose, *The Rehearsal for Reconstruction: The Port Royal Experiment* (New York: Oxford University Press, 1964); Ludlum, *Early American Hurricanes*, 101–102; John D. Hayes, ed., *Samuel Francis Du Pont: A Selection from His Civil War Letters* (Ithaca, NY: Cornell University Press, 1969), 1:207.

11. *Macon Daily Telegraph*, June 5, 1863; Michael Chenoweth and Cary J. Mock, "Hurricane 'Amanda': Rediscovery of a Forgotten U.S. Civil War Hurricane," *Bulletin of the American Meteorological Society* 94 (November 2013): 1735–1742; Ella Lonn, "The Extent and Importance of Federal Naval Raids on Salt-Making in Florida, 1862–1865," *Florida Historical Society Quarterly* 10 (1932): 167–184.

12. Mart A. Stewart, "Walking, Running, and Marching into an Environmental History of the Civil War," in *The Blue, the Gray, and the Green: Toward an Environmental History of the Civil War*, ed. Brian Allen Drake (Athens, GA: University of Georgia

Press, 2015), 214–215; Clarke, *Dwelling Place*, 415–416; Hattie Rogers, *Federal Writers' Project: Slave Narrative Project*, vol. 11, *North Carolina*, pt. 2, 227–228; Silkenat, *Driven from Home*, 16.

13. David W. Blight, *A Slave No More: Two Men Who Escaped to Freedom* (Boston: Mariner, 2007), 216–217, 251–257.

14. Elizabeth Hyde Botume, *First Days amongst the Contrabands* (Boston: Lee & Shepard, 1893), 178–180.

15. Ira Berlin et al., eds., *Freedom: A Documentary History of Emancipation, 1861–1867* (New York: Cambridge University Press, 1995), ser. 1, 1:217; Joseph T. Wilson, *The Black Phalanx: A History of the Negro Soldiers of the United States in the War of 1775–1812, 1861–1865* (Hartford, CT: American Publishing, 1888), 70; Buman, "Two Histories, One Future," 235–236; Reidy, *Illusions of Emancipation*, 100–101.

16. *Marion Star*, June 18, 1861, quoted in Howell M. Henry, *The Police Control of the Slave in South Carolina* (Emory, VA: n.p., 1914), 121.

17. *The War of the Rebellion: A Compilation of the Official Records of the Union and Confederate Armies* (Washington, DC: GPO, 1880–1901), ser. 2, 1:812; Matthew J. Graham, *Ninth Regiment New York Volunteers* (New York: E. P. Cody, 1900), 216; Vincent Colyer, *Brief Report of the Services Rendered by the Freed People to the United States Army* (New York: V. Colyer, 1864), 19–20; Silkenat, *Driven from Home*, 18–19.

18. Colyer, *Services Rendered*, 22; Silkenat, *Driven from Home*, 16; Berlin et al., *Freedom*, ser. 1, 1:325–326.

19. Manning, *Troubled Refuge*, 106–107; Taylor, *Embattled Freedom*, 65–66; *New York Times*, November 8, 1862; George David Schieffler, "Civil War in the Delta: Environment, Race, and the 1863 Helena Campaign" (PhD diss., University of Arkansas, 2017), 135–138, 169–174. In 2013, the site of Helena's contraband camp was rededicated as Freedom Park.

20. Taylor, *Embattled Freedom*, 87–92.

21. Berlin et al., *Freedom*, ser. 2, 267–271; Amy Murrell Taylor, "How a Cold Snap in Kentucky Led to Freedom for Thousands: An Environmental Story of Emancipation," in *Weirding the War: Stories from the Civil War's Ragged Edges*, ed. Stephen Berry (Athens, GA: University of Georgia Press, 2011), 191–214; Downs, *Sick from Freedom*, 18–21; Reidy, *Illusions of Emancipation*, 83–84.

22. Colyer, *Services Rendered*, 8; Berlin et al., *Freedom*, ser. 1, 1:138–139, 179.

23. Coyler, *Services Rendered*, 24–25.

24. *War of the Rebellion*, ser. 1, 15:27–33; "Letters of General Thomas Williams, 1862," *American Historical Review* 14 (1909): 322–328; Edward Bacon, *Among the Cotton Thieves* (Detroit: Free Press, 1867), 15–16; Brady, *War Upon the Land*, 35–46; Kate Stone, *Brokenburn: The Journal of Kate Stone, 1861–1868* (Baton Rouge: Louisiana State University Press, 1953), 134; William F. Messner, "Vicksburg Campaign of 1862: A Case Study in the Federal Utilization of Black Labor," *Louisiana History*

16 (1975): 371–381; Reidy, *Illusions of Emancipation*, 71; *National Anti-Slavery Standard*, August 16, September 27, 1862; *New York Tribune*, August 2, 1862.

25. Grant to Col. George W. Deitzler, February 2, 1863, Grant to Col. John C. Kelton, 4 February 1863, John Y. Simon, *Papers of Ulysses S. Grant* (Carbondale: Southern Illinois University Press, 1967–2012), 7:278–279, 282; Halleck to Grant, March 30, 1863, Simon, *Papers of Ulysses S. Grant*, 8:93; Nicholas W. Sacco, "'I Never Was an Abolitionist': Ulysses S. Grant and Slavery, 1854–1863," *Journal of the Civil War Era* 9 (2019): 431–432.

26. Mildred Throne, ed., *The Civil War Diary of Cyrus F. Boyd: Fifteenth Iowa Infantry, 1861–1863* (Iowa City: State Historical Society of Iowa, 1953), 118; Donald L. Miller, *Vicksburg: Grant's Campaign that Broke the Confederacy* (New York: Simon & Schuster, 2019), 266–268; Jane Turner Censer, ed., *Papers of Frederick Law Olmsted* (Baltimore: Johns Hopkins University Press, 1986), 4:571.

27. Ulysses S. Grant, *Personal Memoirs of U.S. Grant* (New York: Charles L. Webster), 1:447–450; William T. Sherman, *Memoirs of General William T. Sherman* (New York: D. Appleton, 1875), 1:333.

28. Benjamin E. Humphreys, *Floods and Levees of the Mississippi: Supplemental Report* (Washington, DC: GPO, 1914), 17; Campanella, *Bienville's Dilemma*, 309; Morris, *Big Muddy*, 147–149; George S. Pabis, "Delaying the Deluge: The Engineering Debate over Flood Control on the Lower Mississippi River, 1846–1861," *Journal of Southern History* 64 (1998): 450; Matthew P. Carlin, "The Hydraulic Dimension of Reconstruction in Louisiana, 1863–1879" (master's thesis, University of New Orleans, 2019), 23–30; J. Carlyle Sitterson, *Sugar Country: The Case Sugar Industry in the South, 1753–1950* (Lexington: University of Kentucky Press 1953), 209–226; Martin Reuss, *Designing the Bayous: The Control of the Water in the Atchafalaya Basin, 1800–1995* (College Station: Texas A&M Press, 2004), 54–55; Grant, *Memoirs*, 1:458.

29. George Washington Williams, *History of Negro Troops in the War of the Rebellion* (New York: Harper, 1888), 111, 187; David C. Rankin, *Diary of a Christian Soldier: Rufus Kinsley and the Civil War* (New York: Cambridge University Press, 2004), 170.

30. Mauldin, *Unredeemed Land*, 67; Trimble, *Man-Induced*, 27; John Townshend Trowbridge, *The South* (Hartford, CT: L. Stebbins, 1866), 225; John Richard Dennett, *The South As It Is: 1865–1866* (New York: Viking, 1965), 129; Stewart, *What Nature Suffers*, 193.

31. Berlin et al., *Freedom*, ser. 1, 3:331–338; Steven Hahn, *A Nation under Our Feet: Black Political Struggles in the Rural South from Slavery to the Great Migration* (Cambridge, MA: Harvard University Press, 2003), 129–143; *Minutes of the Freedmen's Convention Held in the City of Raleigh* (Raleigh, NC: Standard, 1866), 26; Berlin et al., *Freedom*, ser. 3, 2:361–341.

CONCLUSION

1. Edward King, *The Great South* (Hartford, CT: American Publishing, 1875), 433–434; Tuten, *Lowcountry Tide and Time*, 22–23; Smith, "Rich Swamps and Rice Grounds," 283–284; "A Raid Among the Rice Plantations," *Harper's Weekly* 7 (July 4, 1863): 427; Kate Clifford Larson, *Bound for the Promised Land: Harriet Tubman, Portrait of an American Hero* (New York: Ballantine, 2004), 212–226; Clinton, *Harriet Tubman*, 164–175; Leon F. Litwack, *Been in the Storm So Long: The Aftermath of Slavery* (New York: Knopf, 1979), 93–94.
2. Mauldin, *Unredeemed Land*, 6, 99–128; Browning and Silver, *Environmental History*, 196.
3. Gavin Wright, *Old South, New South: Revolutions in the Southern Economy since the Civil War* (Baton Rouge: Louisiana State University Press, 1997), 34–38; Roger L. Ransom and Richard Sutch, *One Kind of Freedom: The Economic Consequences of Emancipation* (New York: Cambridge University Press, 1977), 149–156; Maudlin, *Unredeemed Land*, 111–112; Timothy Johnson, "Reconstructing the Soil: Emancipation and the Roots of Chemical-Dependent Agriculture in America," in *The Blue, the Gray, and the Green: Toward an Environmental History of the Civil War*, ed Brian Allen Drake (Athens, GA: University of Georgia Press, 2015), 191–208.
4. Frederick Douglass, *Address Delivered by Hon. Frederick Douglass at the Third Annual Fair of the Tennessee Colored Agricultural and Mechanical Association* (Washington, DC: New National Era and Citizen Print, 1873); *Tennessean*, September 19, 1873; Kimberly K. Smith, *African American Environmental Thought: Foundations* (Lawrence: University Press of Kansas, 2007), 74.
5. W. E. B. Du Bois, *The Souls of Black Folk* (Chicago: A. C. McClurg, 1903), 115–134.
6. Brian Williams, "'That We May Live': Pesticides, Plantations, and Environmental Racism in the United States South," *Environment and Planning* 1 (2018): 243–267; Carolyn Merchant, "Shades of Darkness: Race and Environmental History," *Environmental History* 8 (2003): 380–394.

Bibliography

ARCHIVES

Special Collections and Archives, Clemson University, Clemson, SC
   Thomas Green Clemson Papers
Special Collections, College of William and Mary, Williamsburg, VA
   Jerdone Family Papers
   Edmund Ruffin Farm Journal
   Robert Stevens Jr. Letter
Special Collections, Duke University, Durham, NC
   Telfair Papers
Library of Congress, Washington, DC
   James Cook, "A Map of the Province of South Carolina."
   Interview with Fountain Hughes
   Thomas Jefferson Papers
Massachusetts Historical Society, Boston, MA
   Thomas Jefferson Papers
National Library of Scotland, Edinburgh, UK
   "Sale of sugar plantation & slaves, to effect a partition between joint owners," 1852
Ohio History Connection, Columbus, OH
   Wilbur Siebert Papers
South Carolina Historical Society, Columbia, SC
   Smith Family Papers
Special Collections Research Center, University of Kentucky, Lexington, KY
   Francis M. Goddard Diary
Southern Historical Collection, University of North Carolina, Chapel Hill, NC
   Couper Family Papers
   William Dunbar Account Book
   Federal Soldiers' Letters
   Lenoir Family Papers

Andrew McCollum Papers
John Rutledge Papers
Dr. John Scott Papers
William D. Valentine Diary
Henry Clay Warmoth Papers
Special Collections, University of Virginia, Charlottesville, VA
Dr. James Carmichael Papers

NEWSPAPERS AND PERIODICALS

Adams Centennial (Gettysburg, PA)
Albany Gazette
American Farmer
Arator
Carolina Spectator
Charleston Mercury
Connecticut Herald
Daily Constitutionalist (Augusta, GA)
Daily Crescent (New Orleans)
DeBow's Review
Emancipator (New York)
Farmers' Register
Federal Republican (DC)
Fredericksburg News
Georgia Courier (Augusta)
Georgia Gazette
Georgia State Gazette
Harper's Weekly
Le Meschacebe (Louisiana)
Liberator
Louisiana Gazette and New Orleans Mercantile Advertiser
Macon Daily Telegraph
Merchants' Magazine and Commercial Review
National Anti-Slavery Standard
New Orleans Bee
New Orleans Picayune
New York Times
New York Tribune
Niles' Register
North Star
Richmond Daily Dispatch
Richmond Enquirer

Richmond Examiner
Southern Agriculturalist
Southern Federal Union (Milledgeville, GA)
Southern Planter
Spooner's Vermont Journal
Tennessean (Nashville)
Western Democrat (Charlotte, NC)
Winyah Observer (Georgetown, SC)

PUBLISHED PRIMARY SOURCES

Abdy, Edward Strutt. *Journal of a Residence and Tour in the United States of North America.* 3 vols. London: G. Woodfall, 1835.

Agricola [George W. Jeffreys]. *A Series of Essays on Agriculture and Rural Affairs.* Raleigh, NC: Joseph Gales, 1819.

Albert, Octavia V. Rogers. *House of Bondage.* New York: Hunt & Eaton, 1890.

American Husbandry: Containing an Account of the Soil, Climate, Production and Agriculture of the British Colonies in North-America and the West-Indies. 2 vols. London: J. Bew, 1775.

Anburey, Thomas. *Travels through the Interior Parts of America.* 2 vols. London: W. Lane, 1789.

Anderson, William J. *Life and Narrative of William J. Anderson.* Chicago: Daily Tribune Book & Job Printing Office, 1857.

Audubon, John James. *Ornithological Biography.* 5 vols. Edinburgh: Black, 1831–1839.

Avirett, James Battle. *The Old Plantation: How We Lived in Great House and Cabin before the War.* New York: F. Tennyson Neely, 1901.

Bacon, Edward. *Among the Cotton Thieves.* Detroit: Free Press, 1867.

Baker, T. Lindsay, and Julie P. Baker, eds. *The WPA Oklahoma Slave Narratives.* Norman: University of Oklahoma Press, 1996.

Ball, Charles. *Slavery in the United States.* New York: John S. Taylor, 1837.

Banks, Jourden H. *A Narrative of Events of the Life of J. H. Banks, an Escaped Slave.* Liverpool: M. Rourke, 1861.

Barnard, Henry. "The South Atlantic States in 1833, as Seen by a New Englander." *Maryland Historical Magazine* 13 (1918): 267–386.

Bartram, John. "Diary of a Journey through the Carolinas, Georgia, and Florida, from July 1, 1765, to April 10, 1766," ed. Francis Harper. *Transactions of the American Philosophical Society* 33 (1942): 1–120.

Bartram, William. *Travels Through North and South Carolina, Georgia, East and West Florida, the Cherokee Country, the Extensive Territories of the Muscogulges, or Creek Confederacy, and the Country of the Chactaws.* Philadelphia: James & Johnson, 1791.

Berkeley, Edmund, Jr., and Dorothy Smith Berkeley, eds. *The Correspondence of John Bartram, 1734–1777.* Gainesville: University Press of Florida, 1992.

Berlin, Ira, et al. *Freedom: A Documentary History of Emancipation, 1861–1867*. 6 vols. New York: Cambridge University Press; Chapel Hill: University of North Carolina Press, 1995–2013.

Berquin-Duvallon, Pierre-Louis. *Travels in Louisiana and the Floridas*. New York: I. Riley, 1806.

Bibb, Henry. *Narrative of Life and Adventures of Henry Bibb, An American Slave*. New York: Published by the Author, 1849.

Black, Leonard. *The Life and Sufferings of Leonard Black, a Fugitive from Slavery*. New Bedford: Benjamin Lindsey, 1847.

Blake, William P., and Charles T. Jackson, *Gold Placers of the Vicinity of Dahlonega*. Boston: n.p., 1859.

Blight, David W. *A Slave No More: Two Men Who Escaped to Freedom*. Boston: Mariner, 2007.

Botume, Elizabeth Hyde. *First Days amongst the Contrabands*. Boston: Lee & Shepard, 1893.

Brackenridge, Henry M. *Views of Louisiana*. Pittsburgh: Cramer, Spear, & Eichbaum, 1814.

Brown, John. *Slave Life in Georgia*. London: n.p., 1855.

Brown, William Wells. *The Black Man: His Antecedents, His Genius, and His Achievements*. New York: Thomas Hamilton, 1863.

Brown, William Wells. *Narrative of William W. Brown, a Fugitive Slave*. Boston: Anti-Slavery Office, 1847.

Bruce, Henry Clay. *New Man: Twenty-Nine Years a Slave., Twenty-Nine Years a Free Man*. York, PA: F. Anstadt & Sons, 1895.

Bryant, William Cullen. *Letters of a Traveller*. New York: Putnam, 1850.

Buckingham, James Silk. *The Slave States of America*. 2 vols. London: Fisher, 1845.

Byrd, William. "Proposal to Drain the Dismal Swamp." *Farmers' Register* 4 (January 1, 1837): 521–524.

Byrd, William. *The Westover Manuscripts: Containing the History of the Dividing Line Betwixt Virginia and North Carolina*. Petersburg, VA: Edmund & Julian C. Ruffin, 1841.

Carroll, B. R. *Historical Collections of South Carolina*. 2 vols. New York: Harper & Brothers, 1836.

Cartwright, Samuel A. "How to Save the Republic, and the Position of the South in the Union." *DeBow's Review* 11 (1851): 184–197.

Censer, Jane Turner, ed. *Papers of Frederick Law Olmsted*, vol. 4. Baltimore: Johns Hopkins University Press, 1986.

Chambers, William. *Things as They Are in America*. Edinburgh: William & Robert Chambers, 1854.

Champomier, P. A. *Statement of the Sugar Crop Made in Louisiana, 1849–1850*. New Orleans: Cook, Young, 1850.

Charlton, Lewis. *Sketch of the Life of Mr. Lewis Charlton and Reminiscences of Slavery.* Portland, ME: Daily Press, n.d.

Childs, St. Julien R. "A Letter Written in 1711 by Mary Stafford to Her Kinswoman in England." *South Carolina Historical Magazine* 81 (1980): 1–7.

Clarke, Lewis. *Narrative of the Sufferings of Lewis Clarke.* Boston: David H. Ela, 1845.

Clemson, Thomas G. "Gold and the Gold Region." *Orion* 4 (1844): 57–66.

Clifton, James M., ed. *Life and Labor on Argyle Island: Letters and Documents of a Savannah River Rice Plantation, 1833–1867.* Savannah, GA: Beehive, 1978.

Cocke, John Hartwell. "Tobacco the Bane of Virginia Husbandry." *Southern Planter* 19 (August 1859): 482–483.

Cocke, St. George. "Management of Negroes." *DeBow's Review* 14 (1853): 177–178.

Coffin, Levi. *Reminiscences of Levi Coffin.* Cincinnati: Robert Clarke, 1880.

Coleman, W. H. *Historical Sketch Book and Guide to New Orleans and Environs.* New York: W. H. Coleman, 1885.

Colyer, Vincent. *Brief Report of the Services Rendered by the Freed People to the United States Army.* New York: V. Colyer, 1864.

Cooke, George. "Sketches of Georgia." *Southern Literary Messenger* 6 (Nov. 1840): 775–777.

Darby, William. *The Emigrant's Guide to the Western and Southwestern States and Territories.* New York: Kirk & Mercein, 1818.

Davis, Edwin Adams. *Plantation Life in the Florida Parishes of Louisiana, 1836–1846.* New York: Columbia University Press, 1943.

DeBow, J. D. B. *Industrial Resources, Etc., of the Southern and Western States.* 3 vols. Charleston, SC: DeBow's, 1853.

De Brahm's Report of the General Survey in the Southern District of North America. Columbia: University of South Carolina Press, 1971.

A Declaration of the Immediate Causes Which Induce and Justify the Secession of the State of Mississippi from the Federal Union. Jackson, MS: Barksdale, 1861.

Dennett, John Richard. *The South As It Is: 1865–1866.* New York: Viking, 1965.

"Department of Agriculture." *DeBow's Review* 13 (1852): 192–198.

De Villiers, Marc. "A History of the Foundation of New Orleans (1717–1722)." *Louisiana Historical Quarterly* 3 (1920): 157–251.

Douglass, Frederick. *Address Delivered by Hon. Frederick Douglass at the Third Annual Fair of the Tennessee Colored Agricultural and Mechanical Association.* Washington, DC: New National Era & Citizen Print, 1873.

Douglass, Frederick. *The Heroic Slave.* Boston: John P. Jewett, 1853.

Douglass, Frederick. *Life and Times of Frederick Douglass.* Boston: De Wolfe & Fiske, 1892.

Douglass, Frederick. *My Bondage and My Freedom.* New York: Miller, Orton, & Mulligan, 1855.

Douglass, Frederick. *Narrative of the Life of Frederick Douglass, an American Slave.* Boston: Anti-Slavery Office, 1845.

Drayton, John. *A View of South Carolina as Respects Her Natural and Civil Concerns.* Charleston, SC: W. P. Young, 1802.

Drew, Benjamin. *A North-Side View of Slavery.* Boston: Jewett, 1856.

Du Bois, W. E. B. *The Souls of Black Folk.* Chicago: A. C. McClurg, 1903.

Easterby, J. H. "South Carolina through New England Eyes: Almira Coffin's Visit to the Low Country in 1851." *South Carolina Historical and Genealogical Magazine* 45 (1944): 127–136.

Easterby, J. H. *The South Carolina Rice Plantation as Revealed in the Papers of R. W. Allston.* Chicago: University of Chicago Press, 1945.

Eddis, William. *Letters from America,* London: Printed for the Author, 1792.

Elliot, Jonathan. *Debates, Resolutions, and Other Proceedings in Convention on the Adoption of the Federal Constitution.* 4 vols. Washington, DC: Elliot, 1827–1830.

Emmons, Ebenezer. *Report of the North-Carolina Geological Survey.* Raleigh, NC: H. D. Turner, 1858.

Engerman, Stanley L., Seymour Drescher, and Robert L. Paquette, eds. *Slavery.* New York: Oxford University Press, 2001.

"Explosion at the Midlothian Coal Pits." *Mining Magazine* 4 (1855): 316–317.

Featherstonhaugh, George William. *A Canoe Voyage up the Minnay Sotor.* 2 vols. London, R. Bentley, 1847.

Federal Writers' Project: Slave Narrative Project. Library of Congress. https://www.loc.gov/collections/slave-narratives-from-the-federal-writers-project-1936-to-1938/.

Fedric, Francis. *Slave Life in Virginia and Kentucky.* London: Wertheim, Macintosh, & Hunt, 1863.

Fithian, Philip Vickers. *Journals and Letters of Philip Vickers Fithian, 1773–1774: A Plantation Tutor of the Old Dominion.* Williamsburg, VA: Colonial Williamsburg, 1943.

Founders Online. National Archives. https://founders.archives.gov/.

Garnett, James M. "Defects in Agriculture." *Memoirs of the Society of Virginia for Promoting Agriculture.* Richmond, VA: Shepard & Pollard, 1818.

Gonzales, Ambrose E. *The Black Border: Gullah Stories of the Carolina Coast.* Columbia, SC: States Company, 1922.

Gosse, Philip Henry. *Letters from Alabama.* London: Morgan & Chase, 1859.

Gould, E. W. *Fifty Years on the Mississippi.* St. Louis: Nixon-Jones, 1889.

Graham, Matthew J. *Ninth Regiment New York Volunteers.* New York: E. P. Cody, 1900.

Grandy, Moses. *Narrative of the Life of Moses Grandy.* London: C. Gilpin, 1843.

Grant, Ulysses S. *Personal Memoirs of U. S. Grant.* 2 vols. New York: Charles L. Webster, 1885.

Gray, Thomas R. *Confessions of Nat Turner.* Baltimore: T. R. Gray, 1831.

Green Jacob D. *Narrative of the Life of J. D. Green, a Runaway Slave.* Huddersfield, UK: Henry Fielding, 1864.

Greene, Jack P. *Diary of Colonel Landon Carter of Sabine Hall.* 2 vols. Charlottesville: Virginia Historical Society, 1965.

Habersham, James. *The Letters of Hon. James Habersham, 1756–1775.* Savannah, GA: Savannah Morning News, 1904.

Hayes, John D., ed. *Samuel Francis Du Pont: A Selection from His Civil War Letters.* 3 vols. Ithaca, NY: Cornell University Press, 1969.

Heinrich, Oswald J. "The Midlothian, Virginia, Colliery in 1876." *Transactions of the American Institute of Mining Engineers* 4 (1875–1876): 308–316.

Henson, Josiah. *Uncle Tom's Story of His Life: An Autobiography of the Rev. Josiah Henson.* London: Christian Age Office, 1876.

Heyward, Duncan Clinch. *Seed from Madagascar.* Chapel Hill: University of North Carolina Press, 1937.

Higginson, Thomas Wentworth. "Nat Turner's Insurrection." *Atlantic Monthly* 8 (August 1861): 173–187.

Hodgson, Adam. *Letter from North America.* London: Hurst, Robinson, 1824.

Howe, S. G. *Refugees from Slavery in Canada West: Report to the Freedmen's Inquiry Commission.* Boston: Wright & Potter, 1864.

Hughes, Louis *Thirty Years a Slave.* Milwaukee, WI: South Side Printing, 1897.

Humphreys, A. A., and H. L. Abbot, *Report on the Physics and Hydraulics of the Mississippi River.* Washington, DC: GPO, 1867.

Humphreys, Benjamin E. *Floods and Levees of the Mississippi River: Supplemental Report.* Washington, DC: GPO, 1914.

Hurston, Zora Neale. *Barracoon: The Story of the Last "Black Cargo".* New York: Harper Collins, 2018.

Ingraham, Joseph Holt. *The South-West: By a Yankee.* 2 vols. New York: Harpers, 1835.

Ingraham, Joseph Holt. *The Sunny South.* Philadelphia: G. G. Evans, 1860.

Jackson, Andrew. *Narrative and Writings of Andrew Jackson, of Kentucky.* Syracuse, NY: Daily & Weekly Star Office, 1847.

Jackson, John Andrew. *Experience of a Slave in South Carolina.* London: Passmore & Alabaster, 1862.

Jacobs, Harriet A. *Incidents in the Life of a Slave Girl.* Boston: Published for the Author, 1861.

Jefferson, Thomas. *An Account of Louisiana.* Providence: Heaton & Williams, 1803.

Johnston, Hugh Buckner. "The Journal of Ebenezer Hazard in North Carolina, 1777 and 1778." *North Carolina Historical Review* 36 (1959): 358–381.

Kemble, Frances Anne. *Journal of a Residence on a Georgian Plantation in 1838–1839.* New York: Harper & Brothers, 1863.

King, Edward. *The Great South.* Hartford, CT: American Publishing, 1875.

Latrobe, Benjamin Henry. *The Journal of Latrobe.* New York: Appleton, 1905.

Laws of the State of North Carolina, Passed by the General Assembly at the Session of 1846–1847. Raleigh, NC: Thomas J. Lemay, 1847.

Lawson, John. *New Voyage to Carolina.* London: n.p., 1709.

Leeds, Stephen P. "Notes on the Gold Region of North and South Carolina." *Mining Magazine* 2 (1854): 355–369.

Leigh, Frances Butler. *Ten Years on a Georgia Plantation Since the War.* London: Richard Bentley & Son, 1883.

Lemmon, Sarah McCulloh. *The Pettigrew Papers.* 2 vols. Raleigh, NC: State Department of Archives & History, 1971.

LePage du Pratz, Antoine Simon. *The History of Louisiana.* London: T. Becket, 1774.

Lesley, J. Peter. *The Iron Manufacturer's Guide to the Furnaces, Forges, and Rolling Mills of the United States.* New York: J. Wiley, 1859.

"Letters of General Thomas Williams, 1862." *American Historical Review* 14 (1909): 304–328.

"Letters Written during a Journey through North America." *Christian Observer* 23 (1823): 151–156.

Lewis, George. *Impressions of America and the American Churches.* Edinburgh: W. P. Kennedy, 1845.

Lieber, Oscar M. *Report of the Survey of South Carolina.* Columbia, SC: Gibbes, 1856.

Life and Adventures of Zamba, An African Negro King. London: Smith, Elder, 1847.

Lockley, Timothy J. *Maroon Communities in South Carolina: A Documentary Record.* Columbia: University of South Carolina Press, 2009.

Long, John Dixon. *Pictures of Slavery in Church and State.* Philadelphia: Published by the Author, 1857.

Longfellow, Henry Wadsworth. *Poems on Slavery.* Cambridge, MA: John Owen, 1842.

Lovell, Caroline Couper. *The Golden Isles of Georgia.* Boston: Little, Brown, 1932.

Lowery, Irving E. *Life on the Old Plantation in Ante-Bellum Days.* Columbia, SC: State Co. Printers, 1911.

Lyell, Charles. "On the Structure and Probable Age of the Coal-Field of the James River." *Quarterly Journal of the Geological Society* 3 (1847): 261–280.

Lyell, Charles. *A Second Visit to the United States of North America.* 2 vols. New York: Harper & Brothers, 1849.

Mackay, Charles. *Life and Liberty in America.* New York: Harper & Bros., 1859.

Mallory, William. *Old Plantation Days.* Hamilton, ON: n.p., 1902.

McLean, Robert C. "A Yankee Tutor in the Old South." *North Carolina Historical Review* 47 (1970): 51–85.

Minutes of the Freedmen's Convention Held in the City of Raleigh. Raleigh, NC: Standard Book, 1866.

Mitchell, Elisha. *Diary of a Geological Tour.* James Sprunt Historical Monograph 6. Chapel Hill: University of North Carolina Press, 1905.

Nitze, H. B. C., and H. A. J. Wilkens. "The Present Condition of Gold-Mining in the Southern Appalachian States." *Transactions of the American Institute of Mining Engineers* 25 (1896): 661–796, 1021–1023.

Northup, Solomon. *Twelve Years a Slave.* Auburn, NY: Derby & Miller, 1853.

Oldmixon, John W. *Transatlantic Wanderings.* London: Routledge, 1855.

Olmsted, Denison. "Geology and Mineralogy of North-Carolina." *Southern Review* 1 (1828): 235–261.

Olmsted, Frederick Law. *The Cotton Kingdom*. 2 vols. New York: Mason Brothers, 1861.

Olmsted, Frederick Law. *A Journey in the Seaboard Slave States*. New York: Dix & Edwards, 1856.

O'Neall, John Belton. *Annals of Newberry*. Newberry, SC: Aull & Houseal, 1892.

Paine, Lewis W. *Six Years in a Georgia Prison*. New York: printed for the author, 1851.

Parker, Allen. *Recollections of Slavery Times*. Worcester, MA: Chas. W. Burbank, 1895.

Partz, August. "Gold-Bearing Belts of the Atlantic States." *Mining Magazine* 3 (1854): 161–168.

Paschal, George Washington. *Ninety-Four Years: Agnes Paschal*. Washington, DC: M'Gill & Witherow, 1871.

Paulding, James. "The Mississippi." *Graham's American Monthly* 22 (1843): 215–224.

Perdue, Charles L., Jr., Thomas E. Barden, and Robert K. Phillips. *Weevils in the Wheat: Interviews with Virginia Ex-Slaves*. Charlottesville: University of Virginia Press, 1976.

Pickard, Kate E. R. *The Kidnapped and the Ransomed*. Syracuse, NY: William T. Hamilton, 1856.

Pittman, Philip. *The Present State of the European Settlements on the Mississippi*. London: J. Nourse, 1770.

Porcher, Francis P. *Resources of Southern Fields and Forests*. Charleston, SC: Evans & Cogswell, 1863.

Porte Crayon [David Hunter Strother]. "North Carolina Illustrated." *Harper's New Monthly Magazine* 82 (March 1857): 433–450; 84 (May 1857): 741–755; 86 (July 1857): 154–164; 87 (Aug. 1857): 289–300.

Porte Crayon [David Hunter Strother]. "Dismal Swamp." *Harper's New Monthly Magazine* 13 (1856): 441–455.

Porteous, Laura L. "Governor Carondelet's Levee Ordinance of 1792." *Louisiana Historical Quarterly* 10 (1927): 513–514.

Pringle, Elizabeth W. Allston. *Chronicles of Chicora Wood*. New York: Scribner's, 1922.

"A Raid Among the Rice Plantations." *Harper's Weekly* 7 (July 4, 1863): 427.

Ramsay, David. *The History of South Carolina*. 2 vols. Charleston, SC: David Longworth, 1809.

Randolph, Peter. *From Slave Cabin to the Pulpit*. Boston: James H. Earle, 1893.

Rankin, David C. *Diary of a Christian Soldier: Rufus Kinsley and the Civil War*. New York: Cambridge University Press, 2004.

"Records of the Superior Council of Louisiana." *Louisiana Historical Quarterly* 3 (1920): 403–448.

Redpath, James. *The Roving Editor*. New York: A. B. Burdick, 1859.

Report of the Secretary of War. 2 vols. Washington, DC: GPO, 1883.

Reports of the Committees of the House of Representatives, Twenty-Second Congress, First Session. Washington, DC: Duff Green, 1831.

Rogers, George C., ed. *The Papers of Henry Laurens*. 16 vols. Columbia: University of South Carolina Press, 1968–2003.

Roper, Moses. *Narrative of the Adventures and Escape of Moses Roper, from American Slavery*. Berwick-upon-Tweed, UK: Warder Office, 1848.

Rothe, Charles E. "Remarks on the Gold Mines of North Carolina." *American Journal of Science and Arts* 13 (1828): 201–217.

Rowland, Dunbar. *Official Letter Books of W. C. C. Claiborne, 1801–1816*. 6 vols. Jackson, MS: State Department of Archives & History, 1917.

Rowland, Eron. *Life, Letters and Papers of William Dunbar of Elgin, Morayshire, Scotland, and Natchez, Mississippi*. Jackson: Mississippi Historical Society, 1930.

Ruffin, Edmund. *Agricultural, Geological, and Descriptive Sketches of Lower North Carolina*. Raleigh, NC: Institution for the Deaf & Dumb & the Blind, 1861.

Ruffin, Edmund. *Exhausting and Fertilizing Systems of Agriculture*. Charleston, SC: Walker & James, 1853.

Ruffin, Edmund. "Notes of a Steam Journey." *Farmers' Register* 8 (April 30, 1840): 243–254.

Ruffin, Edmund. "Observations Made during an Excursion to the Dismal Swamp." *Farmers' Register* 4 (1 January 1837): 513–521.

Ruffin, Edmund. "On the Sources of Malaria." *Farmers' Register* 6 (1838): 216–228.

Saunders, William L. *Colonial Records of North Carolina*. 10 vols. Raleigh, NC: Hale, 1886–1890.

Saxon, Lyle. *Father Mississippi*. New York: Century, 1927.

Scarborough, William Kauffman, ed. *The Diary of Edmund Ruffin*. 3 vols. Baton Rouge: Louisiana State University Press, 1972–1989.

Schaw, Janet. *Journal of a Lady of Quality: Being the Narrative of a Journey from Scotland to the West Indies, North Carolina, and Portugal, in the Years 1774 to 1776*. New Haven, CT: Yale University Press, 1921.

Schoepf, Johann David. *Travels in the Confederation*. Translated by Alfred J. Morrison. Philadelphia: W. J. Campbell, 1911.

Seabrook, Whitemarsh B. *Agricultural Capabilities of S. Carolina*. Columbia, SC: Bowman, 1848.

Secession of Mississippi from the Federal Union. Jackson: Mississippian Book & Job Printing Office, 1861.

Sherman, William T. *Memoirs of General William T. Sherman*. 2 vols. New York: D. Appleton, 1875.

Simms, William Gilmore. *Geography of South Carolina*. Charleston, SC: Babcock, 1843.

Simon, John Y. *Papers of Ulysses S. Grant*. 31 vols. Carbondale: Southern Illinois University Press, 1967–2012.

Smith, Mark M. *Stono: Documenting and Interpreting a Southern Slave Revolt*. Columbia: University of South Carolina Press, 2005.

Smith, William A. *Lectures on the Philosophy and Practice of Slavery, as Exhibited in the Institution of Domestic Slavery in the United States, with the Duties of Masters to Slaves*. Nashville: Stevenson & Evans, 1856.

Smith, William B. "Can the Culture of Tobacco Be Dispensed With in Eastern Virginia." *Farmers' Register* 6 (1838): 747–753.

Smith, William R. *The History and Debates of the Convention of the People of Alabama.* Montgomery: White, Pfister, 1861.

Smyth, John Ferdinand. *A Tour in the United States.* 2 vols. London: G. Robinson, 1784.

Southard, Nathaniel, ed. *The American Anti-Slavery Almanac for 1838.* Boston: Isaac Knapp, 1838.

Sprague, Stuart Seely. *His Promised Land: The Autobiography of John P. Parker, Former Slave and Conductor on the Underground Railroad.* New York: Norton, 1998.

Spratt, L. W. *The Philosophy of Secession.* Charleston, SC [?]: n.p., 1861.

Stephens, Alexander H. "Cornerstone Address, March 21, 1861." In *The Rebellion Record,* ed. Frank Moore, 1:44–46. New York: Putnam, 1862.

Still, William. *The Underground Rail Road.* Philadelphia: Porter & Coates, 1872.

Stone, Kate. *Brokenburn: The Journal of Kate Stone, 1861–1868.* Baton Rouge: Louisiana State University Press, 1955.

Stowe, Harriet Beecher. *Dred: A Tale of the Great Dismal Swamp.* Boston: Phillips, Sampson, 1856.

Stroyer, Jacob. *My Life in the South.* Salem, MA: Salem Observer, 1885.

Thompson, Charles. *Biography of a Slave.* Dayton, OH: United Brethren, 1875.

Thompson, John. *The Life of John Thompson, a Fugitive Slave.* Worcester, MA: John Thompson, 1856.

Thornton, William. *North Carolina Gold-Mine Company.* Washington, DC: n.p., 1806.

Throne, Mildred, ed. *The Civil War Diary of Cyrus F. Boyd: Fifteenth Iowa Infantry, 1861–1863.* Iowa City: State Historical Society of Iowa, 1953.

Thwaites, Reuben Gold. *Early Western Travels.* 32 vols. Cleveland: A. H. Clark, 1904–1907.

Trowbridge, John Townsend. *The South.* Hartford, CT: L. Stebbins, 1866.

"Turpentine: Hints for Those About to Engage in its Manufacture." *DeBow's Review* 19 (October 1855): 486–489.

Van Doren, Mark. *Correspondence of Aaron Burr and His Daughter Theodosia.* New York: Covici-Friede, 1929.

Van Evrie, John H. *Negroes and Negro "Slavery".* New York: Van Evrie, Horton, 1863.

Walker, William. *Buried Alive (behind Prison Walls) for a Quarter of a Century.* Saginaw, MI: Friedman & Hynan, 1892.

The War of the Rebellion: A Compilation of the Official Records of the Union and Confederate Armies. 70 vols. Washington, DC: GPO, 1880–1901.

Watson, Elkanah. *Men and Times of the Revolution.* New York: Dana, 1856.

Watson, Henry. *Narrative of Henry Watson, A Fugitive Slave.* Boston: Bela Marsh, 1848.

Weld, Theodore Dwight. *Slavery As It Is: Testimony of a Thousand Witnesses.* New York: Anti-Slavery Office, 1839.

Wiley, Calvin H. *Adventures of Old Dan Tucker and His Son Walter: A Tale of North Carolina.* London: Willoughby, 1851.

Williams, George Washington. *A History of Negro Troops in the War of the Rebellion*. New York: Harper, 1888.

Williams, Isaac D. *Sunshine and Shadow of Slave Life*. East Saginaw, MI: Evening News Printing, 1885.

Williams, James. *Narrative of James Williams*. New York: American Anti-Slavery Society, 1838.

Wilson, Clyde N., ed., *The Papers of John C. Calhoun*. Columbia: University of South Carolina Press, 1979.

Wilson, Joseph T. *The Black Phalanx: A History of the Negro Soldiers of the United States in the War of 1775–1812, 1861–1865*. Hartford, CT: American Publishing, 1888.

Yeates, William Smith, S. W. McCallie, and Francis P. King, *Preliminary Report on a Part of the Gold Deposits*. Atlanta: G. W. Harrison, 1896.

SECONDARY SOURCES

Books

Adams, Sean Patrick. *Iron from the Wilderness: The History of Virginia's Catharine Furnace*. Fredericksburg, VA: National Park Service, 2011.

Anderson, Virginia DeJohn. *Creatures of Empire: How Domestic Animals Transformed Early America*. New York: Oxford University Press, 2006.

Bagley, William Chandler, Jr. *Soil Exhaustion and the Civil War*. Washington, DC: American Council on Public Affairs, 1942.

Bancroft, Frederick. *Slave Trading in the Old South*. Baltimore: J. H. Furst, 1931.

Baptist, Edward. *The Half Has Never Been Told: Slavery and the Making of American Capitalism*. New York: Basic Books, 2014.

Barney, William L. *Rebels in the Making: The Secession Crisis and the Birth of the Confederacy*. New York: Oxford University Press, 2020.

Beckert, Sven. *Empire of Cotton: A Global History*. New York: Knopf, 2013.

Beckert, Sven, and Seth Rockman, eds. *Slavery's Capitalism: A New History of American Economic Development*. Philadelphia: University of Pennsylvania Press, 2016.

Bell, Andrew McIlwaine. *Mosquito Soldiers: Malaria, Yellow Fever, and the Course of the American Civil War*. Baton Rouge: Louisiana State University Press, 2010.

Bell, Karen Cook. *Claiming Freedom: Race, Kinship, and Land in Nineteenth-Century Georgia*. Columbia: University of South Carolina Press, 2018.

Bell, Karen Cook. *Running from Bondage: Enslaved Women and Their Remarkable Fight for Freedom in Revolutionary America*. New York: Cambridge University Press, 2021.

Berlin, Ira. *Many Thousands Gone: The First Two Centuries of Slavery in North America*. Cambridge, MA: Harvard University Press, 1998.

Berlin, Ira, and Philip D. Morgan, eds. *The Slaves' Economy: Independent Production by Slaves in the Americas*. London: Frank Cass, 1991.

Berry, Daina Ramey. *Swing the Sickle for the Harvest Is Ripe: Gender and Slavery in Antebellum Georgia*. Champaign: University of Illinois Press, 2007.

Boatright, Sherry L. *John C. Calhoun Gold Mine: An Introductory Report on Its Historical Significance*. Atlanta: Georgia Department of Natural Resources, 1974.

Bolgiano, Chris. *The Appalachian Forest*. Mechanicsburg, PA: Stackpole, 1998.

Bolton, S. Charles. *Fugitivism: Escaping Slavery in the Lower Mississippi Valley, 1820–1860*. Fayetteville: University of Arkansas Press, 2019.

Boster, Dea H. *African American Slavery and Disability: Bodies, Property, and Power in the Antebellum South, 1800–1860*. New York: Routledge, 2013.

Brady, Lisa M. *War upon the Land: Military Strategy and the Transformation of Southern Landscapes during the American Civil War*. Athens, GA: University of Georgia Press, 2012.

Breen, Patrick H. *The Land Shall Be Deluged in Blood: A New History of the Nat Turner Revolt*. New York: Oxford University Press, 2015.

Breen, T. H. *Tobacco Culture: The Mentality of the Great Tidewater Planters on the Eve of the Revolution*. Princeton, NJ: Princeton University Press, 1985.

Brettle, Adrian. *Colossal Ambitions: Confederate Planning for a Post–Civil War World*. Charlottesville: University of Virginia Press, 2020.

Brewster, Lawrence Fay. *Summer Migrations and Resorts of South Carolina Low-Country Planters*. Durham, NC: Duke University Press, 1947.

Browning, Judkin, and Timothy Silver. *An Environmental History of the Civil War*. Chapel Hill: University of North Carolina Press, 2020.

Bullard, Robert D. *Dumping in Dixie: Race, Class, and Environmental Quality*. Boulder, CO: Westview, 1990.

Burke, Diane Mutti. *On Slavery's Border: Missouri's Small Slaveholding Households, 1815–1865*. Athens, GA: University of Georgia Press, 2010.

Bushman, Claudia L. *In Old Virginia: Slavery, Farming, and Society in the Journal of John Walker*. Baltimore: Johns Hopkins University Press, 2001.

Bushman, Richard Lyman. *The American Farmer in the Eighteenth Century: A Social and Cultural History*. New Haven, CT: Yale University Press, 2018.

Camp, Stephanie M. H. *Closer to Freedom: Enslaved Women and Everyday Resistance in the Plantation South*. Chapel Hill: University of North Carolina Press, 2004.

Campanella, Richard. *Bienville's Dilemma: A Historical Geography of New Orleans*. Lafayette: Center for Louisiana Studies 2008.

Campanella, Richard. *Delta Urbanism: New Orleans*. Chicago: American Planning Association, 2010.

Carney, Judith A. *Black Rice: The African Origins of Rice Cultivation in the Americas*. Cambridge, MA: Harvard University Press, 2002.

Cashin, Joan E. *War Stuff: The Struggle for Human and Environmental Resources in the American Civil War*. New York: Cambridge University Press, 2018.

Cate, Margaret Davis. *Early Days of Coastal Georgia*. St. Simons Island, GA: Fort Frederica Association, 1955.

Cecelski, David S. *The Fire of Freedom: Abraham Galloway and the Slaves' Civil War.* Chapel Hill: University of North Carolina Press, 2012.

Cecelski, David S. *The Waterman's Song: Slavery and Freedom in Maritime North Carolina.* Chapel Hill: University of North Carolina Press, 2001.

Censer, Jane Turner. *North Carolina Planters and Their Children, 1800–1860.* Baton Rouge: Louisiana State University Press, 1990.

Chaplin, Joyce E. *An Anxious Pursuit: Agricultural Innovation and Modernity in the Lower South, 1730–1815.* Chapel Hill: University of North Carolina Press, 1996.

Clarke, Erskine. *Dwelling Place: A Plantation Epic.* New Haven, CT: Yale University Press, 2007.

Clinton, Catherine. *Harriet Tubman: The Road to Freedom.* New York: Little, Brown, 2004.

Coclanis, Peter A. *The Shadow of a Dream: Economic Life and Death in the South Carolina Low Country, 1670–1920.* New York: Oxford University Press, 1991.

Cornelius, Janet Duitsman. *Slave Missions and the Black Church in the Antebellum South.* Columbia: University of South Carolina Press, 1999.

Coulter, E. Merton. *Auraria: The Story of a Georgia Gold Mining Town.* Athens, GA: University of Georgia Press, 1956.

Coulter, E. Merton. *Georgia's Disputed Ruins.* Chapel Hill: University of North Carolina Press, 1937.

Covey, Herbert C. *African American Slave Medicine: Herbal and Non-Herbal Treatments.* Lanham, MD: Lexington, 2007.

Cowdrey, Albert E. *This Land, This South: An Environmental History*, rev. ed. Lexington: University of Kentucky Press, 1996.

Craven, Avery. *Soil Exhaustion as a Factor in the Agricultural History of Virginia and Maryland, 1606–1860.* Urbana: University of Illinois Press, 1926.

Cronon, William. *Changes in the Land: Indians, Colonists, and the Ecology of New England.* New York: Hill & Wang, 1983.

Cushman, Gregory T. *Guano and the Opening of the Pacific World: A Global Ecological History.* New York: Cambridge University Press, 2013.

Davis, David Brion. *Inhuman Bondage: The Rise and Fall of Slavery in the New World.* New York: Oxford University Press, 2006.

Davis, Donald Edward. *Where There Are Mountains: An Environmental History of the Southern Appalachians.* Athens, GA: University of Georgia Press, 2003.

Dawdy, Shannon Lee. *Building the Devil's Empire: French Colonial New Orleans.* Chicago: University of Chicago Press, 2008.

Dawson, Kevin. *Undercurrents of Power: Aquatic Culture in the African Diaspora.* Philadelphia: University of Pennsylvania Press, 2018.

Dean, Adam Wesley. *An Agrarian Republic: Farming, Antislavery Politics, and Nature Parks in the Civil War Era.* Chapel Hill: University of North Carolina Press, 2015.

DeRosier, Arthur H., Jr. *William Dunbar: Scientific Pioneer of the Old Southwest.* Lexington: University Press of Kentucky, 2007.

Deyle, Steven. *Carry Me Back: The Domestic Slave Trade in American Life.* New York: Oxford University Press, 2006.

Din, Gilbert C. *Spaniards, Planters, and Slaves: The Spanish Regulation of Slavery in Louisiana, 1763–1803.* College Station: Texas A&M Press, 1999.

Diouf, Sylviane A. *Slavery's Exiles: The Story of the American Maroons.* New York: New York University Press, 2014.

Downs, Jim. *Sick from Freedom: African-American Illness and Suffering during the Civil War and Reconstruction.* New York: Oxford University Press, 2012.

Drake, Brian Allen, ed. *The Blue, the Gray, and the Green: Toward an Environmental History of the Civil War.* Athens, GA: University of Georgia Press, 2015.

Du Bois, W. E. B. *Black Reconstruction in America.* New York: Free Press, 1998.

Dunaway, Wilma A. *The First American Frontier: Transition to Capitalism in Southern Appalachia, 1700–1860.* Chapel Hill: University of North Carolina Press, 1996.

Dunaway, Wilma A. *Slavery in the American Mountain South.* New York: Cambridge University Press, 2003.

Dusinberre, William. *Them Dark Days: Slavery in American Rice Swamps.* New York: Oxford University Press, 1996.

Earley, Lawrence S. *Looking for Longleaf: The Rise and Fall of an American Forest.* Chapel Hill: University of North Carolina Press, 2004.

Edelson, S. Max. *Plantation Enterprise in Colonial South Carolina.* Cambridge, MA: Harvard University Press, 2011.

Egerton, Douglas R. *Death or Liberty: African Americans and Revolutionary America.* New York: Oxford University Press, 2009.

Egerton, Douglas R. *Gabriel's Rebellion: The Virginia Slave Conspiracies of 1800 to 1802.* Chapel Hill: University of North Carolina Press, 1993.

Ellenberg, George B. *Mule South to Tractor South: Mules, Machines, and the Transformation of the Cotton South.* Tuscaloosa: University of Alabama Press, 2007.

Escott, Paul D. *Slavery Remembered: A Record of Twentieth Century Slave Narratives.* Chapel Hill: University of North Carolina Press, 1979.

Evans, Eli N. *Judah P. Benjamin: The Jewish Confederate.* New York: Free Press of Macmillan, 1988.

Fagan, Brian. *The Little Ice Age: How Climate Made History, 1300–1850.* New York: Basic Books, 2000.

Feduccia, Alan J. *Catesby's Birds of Colonial America.* Chapel Hill: University of North Carolina Press, 1985.

Ferguson, Leland. *Uncommon Ground: Archaeology and Early African America, 1650–1800.* Washington, DC: Smithsonian Institution Press, 1992.

Fett, Sharla M. *Working Cures: Healing, Health, and Power on Southern Slave Plantations.* Chapel Hill: University of North Carolina Press, 2002.

Follett, Richard J. *The Sugar Masters: Planters and Slaves in Louisiana's Cane World, 1820–1860.* Baton Rouge: Louisiana State University Press, 2005.

Ford, Lacy K. *Deliver Us from Evil: The Slavery Question in the Old South.* New York: Oxford University Press, 2009.

Forkner, Ben. *Audubon on Louisiana.* Baton Rouge: Louisiana State University Press, 2018.

Forret, Jeff. *Race Relations at the Margins: Slaves and Poor Whites in the Antebellum Southern Countryside.* Baton Rouge: Louisiana State University Press, 2006.

Franklin, John Hope, and Loren Schweninger, *Runaway Slaves: Rebels on the Plantation.* New York: Oxford University Press, 2000.

Fraser, Walter J. *Lowcountry Hurricanes: Three Centuries of Storms at Sea and Ashore.* Athens, GA: University of Georgia Press, 2006.

Frey, Sylvia R. *Water from the Rock: Black Resistance in a Revolutionary Age.* Princeton, NJ: Princeton University Press, 1991.

Fritz, Karen. *Voices in the Storm: Confederate Rhetoric, 1861–1865.* Denton: University of North Texas Press, 1999.

Gates, Paul W. *The Farmer's Age: Agriculture, 1815–1860.* New York: Holt, Rinehart & Winston, 1960.

Genovese, Eugene D. *The Political Economy of Slavery.* New York: Pantheon, 1965.

Genovese, Eugene D. *Roll, Jordan, Roll: The World the Slaves Made.* New York: Vintage, 1976.

Gibson, Abraham H. *Feral Animals in the American South: An Evolutionary History.* New York: Cambridge University Press, 2016.

Gilje, Paul A. *Liberty on the Waterfront: American Maritime Culture in the Age of Revolution.* Philadelphia: University of Pennsylvania Press, 2004.

Gilmore, William C. *The Confederate Jurist: The Legal Life of Judah P. Benjamin.* Edinburgh: Edinburgh University Press, 2021.

Giraud, Marcel. *History of French Louisiana,* vol. 5, *The Company of the Indies, 1723–1731.* Baton Rouge: Louisiana State University Press, 1991.

Goldenberg, Joseph A. *Shipbuilding in Colonial America.* Charlottesville: University Press of Virginia, 1976.

Gomez, Michael A. *Exchanging Our Country Marks: The Transformation of African Identities in the Colonial and Antebellum South.* Chapel Hill: University of North Carolina Press, 1998.

Gray, Cecil Lewis. *A History of Agriculture in the Southern United States to 1860.* Washington, DC: Carnegie, 1933.

Hadden, Sally E. *Slave Patrols: Law and Violence in Virginia and the Carolinas.* Cambridge, MA: Harvard University Press, 2003.

Hahn, Barbara M. *Making Tobacco Bright: Creating an American Commodity, 1617–1937.* Baltimore: Johns Hopkins University Press, 2011.

Hahn, Steven. *A Nation under Our Feet: Black Political Struggles in the Rural South from Slavery to the Great Migration.* Cambridge, MA: Harvard University Press, 2003.

Hahn, Steven. *A Nation without Borders: The United States and Its World in an Age of Civil Wars, 1830–1910.* New York: Penguin, 2017.

Hahn, Steven. *The Political Worlds of Slavery and Freedom.* Cambridge, MA: Harvard University Press, 2009.

Hall, Arthur R. *Early Erosion-Control Practices in Virginia.* Washington, DC: GPO, 1938.

Hall, Gwendolyn Midlo. *Africans in Colonial Louisiana: The Development of Afro-Creole Culture in the Eighteenth-Century.* Baton Rouge: Louisiana State University Press, 1995.

Harris, Lynn B. *Patroons & Periaguas: Enslaved Watermen and Watercraft of the Lowcountry.* Columbia: University of South Carolina Press, 2014.

Hatley, Tom. *The Dividing Paths: Cherokees and South Carolinians through the Era of the Revolution.* New York: Oxford University Press, 1998.

Hawthorne, Walter. *Planting Rice and Harvesting Slaves: Transformations along the Guinea-Bissau Coast.* Portsmouth, NH: Heinemann, 2003.

Henry, Howell M. *The Police Control of the Slave in South Carolina.* Emory, VA: n.p., 1914.

Hilliard, Sam Bowers. *Hog Meat and Hoecake: Food Supply in the Old South, 1840–1860.* Carbondale: Southern Illinois University Press, 1972.

Hogarth, Rona A. *Medicalizing Blackness: Making Racial Differences in the Atlantic World, 1780–1840.* Chapel Hill: University of North Carolina Press, 2017.

Holton, Woody. *Forced Founders: Indians, Debtors, Slaves, and the Making of the American Revolution in Virginia.* Chapel Hill: University of North Carolina Press, 1999.

Hudson, J. Blaine. *Fugitive Slaves and the Underground Railroad in the Kentucky Borderland.* Jefferson, NC: McFarland, 2002.

Hurt, R. Douglas. *Agriculture and the Confederacy: Policy, Productivity, and Power in the Civil War South.* Chapel Hill: University of North Carolina Press, 2015.

Ingersoll, Thomas N. *Mammon and Manon in Early New Orleans: The First Slave Society in the Deep South, 1718–1819.* Knoxville: University of Tennessee Press, 1999.

Inscoe, John C. *Mountain Masters: Slavery and the Sectional Criss in Western North Carolina.* Knoxville: University of Tennessee Press, 1989.

Isaac, Rhys. *Landon Carter's Uneasy Kingdom: Revolution and Rebellion on a Virginia Plantation.* New York: Oxford University Press, 2004.

Isaac, Rhys. *The Transformation of Virginia, 1740–1790.* Chapel Hill: University of North Carolina Press, 1982.

Jennison, Watson W. *Cultivating Race: The Expansion of Slavery in Georgia, 1750–1860.* Lexington: University Press of Kentucky, 2012.

Johnson, Frank Roy. *Tales from Old Carolina.* Murfreesboro, NC: Johnson, 1965.

Johnson, Walter. *River of Dark Dreams: Slavery and Empire in the Cotton Kingdom.* Cambridge, MA: Harvard University Press, 2013.

Johnson, Walter. *Soul by Soul: Life Inside the Antebellum Slave Market.* Cambridge, MA: Harvard University Press, 2001.

Johnson, Whittington B. *Black Savannah, 1788–1864.* Fayetteville: University of Arkansas Press, 1996.

Joyner, Charles W. *Down by the Riverside: A South Carolina Slave Community*. Urbana: University of Illinois Press, 1985.

Joyner, Charles W. *Remember Me: Slave Life in Coastal Georgia*. Athens, GA: University of Georgia Press, 2011.

Kapsch, Robert J. *Historic Canals and Waterways of South Carolina*. Columbia: University of South Carolina Press, 2010.

Karp, Matthew. *This Vast Southern Empire: Slaveholders at the Helm of American Foreign Policy*. Cambridge, MA: Harvard University Press, 2016.

Kaye, Anthony E. *Joining Places: Slave Neighborhoods in the Old South*. Chapel Hill: University of North Carolina Press, 2009.

Kelman, Ari. *A River and Its City: The Nature of Landscape in New Orleans*. Berkeley: University of California Press, 2006.

Kendall, John. *History of New Orleans*. Chicago: Lewis, 1922.

Kennedy, Roger G. *Mr. Jefferson's Lost Cause: Land, Farmers, Slavery, and the Louisiana Purchase*. New York: Oxford University Press, 2003.

Kinzer, Mark. *Nature's Return: An Environmental History of Congaree National Park*. Columbia: University of South Carolina Press, 2017.

Kiple, Kenneth F., and Virginia H. King, *Another Dimension to the Black Diaspora: Diet, Disease, and Racism*. New York: Cambridge University Press, 1981.

Kirby, Jack Temple. *Mockingbird Song: Ecological Landscapes of the South*. Chapel Hill: University of North Carolina Press, 2006.

Kirby, Jack Temple. *Poquosin: A Study of Rural Landscape and Society*. Chapel Hill: University of North Carolina Press, 1995.

Kulikoff, Allan. *Tobacco and Slaves: The Development of Southern Cultures in the Chesapeake, 1680–1800*. Chapel Hill: University of North Carolina Press, 1988.

Kupperman, Karen Ordahl *The Jamestown Project*. Cambridge, MA: Harvard University Press, 2007.

Lamb, H. H. *Climate, History, and the Modern World*. London: Routledge, 1982.

Lamb, Robert Byron. *The Mule in Southern Agriculture*. Berkeley: University of California Press, 1963.

Larson, Kate Clifford *Bound for the Promised Land: Harriet Tubman, Portrait of an American Hero*. New York: Ballantine, 2004.

Lewis, Ronald L. *Black Coal Miners in America: Race, Class, and Community Conflict, 1780–1980*. Lexington: University Press of Kentucky, 1987.

Lewis, Ronald L. *Transforming the Appalachian Countryside: Railroads, Deforestation, and Social Change in West Virginia, 1880–1920*. Chapel Hill: University of North Carolina Press, 1998.

Libby, David J. *Slavery and Frontier Mississippi, 1720–1835*. Jackson: University Press of Mississippi, 2004.

Littlefield, Daniel C. *Rice and Slaves: Ethnicity and the Slave Trade in Colonial South Carolina*. Champaign: University of Illinois Press, 1991.

Litwack, Leon F. *Been in the Storm So Long: The Aftermath of Slavery.* New York: Knopf, 1979.

Ludlum, David M. *Early American Hurricanes,1492–1870.* Boston: American Meteorological Society, 1963.

Majewski, John. *Modernizing a Slave Economy: The Economic Vision of the Confederate Nation.* Chapel Hill: University of North Carolina Press, 2009.

Manning, Chandra. *Troubled Refuge: Struggling for Freedom in the Civil War.* New York: Knopf, 2016.

Marrs, Aaron W. *Railroads in the Old South: Pursuing Progress in a Slave Society.* Baltimore: Johns Hopkins University Press, 2009.

Mathew, William M. *Edmund Ruffin and the Crisis of Slavery in the Old South: The Failure of Agricultural Reform.* Athens, GA: University of Georgia Press, 1988.

Mauldin, Erin. *Unredeemed Land: An Environmental History of Civil War and Emancipation in the Cotton South.* New York: Oxford University Press, 2018.

McCandless, Peter. *Slavery, Disease, and Suffering in the Southern Lowcountry.* New York: Cambridge University Press, 2011.

McCurry, Stephanie. *Confederate Reckoning: Power and Politics in the Civil War South.* Cambridge, MA: Harvard University Press, 2010.

McInnis, Maurie D. *Slaves Waiting for Sale: Abolitionist Art and the American Slave Trade.* Chicago: University of Chicago Press, 2011.

McNeill, J. R. *Mosquito Empires: Ecology and War in the Greater Caribbean, 1620–1914.* New York: Cambridge University Press, 2012.

Meier, Kathryn Shively. *Nature's Civil War: Common Soldiers and the Environment in 1862 Virginia.* Chapel Hill: University of North Carolina Press, 2013.

Memminger, Edward Read. *A Historical Sketch of Flat Rock.* Flat Rock, NC: Stephen, 1954.

Meriwether, Robert Lee. *The Expansion of South Carolina, 1729–1765.* Kingsport, TN: Southern Publishers, 1940.

Miller, David C. *Dark Eden: The Swamp in Nineteenth-Century American Culture.* New York: Cambridge University Press, 1989.

Miller, Donald L. *Vicksburg: Grant's Campaign That Broke the Confederacy.* New York: Simon & Schuster, 2019.

Miller, Mary Carol. *Lost Mansions of the Mississippi.* 2 vols. Jackson: University of Mississippi Press, 1996–2010.

Mooney, Katherine C. *Race Horse Men: How Slavery and Freedom Were Made at the Racetrack.* Cambridge, MA: Harvard University Press, 2014.

Moore, John Hebron. *Andrew Brown and Cypress Lumbering in the Old Southwest.* Baton Rouge: Louisiana State University Press, 1967.

Morgan, Philip D. *Slave Counterpoint: Black Culture in the Eighteenth-Century Chesapeake and Lowcountry.* Chapel Hill: University of North Carolina Press, 1998.

Morris, Christopher. *The Big Muddy: An Environmental History of the Mississippi and Its People, from Hernando de Soto to Hurricane Katrina.* New York: Oxford University Press, 2012.

Mulcahy, Matthew. *Hurricanes and Society in the British Greater Caribbean, 1624–1783.* Baltimore: Johns Hopkins University Press, 2005.

Nelson, Lynn A. *Pharsalia: An Environmental Biography of a Southern Plantation, 1780–1880.* Athens, GA: University of Georgia Press, 2007.

Nelson, Megan Kate. *Ruin Nation: Destruction and the American Civil War.* Athens, GA: University of Georgia Press, 2012.

Nelson, Megan Kate. *Trembling Earth: A Cultural History of the Okefenokee Swamp.* Athens, GA: University of Georgia Press, 2005.

Nevius, Marcus P. *City of Refuge: Slavery and Petit Marronage in the Great Dismal Swamp, 1763–1856.* Athens, GA: University of Georgia Press, 2020.

Nieman Donald G. *From Slavery to Sharecropping: White Land and Black Labor in the Rural South, 1865–1900.* New York: Garland, 1994.

Nobles, Gregory. *John James Audubon: The Nature of the American Woodsman.* Philadelphia: University of Pennsylvania Press, 2017.

Noe, Kenneth W. *The Howling Storm: Weather, Climate, and the American Civil War.* Baton Rouge: Louisiana State University Press, 2020.

Oakes, James. *Ruling Race: A History of American Slaveholders.* New York: Knopf, 1982.

Oast, Jennifer. *Institutional Slavery: Slaveholding Churches, Schools, Colleges, and Businesses in Virginia, 1680–1860.* New York: Cambridge University Press, 2016.

O'Donovan, Susan Eva. *Becoming Free in the Cotton South.* Cambridge, MA: Harvard University Press, 2010.

Olwell, Robert. *Masters, Slaves, and Subjects: The Culture of Power in the South Carolina Low Country, 1740–1790.* Ithaca, NY: Cornell University Press, 1998.

Osterweis, Rollin G. *Judah P. Benjamin: Statesman of the Lost Cause.* New York: G. P. Putnam, 1933.

Ouchley, Kelby. *Flora and Fauna of the Civil War: An Environmental Reference Guide.* Baton Rouge: Louisiana State University Press, 2010.

Owens, Leslie Howard. *This Species of Property: Slave Life and Culture in the Old South.* New York: Oxford University Press, 1976.

Parent, Anthony S., Jr. *Foul Means: The Formation of a Slave Society in Virginia, 1660–1740.* Chapel Hill: University of North Carolina Press, 2003.

Pargas, Damian A. *Slavery and Forced Migration in the Antebellum South.* New York: Cambridge, 2014.

Partagas, Jose F., and Henry F. Diaz. *A Reconstruction of Historical Tropical Cyclone Frequency.* Boulder, CO: NOAA, 1995.

Penningroth, Dylan C. *Claims of Kinfolk: African America Property and Community in the Nineteenth-Century South.* Chapel Hill: University of North Carolina Press, 2003.

Phillips, Ulrich Bonnell. *Life and Labor in the Old South.* Boston: Little, Brown, 1929.

Proctor, Nicholas W. *Bathed in Blood: Hunting and Mastery in the Old South.* Charlottesville: University of Virginia Press, 2002.

Quarles, Benjamin. *The Negro in the American Revolution.* Chapel Hill: University of North Carolina Press, 1961.

Raboteau, Albert J. *Slave Religion: The "Invisible Institution" in the Antebellum South.* New York: Oxford University Press, 1978.

Rainville, Lynn. *Hidden History: African American Cemeteries in Central Virginia.* Charlottesville: University of Virginia Press, 2014.

Ransom, Roger L., and Richard Sutch. *One Kind of Freedom: The Economic Consequences of Emancipation.* New York: Cambridge University Press, 1977.

Reidy, Joseph P. *Illusions of Emancipation: The Pursuit of Freedom and Equality in the Twilight of Slavery.* Chapel Hill: University of North Carolina Press, 2019.

Reuss, Martin. *Designing the Bayous: The Control of Water in the Atchafalaya Basin, 1800–1995.* College Station: Texas A&M Press, 2004.

Rohland, Eleonora. *Changes in the Air: Hurricanes in New Orleans from 1718 to the Present.* New York: Berghahn, 2018.

Rose, Willie Lee. *The Rehearsal for Reconstruction: The Port Royal Experiment.* New York: Oxford University Press, 1964.

Rothman, Adam. *Slave Country: American Expansion and the Origins of the Deep South.* Cambridge, MA: Harvard University Press, 2007.

Rothman, Joshua. *Flush Times and Fever Dreams: A Story of Capitalism and Slavery in the Age of Jackson.* Athens, GA: University of Georgia Press, 2012.

Rowland, Lawrence S., Alexander Moore, and George C. Rogers Jr. *History of Beaufort County, South Carolina*, vol. 1, *1514–1861.* Columbia: University of South Carolina Press, 1996.

Royster, Charles. *The Fabulous History of the Dismal Swamp Company: A Story of George Washington's Times.* New York: Knopf, 1999.

Saikku, Mikko. *This Delta, This Land: An Environmental History of the Yazoo-Mississippi Floodplain.* Athens, GA: University of Georgia Press, 2005.

Salafia, Matthew. *Slavery's Borderland: Freedom and Bondage Along the Ohio River.* Philadelphia: University of Pennsylvania Press, 2013.

Sarris, Jonathan Dean. *A Separate Civil War: Communities in Conflict in the Mountain South.* Charlottesville: University of Virginia Press, 2006.

Saunt, Claudio. *Unworthy Republic: The Dispossession of Native Americans and the Road to Indian Territory.* New York: Norton, 2020.

Savitt, Todd L. *Medicine and Slavery: The Diseases and Health Care of Blacks in Antebellum Virginia.* Champaign: University of Illinois Press, 2002.

Sawyer, Roy T. *America's Wetland: An Environmental and Cultural History of Tidewater Virginia and North Carolina.* Charlottesville: University of Virginia Press, 2010.

Sayers, Daniel O. *A Desolate Place: The Archaeology of Maroons, Indigenous Americans, and Enslaved Laborers in the Great Dismal Swamp.* Gainesville: University Press of Florida, 2014.

Scarborough, William Kauffman. *Masters of the Big House: Elite Slaveholders of the Mid-Nineteenth-Century South*. Baton Rouge: Louisiana State University Press, 2003.

Scott, Julius S. *The Common Wind: Afro-American Currents in the Age of the Haitian Revolution*. New York: Verso, 2018.

Schwalm, Leslie A. *A Hard Fight for We: Women's Transition from Slavery to Freedom in South Carolina*. Urbana: University of Illinois Press, 1997.

Silkenat, David. *Driven from Home: North Carolina's Civil War Refugee Crisis*. Athens, GA: University of Georgia Press, 2016.

Silver, Timothy. *New Face on the Countryside: Indians, Colonists, and Slaves in South Atlantic Forests, 1500–1800*. New York: Cambridge University Press, 1990.

Sinha, Manisha. *The Counter-Revolution of Slavery: Politics and Ideology in Antebellum South Carolina*. Chapel Hill: University of North Carolina Press, 2000.

Sitterson, J. Carlyle. *Sugar Country: The Cane Sugar Industry in the South, 1753–1950*. Lexington: University of Kentucky Press, 1953.

Smith, Julia Floyd. *Slavery and Rice Culture in Low Country Georgia, 1750–1860*. Knoxville: University of Tennessee Press, 1985.

Smith, Kimberly K. *African American Environmental Thought: Foundations*. Lawrence: University Press of Kansas, 2007.

Smith, Mark M. *Mastered by the Clock: Time, Slavery, and Freedom in the American South*. Chapel Hill: University of North Carolina Press, 1997.

Snyder, Christina. *Slavery in Indian Country: The Changing Face of Captivity in Early America*. Cambridge, MA: Harvard University Press, 2012.

Souder, William M. *Under A Wild Sky: John James Audubon and the Making of the Birds of America*. New York: North Point, 2004.

Spears, Ellen Griffith. *Baptized in PCBs: Race, Pollution, and Justice in an All-American Town*. Chapel Hill: University of North Carolina Press, 2014.

Stanton, Lucia. *Those Who Labor for My Happiness: Slavery at Thomas Jefferson's Monticello*. Charlottesville: University of Virginia Press, 2012.

Starobin, Robert S. *Industrial Slavery in the Old South*. New York: Oxford University Press, 1970.

Stewart, Catherine A. *Long Past Slavery: Representing Race in the Federal Writers' Project*. Chapel Hill: University of North Carolina Press, 2016.

Stewart, Mart. *"What Nature Suffers to Groe": Life, Labor, and Landscape on the Georgia Coast, 1680–1920*. Athens, GA: University of Georgia Press, 1996.

Stith, Matthew M. *Extreme Civil War: Guerrilla Warfare, Environment, and Race on the Trans-Mississippi Frontier*. Baton Rouge: Louisiana State University Press, 2016.

Stoll, Steven. *Larding the Lean Earth: Soil and Society in Nineteenth-Century America*. New York: Hill & Wang, 2003.

Stowe, Steven M. *Doctoring the South: Southern Physicians and Everyday Medicine in the Mid-Nineteenth Century*. Chapel Hill: University of North Carolina Press, 2004.

Swanson, Drew A. *Beyond the Mountains: Commodifying Appalachian Environments*. Athens, GA: University of Georgia Press, 2018.

Swanson, Drew A. *A Golden Weed: Tobacco and Environment in the Piedmont South.* New Haven, CT: Yale University Press, 2014.

Swanson, Drew A. *Remaking Wormsloe Plantation: The Environmental History of a Lowcountry Landscape.* Athens, GA: University of Georgia Press, 2012.

Taylor, Alan. *American Revolutions: A Continental History, 1750–1804.* New York: Norton, 2016.

Taylor, Alan. *The Internal Enemy: Slavery and War in Virginia, 1772–1832.* New York: Norton, 2013.

Taylor, Amy Murrell. *Embattled Freedom: Journeys through the Civil War's Slave Refugee Camps.* Chapel Hill: University of North Carolina Press, 2018.

Taylor, Dorceta E. *Toxic Communities: Environmental Racism, Industrial Pollution, and Residential Mobility.* New York: New York University Press, 2014.

Thompson, Michael D. *Working on the Dock of the Bay: Labor and Enterprise in an Antebellum Southern Port.* Columbia: University of South Carolina Press, 2015.

Trimble, Stanley Wayne. *Man-Induced Soil Erosion on the Southern Piedmont, 1700–1970.* Ankeny, IA: Soil Conservation Society of America, 1974.

Tuten, James H. *Lowcountry Time and Tide: The Fall of the South Carolina Rice Kingdom.* Columbia: University of South Carolina Press, 2010.

Usner, Daniel H., Jr. *Indians, Settlers, & Slaves in a Frontier Exchange Economy: The Lower Mississippi Valley Before 1783.* Chapel Hill: University of North Carolina Press, 1992.

Vlach, John Michael. *Back of the Big House: The Architecture of Plantation Slavery.* Chapel Hill: University of North Carolina Press, 1993.

VerCauteren, Kurt C., James C. Beasley, Stephen S. Ditchkoff, John J. Mayer, Gary J. Roloff, and Bronson K. Strickland. *Invasive Wild Pigs in North America: Ecology, Impacts, and Management.* Boca Raton, FL: CRC, 2019.

Wade, Forest C. *Cry of the Eagle.* Cumming, GA: n.p., 1969.

Walsh, Lorna S. *Motives of Honor, Pleasure & Profit: Plantation Management in the Colonial Chesapeake, 1607–1763.* Chapel Hill: University of North Carolina Press, 2010.

Weiner, Marli F., and Mazie Hough. *Sex, Sickness, and Slavery: Illness in the Antebellum South.* Champaign: University of Illinois Press, 2012.

Wells, Jonathan Daniel. *Origins of the Southern Middle Class, 1800–1861.* Chapel Hill: University of North Carolina Press, 2005.

Williams, David. *The Georgia Gold Rush: Twenty-Niners, Cherokees, and Gold Fever.* Columbia: University of South Carolina Press, 1993.

Wilson, Anthony. *Shadow and Shelter: The Swamp in Southern Culture.* Jackson: University Press of Mississippi, 2006.

Wilson, David K. *The Southern Strategy: Britain's Conquest of South Carolina and Georgia, 1775–1780.* Columbia: University of South Carolina Press, 2005.

Wilson, Samuel. *The Vieux Carré: Its Plan, Its Growth, Its Architecture.* New Orleans: Bureau of Government Research, 1968.

Wong, Edlie L. *Neither Fugitive nor Free: Atlantic Slavery, Freedom Suits, and the Legal Culture of Travel.* New York: New York University Press, 2009.

Wood, Betty. *Women's Work, Men's Work: The Informal Slave Economies of Lowcountry Georgia.* Athens, GA: University of Georgia Press, 1995.

Wood, Peter H. *Black Majority: Negroes in Colonial South Carolina from 1650 through the Stono Rebellion.* New York: Knopf, 1974.

Wright, Gavin. *Old South, New South: Revolutions in the Southern Economy since the Civil War.* Baton Rouge: Louisiana State University Press, 1997.

Wright, Gavin. *Slavery and American Economic Development.* Baton Rouge: Louisiana State University Press, 2013.

ARTICLES AND BOOK CHAPTERS

Adams, Natalie P. "A Pattern of Living: A View of the African American Slave Experience in the Pine Forests of the Lower Cape Fear." In *Another's Country: Archaeological and Historical Perspectives on Cultural Interactions in the Southern Colonies*, ed. J. W. Joseph and Martha Zierden, 65–78. Tuscaloosa: University of Alabama Press, 2002.

Ainsworth, Kyle. "Field Hands, Cowboys, and Runaways: Enslaved People on Horseback in Texas's Planter-Herder Economy, 1835–1865." *Journal of Southern History* 86 (2020): 557–600.

Andrews, Thomas G. "Beasts of the Southern Wild: Slaveholders, Slaves, and Other Animals in Charles Ball's *Slavery in United States*." In *Rendering Nature: Animals, Bodies, Places, Politics*, ed. Marguerite S. Schaffer and Phoebe S. K. Young, 21–47. Philadelphia: University of Pennsylvania Press, 2015.

Ayers, Edward L. and Scott Nesbit. "Seeing Emancipation: Scale and Freedom in the American South." *Journal of the Civil War Era* 1 (2011): 3–24.

Barone, John. "Historical Presence and Distribution of Prairies in the Black Belt of Mississippi and Alabama." *Castanea* 70 (2005): 170–183.

Baumgarten, Linda "'Clothes for the People': Slave Clothing in Early Virginia." *Journal of Early Southern Decorative Arts* 14 (1988): 27–70.

Bell, Whitfield J., Jr. "Thomas Anburey's 'Travels Through America': A Note on Eighteenth Century Plagiarism." *Papers of the Bibliographical Society of America* 37 (1943): 23–36.

Bland, Alastair. "The Environmental Disaster That Is the Gold Industry." *Smithsonian*, February 14, 2014. https://www.smithsonianmag.com/science-nature/environmental-disaster-gold-industry-180949762/.

Blassingame, John W. "Using the Testimony of Ex-Slaves: Approaches and Problems." *Journal of Southern History* 41 (1975): 473–492.

Bledsoe, Adam. "Marronage as a Past and Present Geography in the Americas." *Southern Geographer* 57 (2017): 30–50.

Blum, Elizabeth D. "Power, Danger, and Control: Slave Women's Perceptions of Wilderness in the Nineteenth Century." *Women's Studies* 32 (2002): 247–265.

Boime, Albert. "John James Audubon: A Birdwatcher's Fanciful Flights." *Art History* 22 (1999): 728–755.

Boney, F. N. "Doctor Thomas Hamilton: Two Views of a Gentleman of the Old South." *Phylon* 28 (1967): 288–292.

Bradford, S. Sydney. "The Negro Ironworker in Ante-Bellum Virginia." *Journal of Southern History* 25 (1959): 194–206.

Brady, Lisa M. "Environmental Histories." *Journal of the Civil War Era*. https://www. journalofthecivilwarera.org/forum-the-future-of-civil-war-era-studies/the-future- of-civil-war-era-studies-environmental-histories/.

Browning, Judkin, and Timothy Silver. "Nature and Human Nature: Environmental Influences on the Union's Failed Peninsula Campaign, 1862." *Journal of the Civil War Era* 8 (2018): 388–415.

Buchanan, Thomas C. "Levees of Hope: African American Steamboat Workers, Cities, and Slave Escapes on the Antebellum Mississippi." *Journal of Urban History* 30 (2004): 360–377.

Buchanan, Thomas C. "Rascals on the Antebellum Mississippi: African American Steamboat Workers and the St. Louis Hangings of 1841." *Journal of Social History* 34 (2001): 797–816.

Byrd, Dana E. "Motive Power: Fans, Punkah, and Fly Brushes in the Antebellum South." *Buildings and Landscapes* 23 (2016): 29–51.

Cade, John B. "Out of the Mouths of Ex-Slaves." *Journal of Negro History* 20 (1935): 294–337.

Campanella, Richard. "Disaster and Response in an Experiment Called New Orleans, 1700s-2000s." In *Oxford Research Encyclopedias: Natural Hazard Science.* New York: Oxford University Press, 2016.

Campbell, John. "'My Constant Companion': Slaves and their Dogs in the Antebellum South." In *Working toward Freedom: Slave Society and Domestic Economy in the American South*, ed. Larry E. Hudson Jr., 53–76. Rochester, NY: University of Rochester Press, 1994.

Cappon, Lester J. "Lucy Selina's Charcoal Era." *Virginia Cavalcade* 7 (1957): 31–39.

Cashin, Joan. "Landscape and Memory in Antebellum Virginia." *Virginia Magazine of History and Biography* 102 (1994): 477–500.

Cecelski, David S. "The Oldest Living Confederate Chaplain Tells All?" *Southern Cultures* 3 (1997): 5–24.

Cecelski, David S. "The Shores of Freedom: The Maritime Underground Railroad in North Carolina, 1800–1861." *North Carolina Historical Review* 71 (1994): 174–206.

Chenoweth, Michael, and Cary J. Mock. "Hurricane 'Amanda': Rediscovery of a Forgotten U.S. Civil War Hurricane." *Bulletin of the American Meteorological Society* (November 2013): 1735–1742.

Coelho, Philip R. P., and Robert A. McGuire. "Biology, Diseases, and Economics: An Epidemiological History of Slavery in the American South." *Journal of Bioeconomics* 1 (1999): 158–190.

Daley, Suzanne. "Peru Scrambles to Drive Out Illegal Gold Mining and Save Precious Land." *New York Times*, July 25, 2016.

Davis, Donald W. "Historical Perspective on Crevasses, Levees, and the Mississippi River." In Transforming New Orleans and Its Environs: Centuries of Change, ed. Craig E. Colten, 84–106. Pittsburgh: University of Pittsburgh Press, 2000.

Dawson, Kevin. "Enslaved Swimmers and Divers in the Atlantic World." *Journal of American History* 92 (2006): 1327–1355.

Degler, Carl N. "Why Historians Change Their Minds." *Pacific Historical Review* 45 (1976): 167–184.

Dott, Robert H., Jr. "Charles Lyell's Debt to North America: His Lectures and Travels from 1841 to 1853." in *Lyell: The Past is the Key to the Present,* ed. D. J. Blundell and A. C. Scott, 53–69. London: Geological Society, 1998.

Downey, Tom. "Riparian Rights and Manufacturing in Antebellum South Carolina: William Gregg and the Origins of the 'Industrial Mind.'" *Journal of Southern History* 65 (1999): 77–108.

Earle, Carville. "The Myth of the Southern Soil Miner: Macrohistory, Agricultural Innovation, and Environmental Change." In *The Ends of the Earth: Perspectives on Modern Environmental History*, ed. Donald Worster, 175–210. New York: Cambridge University Press, 1989.

Earle, Carville, and Ronald Hoffman. "Genteel Erosion: The Ecological Consequences of Agrarian Reform in the Chesapeake, 1730–1840." In *Discovering the Chesapeake: The History of an Ecosystem*, ed. Philip D. Curtin, Grace S. Brush, and George W. Fisher, 279–303. Baltimore: Johns Hopkins University Press, 2001.

Edelson, S. Max. "Beyond 'Black Rice': Reconstructing Material and Cultural Contexts for Early Plantation Agriculture." *American Historical Review* 115 (2010): 125–135.

Eisterhold, John A. "Charleston: Lumber and Trade in a Declining Southern Port." *South Carolina Historical Magazine* 74 (1972): 61–72.

Eisterhold, John A. "Colonial Beginnings in the Southern Lumber Industry: 1607–1800." *Southern Lumberman* 223 (1971): 150–153.

Ellenberg, George B. "African Americans, Mules, and the Southern Mindscape, 1850–1950." *Agricultural History* 72 (1998): 381–398.

Eltis, David, Philip Morgan, and David Richardson. "Agency and Diaspora in Atlantic History: Reassessing the African Contribution to Rice Cultivation in the Americas." *American Historical Review* 112 (2007): 1329–1358.

Esdaile, Louisa J., and Justin M. Chalker. "The Mercury Problem in Artisanal and Small-Scale Gold Mining." *Chemistry* 24 (2018): 6905–6916.

Espinoza, Mariola. "The Question of Racial Immunity to Yellow Fever in History and Historiography." *Social Science History* 38 (2014): 437–453.

Fiege, Mark. "Gettysburg and the Organic Nature of the American Civil War." In *Natural Enemy, Natural Ally: Toward an Environmental History of Warfare*, ed. Edmund Russell and Richard Tucker, 93–109. Corvallis: Oregon State University Press, 2004.

Follett, Richard. "Heat, Sex, and Sugar: Pregnancy and Childbearing in the Slave Quarters." *Journal of Family History* 28 (2003): 510–539.

Forret, Jeff. "Deaf & Dumb, Blind, Insane, or Idiotic." *Journal of Southern History* 82 (2016): 503–548.

Forret, Jeff. "Slave Labor in North Carolina's Antebellum Gold Mines." *North Carolina Historical Review* 76 (1999): 135–162.

Fountain, Daniel L. "Historians and Historical Archaeology: Slave Sites." *Journal of Interdisciplinary History* 26 (1995): 67–77.

Fussell, Elizabeth. "Constructing New Orleans, Constructing Race: A Population History of New Orleans." *Journal of American History* 94 (2007): 846–855.

Gibbs, Tyson, Kathleen Cargill, Leslie Sue Lieberman, and Elizabeth J. Reitz. "Nutrition in a Slave Population: An Anthropological Examination." *Medical Anthropology* 4 (1980): 175–262.

Giltner, Scott. "Slave Hunting and Fishing in the Antebellum South." In *"To Love the Wind and the Rain": African Americans and Environmental History*, ed. Dianne D. Glave and Mark Stoll, 21–36. Pittsburgh: University of Pittsburgh Press, 2006.

Green, Fletcher Melvin. "Gold Mining: A Forgotten Industry of Ante-Bellum North Carolina." *North Carolina Historical Review* 14 (1937): 1–19, 135–155.

Guterl, Matthew Pratt. "Slavery and Capitalism: A Review Essay." *Journal of Southern History* 81 (2015): 405–420.

Hamer, Fritz, and Michael Trinkley. "African Architectural Transference to the South Carolina Low Country, 1700–1880." *Tennessee Anthropologist* 22 (1997): 1–34.

Hardin, David S. "'The Same Sort of Seed in Different Earths': Tobacco Types and Their Regional Variation in Colonial Virginia." *Historical Geography* 34 (2006): 137–158.

Hauser, Jason. "'A Golden Harvest': Gold Mining and Agricultural Reform in North Carolina, 1799–1842." *Agricultural History* 91 (2017): 469–487.

Hawthorne, Walter. "Black Rice Reconsidered." In *Rice: Global Networks and New Histories*, ed. Francesca Bray, Peter A. Coclanis, Edda Fields-Black, and Dagmar Schaefer, 279–290. Cambridge: Cambridge University Press, 2015.

Helms, Douglas. "Soil and Southern History." *Agricultural History* 74 (2000): 723–758.

Hilliard, Sam B. "Pork in the Ante-Bellum South: The Geography of Self-Sufficiency." *Annals of the Association of American Geographers* 59 (1969): 461–477.

Hines, Elizabeth. "McCulloch's Rock Engine House: An Antebellum Cornish-Style Gold Ore Mill near Jamestown, North Carolina." *Material Culture* 27 (1995): 1–28.

Hines, Elizabeth, and Michael S. Smith. "Gold Is Where You Find It: Placer Mining in North Carolina, 1799–1849." *Earth Sciences History* 21 (2002): 119–149.

Hinke, William J. "Report of the Journey of Francis Louis Michel from Berne, Switzerland to Virginia." *Virginia Magazine of History and Biography* 24 (1916): 1–43, 113–141, 275–303.

Hunt, Raymond F. "The Patrolus Ironworks." *Tennessee Historical Quarterly* 25 (1966): 176–196.

Jacoby, Karl. "Slaves by Nature? Domestic Animals and Human Slaves." *Slavery and Abolition* 15 (1994): 89–99.

Johnson, Timothy. "Reconstructing the Soil: Emancipation and the Roots of Chemical-Dependent Agriculture in America." In *The Blue, the Gray, and the Green: Toward an Environmental History of the Civil War*, ed. Brian Allen Drake, 191–208. Athens, GA: University of Georgia Press, 2015.

Jones, Alice Simms and E. Gibbes Patton. "Forest, 'Prairie,' and the Soils in the Black Belt of Sumter County, Alabama, in 1832." *Ecology* 47 (1966): 75–80.

Jordan, Weymouth. "Early Ante-Bellum Marion, Alabama: A Black Belt Town." *Alabama Historical Quarterly* 5 (1943): 12–31.

Jordan, Weymouth. "Peruvian Guano Gospel in the Old South." *Agricultural History* 24 (1950): 211–221.

Kaye, Anthony E. "Neighborhoods and Nat Turner: The Making of a Slave Rebel and the Unmaking of a Slave Rebellion." *Journal of the Early Republic* 27 (2007): 705–720.

Kelman, Ari. "Forests and Other River Perils." In *Transforming New Orleans and Its Environs: Centuries of Change*, ed. Craig E. Colten, 45–63. Pittsburgh: University of Pittsburgh Press, 2000.

Knapp, Richard F. "Golden Promise in the Piedmont: The Story of John Reed's Mine." *North Carolina Historical Review* 52 (1975): 1–19.

Kutzbach, John E., and Thompson Webb III. "Climate and Climate History in the Chesapeake Bay Region." In *Discovering the Chesapeake: The History of an Ecosystem*, ed. Philip D. Curtin, Grace S. Brush, and George W. Fisher, 15–39. Baltimore: Johns Hopkins University Press, 2001.

LaFay, Elaine. "The Wind Can Blow Through and Through: Ventilation, Public Health, and the Regulation of Fresh Air on Antebellum Southern Plantations." In *Atlantic Environments and the American South*, ed. Thomas Blake Earle and D. Andrew Johnson, 38–62. Athens, GA: University of Georgia Press, 2020.

Lander, Ernest M. "The Iron Industry in Ante-Bellum South Carolina." *Journal of Southern History* 20 (1954): 337–355.

Lewis, David Rich. "American Indian Environmental Relations." In *A Companion to American Environmental History*, ed. Douglas Sackman, 191–213. Hoboken, NJ: Wiley-Blackwell, 2010.

Lewis, Ronald L. " 'Darkest Abode of Man': Black Miners in the First Southern Coal Field, 1780–1865." *Virginia Magazine of History and Biography* 87 (1979): 190–202.

Lockley, Timothy J. " 'The King of England's Soldiers': Armed Blacks in Savannah and Its Hinterlands during the Revolutionary War Era, 1778–1787." In *Slavery and Freedom in Savannah*, ed. Leslie M. Harris and Daina Ramey Berry, 26–41. Athens, GA: University of Georgia Press, 2014.

Lockley, Timothy J. "Trading Encounters Between Non-Elite Whites and African Americans in Savannah, 1790–1860." *Journal of Southern History* 66 (2000): 25–48.

Lockley, Timothy J., and David Doddington, "Maroon and Slave Communities in South Carolina before 1865." *South Carolina Historical Magazine* 113 (2012): 125–145.

Lonn, Ella. "The Extent and Importance of Federal Naval Raids on Salt-Making in Florida, 1862–1865." *Florida Historical Society Quarterly* 10 (1932): 167–184.

Lussana, Sergio. "Reassessing Brer Rabbit: Friendship, Altruism, and Community in the Folklore of Enslaved African-Americans." *Slavery and Abolition* 38 (2018): 123–146.

Maris-Wolf, Ted. "Hidden in Plain Sight: Maroon Life and Labor in Virginia's Dismal Swamp." *Slavery and Abolition* 34 (2013): 446–464.

Marcus, Alan I. "The South's Native Foreigners: Hookworm as a Factor in Southern Distinctiveness." In *Disease and Distinctiveness in the American South*, ed. Todd L. Savitt and James Harvey Young, 79–99. Knoxville: University of Tennessee Press, 1988.

Masur, Kate. "'Rare Phenomenon of Philological Vegetation': The Word 'Contraband' and the Meanings of Emancipation in the United States." *Journal of American History* 93 (2007): 1050–1084.

Masur, Louis. "Olmsted's Southern Landscapes." *New York Times*, July 9, 2011. opinionator.blogs.nytimes.com /2011/07/09/olmsteds-southern-landscapes.

Mercantini, Jonathan. "The Great Carolina Hurricane of 1752." *South Carolina Historical Magazine* 103 (2002): 351–365.

Merchant, Carolyn. "Shades of Darkness: Race and Environmental History." *Environmental History* 8 (2003): 380–394.

Messner, William F. "Vicksburg Campaign of 1862: A Case Study in the Federal Utilization of Black Labor." *Louisiana History* 16 (1975): 371–381.

Mock, Cary J., Michael Chenoweth, Isabel Altamirano, Matthew D. Rodgers, and Ricardo Garcia-Herrera. "The Great Louisiana Hurricane of August 1812." *Bulletin of the American Meteorological Society* (2010): 1653–1663.

Moore, John Hebron. "The Cypress Lumber Industry of the Lower Mississippi Valley during the Colonial Period." *Louisiana History* 24 (1983): 25–47.

Morgan, David T. "Philip Phillips and Internal Improvements in Mid-Nineteenth-Century Alabama." *Alabama Review* 34 (1981): 83–93.

Morgan, Philip D. "The Ownership of Property by Slaves in the Mid-Nineteenth Century Low Country." *Journal of Southern History* 49 (1983): 399–420.

Morris, Christopher. "Impenetrable but Easy: The French Transformation of the Lower Mississippi Valley and the Founding of New Orleans." In *Transforming New Orleans and Its Environs: Centuries of Change*, ed. Craig E. Colten, 22–44. Pittsburgh: University of Pittsburgh Press, 2000.

Morris, Christopher. "A More Southern Environmental History." *Journal of Southern History* 75 (2009): 581–598.

Mulcahy, Matthew. "'Miserably Scorched': Drought in the Plantation Colonies of the British Great Caribbean." In *Atlantic Environments and the American South*, ed. Thomas Blake Earle and D. Andrew Johnson, 65–89. Athens, GA: University of Georgia, 2020.

Nelson, Megan Kate. "Looking at Landscapes of War." *Journal of the Civil War Era* 3 (2013): 439–449.

Nelson, Scott Reynolds. "Who Put Their Capitalism in My Slavery?" *Journal of the Civil War Era* 5 (2015): 289–310.

Nuwer, Deanne Stephens. "'I'll be blame ef I hanker after making my bowels a brick-yard': Dirt Eating in the Antebellum and Early Modern South." *Southern Quarterly* 53 (2016): 141–155.

O'Brien, Greg. "Satire and Politics in the New Orleans Flood of 1849." In *Environmental Disaster in the Gulf South*, ed. Cindy Ermus, 14–36. Baton Rouge: Louisiana State University Press, 2018.

O'Donovan, Susan Eva. "Finding a New War in an Old Image." In *Lens of War: Exploring Iconic Photographs of the Civil War*, ed. J. Matthew Gallman and Gary W. Gallagher, 143–148. Athens, GA: University of Georgia Press, 2015.

Outland, Robert B., III. "Slavery, Work, and the Geography of the North Carolina Naval Stores Industry, 1835–1860." *Journal of Southern History* 62 (1996): 27–56.

Outland, Robert B., III. "Suicidal Harvest: The Self-Destruction of North Carolina's Naval Stores Industry." *North Carolina Historical Review* 78 (2001): 309–344.

Pabis, George S. "Delaying the Deluge: The Engineering Debate over Flood Control on the Lower Mississippi River, 1846–1861." *Journal of Southern History* 64 (1998): 421–454.

Pabis, George S. "Subduing Nature through Engineering: Caleb G. Forshey and the Levees-Only Policy, 1851–1881." In *Transforming New Orleans and Its Environs: Centuries of Change*, ed. Craig E. Colten, 64–83. Pittsburgh: University of Pittsburgh Press, 2000.

Paquette, Robert L. "'A Horde of Brigands?': The Great Louisiana Slave Revolt of 1811 Reconsidered." *Historical Reflections / Réflexions Historiques* 35 (Spring 2009): 72–96.

Pargas, Damian Alan. "In the Fields of a 'Strange Land': Enslaved Newcomers and the Adjustment to Cotton Cultivation in the Antebellum South." *Slavery and Abolition* 34 (2013): 562–578.

Parramore, Thomas C. "Muslim Slave Aristocrats in North Carolina." *North Carolina Historical Review* 77 (2000): 127–150.

Parry, Tyler D., and Charlton W. Yingling. "Slave Hounds and Abolition in the Americas." *Past and Present* 246 (2020): 69–108.

Paterson, David E. "Slavery, Slaves, and Cash in a Georgia Village, 1825–1865." *Journal of Southern History* 75 (2009): 879–930.

Patrick, Vanessa E. "Partitioning the Landscape: The Fence in Eighteenth-Century Virginia." *Colonial Williamsburg Foundation Library Research Report Series* 134 (1983): 1–47.

Pearson, Edward A. "'A Countryside Full of Flames': A Reconsideration of the Stono Rebellion and Slave Rebelliousness in the Early Eighteenth-Century South Carolina Lowcountry." *Slavery and Abolition* 17 (1996): 22–50.

Percy, David O. "Ax or Plow?: Significant Colonial Landscape Alteration Rates in the Maryland and Virginia Tidewater." *Agricultural History* 66 (1992): 66–74.

Perry, Perceval. "The Naval-Stores Industry in the Old South, 1790–1860." *Journal of Southern History* 34 (1968): 509–526.

Perry, Tony C. "In Bondage when Cold was King: The Frigid Terrain of Slavery in Antebellum Maryland." *Slavery and Abolition* 38 (2017): 23–36.

Phifer, Edward W. "Champagne at Brindletown: The Story of the Burke County Gold Rush, 1829–1833." *North Carolina Historical Review* 40 (1963): 489–500.

Phifer, Edward W. "Slavery in Microcosm: Burke County, North Carolina." *Journal of Southern History* 28 (1962): 137–165.

Pritchard, James. "The Last Island Disaster of August 10, 1856." *Louisiana Historical Quarterly* 20 (1937): 690–737.

Reitz, Elizabeth J., Tyson Gibbs, and Ted A. Rathbun. "Archaeological Evidence for Subsistence on Coastal Plantations." In *The Archaeology of Slavery and Plantation Life*, ed. Theresa A. Singleton, 163–191. Orlando: Academic Press, 1985.

Roediger, David R. "And Die in Dixie: Funerals, Death, and Heaven in the Slave Community, 1700–1865." *Massachusetts Review* 22 (1981): 163–183.

Rogers, J. D. "Development of the New Orleans Flood Protection System prior to Hurricane Katrina." *Journal of Geotechnical and Geoenvironmental Engineering* 134 (2008): 602–617.

Rohland, Eleonora. "Hurricanes in New Orleans: Disaster Migration and Adaption, 1718–1794." In *Cultural Dynamic of Climate Change and the Environment in Northern America*, ed. Bernd Sommer, 137–158. Leiden: Brill, 2015.

Rood, Daniel. "Bogs of Death: Slavery, the Brazilian Flour Trade, and the Mystery of the Vanishing Millpond in Antebellum Virginia." *Journal of American History* 101 (2014): 19–43.

Rostlund, Erhard. "The Myth of a Natural Prairie Belt in Alabama: An Interpretation of Historical Records." *Annals of the Association of American Geographers* 47 (1947): 392–411.

Sacco, Nicholas W. "'I Never Was an Abolitionist': Ulysses S. Grant and Slavery, 1854–1863." *Journal of Civil War Era* 9 (2019): 410–437.

Savitt, Todd L. "Slave Life Insurance in Virginia and North Carolina." *Journal of Southern History* 43 (1977) 583–600.

Sayers, Daniel O., P. Brendan Burke, and Aaron M. Henry. "The Political Economy of Exile in the Great Dismal Swamp." *International Journal of Historical Archaeology* 11 (2007): 60–97.

Schob, David E. "Woodhawks and Cordwood: Steamboat Fuel on the Ohio and Mississippi Rivers, 1820–1860." *Journal of Forest History* 21 (1977): 124–132.

Schweninger, Loren. "Slave Independence and Enterprise in South Carolina, 1780–1865." *South Carolina Historical Magazine* 93 (1992): 101–125.

Schweninger, Loren. "The Underside of Slavery: The Internal Economy, Self-hire, and Quasi-freedom in Virginia, 1780–1865." *Slavery and Abolition* 12 (1991): 1–22.

Shoeppner, Michael. "Peculiar Quarantines: The Seaman Acts and Regulatory Authority in the Antebellum South." *Law and History Review* 31 (2013): 559–586.

Silver, Timothy. "Learning to Live with Nature: Colonial Historians and the Southern Environment." *Journal of Southern History* 73 (2007): 539–552.

Singleton, Theresa. "Archaeology and Slavery." In *The Oxford Handbook of Slavery in the Americas*, ed. Mark M. Smith and Robert L. Paquette, 702–724. New York: Oxford University Press, 2012.

Sitterson, J. Carlyle. "Magnolia Plantation, 1852–1862: A Decade of a Louisiana Sugar Estate." *Mississippi Valley Historical Review* 25 (1938): 197–210.

Smith, Kimberly K. "Environmental Criticism and the Slave Narratives." In *The Oxford Handbook of the African American Slave Narrative*, ed. John Ernest, 315–327. New York: Oxford University Press, 2014.

Spruill, Larry H. "Slave Patrols, 'Packs of Negro Dogs' and Policing Black Communities." *Phylon* 53 (2016): 42–66.

Stange, Marion. "Governing the Swamp: Health and the Environment in Eighteenth-Century Nouvelle-Orléans." *French Colonial History* 11 (2010): 1–21.

Sternhell, Yael A. "Emancipation." In *A Companion to the U. S. Civil War*, ed. Aaron Sheehan-Dean, 965–986. Malden, MA: Wiley-Blackwell, 2014.

Stewart, Mart A. "If John Muir Had Been an Agrarian: American Environment History West and South." *Environment and History* 11 (2005): 139–162.

Stewart, Mart A. "Walking, Running, and Marching into an Environmental History of the Civil War." In *The Blue, the Gray, and the Green: Toward an Environmental History of the Civil War*, ed. Brian Allen Drake, 209–224. Athens, GA: University of Georgia Press, 2015.

Stith, Matthew M. "'The Deplorable Condition of the Country': Nature, Society, and War on the Trans-Mississippi Frontier." *Civil War History* 58 (2012): 322–347.

Swanson, Drew A. "Fighting Over Fencing: Agricultural Reform and Antebellum Efforts to Close the Virginia Open Range." *Virginia Magazine of History and Biography* 117 (2009): 104–139.

Taylor, Amy Murrell. "How a Cold Snap in Kentucky Led to Freedom for Thousands: An Environmental Story of Emancipation." In *Weirding the War: Stories from the Civil War's Ragged Edges*, ed. Stephen Berry, 191–214. Athens, GA: University of Georgia Press, 2011.

Thomas, Phillip Drennon. "Endangered Species." In *The New Encyclopedia of Southern Culture*, vol. 8, *Environment*, ed. Martin Melosi, 47–54. Chapel Hill: University of North Carolina Press, 2007.

Thornton, John K. "African Dimension of the Stono Rebellion." *American Historical Review* 96 (1991): 1101–1113.

Twyman, Robert W. "The Clay-Eater: A New Look at an Old Southern Enigma." *Journal of Southern History* 37 (1971): 439–448.

Usner, Daniel H., Jr. "From African Captivity to American Slavery: The Introduction of Black Laborers to Colonial Louisiana." *Louisiana History* 20 (1979): 25–48.

Vollmers, Gloria. "Industrial Slavery in the United States: The North Carolina Turpentine Industry, 1849–61." *Accounting, Business and Financial History* 13 (2003): 369–392.

Wall, Bennett H. "Medical Care of Ebenezer Pettigrew's Slaves." *Journal of American History* 37 (1950): 451–470.

Walsh, Lorna S. "Land Use, Settlement Patterns, and the Impact of European Agriculture, 1620–1820." In *Discovering the Chesapeake: The History of an Ecosystem*, ed. Philip D. Curtain, Grace S. Brush, and George W. Fisher, 220–248. Baltimore: Johns Hopkins University Press, 2001.

Walsh, Lorna S. "Plantation Management in the Chesapeake, 1620–1820." *Journal of Economic History* 49 (1989): 393–406.

Watts, Susan J. "Dracunculiasis in the Caribbean and South America: A Contribution to the History of Dracunculiasis Eradication." *Medical History* 45 (2000): 227–250.

Watts, Susan J. "Population Mobility and Disease Transmission: The Example of the Guinea Worm." *Social Science Medicine* 25 (1987): 1073–1081.

West, Emily. "He come sometime widout de pass: Rethinking Cross-Plantation Marriages and Enslaved Families in Antebellum South Carolina." In *Family Values in the Old South*, ed. Craig Thompson Friend and Anya Jabour, 42–61. Gainesville: University of Florida Press, 2010.

Williams, Brian. "'That We May Live': Pesticides, Plantations, and Environmental Racism in the United States South." *Environment and Planning* 1 (2018): 243–267.

Williams, Clanton W. "Early Ante-Bellum Montgomery: A Black Belt Constituency." *Journal of Southern History* 7 (1941), 495–525.

Williams, David. "Georgia's Forgotten Miners: African-Americans and the Georgia Gold Rush." *Georgia Historical Quarterly* 75 (1991): 76–89.

Williams, H. David. "Gambling Away the Inheritance: The Cherokee Nation and Georgia's Gold and Land Lotteries of 1832–33." *Georgia Historical Quarterly* 73 (1989): 519–539.

Willoughby, Christopher D. "'His Native, Hot Country': Racial Science and Environment in Antebellum American Medical Thought." *Journal of the History of Medicine and Allied Sciences* 72 (2017): 328–351.

Yetman, Norman R. "Ex-Slave Interviews and the Historiography of Slavery." *American Quarterly* 36 (1984): 181–210.

Young, Amy L., Michael Tuma, and Cliff Jenkins. "The Role of Hunting to Cope with Risk at Saragossa Plantation, Natchez, Mississippi." *American Anthropologist* 103 (2001): 692–704.

Young, Jeffrey R. "Ideology and Death on a Savannah River Rice Plantation: Paternalism amidst 'a Good Supply of Disease and Pain.'" *Journal of Southern History* 59 (1993): 673–706.

THESES AND DISSERTATIONS

Allen, Dan Sumner. "'Yea, Though I Walk Through the Valley of the Shadow of Death': Mortuary and Material Culture Patterning at the Donelson Slave Cemetery." Master's thesis, Middle Tennessee State University, 2013.

Buman, Nathan A. "To Kill Whites: The 1811 Louisiana Slave Insurrection." Master's thesis, Louisiana State University, 2008.

Buman, Nathan A. "Two Histories, One Future: Louisiana Sugar Planters, Their Slaves, and the Anglo-Creole Schism, 1815–1865." PhD diss., Louisiana State University, 2013.

Carlin, Matthew P. "The Hydraulic Dimension of Reconstruction in Louisiana, 1863–1879." Master's thesis, University of New Orleans, 2019.

Cowan, William Tynes. "The Slave in the Swamp: Disrupting the Plantation Narrative." PhD diss., College of William and Mary, 2001.

Cramer, Jerame Joseph. "Logs, Labor, and Living: An Archaeological Investigation of African-American Laborers at the Upper and Middle Landing Sawmills at Natchez-under-the-Hill." Master's thesis, Louisiana State University, 2003.

Downer, Joseph A. "Hallowed Ground, Sacred Space: The Slave Cemetery at George Washington's Mount Vernon and the Cultural Landscapes of the Enslaved." Master's thesis, George Washington University, 2015.

Golden, Kathryn Elise Benjamin. "Through the Muck and Mire: Marronage, Representation, and Memory in the Great Dismal Swamp." PhD diss., University of California, Berkeley, 2018.

Gritzner, Janet Bigbee. "Tabby in the Coastal Southeast: The Culture History of an American Building Material." PhD diss., Louisiana State University, 1978.

Hauser, Jason L. "Agrarianism, Industry, the Environment, and Change: Gold Mining in Antebellum North Carolina, 1799–1860." Master's thesis, Appalachian State University, 2012.

Hauser, Jason L. "By Degree: A History of Heat in the Subtropical American South." PhD diss., Mississippi State University, 2017.

Manganiello, Christopher John. "Dam Crazy with Wild Consequences: Artificial Lakes and Natural Rivers in the American South, 1845–1990." PhD diss., University of Georgia, 2010.

McGowan, James Thomas. "Creation of a Slave Society: Louisiana Plantations in the Eighteenth Century." PhD diss., University of Rochester, 1976.

McKee, William L. "Plantation Food Supply in Nineteenth Century Tidewater Virginia." PhD diss., University of California – Berkeley, 1988.

Munger, Sean Michael "1816: 'The Mighty Scourge of Nature': An Environmental History of the Year Without a Summer." Master's thesis, University of Oregon, 2012.

Owens, Jeffrey Alan. "Holding Back the Waters: Land Development and the Origins of Levees on the Mississippi, 1720–1845." PhD diss., Louisiana State University, 1999.

Quintana, Ryan A. "'The Plantation All in Disorder': Black Carolinians' Spatial Practices and the Construction of the Lowcountry Landscape, 1739–1830." PhD diss., University of Wisconsin – Madison, 2010.

Schieffler, George David. "Civil War in the Delta: Environment, Race, and the 1863 Helena Campaign." PhD diss., University of Arkansas, 2017.

Smith, Hayden Ros. "Rich Swamps and Rice Grounds: The Specialization of Inland Rice Culture in the South Carolina Lowcountry, 1670–1861." PhD diss., University of Georgia, 2012.

Smith, James Larry. "Historical Geography of the Southern Charcoal Iron Industry, 1800–1860." PhD diss., University of Tennessee, 1982.

Index

For the benefit of digital users, indexed terms that span two pages (e.g., 52–53) may, on occasion, appear on only one of those pages.